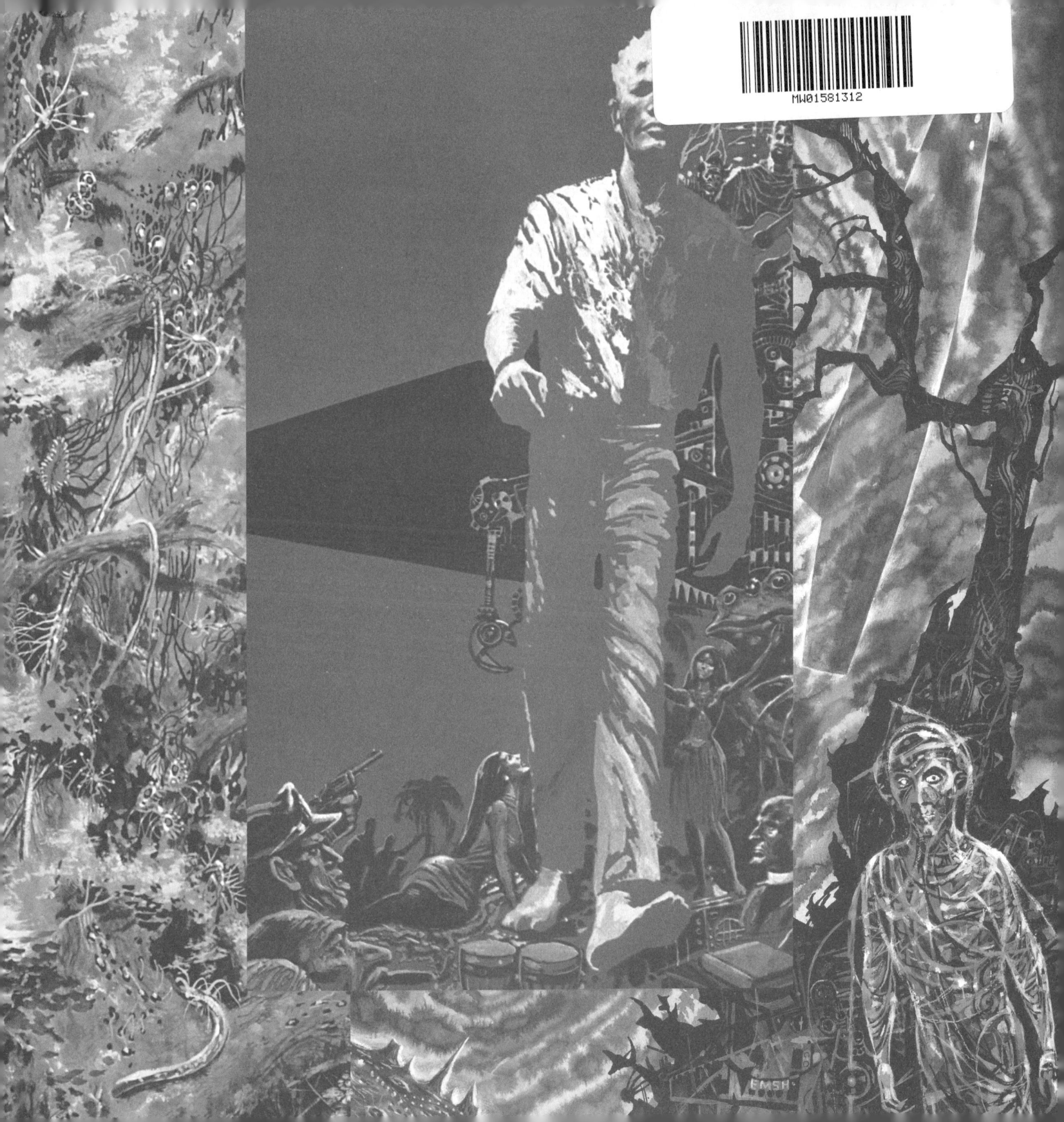

EMSH WILLER
INFINITY X TWO

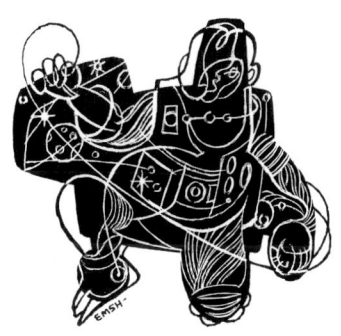

Luis Ortiz

introduction by
Carol Emshwiller

foreword and artwork captions by
Art Consultant Alex Eisenstein

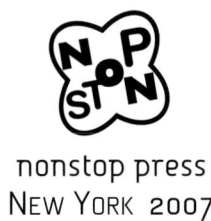

nonstop press
NEW YORK 2007

FOR KARAN

Library of American Artists, vol. two

EMSHWILLER: *Infinity x Two*

First edition

Copyright ©2007 Luis Ortiz

Art copyright ©Ed Emshwiller Estate

Introduction ©2007 Carol Emshwiller

Alex Eisenstein foreword & captions
©2007 Alex Eisenstein

No part of this publication may be
reproduced or transmitted in any form
or by any means, including photocopy,
recording, or any other information storage
and retrieval system, without prior permission
in writing from the publisher and
the artist's estate.

Nonstop Press
nonstop@nonstop-press.com

publisher's catalog-in-publication available upon request

BOOK & JACKET DESIGN
Luis Ortiz

COPY EDITOR
Beret Erway

PRODUCTION BY NONSTOP INK

ISBN-13: 978-1-933065-08-3
ISBN-10: 1-933065-08-7

Printed in S. Korea

CONTENTS

Acknowledgments	6	
Introduction	7	Carol Emshwiller
Foreword	9	Alex Eisenstein

1: Looking into The Future	17
2: Infinity x 2	23
3: The Art of Things to Come	29
4: Red Maple Drive	45
5: Science Fiction Boom	55
6: Art first, Story second	67
7: So be a Camera	75
8: "Oh, there he goes again"	91
9: Rainy day scenarios	107
10: Take a number	121
11: All kinds of branches	131
12: Illusion of reality	141
13: Digital blobs	147
14: Avantopia	155
Notes	164
Ed Emshwiller Filmography	169
Index	170

Captions for Emsh artwork, unless indicated, are by Alex Eisenstein

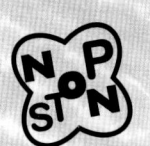

Acknowledgments

THERE ARE MANY people that helped in bringing this book about. Foremost, I would like to thank Carol for always taking the time to answer more of my errant queries — and also for reading and commenting on the manuscript. My thanks also to Susan Emshwiller for her help in filling in details of her father's CalArts days, and for supplying images and family letters. Peter "Stoney" Emshwiller, for his reminiscences of family life in Levittown. And Mac Emshwiller for giving me many details of his brother's early life. Many thanks also to Harlan Ellison, Robert Silverberg, and Alex Eisenstein for the sharing of Emsh stories. I am also beholden to Alex for making many Emsh images, which he has collected over the years for his own delayed Emsh book, available to me. To Robert Haller, of the Anthology Film Archives, my appreciation for allowing me to dig through their Emshwiller film and video library, and also for supplying slides of Emsh art from his personal SF collection. A special thank you to Aniko "Coco" Halverson, Reference Coordinator and Instruction Librarian, California Institute of the Arts, for going above and beyond the call of duty to track down Emshwiller's personal and professional papers, and expediting access to them. And Alvy Ray Smith for all his help in filling in details of Ed's work at NYIT. I would also like to acknowledge the bibliographical work on Ed Emshwiller done by Kathryn Elder through the Anthology Film Archives. Her efforts saved me much wear and tear.

Special thanks are also due to: Earl Kemp, Gary Lovisi, Bill Griffith, Jane Frank, Paul Di Filippo, Andrew Porter, Joe Wrzos, Dick Eney, Todd Mason, Curt Phillip, Michael Waite, John Boston, Stephen Jones, Hagit Hadaya, Robert Weinberg, Jonas Mekas, Lee Gold, Ted White, Greg Pickersgill, Ned Brooks, Anne Panning of the Brockport Writers Forum, Vibeke Sorensen, Eric Solstein, and Ed Hulse.

Introduction

Wanderings and Wonderings

Carol Emshwiller

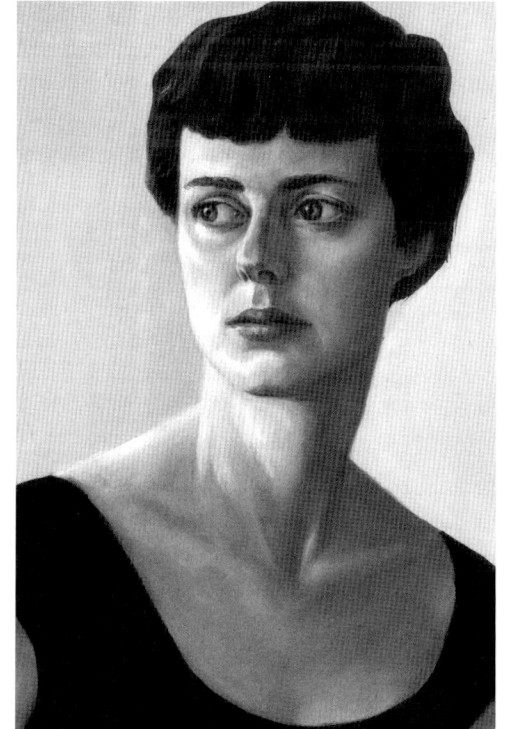

Carol painted by Ed Emshwiller, 1957.

I CAN'T IMAGINE all the work Luis did for this book … some of it with me. He must have taken dozens of tapes interviewing me. I enjoyed our meetings. He always brought me coffee from the Starbucks on the corner. Sometimes a couple of bottles of sparkling water. He knew I liked that. Then there were his calls to Ed's brother and to my son. We had one meeting with my daughter when she was visiting NY. Also calls to our neighbors in Levittown, and then to the people who worked with Ed on his first videos, and I'm sure to many more people than I know about. So much material! I'd have given up long before, or tried to whittle things down to some small part of Ed's life, but Luis, instead, enlarged his research, going out to a history of the science fiction magazines, and then of the movie people and companies Ed worked with, and then the video people. I can't think of anything that *isn't* in this book.

Well, here's one thing, there's a book that influenced us both a lot: Robbe-Grillet's book FOR A NEW NOVEL. I read it to Ed over and over. That's one thing we both loved, me reading to him. He hardly ever read except for the magazine *Scientific American*. Reading to him, I could share the things I loved with him and he liked being read to, sometimes as he was painting or in the car when he was driving.

I've forgotten that book by Robbe-Grillet though I think it's part of me now. I do remember part of it was about not personifying things. I remember one example of what not to do. Don't have the mountain *glowering* or *frowning* down on the village below. Also, don't have similes, though in my class with Kenneth

Koch, he said always "simile" things "down." Don't say the ice cream cone is like a snowy mountain, say the mountain is like an ice cream cone. Ed fit right in with that idea when he had, in *Relativity*, a planet that, as it came closer, became a golf ball. (But, actually, in my own writing I don't have similes at all unless one of my characters thinks them.) Ed and I already believed what was in Robbe Grillet's book, but he clarified it for us.

Our whole life together was mostly discussing art and movies…and our children. Those are all we talked about … and we talked about them ALL the time. Having gone to the same Bauhaus oriented art school, we mostly agreed on art and movies and music so we just reinforced each other. The University of Michigan Art School was into avant-garde art, but also strong on the old techniques, too. Ed's realistic painting of an old army boot that so impressed the art editor, Washington Irving van der Poel, at *Galaxy Magazine* was done in a class called rendering, where you had to paint something — just about anything you picked — as realistically as possible. I never took that class so I was always awed by what came out of it.

Actually I was always awed and impressed by just about everything Ed did. Watching his paintings developing little by little was like magic. And later the movies impressed me, too, and then the video work. I may have gotten mad at him plenty of times, and we had plenty of arguments, but I never, ever, ever stopped admiring his work.

That last trip, driving across the country with Ed a few months before he died was awful. Ed was in a lot of pain the whole time. I think I did most of the driving, but I don't remember much about it. We had just had a wonderful visit at our daughter's in Maine and with our grandchild adopted from India. Ed had some pain then, but not as much as a few days later when we were half way across the country. I remember one rainy night going out to try and find an open drug store to find something for him for pain. Aside from that cold rainy night I don't remember anything more about the trip. I do remember, back at his house near CalArts, taking him to doctor after doctor and test after test—in a wheel chair. He could hardly walk because of the pain. Finally they put him in the hospital. There he stayed for about two months. Later, for a week or so he was in the recovery part of the hospital. Then, one morning they sent him home, but by evening he said, "I have to go back to the hospital." He couldn't say why, just said he had to go back, and they came and got him. Our kids came out to see him one last time. Shortly after that he lapsed into a coma. The night he died, the nurses told our daughter Susan and me to go home. Early the next morning, they called and told us that he had died.

CalArts gave him a wonderful, beautiful memorial service. It was outside. People sat all along a large bank, everybody with candles. There were lots of poems and serious talks, but what I remember best is Sandy McKendrick's. He did the Irish thing. And what a relief. We laughed through it all. (My family isn't Irish, but that's what we did, too, when my father and later my mother died.)

We had Ed cremated. He had just learned to fly after wanting to for years. We hired a small plane and had his ashes thrown out the plane window. We thought he'd have liked that.

Foreword

The Artist Formerly Known as Emsh

Alex Eisenstein

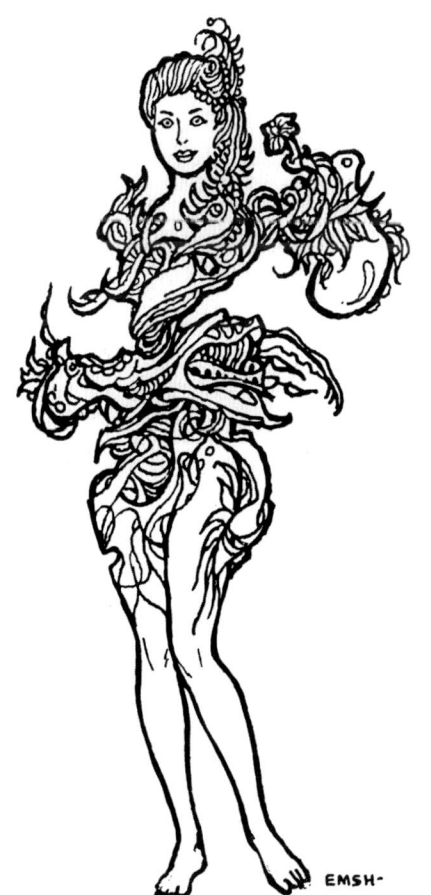

Ink spot art c. 1960s. Possibly done for the MAGAZINE OF FANTASY & SCIENCE FICTION.

Aficionados of a certain age will recall searching, in science fiction covers of the mid-Fifties, for the block-letter chop of "Emsh" tucked among the details of cityscapes, robocars, derelict spaceships, and post-atomic wreckage, or worked into the filigree of utility belts, gizmo arm-bands, gun handles, gear wheels, collars and boot tops, and other paraphernalia of vintage science fiction. At first, this sigil lay out in the open, in a barren spot of the cover. But after a few years Ed began to secrete it in the aforementioned nooks and niches — in one instance, carved into the rough grain of a fencepost on a backwater world. A small conceit, perhaps; but also a game he played with his audience, and we youthful types in readerland would seek out his emblem like beady-eyed ferrets. We knew his solid work on the Ace Double paperbacks, and on digest-size magazines like *Galaxy, If, Infinity, Science Fiction Stories, Fantasy and Science Fiction, Venture,* and even the surviving pulp-era dinosaurs like *Startling* and *Thrilling Wonder*. When his sigil wasn't clearly evident, any three fans at a bus stop might challenge each other to find it, and the hunt would begin. Thus we sought out the mark of The Good that we knew and loved, the slyly camouflaged trademark that was a guarantee of imagination and quality in the rendering of thrilling adventures in space and time.

This hidden signet was a wink-and-nudge from an illustrator we knew had to be "one of us" — a guy in the know, an insider's insider; a fellow-traveler, not just a competent craftsman churning out yardgoods. Because, after all, he was better than that; better even than we realized. The wonder and the paradox of being a fan of Ed Emsh was that you loved his stuff, yet because he was omnipresent, you tended to take him for granted. He established not a gold standard, exactly, but a hard baseline by which everything else was judged. This applied to his own cover art, too, on those occasions when it fell below his usual excellence. The prevalence of his work on newsstands and spinner racks formed, at least in our young minds, a kind of terrific SF wallpaper, a continual surround of space adventure and the far future. Back then, the 21st century seemed a far horizon from the dreary here-and-now, but Ed Emsh brought us there and beyond.

We knew and savored Emsh's flare for neo-modern design, his engaging lifelike people and idiosyncratic extraterrestrials. Even the engineering savvy of his plausible robots, air-cars, out-of-beyond artifacts, and architectures which sometimes melded classical with Mayan-Aztec or de Chirico with Euclid. We admired his visual resourcefulness, the contained energies of his layouts, his smart contemporary graphic sense, and of course his crafty wit. In particular that last: who else could have given us a four-armed Santa Claus distributing toys to human and alien tots? Or the jazzy-surreal, immensely charming "Chamber Music Society of Deneb" (Feb. 1955 *Galaxy*), with its tuxedoed Benny Goodman surrogate riffing with the hepcats of an alien quintet (pg. 88)? And these are only two of the jolts of "alternity" that Emsh produced before our gaping eyes. For SF fanatics coming of age in the 1950s, he seemed to scour the gray matter from the back of our skulls, shaping it into bold adventure and scintillant wonder, giving us what we wanted before we knew what it was. Though hardly ever resolutely photo-realist, the result was real-seeming, possessing an indisputable *there*-ness.

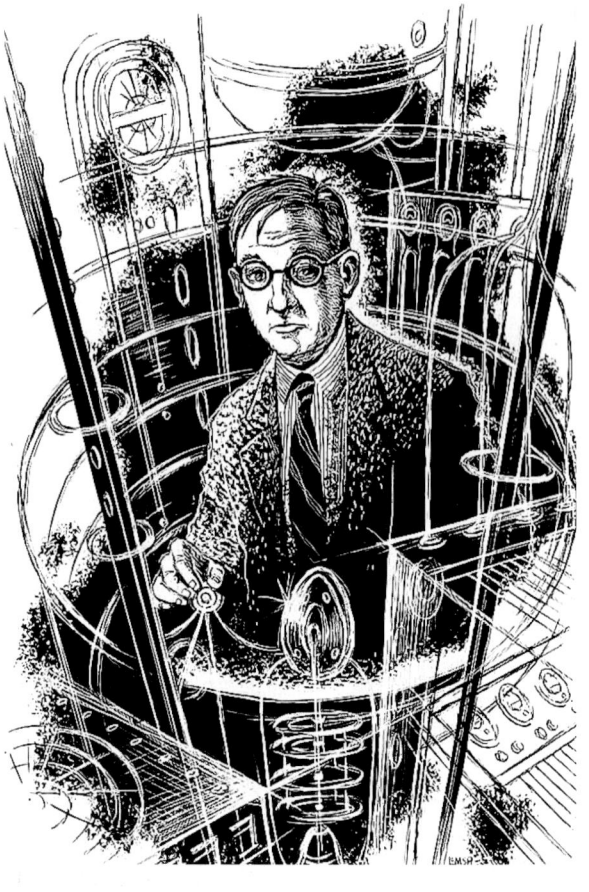

Amazingly, his sure grip on our sciencocratic predilections and that sly wit were there from the beginning, shining through even the quasi-primitive early cover paintings he placed with *Galaxy* and *Fantasy and Science Fiction* (*F&SF*). This is strikingly apparent in Ed's first SF cover sale (to *Galaxy* in 1951): the fossil remnants of an extinct species, Man, are embedded in a multi-layered mesa under a black sky, the top frosted with a baleful slag. A cadre of saurian archaeologists happens upon the record of our warring history exposed in the strata. We see a hand grenade, an M-1 rifle, bullet traces embedded in the rock; farther down a medieval battle-axe, the stone weapons of prehistory at the bottom. One senses the shock of the squat aliens, a hint even of their dismay at arriving a few thousand years too late. Emsh titled it, "Relics of an Extinct Race," and this simple tableau unfolds its story with great immediacy: at once mordant and wistful, grim but cleanly so (pg. 37). In our encounter with its sardonic brilliance, the grimness hardly fazed us. We took this cautionary tale in stride, in part because of Ed's clear, no-nonsense vision. Nowadays this atom-age fable could be a sociopolitical cartoon in *The New Yorker*, *Harper's*, or *Playboy*. Back then, being too strong for mainstream, it had to appear on the upstart *Galaxy*.

Ed produced this bright tableau of the End of the World as a show sample, and the magazine's art director bought it straight out of his portfolio, not a typical action at the time. This happened more than once: Ed's samples were so vibrant and arresting that the newer SF magazines, desperate for unusual and "catchy" cover art, would take them as is. On occasion a visiting author would be given the assignment of writing a story around one of these concept paintings, and thus be assured of selling the resulting manuscript. This occurred several times at *Galaxy*, though often editor H.L.

(top R) PLANET STORIES. "The Toy" by Bryan Berry. Mar. 1954.

Gold would let an Emsh cover run without an accompanying tale. Ed's first sale to *F&SF* (June 1952), showing a young blonde woman holding hands with a spindly green Martian, was another sample piece, but here the editors commissioned Richard Wilson to write a short tale, "Love," around it. Typically for Ed, the featured subject — an interracial couple — might have provoked a swirl of controversy in a mainstream context (pg. 39). However, mid-century SF readers absorbed this poignant image, and the story spun from it, without blinking. The painting, rendered in a naif style, testifies to the lovers' faith in each other, as they stand before a glimmering doorway to the unknown. Let's be frank: you wouldn't

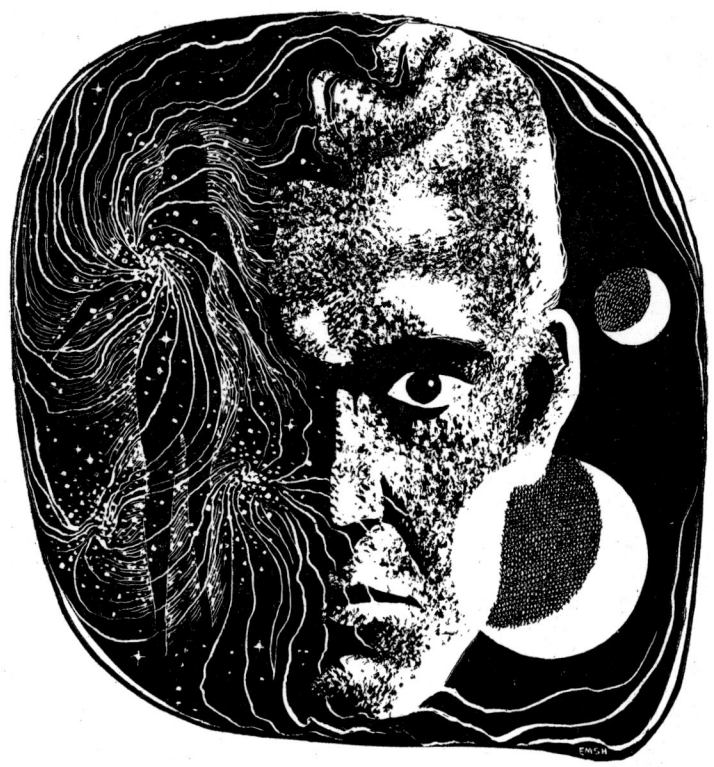

have seen this theme on the cover of *Good Housekeeping*. Although Ed's early, folklorish style may have softened the shock, such a cover could only have seen daylight in that era on a magazine like *Galaxy* or *F&SF*. Ed was also standing a pulp-mag cliche on its head, for this artwork was a reversal of the "Monster and Maiden" theme so prominent in earlier years, used by pulp artists like Erle Bergey to hook adolescent (or even older) readers.

Ed was not above indulging this monster formula, if required by a pulp art director: for example, the fabulous eldritch crab breaking through Martian crust on *Space Stories* (re-painted from one of his portfolio samples), or any number of humanoid beasts on *Super Science*. For the stylish *Galaxy* — where Gold & Co. let him paint and draw largely as he wished — he addressed the subject only once ("Granny Won't Knit," May 1954) but made it distinctly his own: the creature's frightful form is indicated only by a baroque shadow stretching across a lavender plain, while a barelegged blonde is caught in the instant of her first glimpse of the monster, all under the blaze of a chartreuse sky. A molten red stream cuts the landscape, while tall green spikes punctuate the distant plain. Her nominal hero is stepping out of a translucent doorway, his body still insubstantial. The scene is superbly surreal; the hideous creature, like a great rampant beetle, only hinted at. Once more, Emsh does it his way.

This wasn't the first time Ed Emsh referenced Dali, Tanguy, or Ernst, nor was it the last. A vibrant strain of Surrealism was a major influence on his development; more than a hint is rarely absent from his best cover art, and it shows up with some frequency in his better interiors. A bold surrealism is

(top R) STARTLING STORIES. June 1955. "The Black Deep Thou Wingest" by Robert F. Young.

present in the sandy desert and mirror-orbs of "The Silver Eggheads" (Jan. 1959 *F&SF*) (pg. 84), and in the eerie deep-field cosmos and skeletal badlands of "It Opens the Sky" (Nov. 1957 *Venture*) (pg. 72).

Ed was not the only SF artist to use surrealism or abstraction to generate science fictional ambience and subject matter. Notably, Richard Powers took up the gauntlet laid down by Matta and Tanguy; and surrealist elements or strategies crop up in other name SF illustrators, including John Schoenherr, Mel Hunter, Virgil Finlay, and the redoubtable Frank Kelly Freas (who was perceived as Ed's main competition for the title "dean of SF artists"). These fellows were and are considerable talents, in and outside the SF field. And one may argue about who influenced whom. Some maintain that Powers was the most influential cover artist, and it's true that his SF career lasted longer than Ed's. But many of these artists, including Powers, plied a special style or approach. They all have their strong points, and they brought craftsmanship and knowledge, deep feeling, atmosphere, and a special spirit, to their work in science fiction. No one drew better rococo aliens and gnomes, or tortuous trees for that matter, than the dry-brush virtuoso Edd Cartier. Virgil Finlay, subject of a devoted cult following, was past master of a Doré-like engraved look, as well as batwinged demons, wattled amphibians, and so forth.

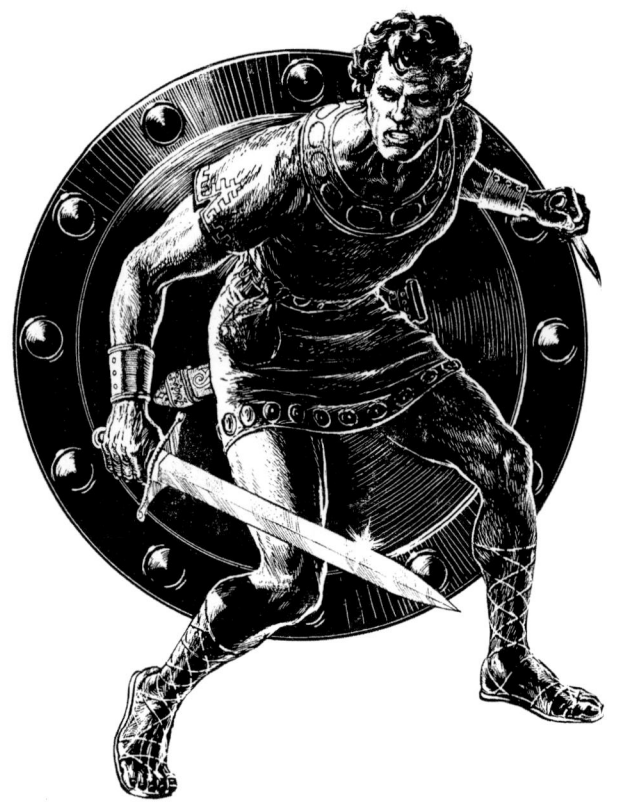

(top R) Jacket art for TALES OF CONAN by L. Sprague de Camp & Robert E. Howard, Gnome Press 1955

Among them all, though, Emshwiller was the most natural and naturalistic purveyor of the futuristic and interstellar. In a field that dotes on the camera-eye view, he could be that snapper of Kodachromes of future and cosmic worlds. Yet he often went beyond this to graphic and painterly intensities that much of his audience was hardly aware of, giving punch and sparkle to otherworld visions as he externalized the landscapes of his inner mindscape. To quote an old television series, it was all about going from the inner mind to the outer limits.

And then, for John Campbell and his good gray *Astounding*, nominal leader of the field, Ed could turn in a bucolic, almost Grandma Moses scene called "Pastoral" (June 1958), which demonstrates that even for an alien camelid the buttercups are always tastier on the other side of the fence (pg. 79). What could be more postcard prosaic, nostalgic, whimsical? Or in "Exploration Team" (March 1956), he could render, with clinical precision, a shaggy beast with enormous fangs roaring at a passel of ranger bears, the lead bear rearing up in snarling defense. Or portray — in "What's Eating You?" (May 1957) — a space traveler stuck on the Moon, pining for the blue-green Earth overhead. Some part of the kick of Emsh's art is that the wild and woolly is often balanced against the prosaic and ordinary. The exact balance between these poles may vary from one image to another, but it remains a constant factor in the success of his covers. And as in "Pastoral," a related element is often their wry humor. In a well-known cover for *If*, "Get a Horse" (Aug. 1958), the largest percheron in the galaxy is hauling a nonfunctional rocket-car across an Earthlike world, its dejected pilot riding the ship's canopy. Even a hundred years from now, says Emsh, the humiliations of owning an auto will be with us.

If Emsh didn't drag High Modernism into the field in 1951, it wasn't for lack of trying. The fractured look of "Beyond Bedlam" (Aug. 1951 *Galaxy*) calls up for many the shade of Picasso (pg. 51); but as an experiment in injecting Modernism into SF, it failed to gain a foothold, and Ed never repeated this attempt with anything so extreme. And maybe a great deal of Modernism wasn't really worth importing into SF. The fans, editors, and writers valued above all Ed's ability to visualize, his skill in portraying people, places and things with hyper-pellucid clarity; especially things that didn't yet exist. In the process of using these talents, however, Ed brought all that he knew to the service of our grand desires: everything from Pointillism to Art Moderne to woodcut to Action Painting became grist for at least the backgrounds of his cover compositions, and sometimes much more.

In his later work, he integrated bits of Modernism well enough that, although we might not care for the way it was done by Picasso, Braque, or Paul Klee, we lapped it up from the hand of Ed Emsh. Coruscations of cosmic fire and dimensional warps, searing blast effects, oceanic nebulae and sinuous trails of stellar gas and starclouds, even the flaring track of a volley of missiles (see "Women's Work," pg. 44, and "Blonde and Robot," pg. 57), are often passages of the purely abstract which Emsh has unleashed to fill out the bright illusions of our SF dreams. In "Collapse of a Field Force" (Feb. 1957 *F&SF*), it promotes the visceral impact of a sudden concussion (pg. 71); while such effects are at their most haunting and allegorical in "It Opens the Sky." Even in one of his tightest paintings, the doubly surreal "Soft Landing" (June 1960 *F&SF*), the smooth undulations of a planetary surface display an abstract rolling flow, promoting this scene's organic, sensual, and erotic content (pg. 93).

To put across a visceral impression, Ed was willing to employ almost any mode or technique. To give a composition impact, he would use any contrast of color or form that would do the job: a swath of complements, a palette of primary colors; a slash of bright yellow; a clash of textures or shapes. Over the years he evolved a theory of "dynamic contrasts" (as he termed it) to cover this

Early 1950s line art from GALAXY SCIENCE FICTION.

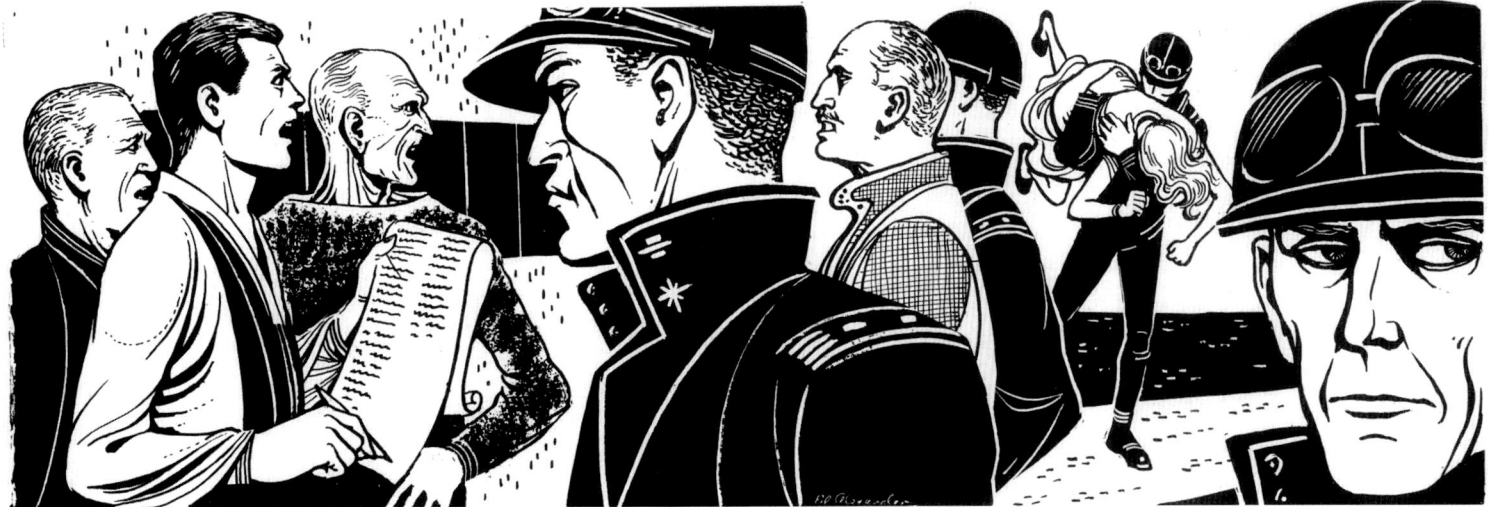

aspect of his aesthetic practice. The raw signs of this strategy can be discerned even in his teen-age efforts (where they were not always wholly successful).

Robert Haller has pointed out one of Emsh's recurring themes, of a woman hurtling through starry space or merging with/engulfed by her environment. Several times he depicts a woman, a dryad it seems, yearning toward or embraced by animate foliage, as in "Hunter, Come Home" (March 1963 *F&SF*) (pg. 90), or encircled by clinging vines — cool and decorous in "The Garden of Time" (Feb. 1962 *F&SF*) (pg. 81), more enveloping and erotic in "The Fellow Who Married the Maxill Girl" (Feb. 1960 *F&SF*). At times, the young woman, with hair streaming, seems to join earth and sky, become a magical link between these zones ("Maxill Girl" again, and hinted at in "Women's Work"). The relationship between figure and environment is an important feature of much of Emsh's art, even some interiors, notably several pieces from *Galaxy* for *The Stars My Destination* that show its hero caught in the twisting maze of a space-wreck or in the debris of a bombed-out cathedral (pg. 36), or confronting an electromagnetic light-storm.

I can't recall when I first saw an Emshwiller cover on an SF magazine or paperback, but it had to be one for the monthly *Galaxy* in the early Fifties. A Christmas cover, featuring Emsh's jovial four-armed Santa (pg. 62)? Maybe the one where spacesuited reindeer haul his rocket-powered sleigh over a bungalow dome on the Moon. Or was it the issue with a rocketship that has crushed a purple cow under one landing fin, while its pilot offers a lame apology to an irate native? Or possibly the one showing a sleek vanadium-steel raygun being fired by a sprawled-in-the-dust space marine, its violet beam sizzling past the viewer's head. Did I say there was something electric about the creations of Ed Emsh? (Other examples: a soft planet opens its brown eye to focus on a human explorer; or a battle rages between space-armored soldiers and hostile insectoids within the super-heated blaze of a nuclear firestorm.) I was nine, I suppose, when a friend of my parents gave me a clutch of these glossy mags after he noticed me staring at their chrome-kote covers. "You can have these now," said soft-spoken Mr. Solomon, "and these others later, when I finish reading them." There's always a kindly pusher to help you on the road to meta-utopia and the stars. There were other scenes of note by Emsh's competitors: a marvelous Mel Hunter of a jet-copter flight over magma seas on Mercury; a Jack Coggins ironwork space vehicle; a foggy, romance-tinged Powers; and on *F&SF*, a sexy, beribboned, floating woman in a montage by George Salter. Nothing to sneeze at, artwise; each of these men a worthy craftsman of the speculative fantastic.

All these artists exerted a magnetic tug on my malleable young mind. And yet, it must have been an Emsh scene, of intense men and women landing on other planets, battling elemental forces on Venus, Mercury, or some other far-flung world, that sealed my fate. For all the grand imaginative views produced by those other wizards, Emsh grabbed deeper at your gut. His art possessed a rare psychological dimension; he could pluck the vital cords hidden inside you to produce a resonant response. And once his visions got under

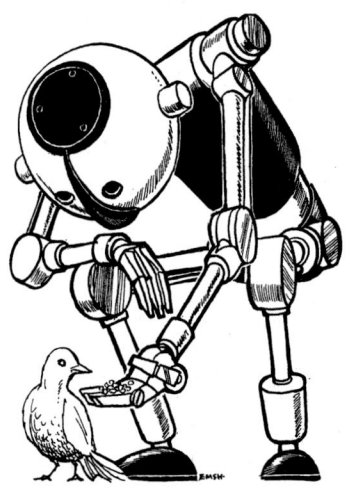

(bot R) Line art from GALAXY. Febuary 1963. For "Comic Inferno" by Brian Aldiss.

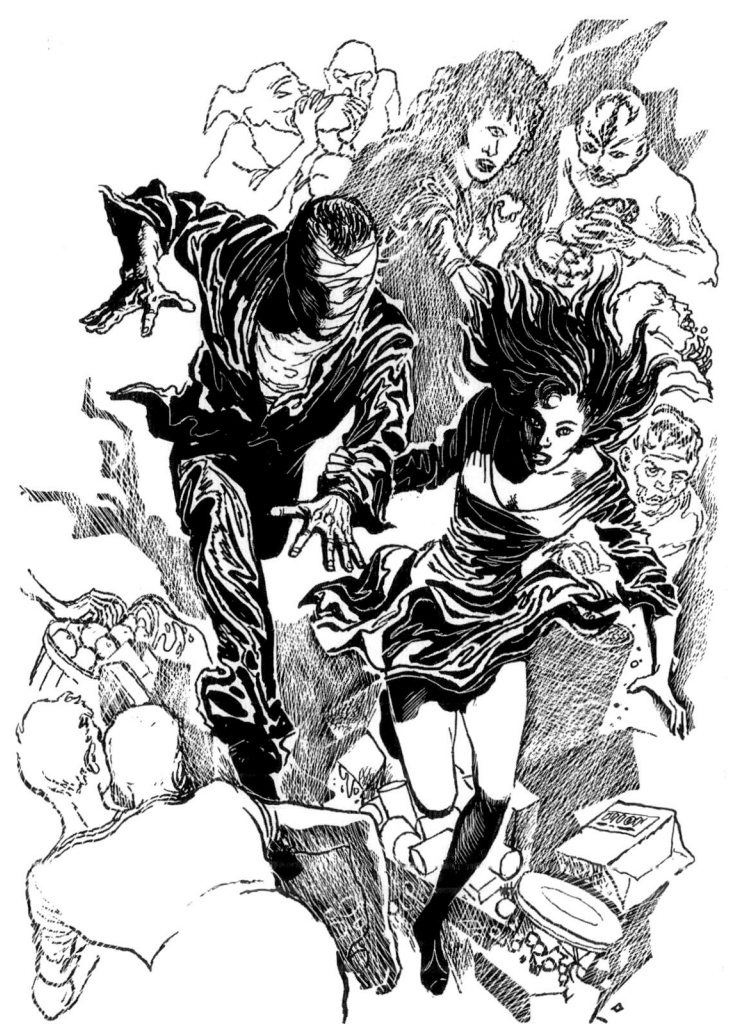

Line art from GALAXY Nov. 1956, THE STARS MY DESTINATION (Pt. 2)

your skin, they didn't let go; as you absorbed Emsh, the universe he was building scene by scene, he would assimilate you — your cortex, your limbic system, your sense of the conceivable and possible. Once he's permeated your bloodstream, he's there to stay. Having gotten down into your neural ganglia, he becomes a psychic symbiont who travels with you wherever you go.

Yes, this is a partisan view, not a clinically detached stance, nor one held with any pseudo-objectivity. Yet, as said earlier, there was a time when I almost took Ed Emsh for granted, his work was so ubiquitous in my pop-cultural environment. And I think that, within the fraternity of science fiction readers, fans, authors and editors, to some extent we all did; we never imagined he would leave us. When he virtually quit the SF game after copping four major awards in a row, he left some consternation in his wake. Many aficionados, and not a few editors, felt he had given up too soon. He kept on painting a new cover every few years for *F&SF*, on request of the owners, his friends the Fermans. Thus he kept a finger, if not a whole hand, in the science fiction pond. And a few of these later works are among his very best. So a work of genius could pop up occasionally, to remind us that the Emsh universe we'd known could no longer be taken as given. It was vanishing like the Cheshire cat, and soon we'd have not even an Emshian grin in our evening sky. The Emsh world was migrating over to the more rarefied continuum of experimental film, which became the new Emshwiller universe, the new Emsh visual discourse. He wasn't saying goodbye to us, though. He gave every sign of waving us on, to follow him and revel in his newest inventions and discoveries. Some SF people did, and others tried to, and much was gained by those who made the crossing. But it was clear to the devotees of his SF art that much was also lost. Of course, Emsh's science-fictional creativity was funneled right into his films and videos. The groundbreaking computer-animation "Sunstone" is proof of that, as well as "Thanatopsis," "Life Lines," "Relativity," "Fusion," and many more among his major films.

It can be said that Ed did it all in his 14-year, 700-odd-cover career in illustration, including men's adventure work and mystery mag covers. Simultaneously, he conducted a modestly successful career as a New York gallery painter in the Abstract mode. After 1965 (except for a handful of *F&SF* covers spread over the next fourteen years), he left illustration and gallery painting to be a full-time creator of art cinema. Ultimately he became a university dean, who continued to create innovative films and videos while he taught. Although he was more than competent at all forms of drawing and painting, and a skilled incidental portraitist, it is probably safe to say that, outside film and video art, Ed will be remembered best for his science fiction work. Especially that vast, varied array of stunning SF covers. In the words of Samuel R. Delany: "for thousands on thousands of readers, Emsh provided the vision of a vivid, material, and living world, a world that ranged from newly imagined subjects to newly imagined objects, a nature and a culture, an organicism and a technology, that ... no one had seen before."

Ed Emshwiller — the artist formerly known as Emsh — was a leader in this once-dismissed artform, arguably a master; an artist with peers but no true equal. He brought fun and drollery, and high adventure and high seriousness to SF; fine hard-edge painting, and a softer-edged, ethereal style, too. For all this we must thank him, and thank him again. He came along at a crucial juncture, a tipping point between thumping pulp and more thoughtful SF literature, and cannily remolded much of its cover and interior art into something more vital, more meaningful, more interesting and involving. It's not easy to say "No" to an Emsh cover, as so many of them cause us to dream with eyes wide open.

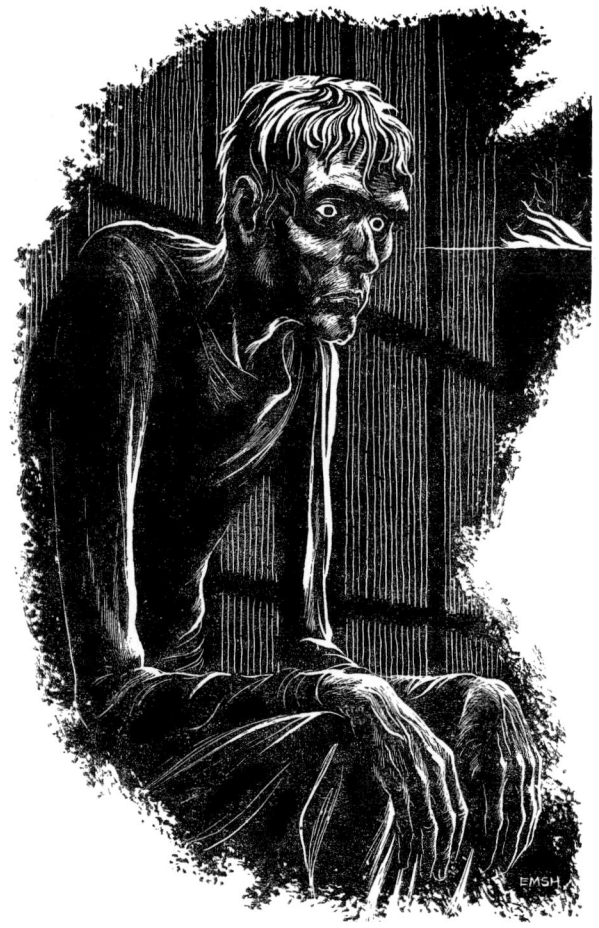

Since his untimely death at age 65 in 1990, his SF art has been increasingly collected by connoisseurs of the form; some experts claim that he is the most collected artist in the field. His films and videos still enthrall many, and with every new viewing their connections to his SF oeuvre are more readily grasped. So he has not disappeared from our ken, after all, because his multifaceted legacy is with us still. His SF art continues to gain younger adherents, fans, and avid collectors ... and someday soon will catch the eye of museum curators as well.

He was a groundbreaker, a pointer to and unveiler of potent worlds beyond the current map. Was then, and still remains. Because his art has life and meaning beyond the transitory and superficial, because it concerns itself with our place in the universe and our possible destinies, it will always attract alert eyes and minds. Though some aspects of his art may be time-bound, the best of it will never grow old or quaint or stale. It will speak to us always in a clear, strong voice about our ceaseless fascination with the future.

INFINITY SCIENCE FICTION. Apr. 1957. "Deeper than the Darkness" by Harlan Ellison.

EMSHWILLER
INFINITY X TWO

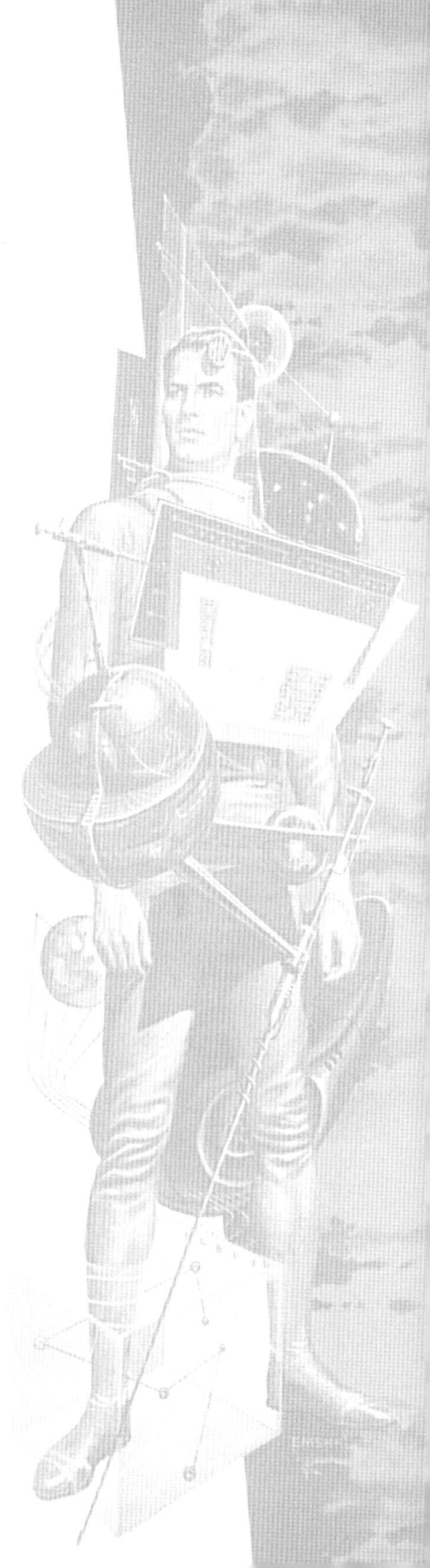

One

Looking into the Future

When the first short Edison films were projected onto a white sheet at the turn of the 20th Century an early shot was of a train pulling head-on into a station; a few people in the audience jumped out of the train's path – momentary fooled by the novelty of the moving image. People in downtown Manhattan witnessing the fall of the World Trade Towers later compared the experience to a scene from a science fiction movie. In less than a hundred years the experience of reality had been inverted.

IN THE WINTER OF 1950-1951 Edmund Alexander Emshwiller was twenty-six, and married for just over a year, when he appeared at the Manhattan offices of *Galaxy Science Fiction* with a portfolio of paintings. Washington Irving van der Poel Jr., the art editor of *Galaxy Science Fiction*, was impressed enough to buy a few ready-made pieces to use as covers for the magazine. Fresh out of art school, Emsh had spent that summer creating the art samples at his in-laws' home in Ann Arbor, Michigan — the whole time worrying at the reception his work might receive. One piece in with his samples was a hyper-realistic painting of his army boot. It was just a lone boot on a white background, but the feel of the leather nappa was palpable. The picture was impressive in its technique — surpassing a photograph. Poel sat back and gazed at the image. He appreciated the talent that went into depicting so ordinary an object. "Where have you worked before?" Poel asked. Ed did not have a ready answer.

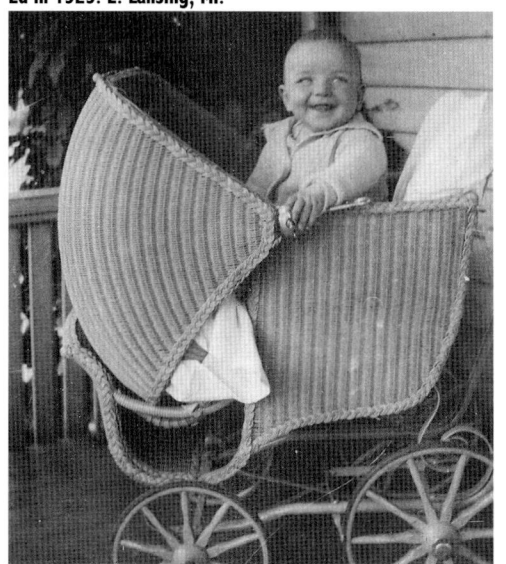

Ed in 1925. E. Lansing, MI.

Errol Emshwiller and Susie MacLellan had met as students at Michigan State University in the early 1920s and married soon after they graduated. Errol had been able to enroll at MSU under a government dispensation for wounded World War I vets. During the Great War he had been stationed near Argonne, France, in an artillery unit, manning a 155mm gun, when a shell exploded next to his embankment and a steel fragment tore into his left arm. Without sulfa drugs (the discovery of penicillin was a decade away) the arm developed gangrene and had to be amputated.

Ed Emshwiller was born in East Lansing, Michigan, on February 16, 1925. He was just Eddy then. Years later he would go by many names, always a variation of his surname. Ed's father Errol taught engineering and physics at Ferris State, a small college in Big Rapids. The Emshwillers were a scientific family, but encouraged Ed's artistic ambitions. Ed did well in science classes, but he also had an artistic bent and always looked to combine the two. His mother Susie used to say he must have "art in his soul."

The early years of the Great Depression had seen reduced enrollment at all colleges across the country and Ferris State didn't need many teachers. By 1932 Errol had moved his family to Chicago where he began studies towards an advanced degree in physics. At home he read magazines, including science fiction pulps *Amazing Stories* and *Astounding Science Fiction*. These would find their way into the hands of Ed and his younger brother Mac.

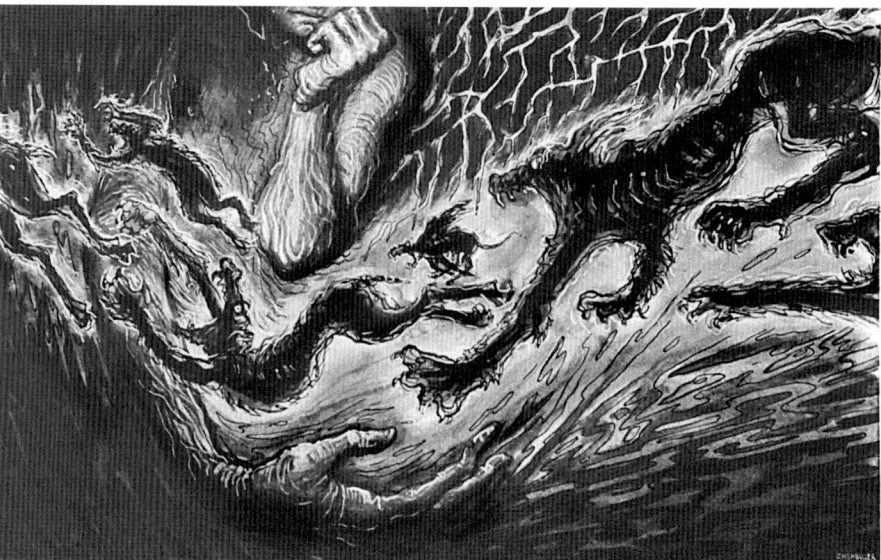

(top R) (Student art, 1948) - Primitive storming vitality, delivered with an underhand caress. This could be the youthful artist summoning his own creative demons. These electric dogs, cats, and flying rats, which flow and twist with the lightning they seem to ride, would surface again in Emsh's SF work some years later.

(bot L) AMAZING STORIES. Jan. 1929. One of the pulp magazines that Ed's father was reading.

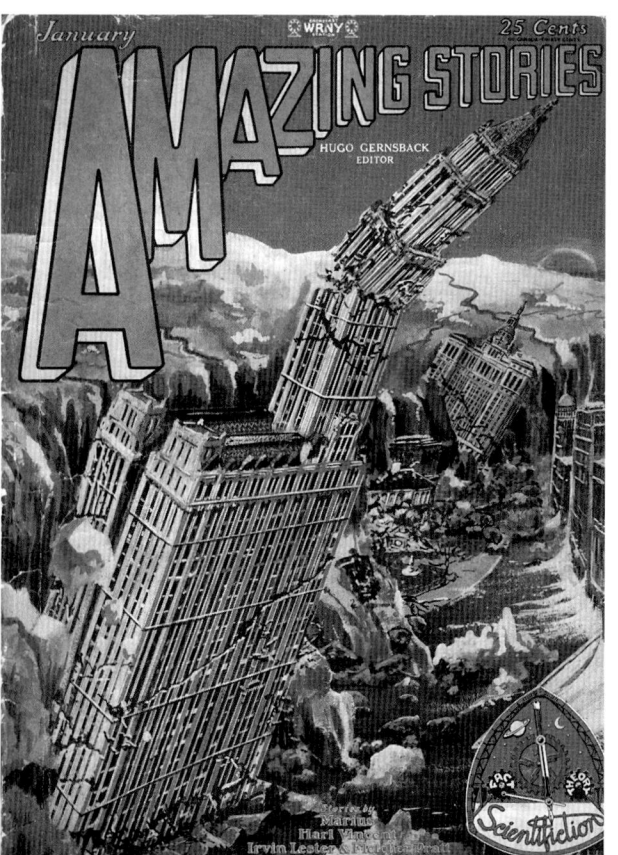

Early science fiction pulp magazines were a dime's worth of scientific wonders, and in most American cities could be found just around the corner. How could readers with a scientific bent and a sense of wonder not be attracted to these monthly, bi-monthly, and quarterly glimpses at the future? The titles tell all: *Amazing Stories*, *Science Wonder Stories*, and *Astounding Stories of Super Science*. As a boy Ed was captivated by the covers and illustrations in these magazines: the giant, super machines; rockets speeding through space; men of action reacting to some imminent disaster–all subjects that would later turn up in his SF art.

In Chicago during the summer of 1934, Errol paid the 50 cents admission to the *Century of Progress* World's Fair, 25 cents each for Ed and Mac. Ed was attracted to the theatrical performances, films and futuristic exhibits, and stared longingly at the flying machines. (A dirigible or airplane ride could be had for $3—an

(top R) Student art by Ed. 1948 done in a rendering class.

(bot L) Susie, Errol, Eddy, and Mac Emshwiller. 1928.

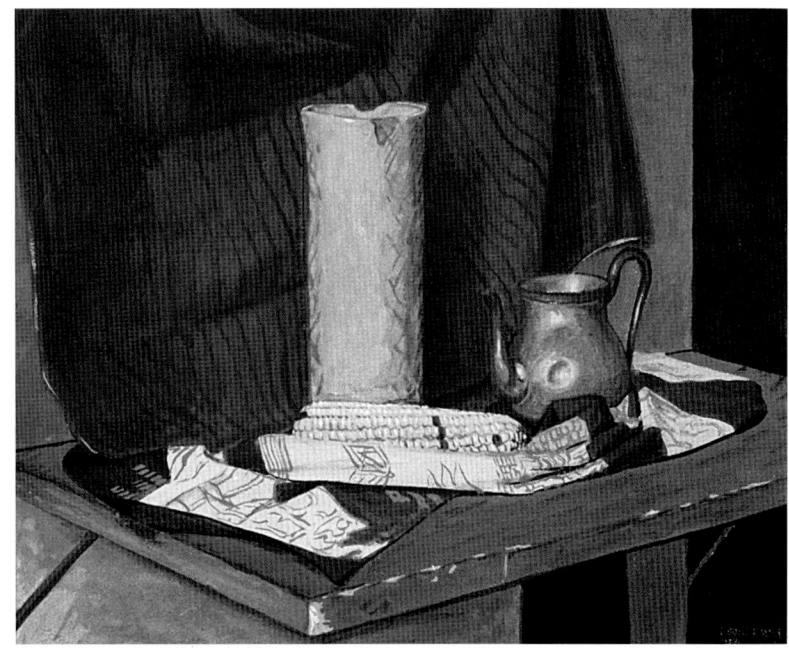

impossible sum for the family.) Inside the fair grounds Errol's first stop was the U-shaped Hall of Science building. Just beyond the entrance stood a transparent man (the clear skin made out of "cellon"—the same material used for film stock), six feet tall, on a pedestal, every organ, every bone and muscle visible, and the whole thing mechanically operational. (A *Galaxy* Magazine cover that Ed would do twenty years later would show a woman with her synthetic flesh removed to expose the gears and metalworks.) Further along, in the medical section, they were greeted by the smell of alcohol and ether, to simulate a hospital, and came across a gigantic animated robot giving a lecture on nutrition in sync with a movie projector. They also saw a demonstration of an early primitive television and broadcast studio.

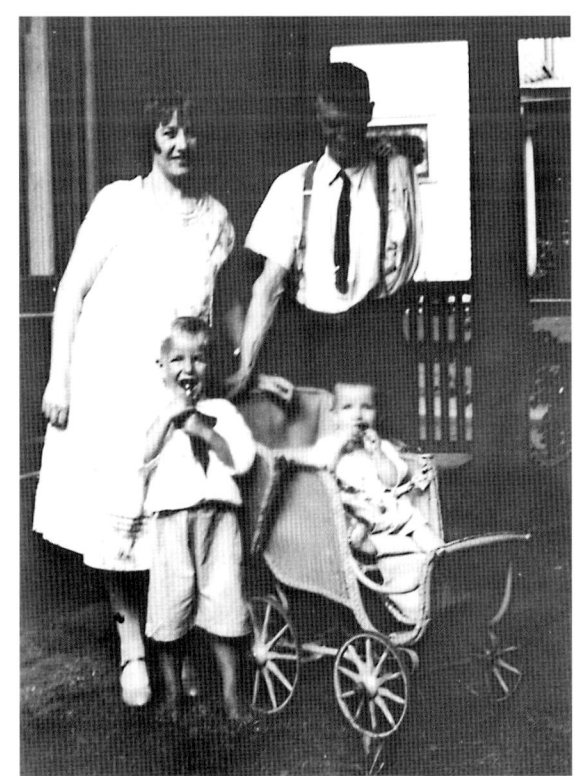

After the Exposition, Ed was inspired to create flipbooks and animated his own little movies, including one of an egg sprouting arms and legs. By the third grade, Ed was taking lessons at the Art Institute of Chicago where he joined a special art class for gifted schoolchildren. He was also making his own action figure cutouts, from drawings of comic strip characters glued onto flattened tin cans.

Like many small children, Ed was aware of the mythic power of images: "…we had a *Natural History* book, a very thick, big book, and it had engravings of all kinds of animals. I remember the ones that were most attractive to me were of jungles, with animals hidden here and there – it was mysterious and not wholly and clearly grasped. And that kind of image was very attractive, and was fascinating. I think that all along the line I had a fascination with the fantastic."

Early in 1937 Susie Emshwiller talked Errol into taking the civil service test for patent examiner. She was tired of the job insecurities of two parents working as teachers. With the extra test points Errol received as a wounded World War I veteran he scored high enough to get the job and the family moved into the Dyer Apartments in Washington, D.C. Before long, his mother enrolled Ed in Saturday art classes at the Corcoran Art School.

In the summer of 1938, a thirteen-year old Ed was selling magazine subscriptions door-to-door and saving his money. His plan was to earn enough to buy a used 8mm movie camera. Once he collected the required sum Ed informed his parents about his plans. *Why did he need a movie camera?*, he was asked. A portable radio, advertised as "electric-tuning!", then fresh on the market, would be more useful.

He got the radio and immediately regretted it. The music and radio plays were no different from those heard on the family's big cathedral radio. With some money left over and no one objecting, Ed bought a used 16mm projector, which came with a few silent Keystone western short-films. He tried his hand at making movies by drawing on strips of paper he had cut to match the 16mm gauge and poked holes along the edge to imitate real film. After a few passes through the projector's gates the paper shredded into pieces and jammed in the gear works where it was charred by the hot lamp. After these early failures, he realized he could draw on clear leader film—this was a few years before Norman McLaren became famous for doing the same thing at the Canada Film Board, and concurrent with the work of Len Lye.

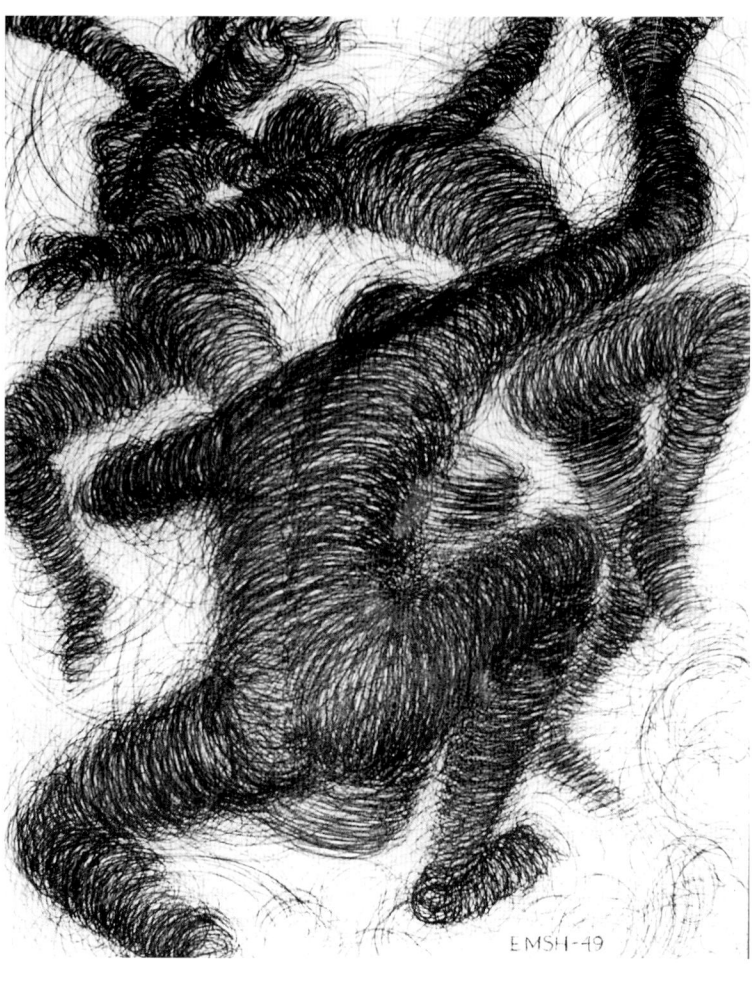

Ed's early passion for film was not just a schoolboy's infatuation with movie cowboys, cartoons, Flash Gordon serials, or horror stars like Bela Lugosi and Lionel Atwill playing cinematic monsters. In his own "movie making" he was already thinking of movement in terms of art, messing around with drawings that evolved in terms of kinetic manipulation of shapes and lines. In his own little experiments, Ed was always amazed at the finished film projected on screen. Some years later, when he finally got his first movie camera, he filmed the evolution of some of his paintings using stop-motion "… at 24 frames a second, in their growth like a blossoming flower, sometimes moving or growing […] that evolved and changed

(top R) (Student art, 1949) - Another highly expressive early drawing, a veritable hurricane of samba/calypso dancers and their vibrant rhythms. This exemplifies Ed's early enthusiasm for lively cinematic movement in his art … a promise of things to come.

(bot L) Art by Carol from the mid 1950s. This was the time she was studying art at the New School in New York City with the social realist artist Robert Gwathmey.

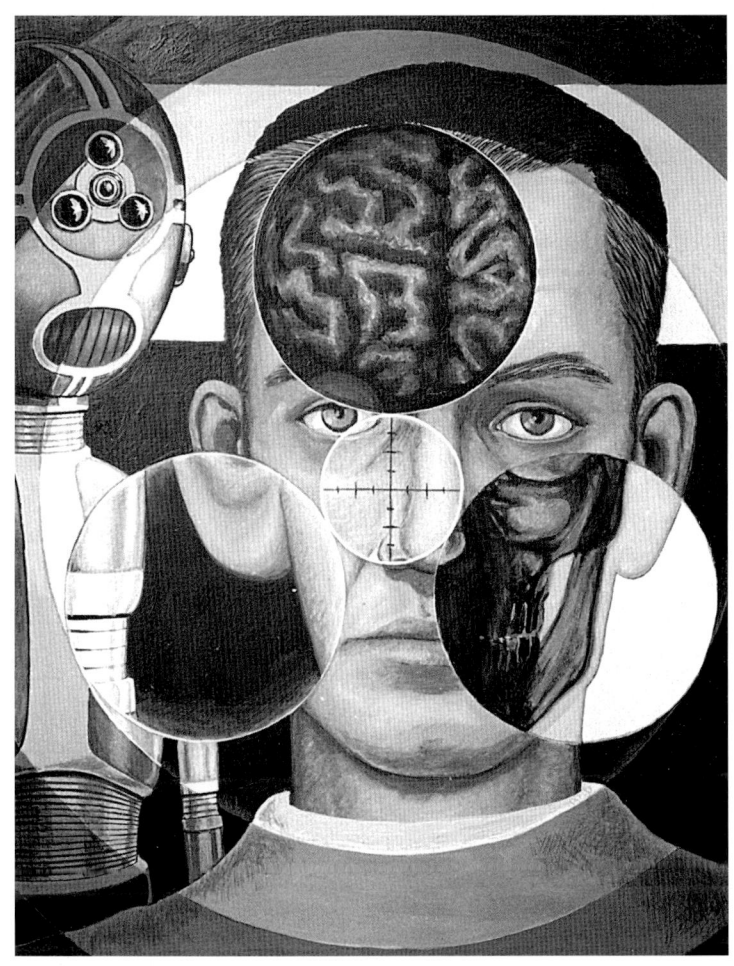

(Early SF art sample, c. 1950) - In this early assault on the heights of professional-style SF cover art, Ed fell into a labored formality. The subject of man vs. robot would crop up several times in years to come. The X-ray views were picked up and applied again to several later themes (including the man/robot partnership detailed in Isaac Asimov's stories in GALAXY SF).

and changed and changed." This was the inverse of the experiment with motion that Eadward Muybridge had done in the 19th century. Muybridge wanted to see how things really move by intersecting motion. Ed wanted to make static things move.

Ed also had a particular fondness for adventure, including movies starring Errol Flynn, and was closely following the exploits of *Terry and the Pirates* and *Prince Valiant* on the comic pages. Like many a teenager of the time, he began thinking of himself as a fearless world adventurer.

While Ed was creating his first images directly on celluloid film, Charles C. Fries was shooting home movies of his family with a Bell & Howell Filmo camera. Professor Fries taught linguistics at the University of Michigan. Throughout the 1930s the family alternated living in Ann Arbor, Michigan, with Germany, France, and England, where Charles worked on and off on the Oxford English Dictionary, and helped to set up language schools in the United States.

His daughter Agnes Carolyn Fries was born on April 12, 1921. As she got older she preferred to be called Carol – *in order to be more like a boy.*

Carol's mother (also named Agnes) was considered a piano prodigy as a child, though she was kept from performing professionally by her own mother. Agnes, at the age of eight, had seen her father drown in a river trying to save her niece. After this time, she and her mother moved from relative to relative. Agnes learned how to play the piano when a resident in a boarding house, where her mother worked, gave her free piano lessons. Carol remembers, *my mother and grandmother just had each other, everybody else was dead, her baby brother was dead and her father was dead.*

Many nights Carol and her brothers would fall asleep to her mother's piano playing. *We were one of those old-fashioned families who stand around the piano and sing songs,* Carol said, *with everybody playing some instrument or other.* Much later, Carol's own children would fall asleep to the clacking of her typewriter.

Fries thought his children should learn languages first hand. When he was working in England, Carol and her brothers were shipped to France. One of the places Carol stayed was a small chateau in the countryside. Carol remembers peeing into a large vat that was emptied on the fields outside. They stayed in another chateau filled with old marble statues and a two-hole outhouse just inside the front entrance. The rest of the house was closed off to save on heating during the cold season and on upkeep during warm months. Carol and her little brother Charley had only the use of the heated parts of the house: a tiny playroom, the kitchen, and the dining room. In the streets some of the French children would greet the American kids by throwing stones at them, and calling Charley "*Américain, tete de chien,*" but Carol's brother was a baseball player back in the states, and had much better aim when he returned the rocks.

All this time, traveling back and forth between America and Europe, she had been confused, hopelessly, badly. *I remember the exact word where I decided I couldn't learn and so gave up: address/adresse. Another was: syrup/sirop.... It was as if a curtain came down ....*

In 1937, on Carol's sixteenth birthday, her father told her that no woman had ever done anything significant or original. Women could only serve as inspiration for men. *I'm sure he thought he was doing me a favor....* Her musician brother became the black sheep of the family by *not* becoming a doctor, lawyer, or professor. In her case, a profession was not expected or necessary.

In France, she had once overheard Liline, the Frenchwoman taking care of her, telling the fourteen-year-old cleaning girl how clever she was – and how good a maid she would make one day. Carol was surprised between the old world thinking of the French and Americans who expected their children to leapfrog far ahead in careers. Liline would later serve as a motherly role model to Carol for her own children.

While growing up, Carol read Tarzan and John Carter of Mars books as they came out, and the westerns of Zane Grey and Will James, and would fantasize being a cowboy. She always thought of herself as one of the boys, albeit a "defective" one, who could excel at whatever she put her mind to. *I would daydream while walking down the street, and if someone was coming towards me I would cross the street so as not to be interrupted.*

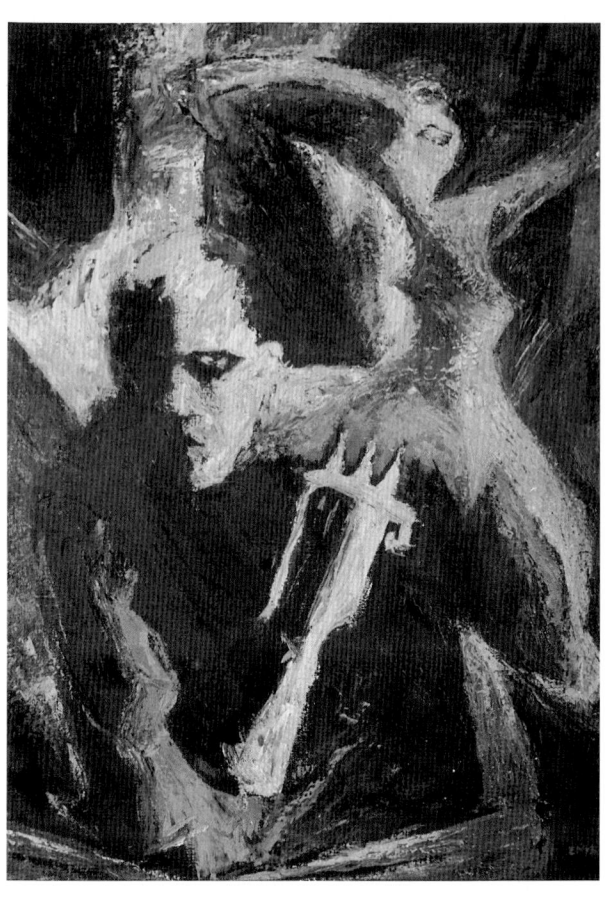

(top R) **Student art by Ed. 1949.**

(bot L) **Student art by Ed. 1948.**

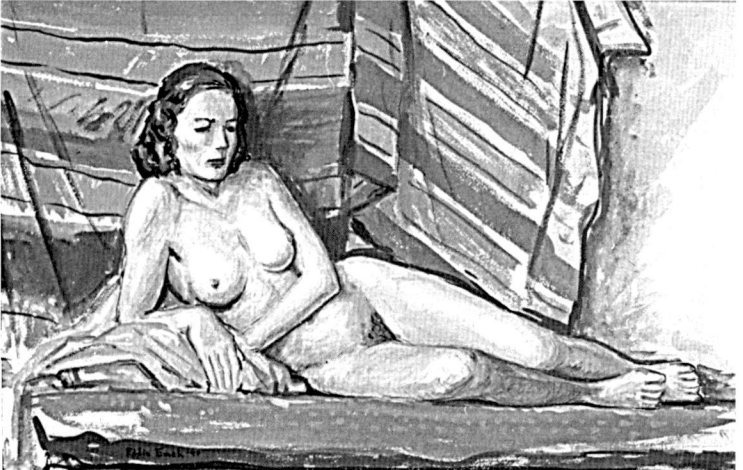

At home, her father dominated. He had trained at the Chicago Divinity School to become a Baptist minister and lost his religion there. *My dad was one who thought to argue was to love. Dad always won.* Carol lost these debates to the Socratic arguments he used. As a grown-up Carol once heard someone call Socrates a bully and she shouted, *Yes!*

Two

2 × Infinity

IN THE LATE SUMMER OF 1939, Charles C. Fries was in Freiburg, Germany, and was at the end of his sabbatical year there. War had begun in Czechoslovakia, Spain, and Albania. He was aware of Hitler's Luftwaffe giving support to Franco in Spain. The news coming in over the radio was bad—things were heating up in Poland, and freighters were being sunk by German U-boats in the Atlantic. Most non-Frenchmen in France knew well the weakness of the Maginot Line and how the Low Countries between France and Germany were little more than a speed bump to Hitler's army.

Charles feared being stranded in a German-occupied France. He began hording petrol. One night he put as many cans of it as he could fit into their automobile, and left the surplus with Liline, who later used it to escape the Nazis before they reached her town. Charles drove all night with his headlights out through countryside and towns under blackout restrictions. All their non-essentials were left behind, including the Filmo movie camera.

They managed to embark on the last civilian ships out of Le Havre. The ship was crowded with Americans fleeing Europe

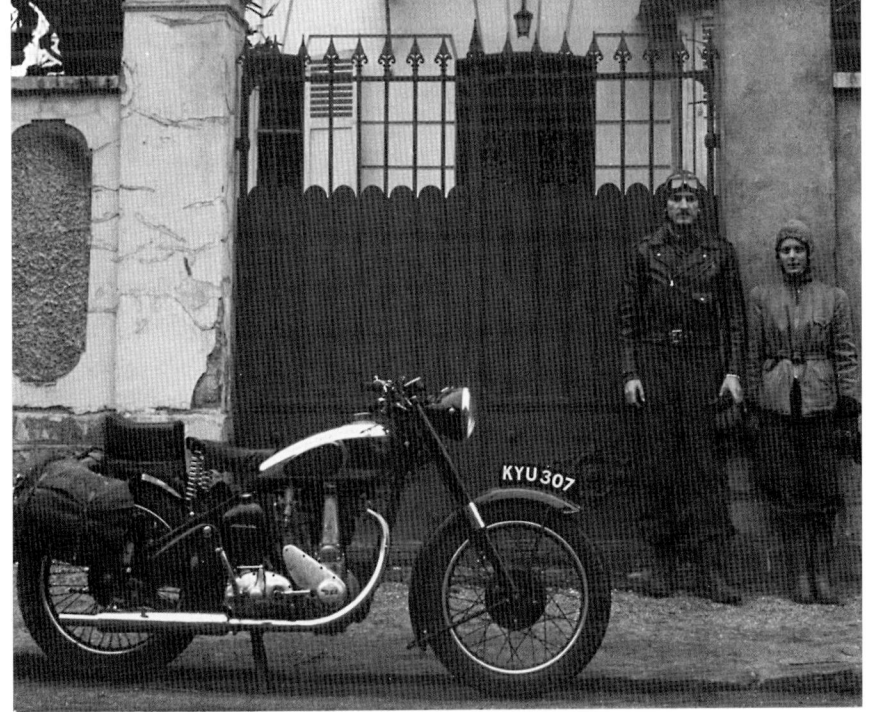

Ed and Carol in France with their BSA motorcycle. 1950.

and cots were set up in the drained pool. At the end of the week, they were back in America within the safe confines of Ann Arbor. Carol entered the freshman class at the University of Michigan in the fall. Since the age of twelve she had practiced violin four to five hours a day, and the music school at the university seemed the obvious choice. Besides music classes, she was also taking classes recommended by her father—including his own linguistics class.

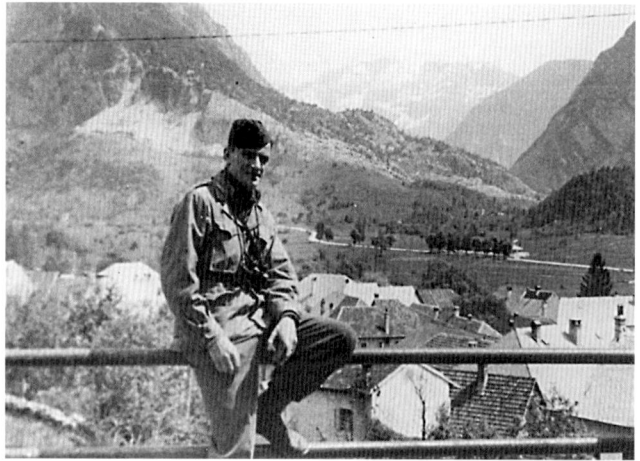

(top) **Ed in Piezzo, Italy, Zone B. July 1945.**

(L) **Student art by Carol. C. 1950.**

By 1942 the patent office had moved part of its operations to Richmond, Virginia, and the Emshwillers were now residents of that sleepy city. Taking classes at Thomas Jefferson High School, Ed was getting interested in girls and had a one-sided crush on the daughter of a local congressman. At this time Ed had begun a swing band where he played the violin — an instrument he could just barely play — with some high school classmates. (The violin was more commonly found in European bands emulating American jazz.) They spent more time practicing than performing before an actual audience, and the band could only play five pieces.

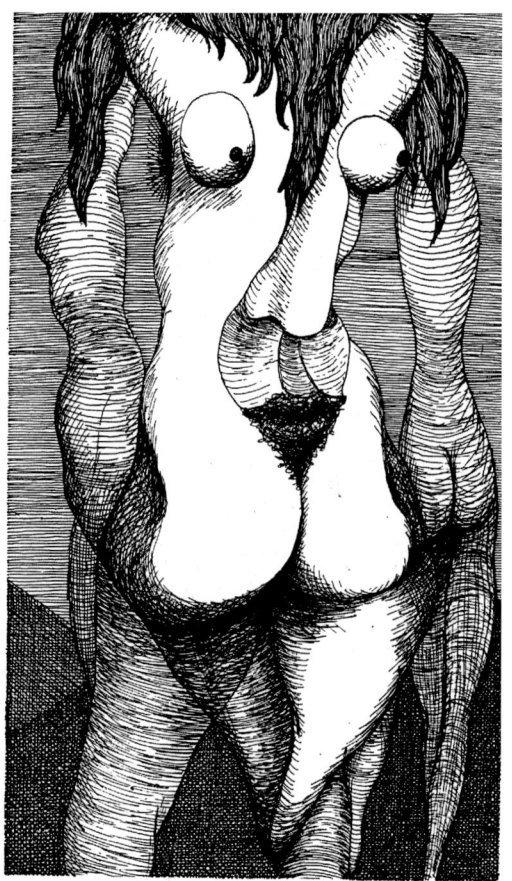

Ed enlisted in the Army on June 25, 1943 soon after graduating high school, and after being rejected by the Rangers branch of the army. (His eyesight was not considered sharp enough.) After boot camp, he was at North Dakota Agriculture College in the Army Special Training Program learning civil engineering. In March 1944, he began officer candidate school at Fort Benning, Georgia, with the rank of corporal and by May 1944 had made 2nd Lieutenant before entering active service. Barely nineteen years old, he was one of the youngest Lieutenants in the army and was considered too young to command soldiers. The army forced him to repeat officer school. This time he had a Captain Queeg-like superior who was disliked by all the men. The group made a concerted effort to have this head officer removed from his duties. When this action failed, the bad marks all the men, including Ed,

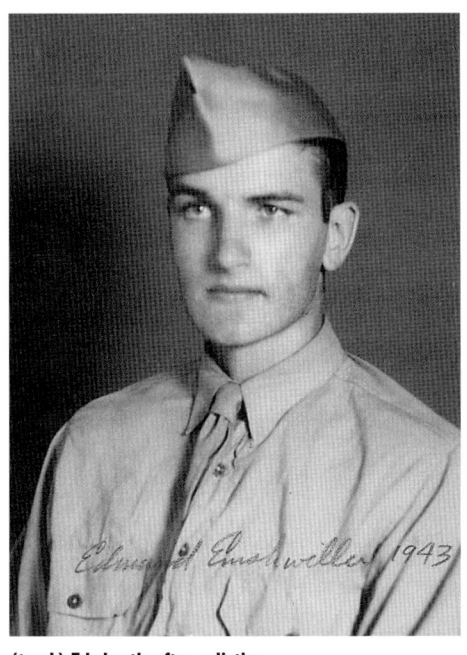
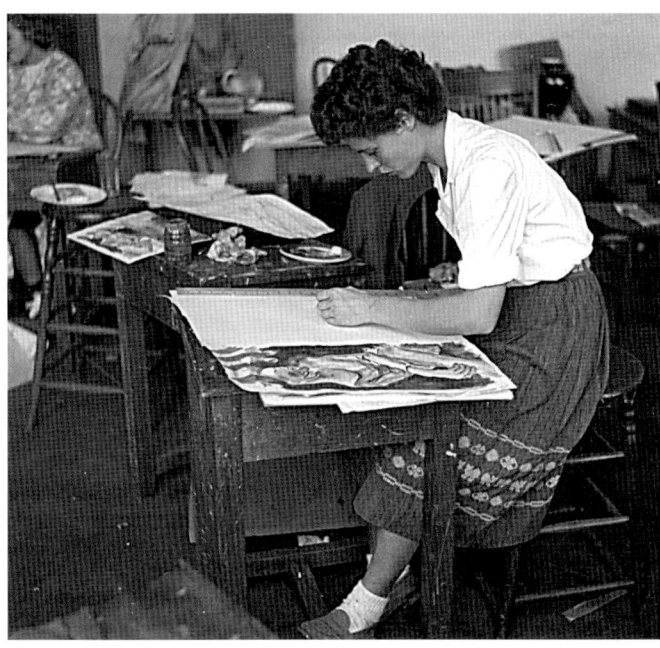

received kept them from further advancement in rank.

Now part of the 3rd Battalion, 351st Infantry 88th Division (nicknamed the "Blue Devils"), Ed was shipped to Italy. His unit was supporting the 350th, which was attacking German forces all along the northern Apennines Mountains. News of the capitulation of Germany broke while Ed was having supper on May 2, 1945. Ed spent the next few months of Italian occupation stationed along the Isonza River Valley between Plezzo and Tolmino. His division was in close proximity to the volatile Yugoslav border where a small cold war was brewing.

(top L) Ed shortly after enlisting in Army. 1943.

(top R) Carol at University of Michigan. 1948.

(bot L) Art by Carol. C. 1950.

War-weary troops now found themselves with plenty of free time and no entertainment or recreational outlets except for local *vino* shops. Captured German soldiers assured the American G.I.s that venereal disease was rare in the area. The army looked for other distractions for its solders.

Ed was made a unit commander supervising operations of entertainment facilities: bars, clubs, and movie theatres. Ed had entered the army harboring the ambition of becoming a wartime cameraman, but at this stage of the war it was too late. (His military qualification was as a heavy machine gunner.)

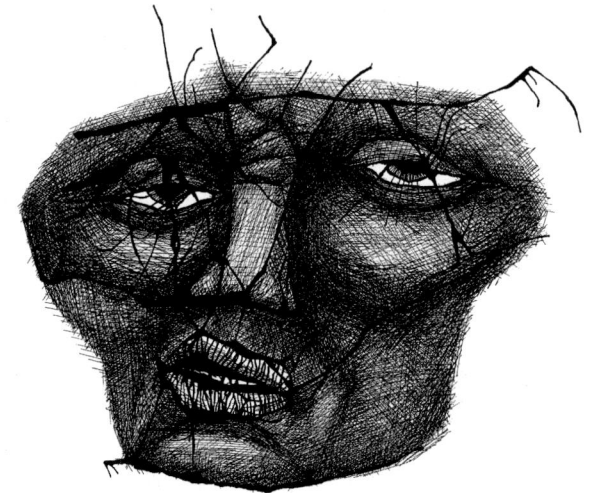

His artistic talents were noticed by one of his superiors and he was made the director of the training aid shop in Trieste, where he created posters and instructional materials for the Army Education Program.

Before going to college Carol had cut her hair short (a style she would keep from then on). She was still too shy, even failing to speak up when she got undeserved bad grades for missing classes while sick. By 1944, she had noticed that many of the men around the University were disappearing. *They were either in Canada ... or in jail for conscientious objecting, or in the war.* She thought of her-

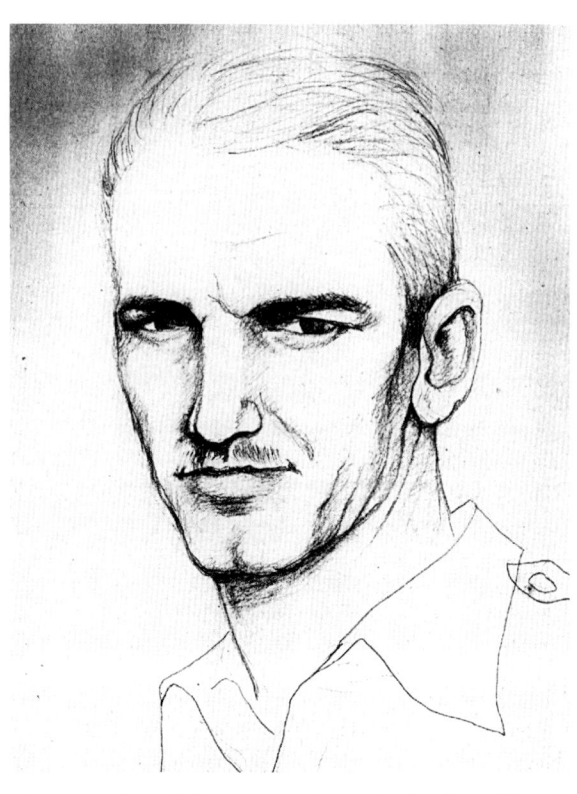

self as a pacifist, but soon after leaving the music school joined the Red Cross. *I wanted to experience what my generation was experiencing.* Many college-age people saw the war as an initiation rite.

Carol worked in a Red Cross rest and relaxation camp on the Isle of Capri, and later in Tarcento ran a club for soldiers and recruited girls for dances. She sometimes drove a truck to pick up supplies. She played pinochle with soldiers and took group hikes on the Italian cliffs. Most of the time she went without her Red Cross uniform, and at times was insulted by American soldiers who took her for an Italian *mujer*. *I was cursed at and spit on by some of our guys [....] They called me words I'd never heard until then...*

When Carol returned to America, at the end of the war, she reentered the music school at the University of Michigan. *I was not a good violinist, mainly because I have slow fingers.* Carol was also a slow reader of sheet music and a bad speller. Growing up in an era before dyslexia became a familiar diagnosis, she always had trouble with words and anything to do with a progressive "reading" of anything on paper. Though she had trouble with reading material, she could draw. *I was dexterous in art in a different way than is required by music.*

Ed left active duty in October 1946, and came home anxious to catch up with his life. Like many returning servicemen, he rarely referred to his war years. The sixties would find him marching in antiwar rallies. If Ed was not able to become a battlefield cameraman, demobilization did bring the Servicemen's Readjustment Act, better known as the G.I. Bill, and with other stipends from the army he could now afford to go to art school. He was ready to enroll at the Pratt School of Art in New York City, but his mother Susie did not approve of this choice. She wanted Ed to have a university degree. It seemed that Susie Emshwiller played a strong assertive influence on Ed during his early years.

Twenty-one years old, in his first year at the University of Michigan Art School, Ed joined all the cine clubs on campus.

(top L) Pencil sketch of Ed done by Carol c. 1949.

(bot R) Ed and Carol on camping trip in France. 1950.

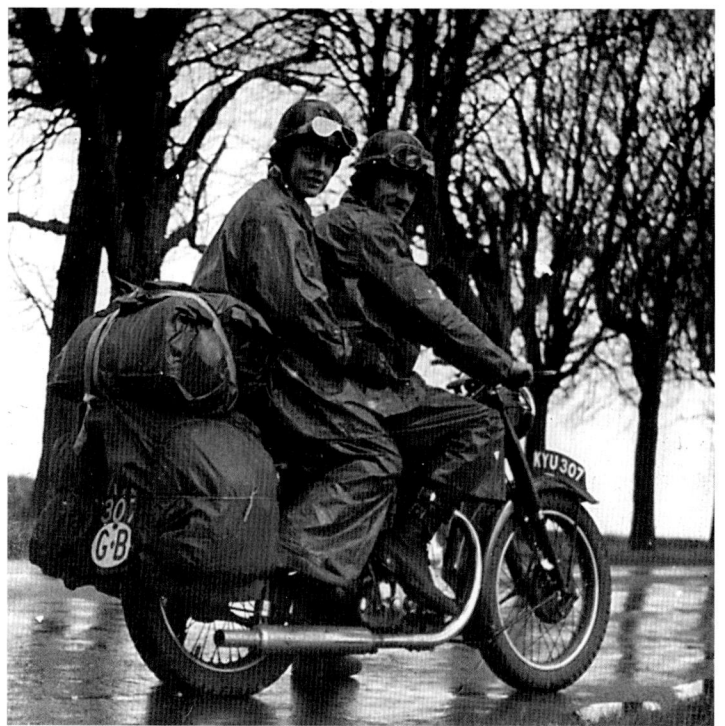

(top R & bot R) Student art by Ed. 1948.

(bot) Ed in Professor Lopez' oil painting class at the University of Michigan. 1948.

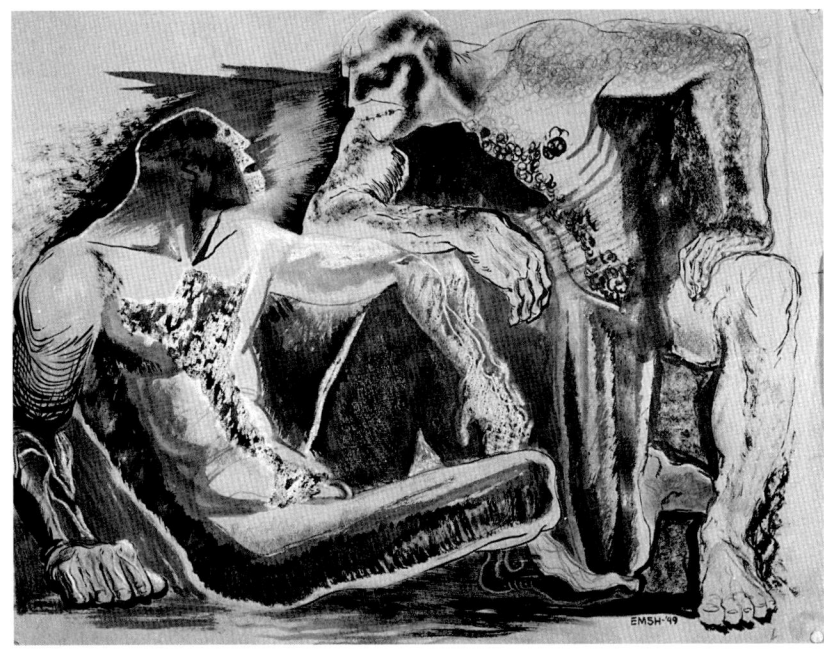

Before long he had decided that a career as a commercial artist might be an easier road for someone with his drawing skills than attempting to get into film work.

The University of Michigan's art curriculum used the Bauhaus school of modernism and contemporary design. Bauhaus avoided using many of the traditional notions of classical art and Ed and Carol were trained as much in modern art and abstraction as in classical art. In the sixties Ed would be accused of taking lysergic drugs to paint some of his wilder abstractions, but he had assiduously learned this style of art as a college student.

In the fall of 1947 Ed was in a life drawing class. During a model break, he was talking with a classmate when he mentioned being stationed in Travesio, Italy, during the war.

I was stationed in Tarcento, near the Yugoslavian border, a pretty, petite, shorthaired brunette called out. *That's near there.* The brunette identified herself as Carol Fries.

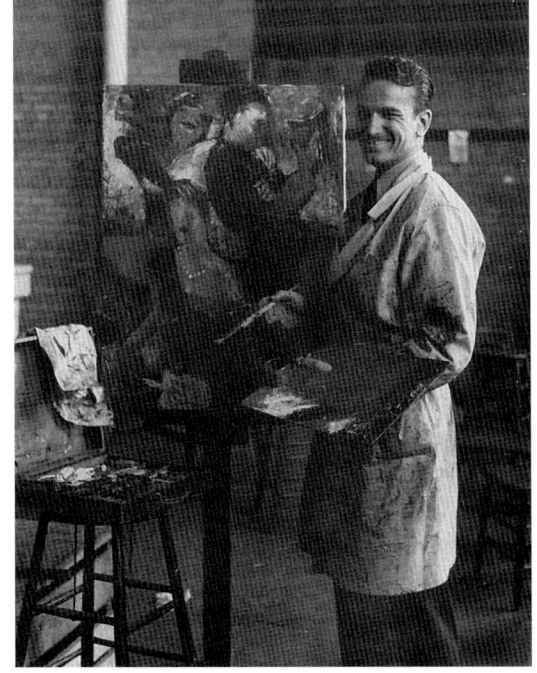

When they met, Ed was a strapping, handsome man with straight shoulders, a Robert Donat-style mustache, and a big smile. By the time he had left the army he was six feet tall and weighed 165 pounds. Carol was thin and delicate-looking, and didn't seem particularly like a woman who would fantasize being a cowboy or enjoy driving trucks. She appeared shy, and sensible, but struck Ed as someone who could pursue a notion with relentless intensity.

They were married August 30, 1949, on Ed's parents back porch in Silver Springs, Maryland, two months after both had received bachelor of art degrees from the University of Michigan. Ed was recovering from a bout of mononucleosis, and was still feeling the effects during the ceremony. Carol's father and her brother Charley drove

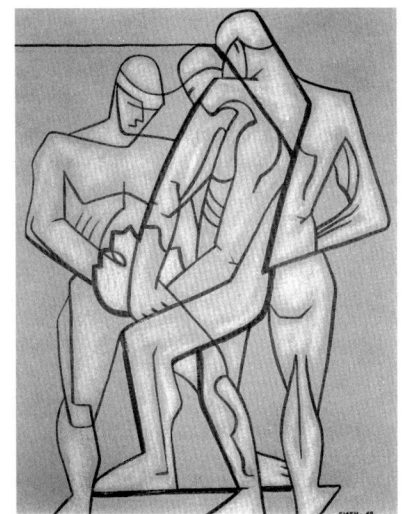

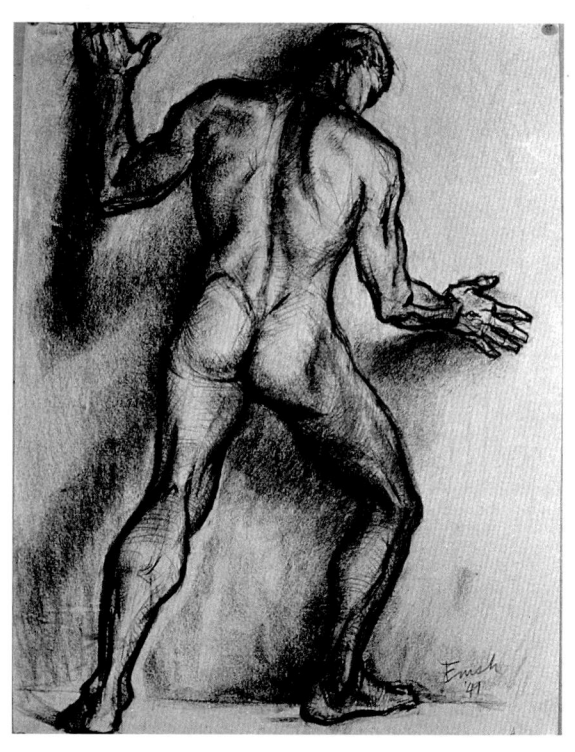

down from Ann Arbor. Carol had won a Fulbright scholarship, and Ed had a year of paid education left on the G.I. Bill, so they decided to go to Paris. (The British author and critic Clive James has noted how America became an artistic world power after the war through the G.I. Bill.)

Before getting to France they bought a 450cc BSA motorcycle in England. (In this he was emulating his brother who was a motorcycle enthusiast.) Ed also bought camping equipment and a small tent. In the spring and summer of 1950 the newlyweds motored to French campgrounds when not taking classes at the Ecole des Beaux-Arts, where Ed was studying graphics while Carol took painting classes. When Ed mentioned that he wanted to buy a movie camera, Carol remembered her father's old Filmo left at Liline's ten years earlier. As soon as he held it in his hands, the camera became a familiar object. Ed examined the camera thoroughly, taking it apart and putting it back together like an army rifle.

Ed's first films were home movies of Carol in Paris and around the Beaux Arts building. One reel of film, stolen in France, was a travelogue of Paris streets and people that Ed shot using short bursts of the shutter — this gave everything a speeded-up, pixilated look. While in France, Ed joined three cine clubs and was a regular at the French Cinematheque.

By the end of their year overseas, they had put thirteen thousand miles on the BSA and set up their camping tent in eleven countries. (In a few places, like Albania, Ed would swing over the border long enough to say he had been there.) Before boarding the ship back home, Ed bought some American periodicals in a Paris bookstall to read during the trip — including a few science fiction magazines. "Between waves (I'd never make a good sailor), I let the obvious idea grow. As soon as I hit shore I started knocking out samples."

(top L) (Student art, 1949) - A strong expressive study of male anatomy, with many indicators that this art student is destined for a life of painting and drawing tied to the figure and human struggle. Note that the powerful, boldly rendered figure is pushing against a wall, a physical barrier, which may be a metaphor for the resistance creative artists often (always?) encounter. Here, clearly, Atlas doesn't shrug.

(bot R) NAKED FEAR: DON'T FEED THE ANIMALS by John Farr. A Mercury Mystery Publication.

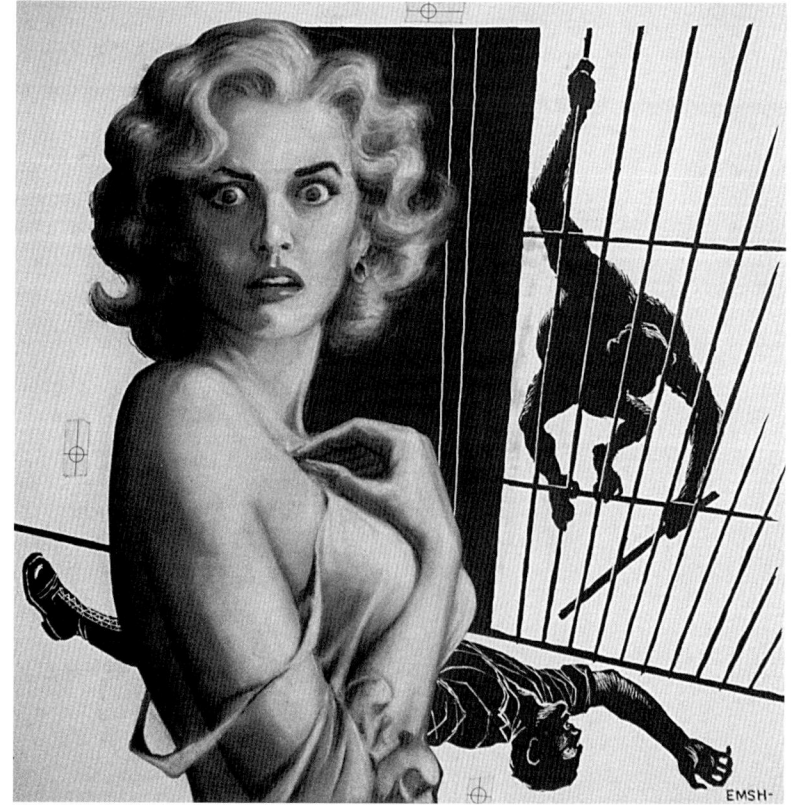

Three

THE ART OF THINGS TO COME

IN 1949, A FRENCH-ITALIAN publisher Edizioni Mondiale (World Editions), had decided that the American market was ripe for *Fascination,* a heavily illustrated, romance-themed magazine it was publishing in Europe. The American edition of *Fascination* was launched and immediately failed in selling to a jaded post-war American audience. Salacious gossip magazines like *True Confessions* were what Americans were reading. A knitting magazine was attempted and also floundered. Casting around for alternative publishing ideas, one of World Editions' New York-based editors suggested a science fiction magazine. *Galaxy Science Fiction* was born in October 1950 with that editor, Horace L. Gold, at the *de facto* helm.

Galaxy had to go up against the gold standard of science fiction periodicals: John W. Campbell, Jr.'s long-established and popular *Astounding Science Fiction,* as well as Anthony Boucher and Mick McComas's more literate *Magazine of Fantasy & Science Fiction.* To fans, Campbell was an science fiction godhead. He was believed to have the magic touch when it came to finding and publishing the best science fiction, but by the early fifties Campbell was beginning to take a bizarre turn into metaphysical quasi-science, including Dianetics, the creation and pet project of pulp writer L. Ron Hubbard.

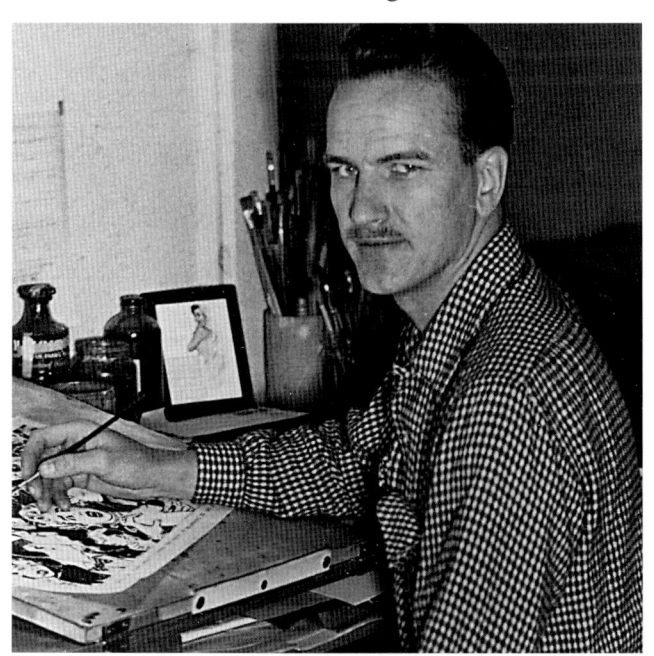

Ed in Levittown attic studio. C. 1953.

Canadian-born Gold had little editorial experience before *Galaxy.* He did have an eclectic writing background: science fiction and fantasy, radio, comic books, and true-life detective tales. Many of *Galaxy*'s authors remember Gold as a "nagging presence." Frederik Pohl, an author's agent at the time, and an SF writer, wrote, "Before *Galaxy* was a year old it was clearly the place where the action was." It didn't hurt that *Galaxy* was also paying the best rates for the material it published, and this forced Campbell to play catch up. Gold had bigger ambitions for *Galaxy.* As author Barry Malzberg once pointed out, "Horace Gold earnestly believed that *Galaxy* could eventually appeal to as many people as *The Saturday Evening Post.*"

The man who directed *Galaxy* and made it an immediate contender on newsstands was looking to publish upscale science fiction

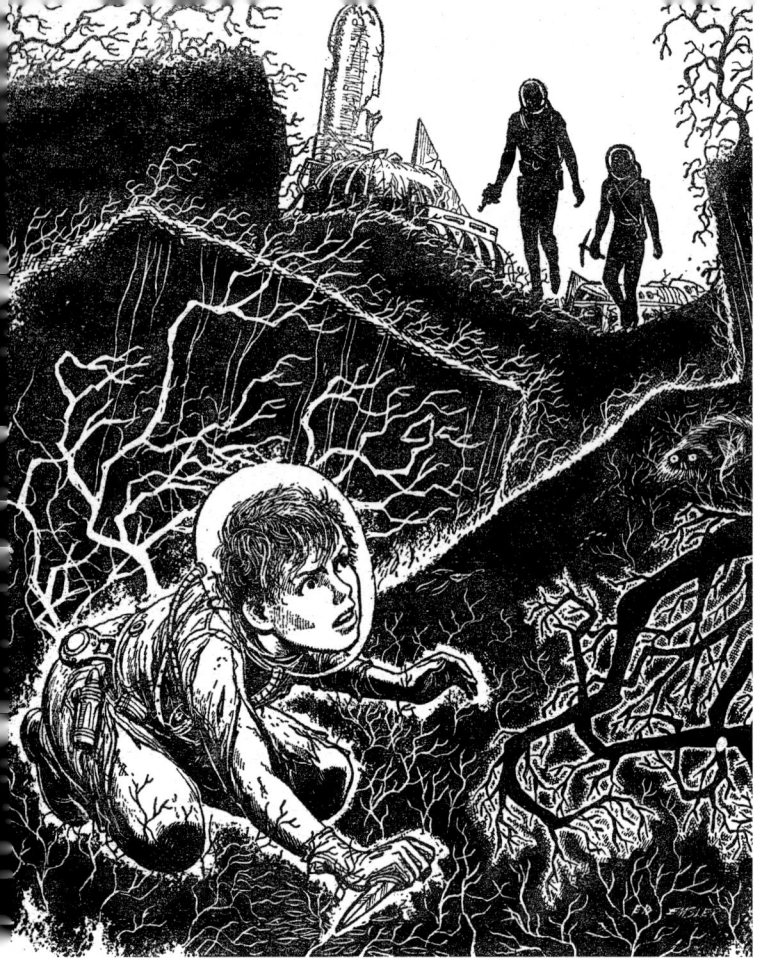

that was intelligent and socially aware. Physically and emotionally, Gold seemed unsuitable for the job. A spinal injury during an army stint in the Pacific would handicap him throughout his life. The whole time he worked on *Galaxy,* Gold admitted that due to "… being so high on anxiety and Seconal — and having agonizing back pains….my mind was in a constant fog." Gold also suffered from severe agoraphobia and rarely left his Manhattan apartment.

Isaac Asimov recalled his first meeting with Gold. The two were sitting in Gold's living room when the editor excused himself. After a long wait Gold's wife Evelyn came into the room and told Asimov he would have to leave. Asimov thought he had made some *faux pas.* As he was taking his leave the phone rang, it was Gold calling him from the phone in the bedroom, now prepared to continue their talk over the phone. Gold's panic attacks only occurred in face-to-face encounters.

Unknown to many of its writers and artists, *Galaxy's* future was on shaky ground during that first year. Behind the scenes there were rumors that the magazine was going under. In September, 1951, the magazine was sold to print broker Robert M. Guinn, who formed Galaxy Publishing Corporation, and for all intents and purposes World Editions left the North American magazine market. *Galaxy* found its footing with Gold in complete editorial control, and became an outlet for Ed's art and the source of a regular paycheck when he needed it most.

Carol remembers Ed voicing his feelings of trepidation about his art samples when they came to New York. Between his time as a G.I. in the "big blow" and college, Ed admitted that he "… had been pretty well sheltered from having to earn a buck." Most of the editors and art directors (some like Campbell did double duty as their own a.d.) of science fiction

THIS PAGE
(top) PLANET STORIES, Mar. 1952, ink and scratchboard. "Return of a Legend" by Raymond Z. Gallun. (Signed as Ed Emsler.)

(bot) (FANTASTIC, May/June 1953, scratchboard interior, "Sally" by Isaac Asimov) - In a world of white, a group of sentient cars dominate anxious, fearful men. A great example of Emsh's sophisticated line and spot-black design, and his dynamic use of space. These three starkly limned men could be running through an auto showroom…but we can tell more than that is going on. Again and again, Ed's graphic interiors would evoke the Techno-Age intersection of Man and Machine.

PAGE 31
(top R) THE FORGOTTEN PLANET by Murray Leinster, Gnome Press.

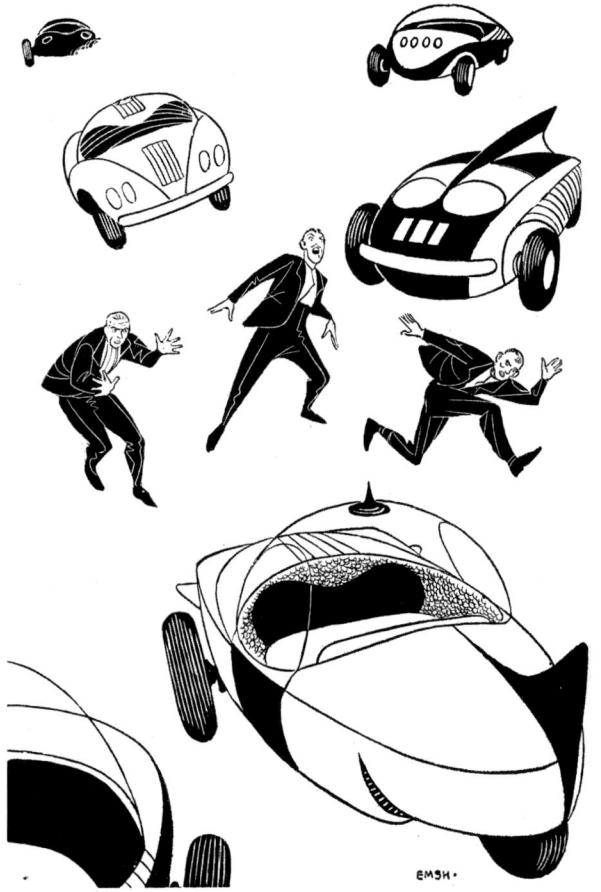

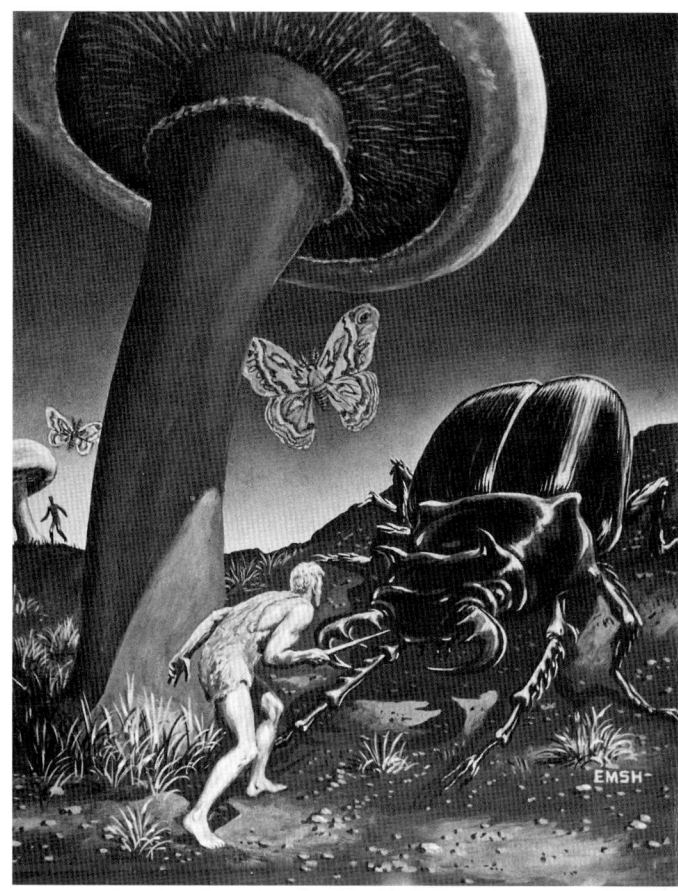

A giant mushroom overshadows a battle between primitive man and beast - in this case a beetle as big as a rhinoceros. The monster slayer, a timeless image from ancient mythology, is presented in light of Swiftian changes in scale: The man may be the miniature, or the insect may have evolved to monstrous size. (Though the grass blades imply the truth.) Emsh gives us tree-size fungi, dazzle-winged moths, a heroic warrior…and one great bug with wicked pincers and terrific highlights. This lively art was deemed too scary by librarians, so a tamer jacket was substituted on many copies of the book.

(bot L) unknown publication. C. 1953.

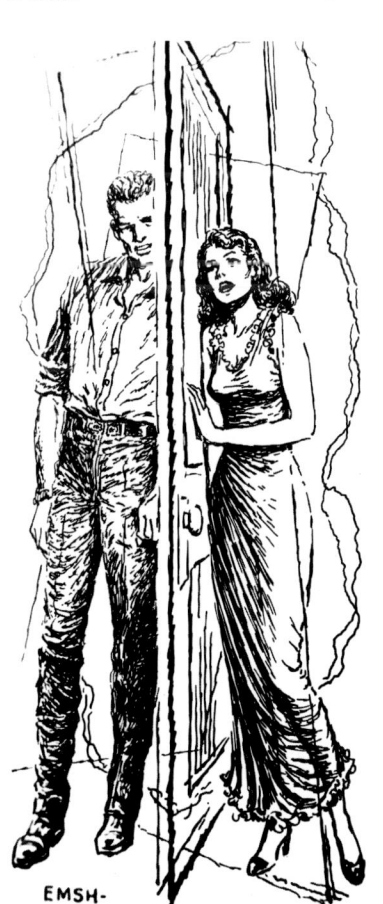

magazines ran loose ships: authors and artists were permitted to wander into offices without notice. Emsh's art already fitted in with Gold's notions of science fiction as social discourse through ideas.

At the start of his art career, Ed fixed on the SF field — feeling more comfortable with the familiar images and subject matter he had grown up with. Ed had decided that fine art was too risky a proposition, and correctly realized that slick magazines like *Saturday Evening Post, Look*, and *Colliers* would allow him little freedom. He also thought that in smaller venues, like pulp magazines, he would be free to explore his own ideas. By the early fifties, the physical format called pulp magazines, 7 by 10 inches in dimension, printed on low-grade pulpwood paper, were already looked upon as old-fashioned and newsstand distributors mostly saw them as unprofitable. To survive, most of the pulps were moving to a digest size 5.5 by 7 inches format.

The art director of *Galaxy*, Washington Van der Poel, appreciated Ed's ability to create evocative cover art that contained a narrative hook. Emshwiller's appearance at *Galaxy*'s midtown offices with ready-to-use paintings in hand was any art director's dream. From the get-go Ed had no trouble understanding the economics of pulp publishing, especially "ghetto science fiction" as it was called by one of its early women practitioners, Judith Merril.

Ed's debut as an artist was the June 1951 *Galaxy* science fiction magazine, with a gouache pulled from his portfolio. The piece was titled "Relics of an Extinct Race" (pg. 37). It is hard to imagine today that the scene it presented, of alien archeologists coming across the historical record of mankind's self-destruction — as depicted through the strata of weapons deposited by successive epochs of violent human civilizations — was not painted with *Galaxy* in mind, but this painting was done at Carol's parents' home in Ann Arbor while the first issues of *Galaxy* were hitting newsstands.

Science fiction is a by-product of the 20th century. Some critics have tried to link it to Edgar Allen Poe's weird stories and Mary Shelley's *Frankenstein*, or an earlier precedent such as

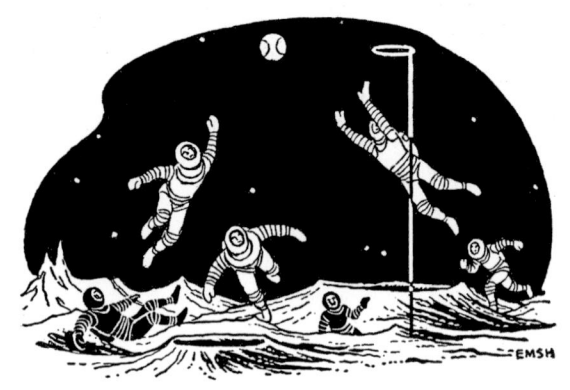

Gulliver's Travels, but these are isolated examples and belong within the literature of their own time. An early radio enthusiast named Hugo Gernsback has a better claim to the title of the *father of science fiction* by creating a Jim Crow society for this type of fiction in the spring 1926 issue of *Amazing Stories*. Whether this was a good or a bad thing has been the crux of an old but cherished fan-nish argument ever since. Debators scores points for both sides, but the reality is—outside of science fiction fandom—no one cares.

Early pulp science fiction magazines did make their readers hungry for more of the same. Beyond the gaze of mainstream literature, SF had a chance to laser-focus its intensity within a clannish subculture made up of fans, brand new writers, fans turned editors, and specialized artists. Some SF writers that would never have appeared without a pulp ghetto include: H.P. Lovecraft, John W. Campbell, Jr., Philip K. Dick, J.G. Ballard, and SF fellow travelers like Thomas Pynchon, Doris Lessing, and Margaret Atwood, would have been very different writers.

One of the tenets of the field—*science fiction is visionary*—is usually applied to the prescience of the fiction and not the art—indeed, just about all histories of science fiction overlook or minimize the visual component. To this day, cover art has not gotten the proper recognition in helping to jumpstart the SF field. Early science fiction art—like the fiction—had less to do with character and technique than with ideas and imagination.

On Depression era newsstands the science fiction pulps, with covers showing exotic scenes of alien creatures, other worlds, interplanetary spaceships, and bizarre contraptions, easily outdid the curiosity factor of standard cliché scenes on other pulps, which were limited to gun-toting heroes and thugs blazing away at each other, or scantily dressed women in peril. Many early fans have remarked on how they discovered SF by sighting some enticing cover. Asimov discovered SF in his father's candy store in Brooklyn when, during the Depression, they began selling pulp magazines.

Without the fantastic showcase of images in Gernsback's

THIS PAGE
(top L) Spot illustration for unknown SF magazine. C. 1955. Ink and scratchboard.

(Bot.R) (c. 1955.) Although this painting may be SF-related, the opposing elements, drawn in white-line and dark over bleeding color-fields, relate to techniques in Ed's early films. This could be a trial balloon aimed at "slick" magazines. The female guard and spiky fence-line suggest a post-collapse scenario, where women have organized for protection against bands of male

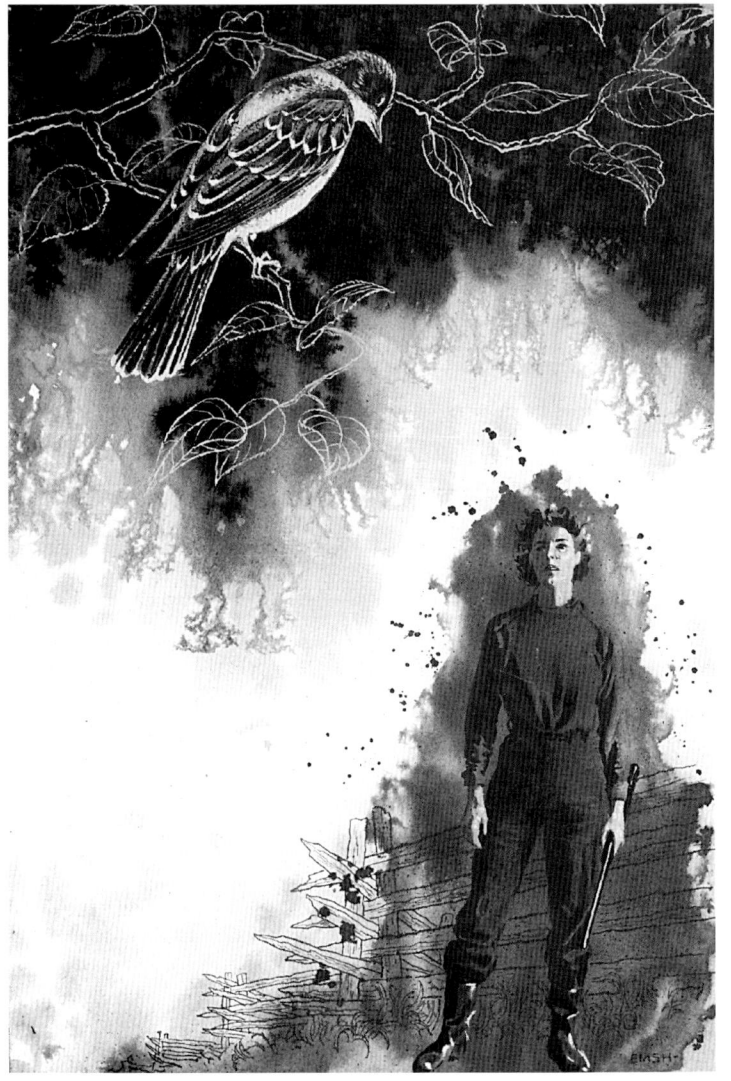

marauders. The contrast of sparrow on tree branch with the menace-laced scene below tells the tale without any barbarian in sight - and also demonstrates Emshwiller's principle of "dynamic contrasts."

THIS PAGE
(top r) UNDERSEA QUEST. By Frederik Pohl & Jack Williamson 1954. Gnome Press.

(Bot.L) PEON, Nov. 1953. Cartoon "illo" for fanzine cover. A relaxing game of chess follows a "good landing" on the Moon - i.e., one the guys walked away from. Ed was a master at delineating wreckage, in both cartoons and serious illustration. (Emsh fanzine art is not all that common, but some fan editors were persuasive; and these casual pieces for zines made fans view him as a good sport.) Though only a scribble for the amateur press, the spaceship is so well-wrought that one feels, with some study and a decent monkey wrench, any handy person could put it in working order.

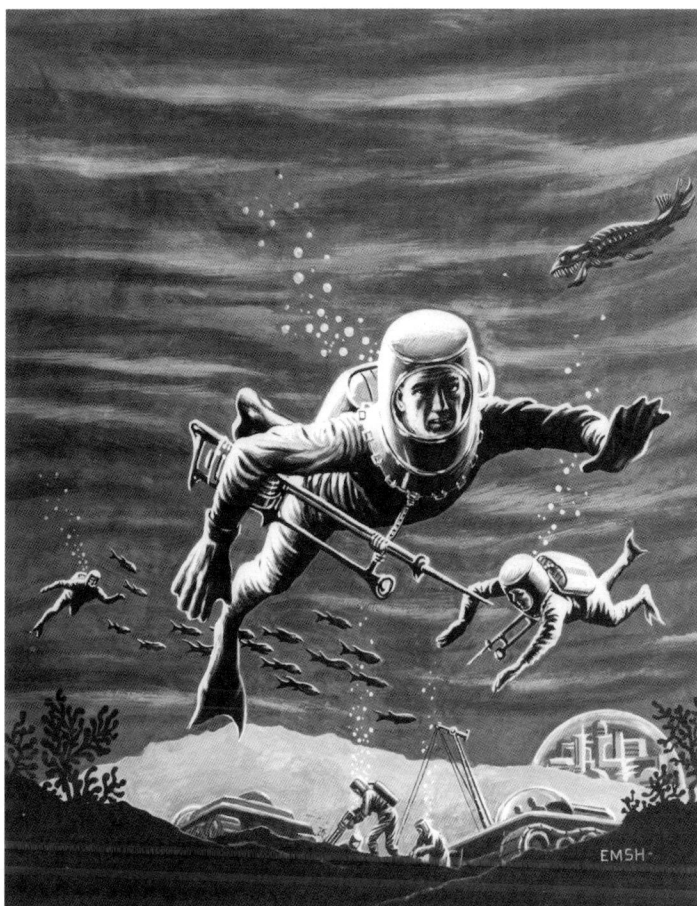

science fiction magazines there would not be a SF field as we now know it. Hugo Gernsback certainly became the father of science fiction art when he discovered Frank R. Paul, the world's first true science fiction artist and the first to define the look and set the raw standards of science fiction art. This rawness gave Paul's work the appeal of primitive art. It was the fusing of science and art that was seductive to people like Ed Emshwiller.

An exemplary Paul cover is the January 1929 issue of *Amazing Stories* (for the story "The Sixth Glacier" by Marius) that shows a realistically done scene of downtown Manhattan buildings toppling before the advance of a gigantic glacier. In the foreground the Woolworth Building is seen collapsing as a thousand foot wall of ice reaches it. In the background, City Hall, all of lower Broadway, Park Row, and the Municipal

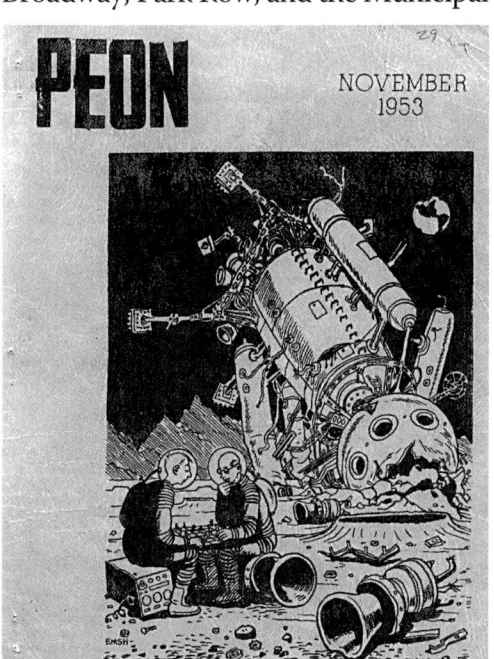

Building are overwhelmed. This scene is prescient in an uncanny way: the point-of-view is exactly where the observation deck of the World Trade Center's north tower was situated (pg. 18).

SF author R.A. Lafferty heralds the patent-medicine shill of pulp covers: "SF pulps leave me puzzled.... [SF] had the air of being very near, but there wasn't much of it within the covers of those magazines. There was more of it on the covers themselves. Lots of those who carry on about their early encounters with SF have recounted their embarrassment at the gaudy and garish covers, have told about themselves hiding the magazines when they carried them home.... The covers were the best part of those old magazines, by a long ways."

English author Brian Aldiss said, "Paul made amends

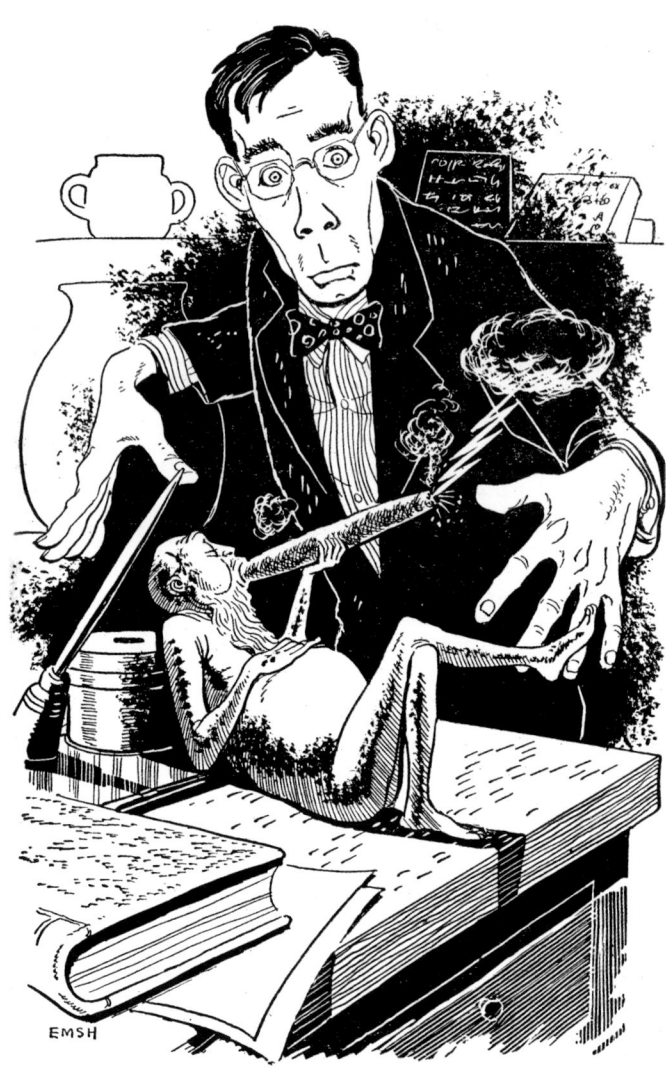

for the inadequacies of the writers…. The images are what attracted me in science fiction, more even than the surprises and the ideas and the crazy plots."

This from Philip José Farmer upon discovering *Amazing Stories* in 1929: "How marvelous were Paul's illustrations…. I've forgotten most of the fiction, but the Pauls were forever burned into my brain."

For the most part, H. L. Gold worked out of his apartment in Stuyvesant Town on East 14th Street where it seemed that much of *Galaxy's* business revolved around the weekly poker games that Gold held in his dining room. There, between manuscripts, galley proofs, cover press sheets, beer, and make-ready copies of the magazine, the Friday night games of fifteen-cent-limit, seven-card high-low, Stud, Anaconda, or Iron Cross (all played on a green baize cloth that covered the dining-room table) would engage regulars, and such semi-regulars as Jerome Bixby, Fred Pohl, Algis Budrys, Robert Sheckley, avant-garde composer John Cage — even Tony Boucher would sit in when he was in town from the west coast. Ed was one of the semi-regulars. (Carol remembers, *I got mad cause he always lost*.)

Like John Campbell, Gold badgered his writers with story ideas. Both editors were constantly polling their readers for their preferences in stories. Gold had even asked the opinions of writers regarding the layout and logo of *Galaxy* before the first issue came out. Boucher commented once that the SF field was rich in editors that "truly edit rather than merely assemble" by stimulating authors with seed-ideas, then reaping the harvest. Some *Galaxy* authors appreciated Gold's coaching more than others.

One writer, William Tenn, wrote of Gold's housebound working arrangement: "Horace created a unique milieu in that cave in Stuyvesant Town […] just as Campbell had earlier created one in his Street & Smith office. If you lived in that milieu, if you moved in it at all, if you did nothing more than correspond with it from time to time, you were enlarged in special ways and began to move in direc-

FANTASY MAGAZINE. Mar. 1953, ("Ashtaru the Terrible"). -A fine instance of Emsh's mature ink-line drawing, in the manner of **UNKNOWN WORLDS** and bearing the influence of Edd Cartier's work for that magazine. Very Cartier-like are the splayed right hand and the horse-faced Ph.D.; everything else is characteristic Emsh, from outline crockery to graven tablets. The potbellied gnome's cigar-lighting routine is surely from the story, but the professor's flummoxed look is pure Emsh in jocular mode. Though a caricature, the prof is so real one might expect to meet him on the street. Deceptively simple, this drawing has every line and shadow exactly in place and cunningly managed. Ed created hundreds of interiors like this one, sharply organized to the point.

(top R) STARTLING STORIES. Summer 1954, (b&w photo of prelim.). The goddesses of fire laugh as a downed spaceship burns like a strafed oil tanker. In this early version of a pulp-mag cover with a typical subject, one point of interest is the oddly laminated outcrop on which the astronauts stand. This rock is made up of purely abstract shapes and textures flowing into and over one another - a shard of Max Ernst intruding into this standard scene. Unusual, too, is the row of slanting background peaks, which subtly echoes the tongues of flame.

(bot) Ed in Levittown on his BSA motorcycle.

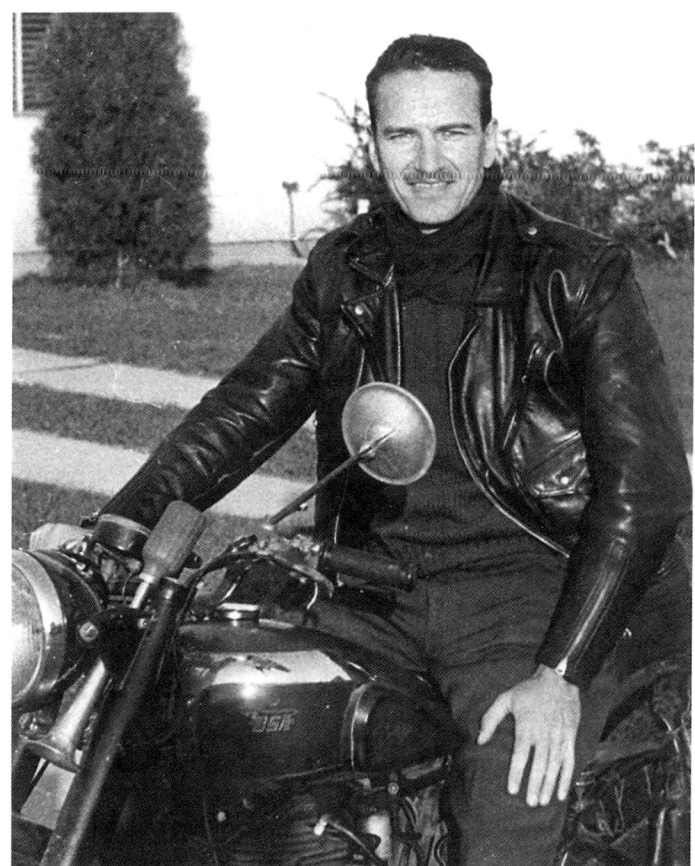

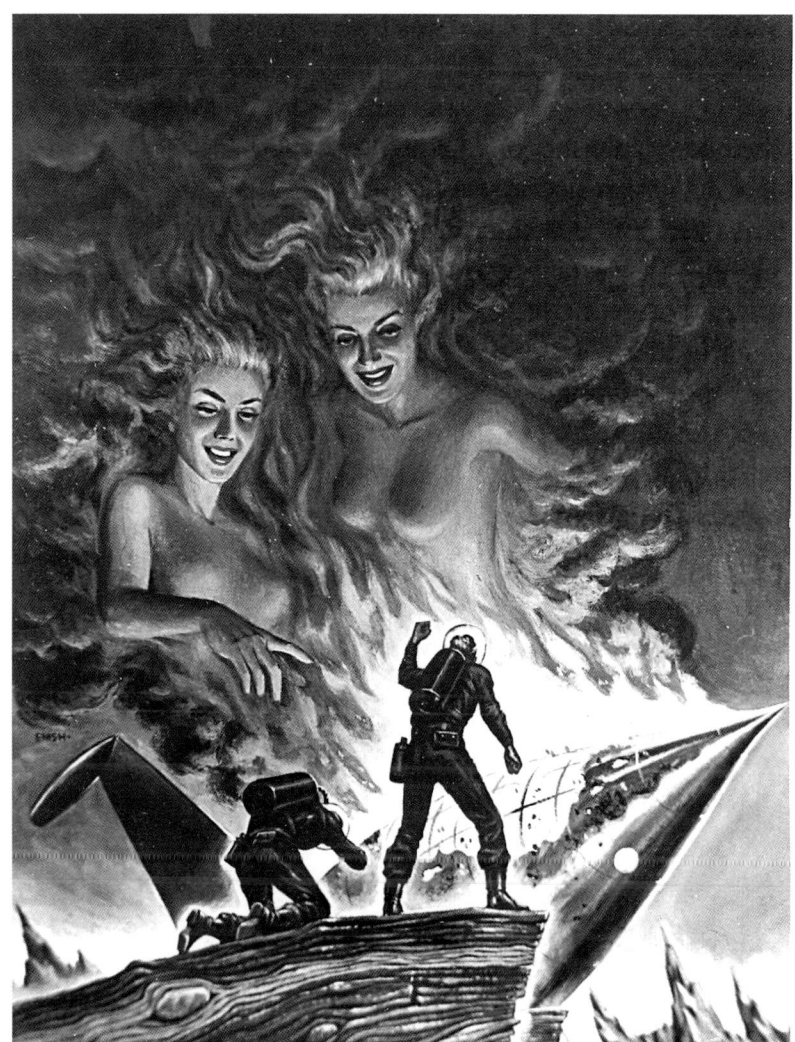

tions that were novel to you and remarkably exciting." Tenn also called Gold "[…] one of the most irritating and aggravating men I've ever known."

Gold had many contradictions: as an ex-radical he was afraid, at the height of McCarthyism, to publish fellow traveler William Tenn's "The Liberation of Earth," a story attacking both American and Russian involvement in the Korean War (Robert "Doc" Lowndes wound up taking it for *Science Fiction*). To be fair, Gold did publish other stories attacking McCarthy's methods, including Asimov's "The Martian Way" and Bernard Wolfe's neglected "Self Portrait," about the sort of person who would thrive in a McCarthy world. However, by the end of the decade Gold was allowing his emotional predilections to color his selection of stories, and authors who knew which buttons to press believed they had an advantage in selling to *Galaxy*.

By the end of 1952 Ed had achieved a big measure of recognition for himself in the science fiction field. Twenty-nine different American science fiction titles appeared in that year, with a total of 153 individual issues — Ed's art was in a *third* of all

35

those SF magazines. He had also begun to create dust jacket art and design for the small SF publisher Avalon Books and in December 1953 Marty Greenberg, publisher of Gnome Press, most successful of the science fiction specialty houses, ordered four hardcover dust jackets. These were black and white paintings that would be converted into color by the printer. On February 3, 1954, Greenberg invited Ed on a trip to Lebanon Pa., where Gnome Press did its four color printing, to see how monochromatic artwork was turned into color. Ed learned the printer's trick of "faking of color" by using overlays to indicate where a particular color ink will appear.

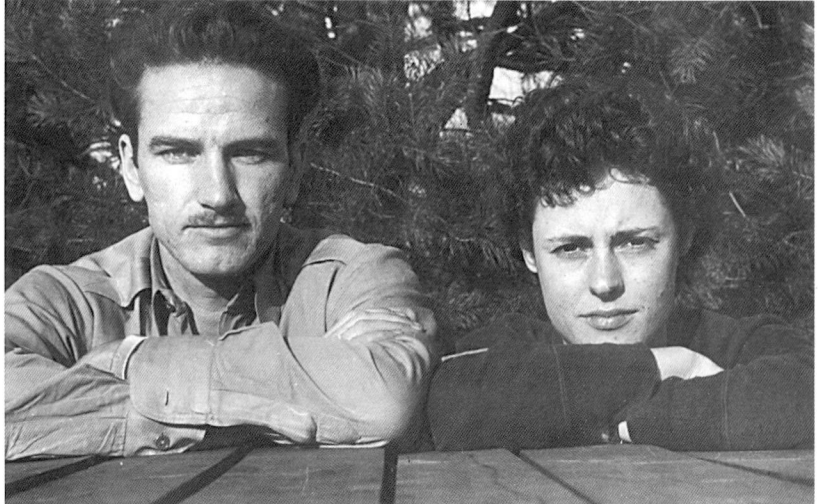

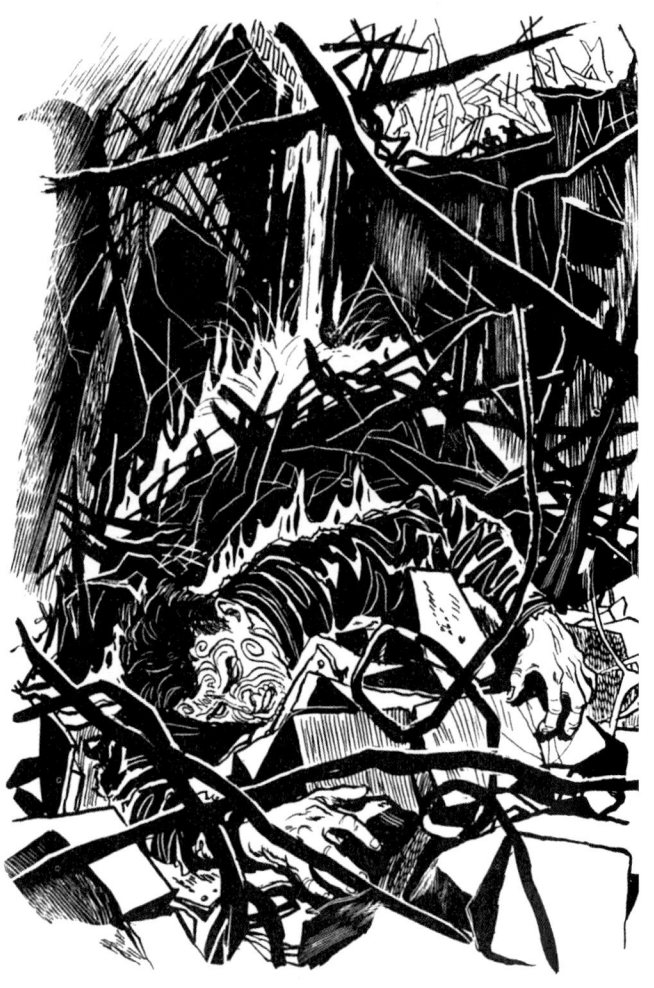

The Emsh name was cropping up in many fan publications, called fanzines, where he was mentioned in the same breath with longtime fan favorites Virgil Finlay, Edd Cartier, and Hannes Bok. Throughout the history of SF there has been a thin wall between professionals and fans, with many pros coming from the ranks of fandom, and fanzines serving as training camps. A teenage Harlan Ellison (at this point in time a fierce little fan soon to become a fierce little writer) recalls asking for and getting a cover illustration for his fanzine *Science Fantasy Bulletin* from Ed in 1953. This was a common bit of interaction between pros and the messy little universe of fandom. Artist Red Grooms, a friend of Ed, in writing about De Kooning and the New York fine art scene in the fifties said, "So many contentious, brilliant, and outrageous characters shout for attention that at times the story seems unreal." The same could be said of SF fandom.

It was normal practice for fanzine editors to get material for free. Ed — like many SF pros who were once fans — was an easy

(top R) Ed and Carol in Ann Arbor, August 1949.

(bot L) GALAXY SCIENCE FICTION, Jan. 1957,(interior for Pt. 4 of Alfred Bester's THE STARS MY DESTINATION). Wild chaotic scene composed of jangled black strokes: all twisted rebar and girders and shattered stone. The tattooed Gully Foyle is trapped inside this morass, liquid fire pouring into the pit. Behind the welter and confusion, the pillars of a cathedral can be discerned, and a sense of derangement and hellish torment prevails. The tortured figure of Foyle, aflame, blindly clinging to rubble, seems to merge with the enveloping chaos. The drawing was slashed out of the scratchboard's surface in a furious burst of energy, its mood and handling the diametric opposite of the neat, calm manner of the FANTASY MAGAZINE piece (page 34); yet it makes its point with force and clarity.

(top R) GALAXY, June 1951, ("Relics of an Extinct Race"). The Great and Terrible History of Man, as discovered by extraterrestrial allosaurs on our blown-out world. The best naively styled SF cover ever painted: The viewer reimagines it as an excellent diorama created by grade-school children, then photographed. Were it super-realistic, it might pall as a sick joke, but its clay-model look survives our cynicism and queasiness. Alien archaeologists have come across the record of mankind's suicide, evidenced in increasingly advanced weapons embedded in successive strata. Too bad no warning sign is posted for the kindly aliens: BEWARE OF GLOWING SLAG AT TOP.

(bot L) Early version of art later used for the first issue of ROCKET STORIES. April 1953.

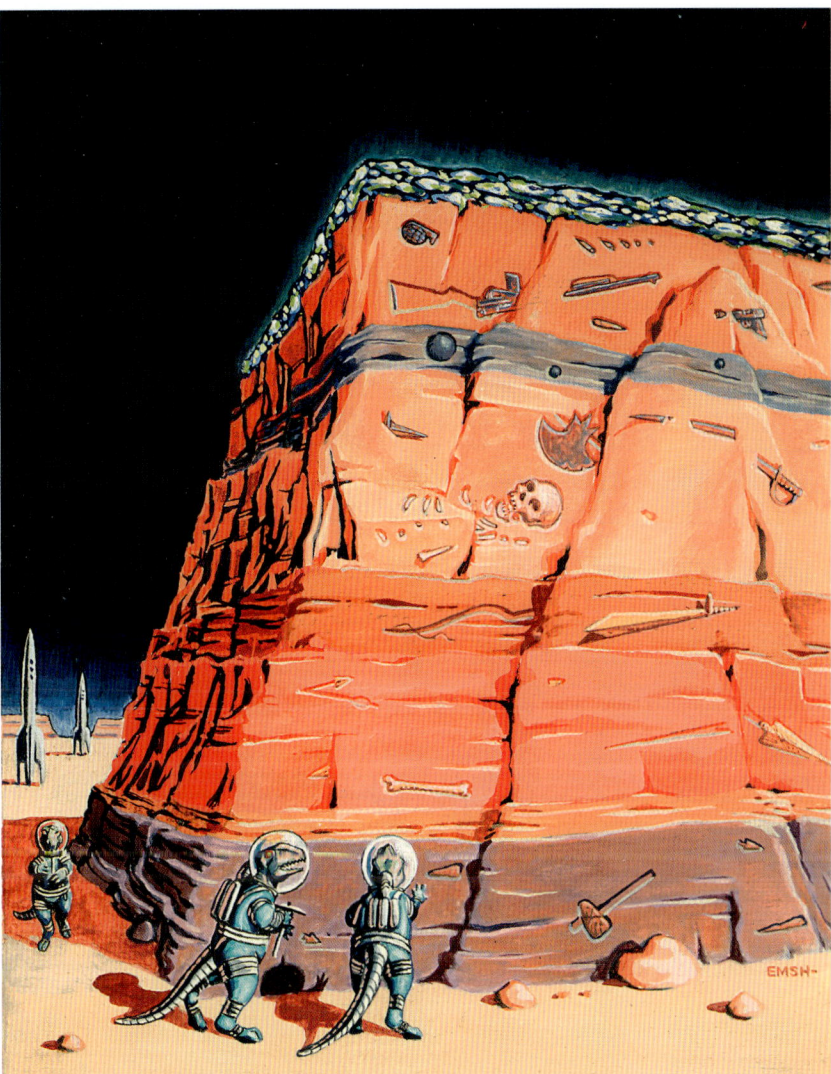

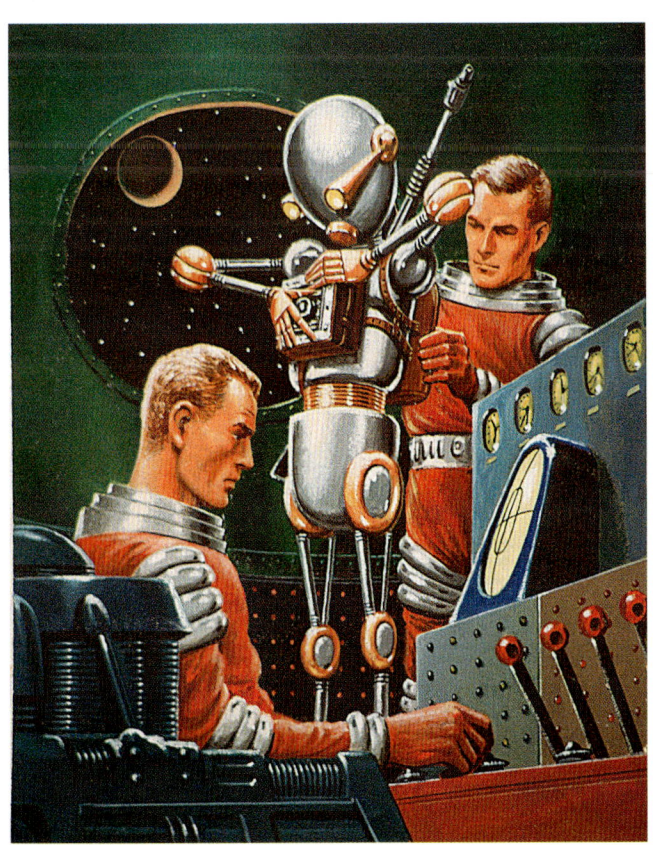

touch for science fiction fans jockeying for bragging rights in fandom. (By the mid-fifties, lack of wider recognition and poverty had sapped Bok's generous spirit after being burned a few times by fan editors, and he swore off giving away his artwork.)

SF fans also yearn for recognition of the genre from the world at large — years later when the field was overtaken by television and Hollywood, some of the same fans would change their opinion, feeling that mass media was stealing science fiction ideas without acknowledging or crediting the source. Brian Aldiss may have said it best, "SF was once impoverished by its isolation. Now it stands in danger of being impoverished by its popularity."

Most of the people seen at SF conventions in the fifties came from a blue-collar background. In many cases the only reading matter, outside of schoolbooks, available while they were growing up were cheap pulp magazines. Depression-hardened fathers and mothers found real books a luxury beyond their means. They wanted better for their children, but had no way to go about insuring this. It was the kind of life

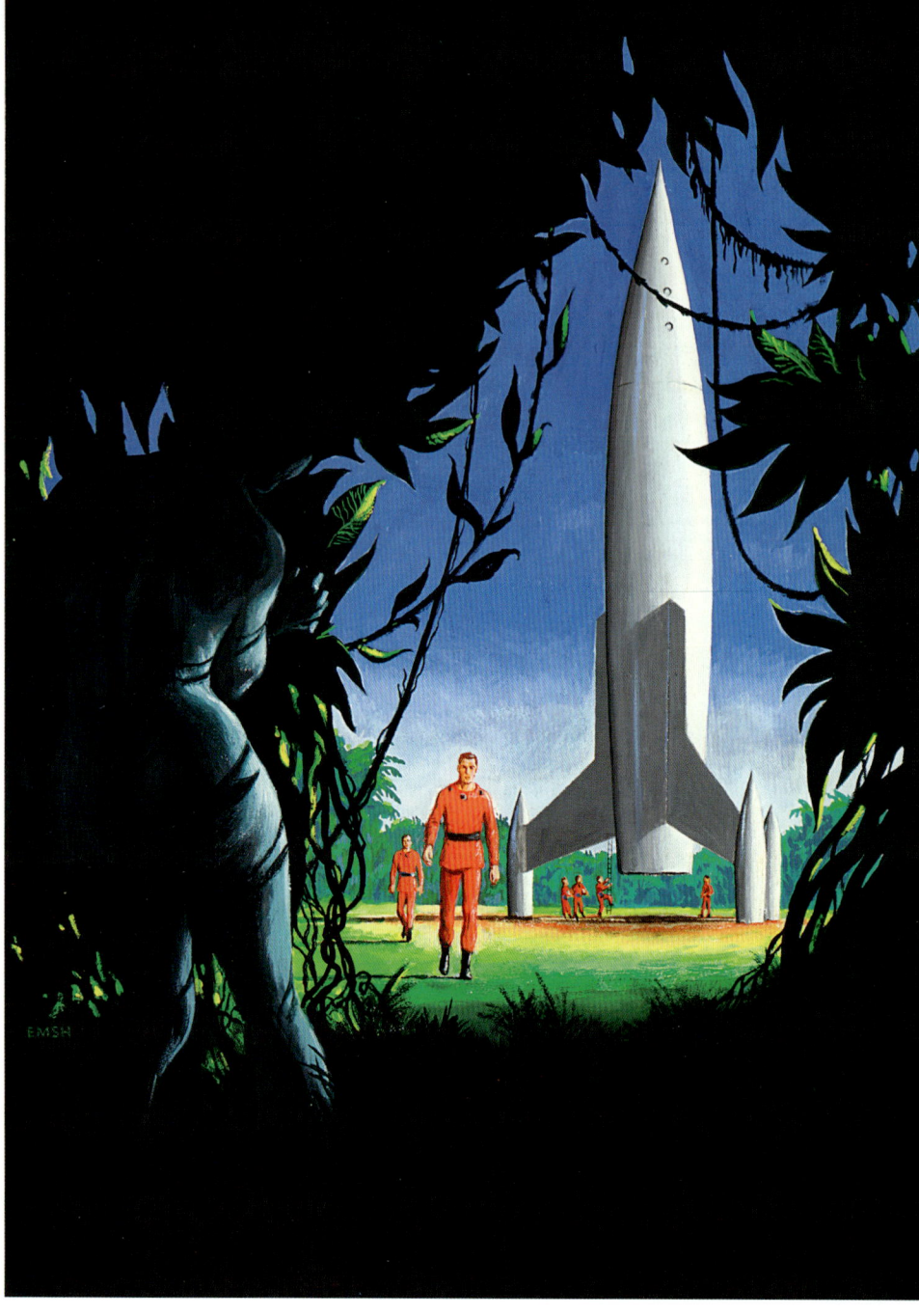

that children ran away from. Some of the brighter ones discovered another escape.

Science fiction changed the life of Asimov, Ellison, Robert Silverberg, Fred Pohl, Damon Knight, Judith Merril, and many other bright children. It is not an accident that most of these people were from a Jewish lineage. Many were already used to a ghetto, or outsider, mindset and felt safe in the science fiction hamlet — a group that pretty much saw itself as superior to "m u n d a n e humans." It seems quite possible that if Kafka had been born a generation later — in America — he would have become a science fiction writer for pulp magazines.

P. Schuyler Miller described the SF mindset, "We were chosen; we were different; we were elite; we didn't want to be the same as other people. And we didn't want them mucking around with our science fiction, when they didn't know what it was all about."

Miller goes on to say of science fiction, "It developed its own code of ethics…its own stereotypes (spacewarps, BEMs, time travel, gimmicks) … its own language … its own inner hierarchy (the sectors

(top L) THE MAGAZINE OF FANTASY AND SCIENCE FICTION, July 1953, "The Hypnoglyph," by "John Anthony" (John Ciardi) — The hoariest cliché of science fiction is the Adam-and-Eve story, where the main characters turn out to be our Old Testament progenitors. Next to that, the toughest chestnut is any scenario set in a Garden of Eden. One might guess the artist didn't know better; however, "Hypnoglyph" is a wonder of double imaging. On the surface, a lush depiction of "first contact": Earthman encounters shapely alien femme blending into the dark jungle - mysterious, faceless, her skull lost in blackness. We see her from inside the forest; she presents herself yet also shrinks into the shadows, all teasing ambivalence. The picture is a wonderland of erotic enticement. But what of the foliage that frames the clearing? Although disguised by looping vines and leaves, this opening strongly resembles the human vulva. Nor is this an accident: a cartoon fox-head on the right seems to laugh at this hidden sexuality.

PAGE 39

(top R) SPACE STORIES. Oct. 1952. (Early version.) A great moment in aerospace defense, using dramatic point-of-view and vaulting perspective. Though the stairs are surely a fast escalator, our boys in yellow mount them two at a time. The scarlet detonation is a visual shock, splaying across the wan evening sky. Oddly, the magazine made Ed repaint this cover almost line-for-line, with minor changes except for deleting the dramatic explosion. The published version (linked to Gordon Dickson's "The Invaders") is sleeker, with cleaner metal-work…but one misses the blood-red eruption.

(bot L) F&SF, June 1952 ("Love" by Richard Wilson) - A portfolio piece: Young lovers holding hands … a Martian and an Earth maid, plus their dog, confront a portal of mystery in the corridors of the Ancient Civilization. The star-crossed lovers await an oracular response from the depths of the glowing cave. Egyptoid bas-reliefs convey a culture of great antiquity; the answer to the sphinx's riddle can't be far away. For this first Emsh scene on F&SF, Richard Wilson got the story assignment and came up with the poignant notion that the girl is blind. The style here is "Gasoline Alley" crossed with "Orphan Annie," of fandom) … gospels (fanzines) … heresies (Shaver, Dianetics, psi) … pilgrimages (conventions). Stories were full of private jokes, and allusions that only the elite could follow…. *We didn't want outsiders."* Once the contour of magazine science fiction was shaped, it does seem that new readers were left out. Eventually, paperback publishers like Ballantine and Ace took notice of these readers.

SF fan and editor Sam Moskowitz said in 1953, "The trouble has been that science fiction editors and publishers have confused science fiction fans with science fiction fandom…

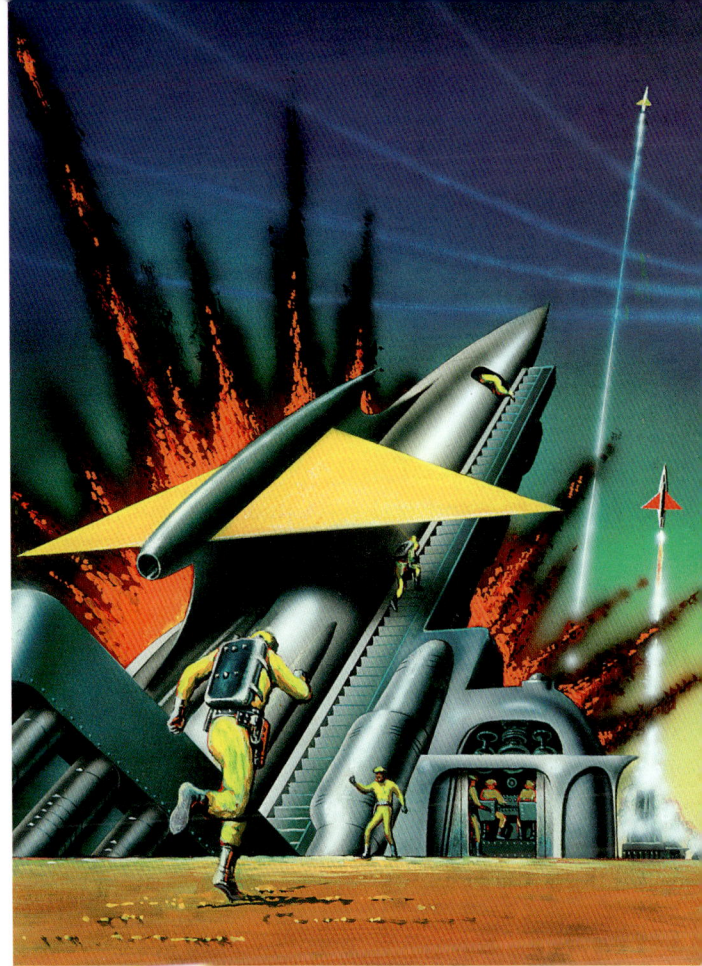

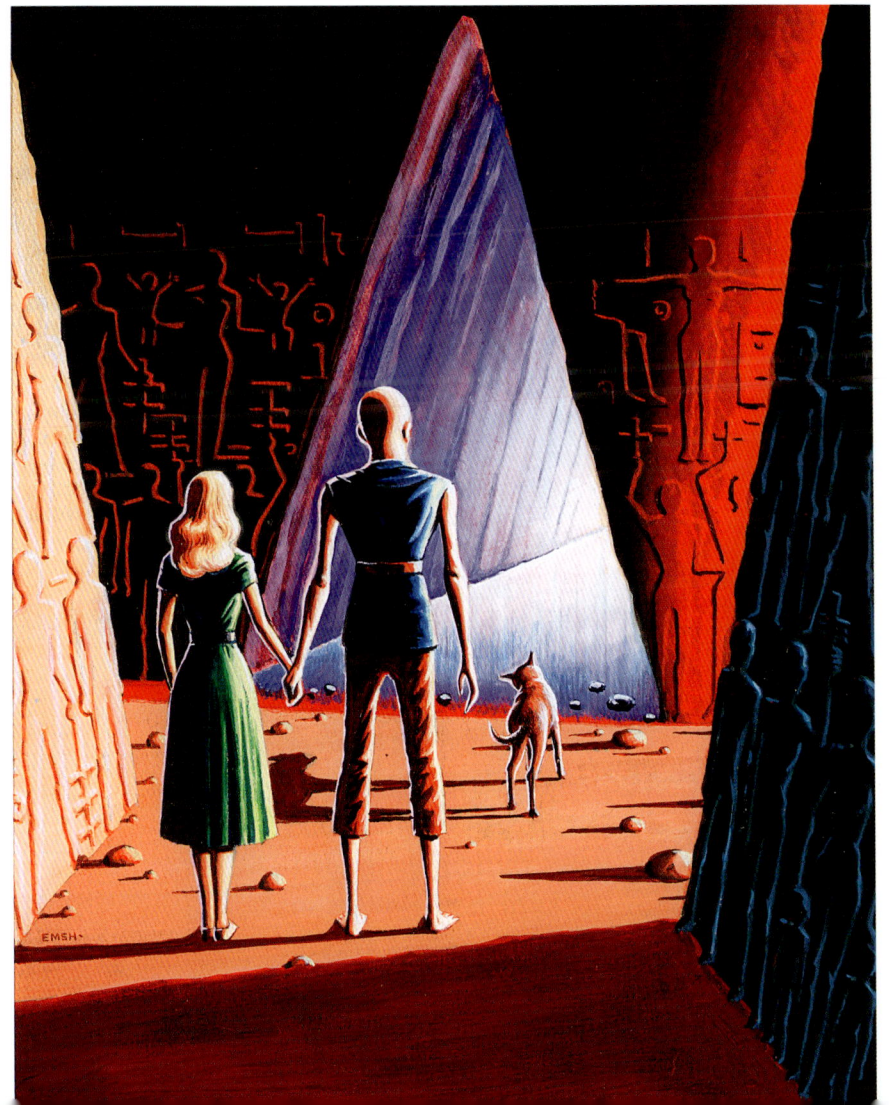

[magazine] publishers have mistakenly taken the number of fans engaged in active fandom as the sum total of the whole."

On September 12, 1952, Ed was one of the people at *Galaxy*'s second anniversary party. Gold knew how big an accomplishment it was to survive two years in the magazine world. The party was held at a steakhouse around the corner from *Galaxy*'s West 40th Street office — without Gold's presence. Ed memorialized the event on the cover of the October 1952 issue of *Galaxy*, but pictured the occasion at Gold's apartment — with Gold at the center of the party.

By any standard the 1952-1953 period was a pretty good time for science fiction. Ed socialized with SF writers but got his directives from the various magazine art editors: W.I. van der Poel at *Galaxy*, and George Salter at *Fantasy & Science Fiction,* were both creative professionals and not real SF fans. Salter at Mercury Press was a German expatriate who had learned his trade in theatre and book publishing, and possessed an almost ethereal sense of design and typography, which gave the early issues of *Fantasy & Science Fiction* a sophisticated and classy look. Ed's early paintings for *F&SF* reflected a more artistic approach, and a general shunning of pulp clichés. Other art directors, like Milton Luros at Columbia Publications (before editor Robert W. Lowndes took over the job), came out of the pulp field, and Ed's work for them reflected this pulpishness.

Rates for cover art ranged anywhere from a high of $150 for the top science fiction magazines like *Galaxy* and *F&SF* to the bottom rate, starting at around $50. Ed could do a cover painting in two or three days and was soon making a comfortable living. For interior black and white line drawings Emshwiller would average $20 an illustration.

The *Magazine of Fantasy & Science Fiction* was the most consciously literate of all the science fiction magazines. Editor Anthony Boucher (a pen name for William Anthony Parker White that may have been a play on "fat check") liked the sophistication he saw in Ed's art. It wasn't long after entering the field that Ed was invited to science fiction conventions. At the big conventions pro editors and fans would mill around, wandering in and out of hotel rooms, clustering together for parties and panel talks, then breaking apart to form new clusters in the suite of a well known fan, pro writer, or editor.

but that only enhances its simple charm. A small joy is the wiry mongrel, cocking its head as it too peers into the mystic tunnel.

THIS PAGE
GALAXY, Aug. 1952, ("The 40-Credit Tour of Earth"). Hold it; I think you're gonna like this shot! Comic, walleyed green men behave like tourists do everywhere. The conceit that the viewer has just been ambushed by one of these guys pulls the scene into sharp relief, with the bumptious alien looming in for the kill from outside the frame. We pause to admire some nice architectural detail; and to note the camera store down the block. In the Big Apple, a customer's a customer, ya know?

PAGE 41
(top R)(GALAXY, Jan. 1953, ("The Defenders" by Philip K. Dick). This famous painting gives us the roboticized battlefield of the future. Chrome-steel warriors have taken over all aspects of combat, including the piloting of rocket planes. The pipe-stem soldier, unfazed by fiery clouds that blot out the sky, projects an omni-competence that will continue fighting until the last enemy city is crushed. We can be sure he will execute efficiently until the job is done, until there's nothing left to destroy. They are an admirable race - and a fearful one.

THIS PAGE
(bot L) THE ORIGINAL SCIENCE FICTION STORIES. May 1956."Living Space" by Isaac Asimov) Mr. & Mrs. Robert Benchley (it seems) inhabit their own private Idaho. A lovely tract home with all the amenities, in eco-harmony under a plexi-dome, forms this single family suburb on a barren world. But a planet-quake in such a locale can spoil your whole day. Things are jumpin' now in this Garden Spot, far from the madding crowds of Old New Jersey. The growing crevasse is a raffish treat, as it brings a dormant world back to crackling life.

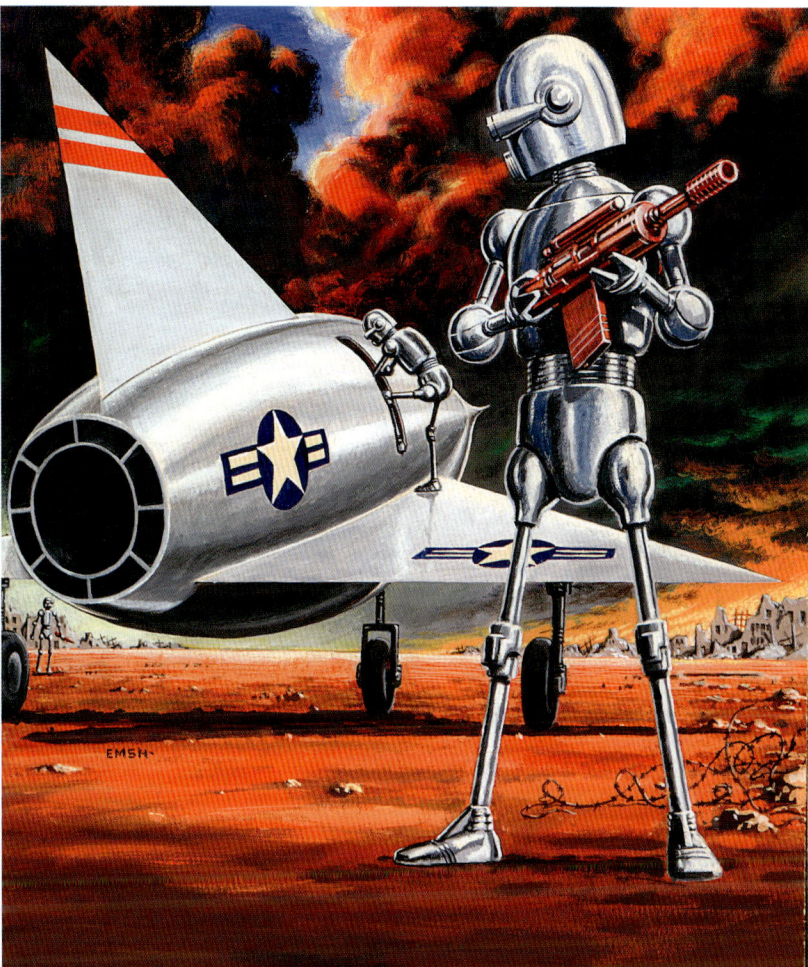

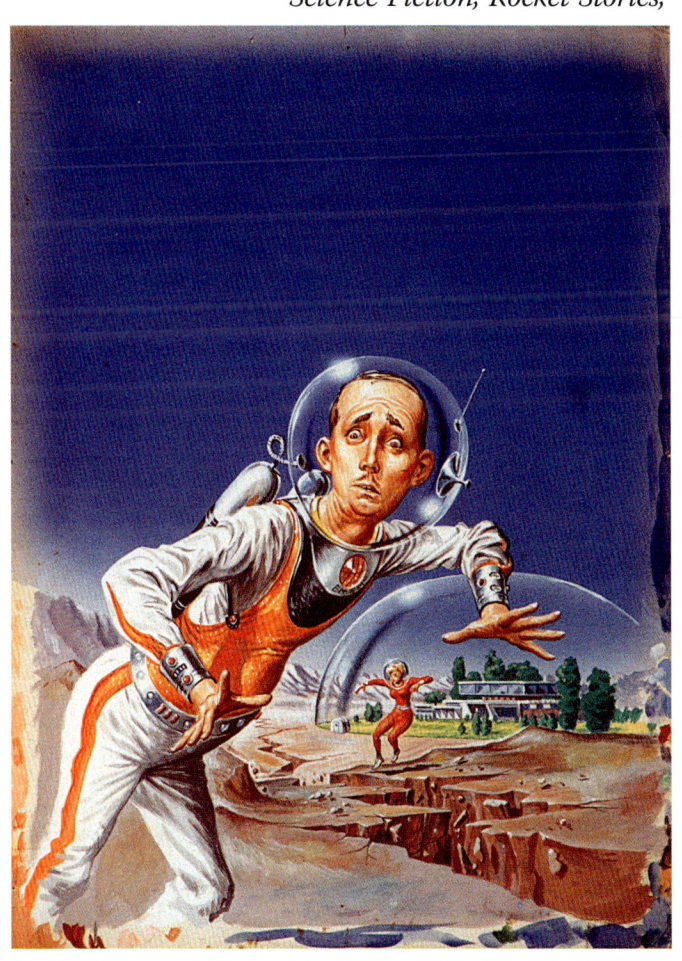

Most of the editors were on friendly terms and did not see each other's magazines as competitors. Ed saw the clubhouse camaraderie among editors, and began studying the various magazines with the intent of doing art for as many as possible. Besides his art appearing in three of the four premiere SF magazines, by mid 1953 Ed was working for *Thrilling Wonder Stories, Space Stories, Startling Stories, Science Fiction, Rocket Stories, Fantastic Story Magazine, Fantasy Magazine,* as well as *Amazing Stories, Galaxy,* and *F&SF.* The only place he had not been able to break into was Campbell's *Astounding Science Fiction.* Street & Smith had its own established artists and Ed was an unknown quantity to them.

Galaxy's policy during the fifties was to keep the original art after getting it back from the printer. Ed, however, needed his samples to show to other art directors and asked to get these paintings back. Van der Poel accommodated Ed. Many magazine publishers had the same almost paranoid tic of not returning art—some created "glory walls" to display art in their offices. The official line given for hanging on to original art was to keep it from being used in other competing publications. Of course, once art began to overwhelm offices and storage rooms, it was routinely tossed into trash bins without a second thought.

Ed's request for the return of his samples saved many of these early paintings and allowed his family to benefit from the sale of original art later. Afterwards, *Galaxy* covers done on commission were not given back. (In an ad in the Jan. 1972 *Galaxy*, publisher Robert M. Guinn made an offer to readers that they could buy art from the magazine as souvenirs, and in this way he managed to get rid of art taking up room in his garage and make a secondary profit at the same time.)

One incident worked to the benefit of both publisher and artist. Ed walked into *F&SF's* offices in Manhattan and as usual spent a little time looking at their "glory wall" of art. He would use his waiting time to examine other artists' work, but this day he noticed that one of his own works had changed. Looking closely he saw that his first piece for F&SF titled "Love" had two inches trimmed from the bottom of the painting. This had been one of his original portfolio samples and Ed hit the roof.

"What have you done to my painting? You have modified it!"

The original painting had a flat expanse of reddish color in the foreground and this area had been trimmed off to fit the frame they had available. In Ed's view, the Procrustean cut had changed his whole composition. "We didn't think it was important," someone in the office said, trying to mollify him.

"It's very important. You can't do that to my art."

An abashed office worker reassured him that such a thing would not happen again.

"If I can't trust you to hold onto my art, I will have to get it all back."

Tony Boucher had an old-fashioned, gentleman's sense of publishing and had no problem with returning art when Ed's request was relayed to him. This began a standing policy that Ed had with *F&SF*. One Emsh art collector, Alex Eisenstein, believes this may have led to Ed doing his best art for that magazine.

In other cases, several of Ed's unused early samples were eventually updated and refined by him for later use. The cover to *Space Stories* for October 1952 showed a group of spacemen racing to board a delta-wing rocket poised on a take-off ramp. In the original sample the spaceport is under bombardment by missiles. In the printed piece all evidence of the space battle has been removed (very likely at the direction of an art editor), but the spacemen are still racing to the spaceship, making the viewer wonder, "what's the rush?" (pg. 39).

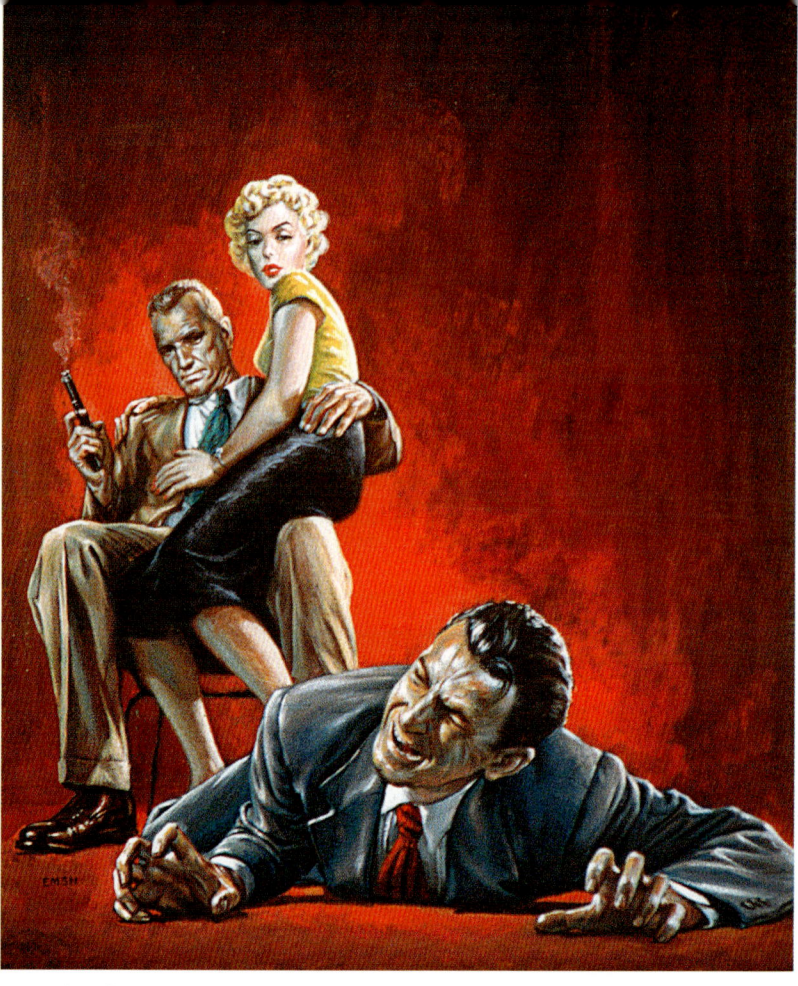

(top R) Unknown. mystery magazine cover art. C. 1959. One of Ed's typical mystery mag paintings, even more polished than some of his SF work. Seductively slick, these habitually involve blatant displays of cruelty and murder - and as here, are anything but subtle. Nevertheless they contain great figural work, with faces that shout out the emotions of the combatants. And the babes…well, they're ultra-hot, and you can tell they know it. This beautiful blonde's raised eyebrow and veiled eyes convey her icy contempt for chumps and saps…and that she doesn't mind watching one die. The red background stands for searing pain, and the anguish of dying in front of people who don't care.

(Top L) Unknown publication. A painting that proves Emsh could find his way around high-tech astronautics. Note the interesting docking mechanism on pod and deep-space vessel, and the artist's mastery of swept-wing perspective.

(Top R) LION ADVENTURE MAGAZINE. May 1960, ("Hell Dogs of the Cheechobie."). Another lovely lady for the tough-tec crowd. And a very unpleasant bulldog. The menace here is magnified by keeping the villainous dog handler out of frame, except for that all-important fist gripping the choke chain.

(Bot. R) F&SF, Sept. 1952, ("Mother" by Alfred Coppel). Landing on the Moon or some other cratered world, the spaceship carries its passenger suspended in an egg-like womb, asleep in fetal position, to be wakened on arrival. At once soothing and startling, this image contrasts deep red and dark blue-greens, hard rectangular with elliptical shapes. Note the massive struts to cushion shocks. A nude man curled into a fetal ball was a provocative image on any magazine in 1952, not just in SF. Decades later, it reminds us of Kubrick/Clarke's Star-Child

(Bot. L) SPACE STORIES, Feb. 1953, ("The Bleak and Barren Land" by Gordon R. Dickson). Nowadays you'd expect to see this on the front of the WEEKLY WORLD NEWS, with a headline of "CRAB MONSTER ATTACKS!" This is another re-do of sample art, improved by innumerable fine-tunings. Among which that grill-work mouth is most chilling

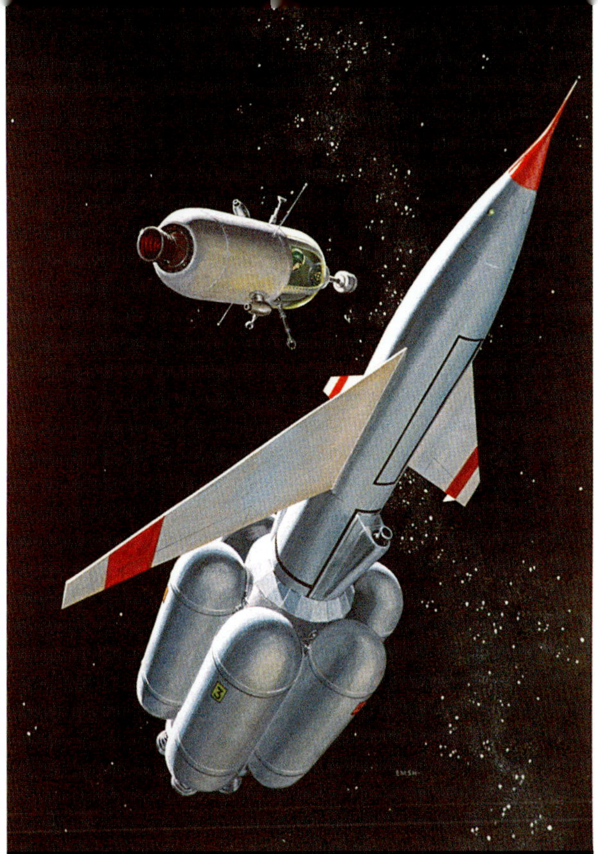

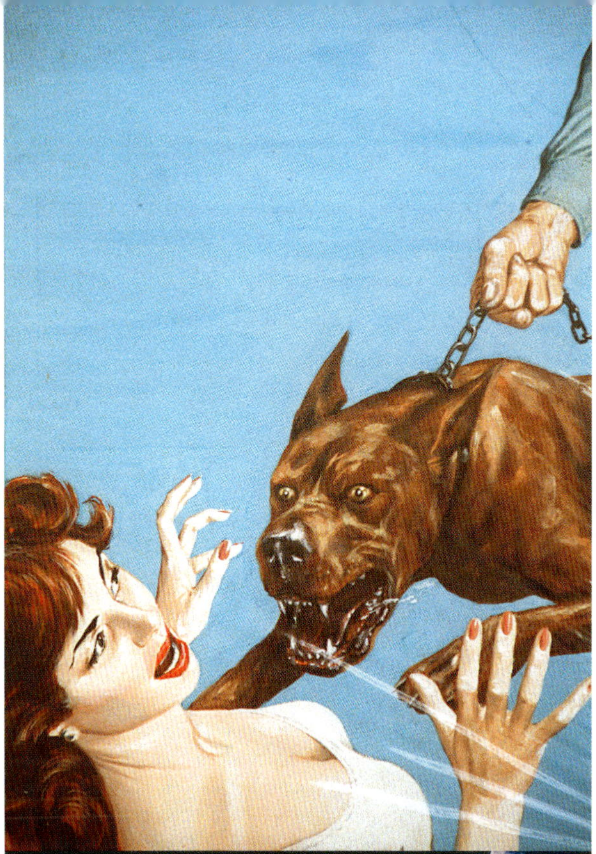

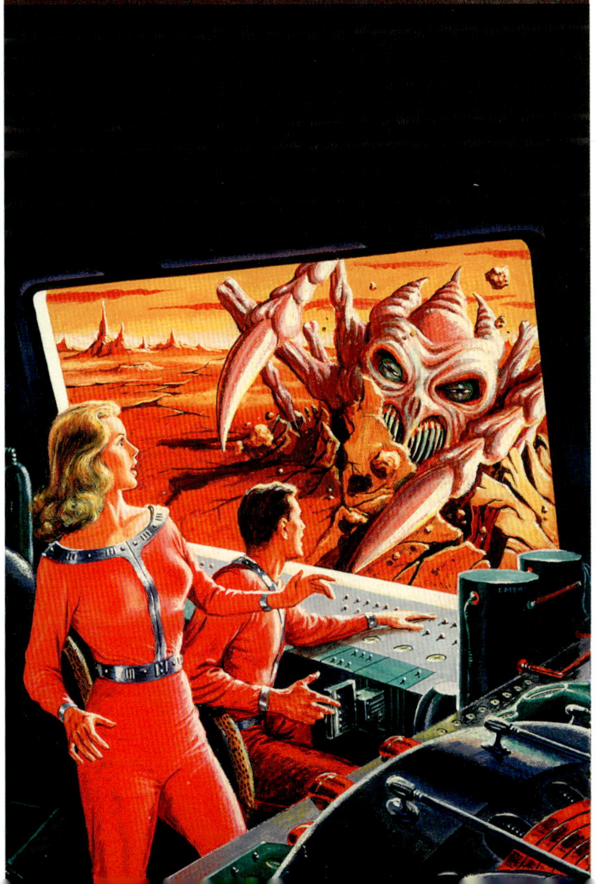

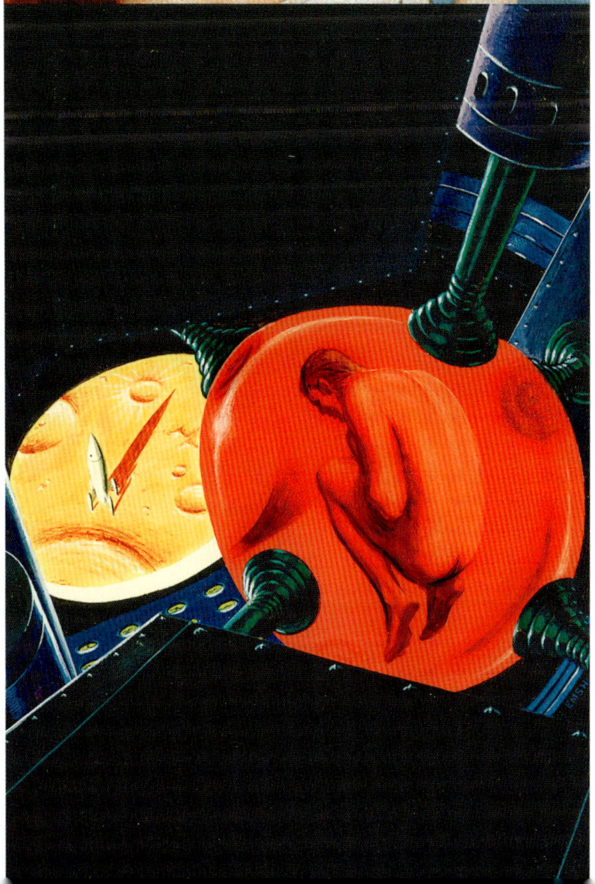

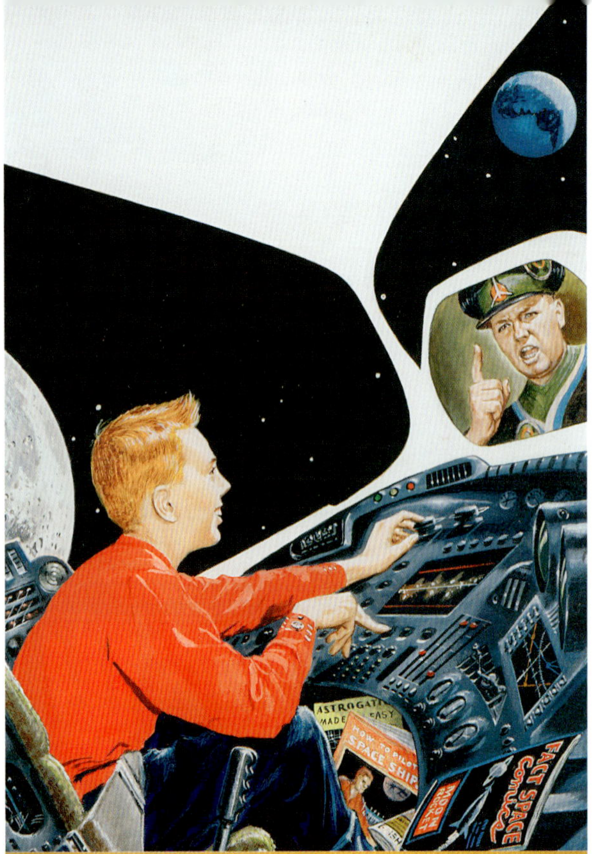

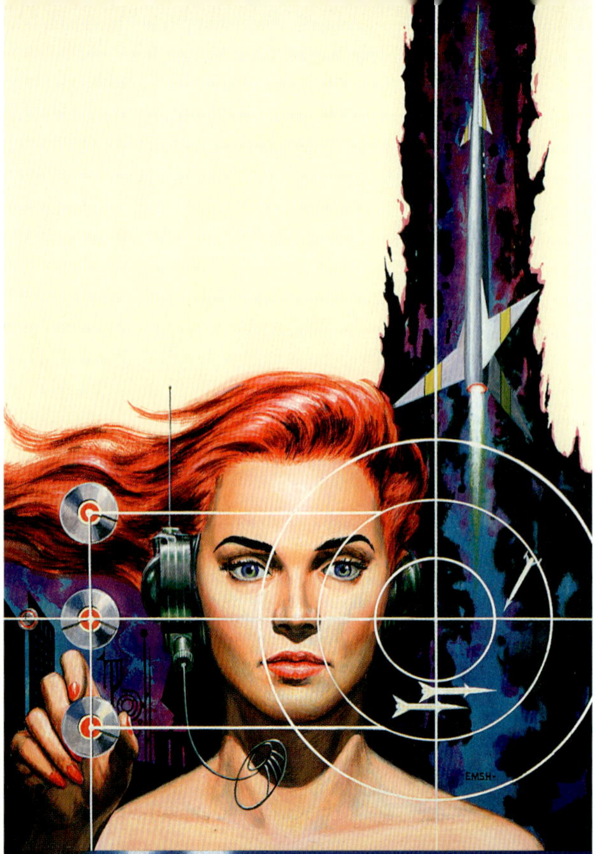

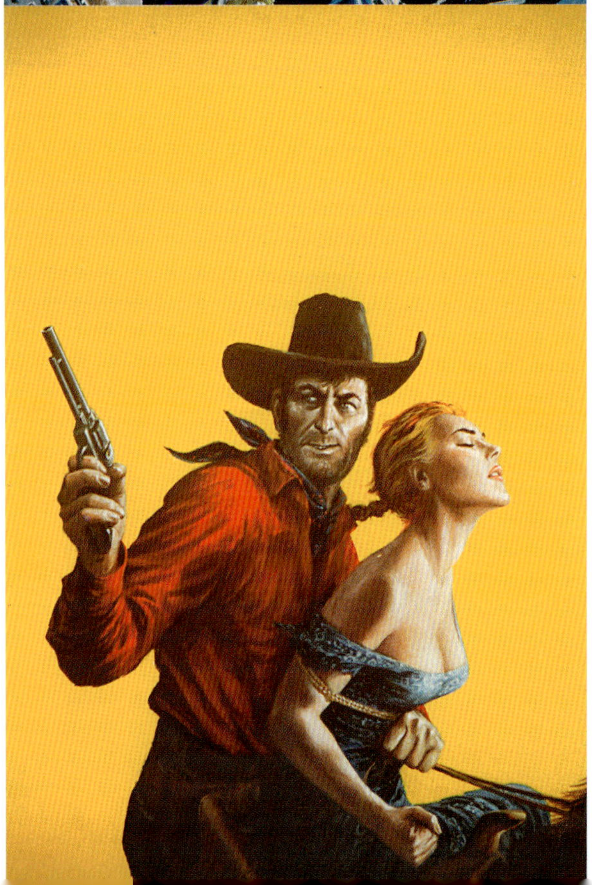

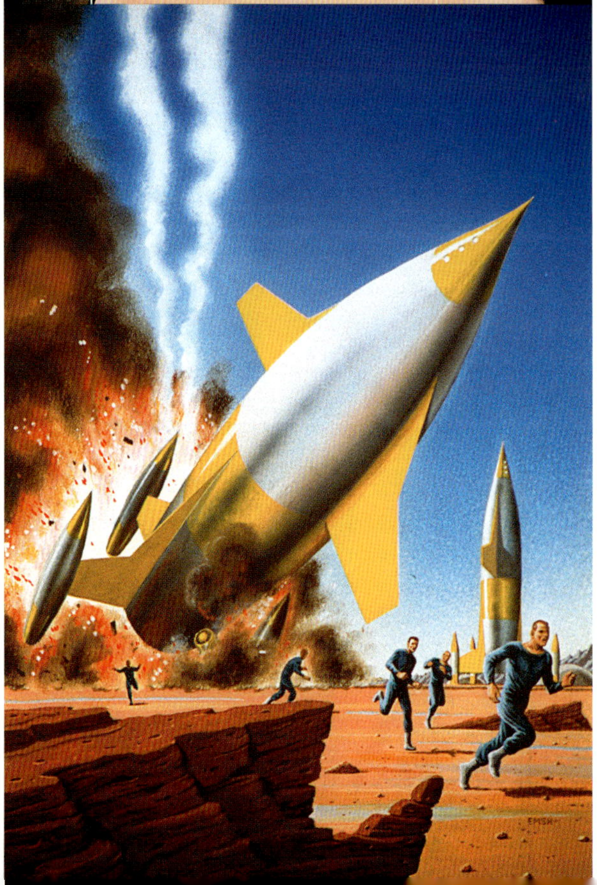

(Top L) ORIGINAL SF. Sept. 1957, "His Head in the Clouds" by "Calvin M. Knox." Every kid's dream, taking a joyride in Daddy's space-coupe. Neighbors posed for this one; that's nine-year-old Bill Griffith, of "Zippy the Pinhead" fame, manning the helm, while his military Dad shakes an angry finger on the vizigraph. Dynamic white surround peps up the design, accentuating the starry void outside.

(Top R) ORIGINAL SF. Nov. 1956. "Women's Work" by Murray Leinster. This scene testifies that all sorts of work qualify as women's work. Dominated by the navigation board and reverse "L" design, the young woman's face is cool, constrained by the rigors of her profession, though her flowing locks suggest a passionate side. Shooting upward through a blue-black channel, a rip in space, an arrow-like rocket vaults onto its outward journey. The woman gazes through the plotting board, through us, focused on the mission...and something beyond.

(Bot. R.) F&SF Apr. 1954 - This disaster at a spaceport is another of Ed's early concept scenes, later repainted for F&SF. The redo is a slight but definite improvement. Ed must have wanted to restyle it, as editors Boucher & McComas would probably not have asked him to. Both versions show Ed's fondness for many-layered rocks (also seen elsewhere).

(Bot. L.) UNTAMED, Mar. 1960, ("Harpe's Last Ride"). A capable Western cover, with a certain pulchritude and bondage quotient.

Four

Red Maple Drive

THE EMSHWILLERS DISCOVERED how challenging a Manhattan tenement apartment is when they moved into a tiny, airless one-room studio, with a shared bathroom at the end of the outside hall, on West 110th Street near Columbia University. Ed's notion of a job went against the grain of what a million other ex-GIs across the country were doing (mostly manufacturing work). He woke early every morning, and after shaving, he would set up his art materials on a small table, along with the photo clippings he had collected from magazines and the Midtown Library Photo Department, and worked on samples or commissions. At night Ed took classes in lithography and silk-screening at the Art Students League on West 57th Street.

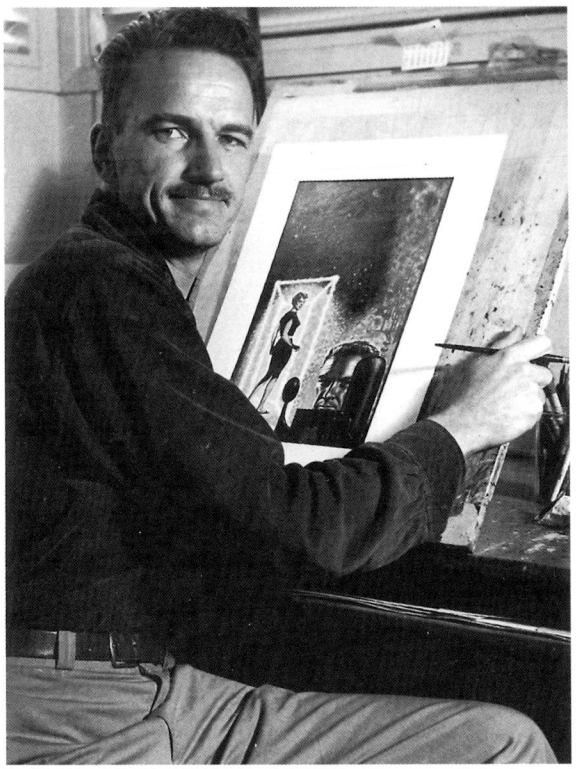

Ed in his studio c. 1956.

Something extraordinary was going on in New York, with art shows of variegated, postwar painters throughout the city intermingling with the exhibition of new films, made by local filmmakers without any studio connections, and poets as easily inspired by a manhole cover as by an abstract painting. It seemed that artists walking the streets of Manhattan could say the word Art aloud, and the public understood. Soon after setting up residence in New York, Ed and Carol joined Cinema 16, "a film society for the adult moviegoer" (to avoid New York State censors it was set up as a private society charging a membership fee). Amos and Marcia Vogel organized cinema 16 in 1947 to present non-commercial movies (encompassing experimental, political, foreign, documentary and avant-garde films) at a succession of rented theatres and auditoriums in Manhattan.

Cinema 16 was modeled after European cine-clubs, like the Cinematheque Francaise, a place that Ed and Carol had become familiar with while living in Paris. Ed would take in the Wednesday night shows at Cinema 16 after a day of making the rounds of art director offices. In an interview, long after Cinema 16's demise, Vogel said, "There were certain things done at the time of Cinema 16 that are simply not being done now."

Cinema 16 offered an alternative to industry-made movies. Ed saw surrealistic films by Salvador Dali and Luis Buñuel, and the early animated films of Norman McLaren and Len Lye. There were complete programs of UPA cartoons, including the work of John Hubley (done in a flat, modernistic graphic style). These were all a revelation to Ed.

These films got Ed interested in the possibilities of single-frame animation. He would see some bit of animation or a scene from an experimental film at Cinema 16, and go home and try the same thing. The availability of portable and sturdy war surplus 16mm film equipment had launched a postwar wave of pioneering American avant-garde and experimental filmmakers, including Maya Deren, James Broughton and Kenneth Anger. Ed admired European neo-realism narrative films like Carol Reed's *The Third Man*, but was drawn to the visual styles and personal expression of most of the experimental films he saw at Cinema 16. This was something he could do.

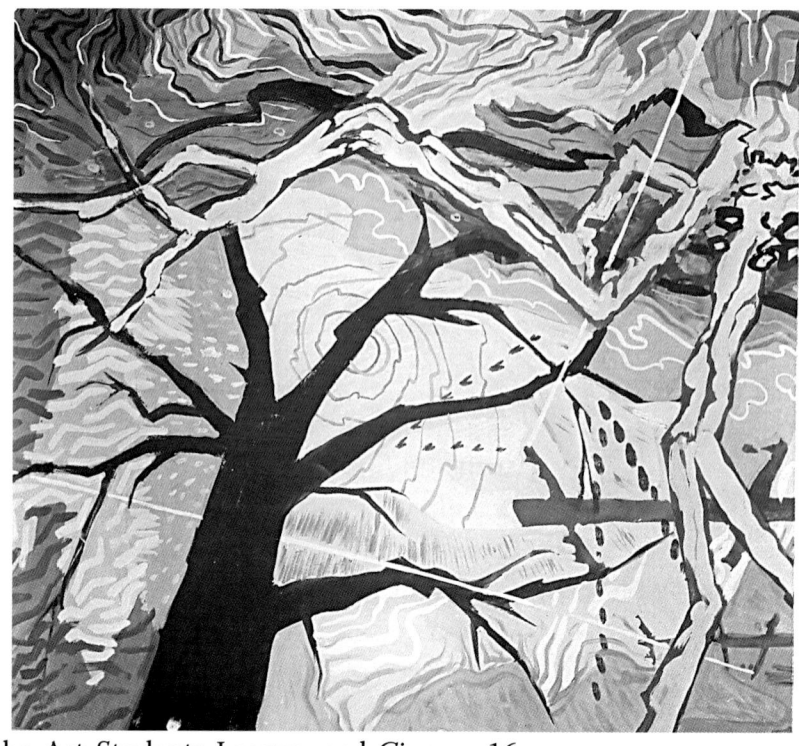

Gotham life, with trips to art museums, classes at the Art Students League, and Cinema 16 screenings, was exciting, but the Emshwillers were not long in Manhattan when in the spring of 1952 Carol noticed an ad in the *New York Times* for affordable houses in a model community being built by William Levitt near Wantagh, Long Island. That weekend they hopped onto the BSA and rode out to see the neighborhood. Their first impression was that there was little to see. The homes were unadorned, assembly-line built, Cape Cod and ranch style frames planted on concrete slabs. However, with G.I. inducements, a $100 down payment and a $9,000 price tag, the monthly mortgage was cheaper than their city apartment and the Levittown homes offered relatively more space to the young couple.

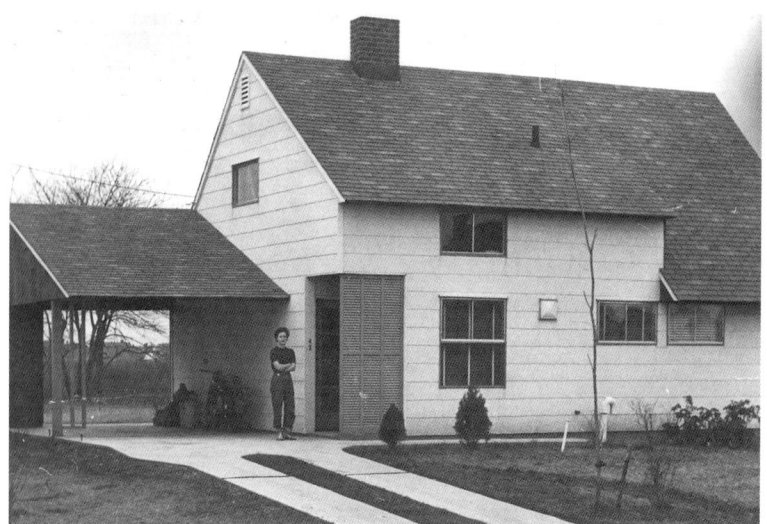

In Levittown no one had fences. Bill Levitt wouldn't allow them. He didn't believe in basements, or garages either, though ultimately popular demand forced him to add carports to the homes. The Emshwillers bought a one-story rancher with a carport, two bedrooms, and one bath at 43 Red Maple Drive and

(top R) Personal art by Ed. C. 1950.

(bot L) Carol in front of Levittown home. C. 1953.

(top R) Ed developing film in his Levittown bathroom.

(bot L) Gnome Press; SCIENCE FICTION TERROR TALES. Edited by Groff Conklin. 1955. According to one source this is the rarest of all Gnome Press titles (despite a larger than normal edition size): "Possibly the rarest Gnome Press book, originally prepared for Crown [publishers], who thought it too scary for its school library market and rejected it."

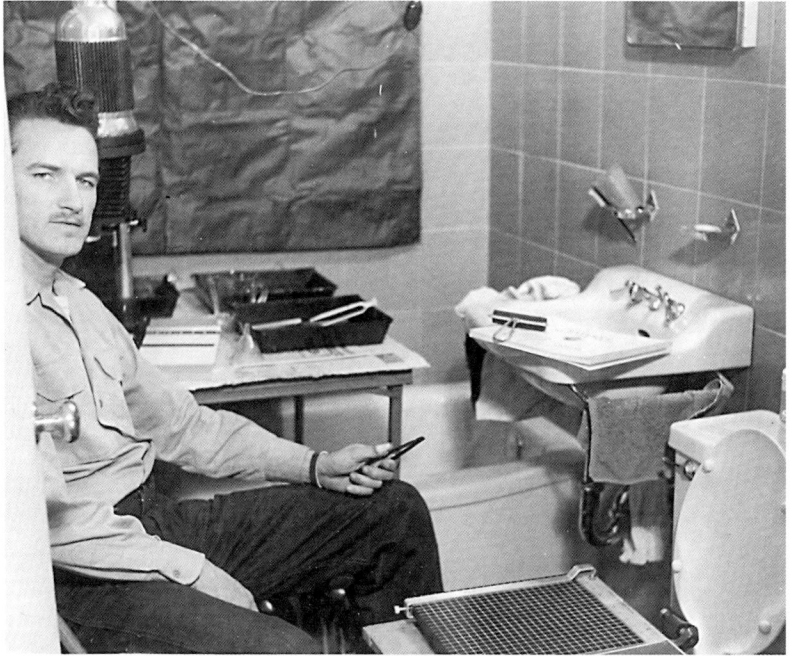

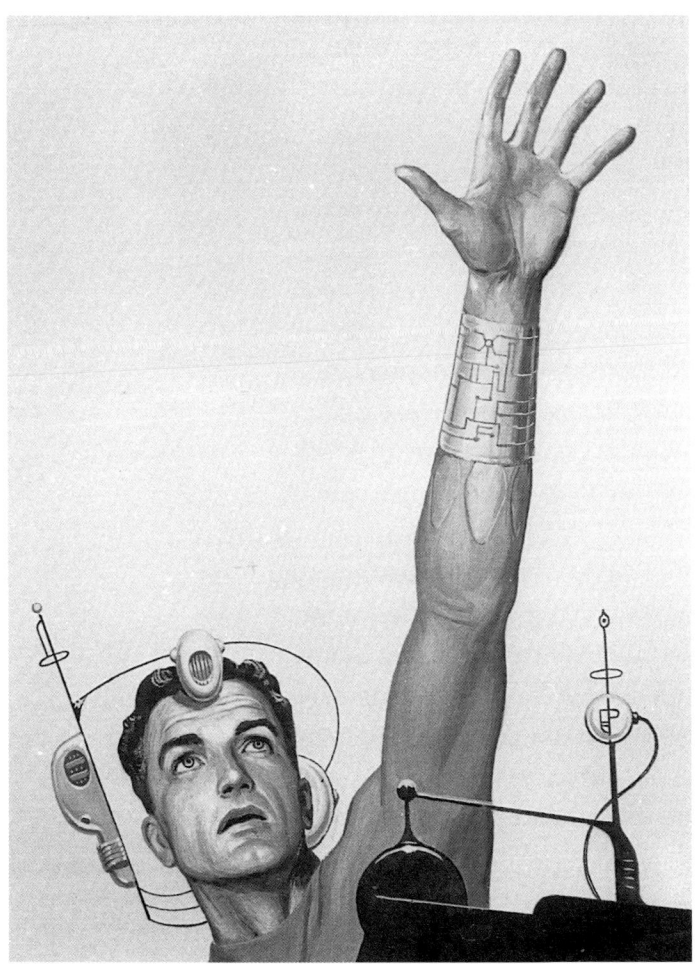

Ed set up a studio in the attic. That first summer, the air hung heavy in the small work place. Even after some remodeling the attic still had an unfinished feel to it. Exposed light fixtures dangling below the rafters lit the center of the room, and left the corners of the room in darkness. In that first year the smell of fresh cut wood was the first thing visitors noticed when they came up the staircase and entered the small studio.

The attic, divided into one small room with a larger room adjacent, was the right size and shape for Ed, who worked alone, though he didn't mind Carol coming up to watch his progress on a painting. Ed's drawing table was at the center of the larger room with flat files and art supplies cabinets under the sloping sides of the ceiling. His ad hoc do-it-himself approach to things began to manifest itself throughout the house when Ed set up a dark room in the bathroom downstairs. Ed had a folding table that fit into the bathtub where he would place his enlarger along with developer and washing trays. A dark cloth would drape the window and mirror to keep out the light. Even the toilet seat, with the lid down, became a work surface.

Ed learned photography mostly from studying photography magazines and used Carol, his brother-in-law's wife, his brother Mac, or any neighbors not at work, as models to work out a pose or figure arrangement for a painting. Ed did his own film developing for pictures where Carol posed in underwear or near nude. He would also pose himself and have Carol snap the photograph. Ed eventually bought a Polaroid camera to speed things up.

Levittown was exciting at first. In its early years it was settled by many artists and writers. One of Ed's best friends was a motor-

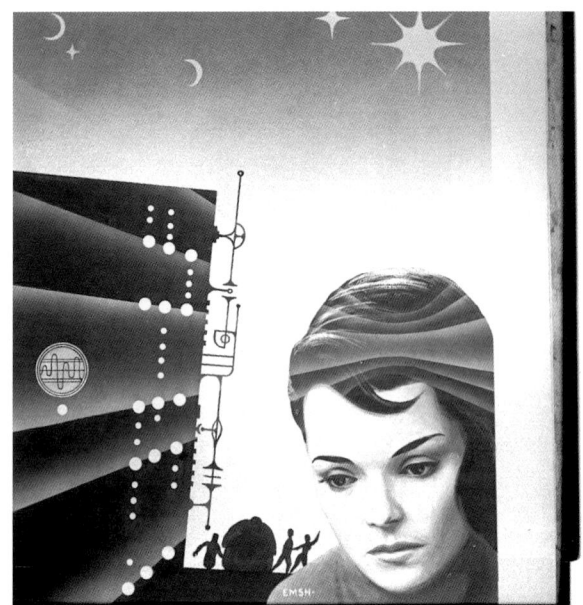 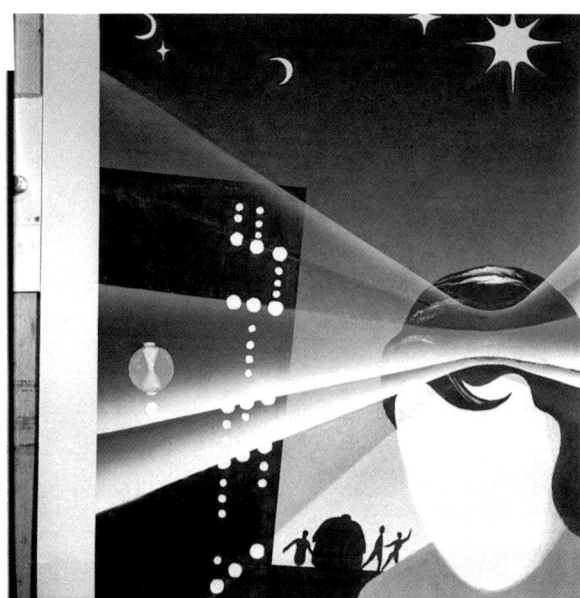

cycle buddy who happened to be a psychiatrist married to a pianist. Everyone was new and eager to find friends. Most of these early settlers would agree that by 1960 most of the artistic types had moved away and the neighborhood had become another suburban commuter enclave to New York City.

The primary ingredients of Ed's art were already in place at this time: inventive hardware of space travel; juxtaposition of large foreground figures with smaller background figures to show depth; abstract elements as science fictional leitmotivs, and imaginative backgrounds.

Ed, who had used the abbreviated "Emsh" since grade school and signed his paintings done at the University of Michigan as Eddy Emsh, divided his labors between science fiction and mystery pulps and digests. After his Bauhaus art studies at the university, and motivated by his appreciation of modernist painters Jackson Pollock, Frank Stella and Franz Kline, it was not long before Ed felt the need to create his own personal art. As a practical child of the Great Depression, he knew his abstract paintings were done for personal reasons. He had realized early on that abstractionists needed heavy-duty fine art coterie promotion to survive.

Emsh's finished abstractions wound up scattered around the house where some visitors, intrigued by this side of Ed's art, would buy them. Ed seemed little interested in exhibiting them in galleries, but did have one show in 1960 at the Sunken Meadow Art Gallery in the town of Sea Cliff, Long Island. An incident at the show is telling: "I was in the gallery when a man came in with his pre-teen son. Like a Rorschach test, he went around the gallery telling the boy what to see: 'This is a painting of a storm at sea. This is a jungle with a great deal of danger, etc. and etc.' This, of course, was the father's projections. I was both amused and horrified by it all because the boy was denied his imagination."

By 1953 Ed's art was everywhere — sophisticated, artistic scenes for *Fantasy & Science Fiction*; monsters threatening spacemen for *Space Stories*; sexy girl art for *Startling Stories*; gigantic rock-

(top) ADDRESS: CENTAURI by F. L. Wallace. Gnome Press, 1955. Three color separations of Emsh art. Photographed by EE.

ets dwarfing the landscape for *Thrilling Wonder Stories*; the witty use of SF tropes for *Galaxy* and *Rocket Stories*. The only other artist in the field nearly as prolific was Frank Kelly Freas. Robert W. Lowndes, editor of *Future Science Fiction* and *Science Fiction Stories*, recalled "Kelly was great fun and came forth with brilliant things; Emsh was more reliable in the long run and could do more with seemingly ordinary scenes – while he seldom matched Freas at Freas' very best, I do not recall him ever being as thoroughly bad as Kelly could be in an off period. I refuse to try to decide which was the better SF artist; both are unforgettable for anyone who was a science fictionist during that time."

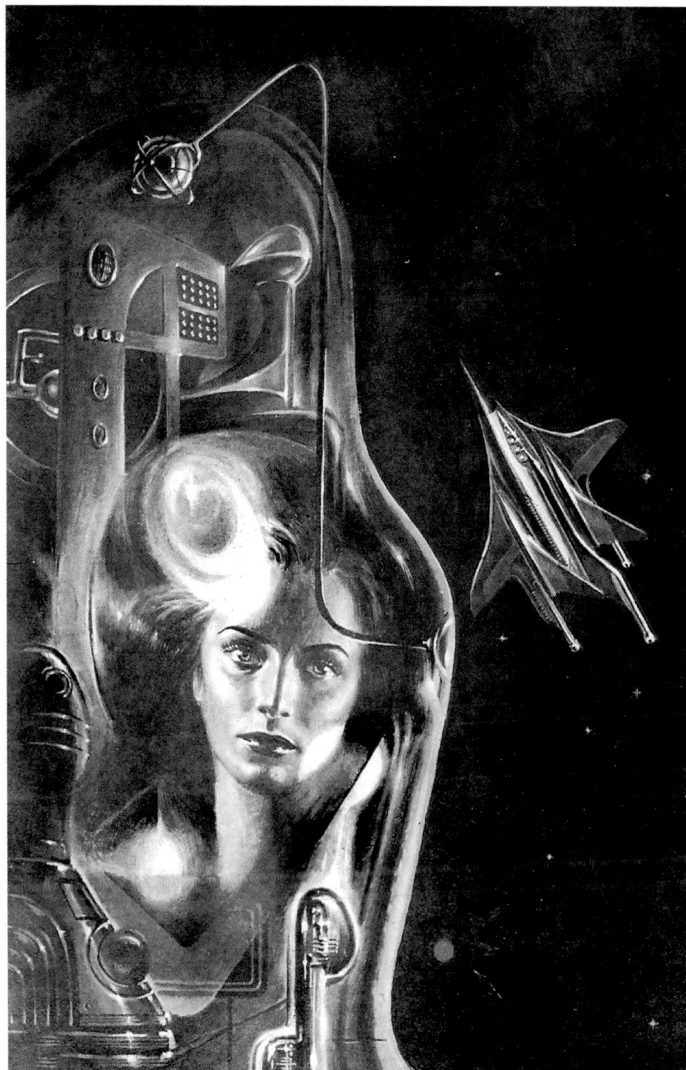

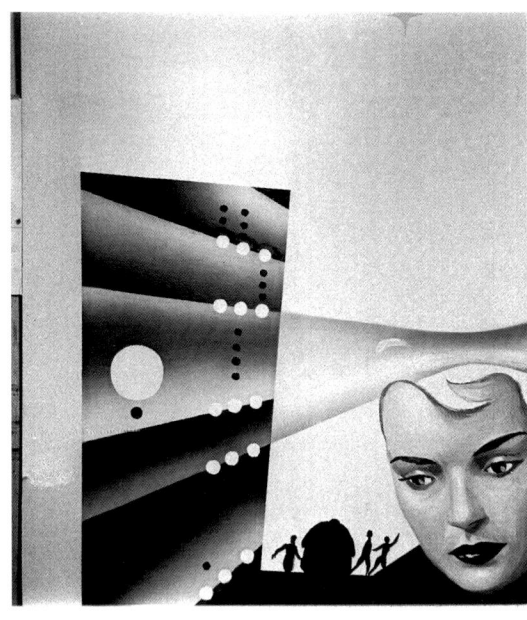

(top R) THE ORIGINAL SCIENCE FICTION STORIES. Aug. 1956.

(bot L) GALAXY SCIENCE FICTION. Aug. 1951. Ink illustration.

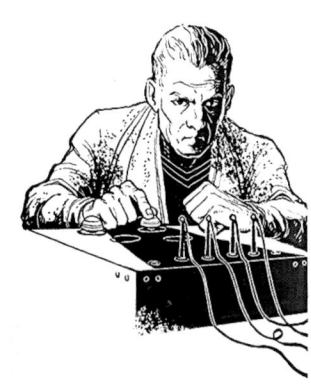

There were times when Ed tried to push other styles of art to his clients. On May 6, 1953, he was in the offices of *F&SF* for an art conference with publisher Lawrence Spivak and George Salter. Ed had the idea to do a symbolic cover for a story called "Letter to a Tiger" (October 1953). At first Spivak and art editor Salter objected to Ed's idea. Ed spent a few hours talking them into going along with his original concept. Ed said afterwards, "As far as I know it is the most symbolic, non-illustrative cover they've used since they have gone in for S.F. covers" (pg. 65). Ed had gotten away with a highly unusual cover for the story "Beyond Bedlam" in *Galaxy*, though here the case could be made that the art matched the story idea of a schizophrenic society (pg. 51).

Even though Van der Poel tried to have a balance of artists in every issue, the June 1953 *Galaxy* included Emsh art on four stories. Ed was prolific enough that magazines began using pseudonyms for him: Ed Emsler in *Amazing Stories* and *Planet Stories*, Ed Alexander and Willer in *Galaxy*; other

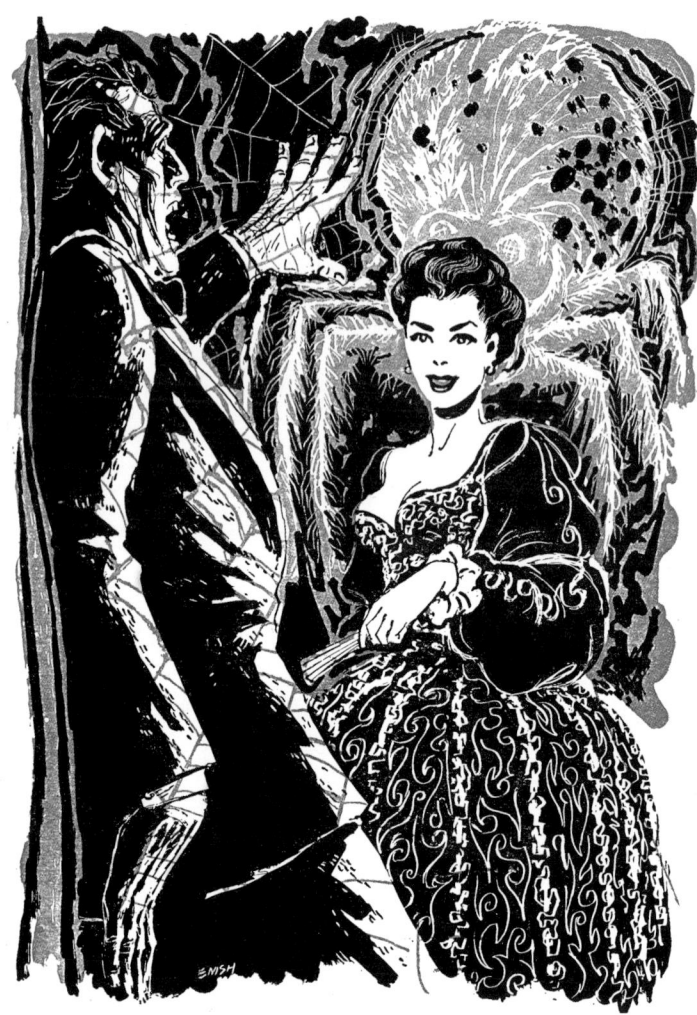

FANTASY MAGAZINE. Aug. 1953. Ink and scratchboard illustration.

pen names included Harry Gars and Ed Emsch. He worked primarily in gouache, opaque watercolors, since most other mediums were too slow drying for the tight deadlines he had to make many times. Most of his black and white interior illustrations were done on scratchboard (a board covered with chalky substrate which is then inked and scratched with a sharp object to reveal white lines in the manner of a woodcut).

Thomas M. Disch once said that the most literate writers in the field during the fifties (he included Damon Knight, James Blish and Alfred Bester in his list) had to write for a naive audience where story ideas were paramount. A sense of wonder could be a scientific idea considered in new ways, or a twist of an old idea. Ed was able to translate this sense of wonder into visual terms in the first few paintings he did for *Fantasy & Science Fiction* and *Galaxy Magazine*.

Ed's SF art was seen to good effect in *F&SF* and *Galaxy* due to the better 4-color printing and cover stock used by both magazines, but he got some unjustified flak from fans at other publications. In response to negative letters for a cover Ed did at *Fantastic Story Magazine*, editor Sam Mines replied, "The story on that Emsh painting for September was mostly one of loss in printing. The original cover was very good and very effective. Otherwise we wouldn't have bought it. But no one could foresee the almost complete loss of detail, which ensued in the printing and the general muddying up." This was a problem Ed would encounter throughout his career. When he became a fulltime filmmaker, the difficulty became one of dealing with film labs.

Over the Labor Day weekend in 1953, the Eleventh World Science Fiction Convention was held at the Bellevue-Stratford Hotel in Philadelphia. Some 650 fans and professionals attended, including Ed Emsh. On Sunday, September 6, Ed served as one of the judges, along with Kelly Freas, at the masquerade. Later that night at the overpriced banquet, with Isaac Asimov serving as toastmaster, the first ever Hugo Awards were handed out (though they were only called achievement awards that night) and there was a tie for professional magazine: *Galaxy* and *Astounding Science Fiction* (which could be considered a rebuke of Campbell's pseudo-science dalliances), and a tie for cover artist: between longtime fan favorite Hannes Bok and Ed Emsh. (The awards were for work done in 1952, a year when Bok had been mostly inactive in the field.) Then, as now, the winners of Hugo awards reflected the best of science fiction as recognized by hardcore fans—making it more of a popularity contest.

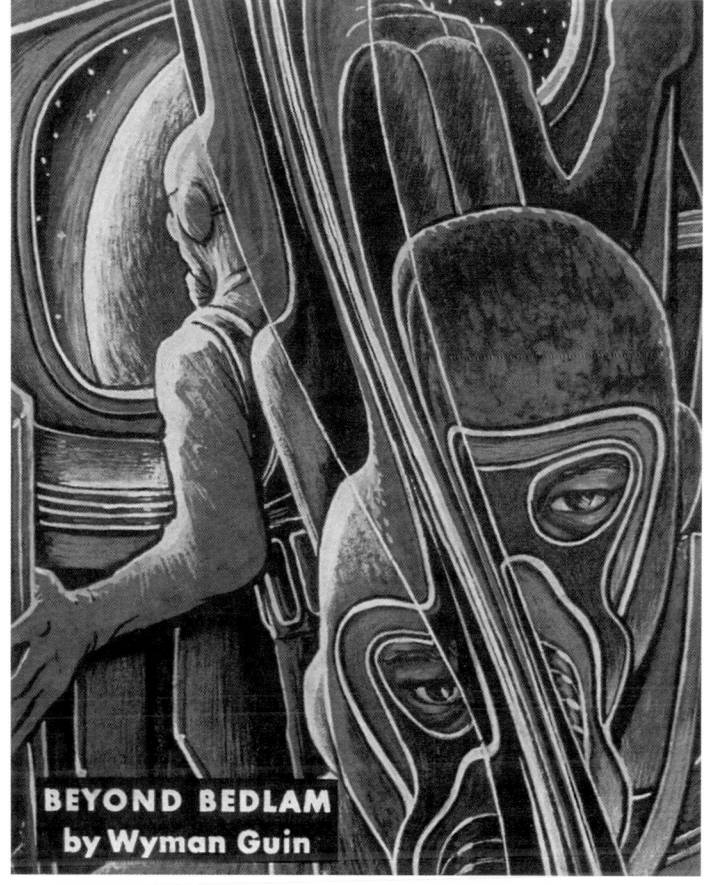

GALAXY SCIENCE FICTION. "Beyond Bedlam" by Wyman Guin. Aug. 1951.

Where artists like Bok looked to older schools of art, Ed, Richard Powers, and Freas were part of a new generation of post-war artists steeped in 20th century art, who had emerged with the general boom in science fiction. As if to underscore this growth, within walking distance, or a short bus ride, of the convention hotel, there were six SF&f movies playing: *It Came from Outer Space; Beast from 20,000 Fathoms; Invaders from Mars; The 5000 Fingers of Dr. T: Scared Stiff;* and *Four-Sided Triangle*. What the general population thought of science fiction could be seen in the Philadelphia movie houses, and in one local newspaper account of the con: *Would Be Zoomies Meet In Philadelphia*.

Many in the science fiction crowd saw Ed as a cool "big-name-pro" on the scene. For one thing artists were still rare at cons: Bok and Finlay avoided crowds, Powers appeared at one 1950s gathering and was not seen again for many years. Freas was one of the few regular artist con attendees during the decade. For many journeymen artists, toiling in the science fiction fields was a minor part of their output. A teenaged Harlan Ellison first met Ed face-to-face at the Philcon after having contacted him by mail to get art for his fanzine.

Many SF artists were based in and around New York, but (with very few exceptions) seemed to lack any interest in the cauldron of modernistic schools of fine art bubbling around them, much less catering to science fiction fans. For these artists, art was a job—the more direction they received, the better they were able to produce. Their point of visual reference was more likely to come from B films, such as *Rocketship X-M* and *Destination Moon*. And of course, Hollywood was not above using images and ideas pilfered from SF magazines.

Commercial artists did not endear themselves to art directors by bringing new ideas into the air. Then as today, art editors saw artists as craftsmen deployed in the service of an idea already fixed, if not fully focused, in the art director's mind. (Richard Powers appears to be the only other artist making any attempt at fusing SF art and modernistic art—in his case, surrealism. Most art directors knew better than to try to give detailed directions to Powers.) Where Ed's drawing skills and his awareness of modern art led him to experiment, most SF artists were content to stick with straightforward figurative and realistic art. Even though he was shot down many times, Ed was always mixing in a few concept sketches that pushed the boundaries of SF art when making the rounds of magazine art directors.

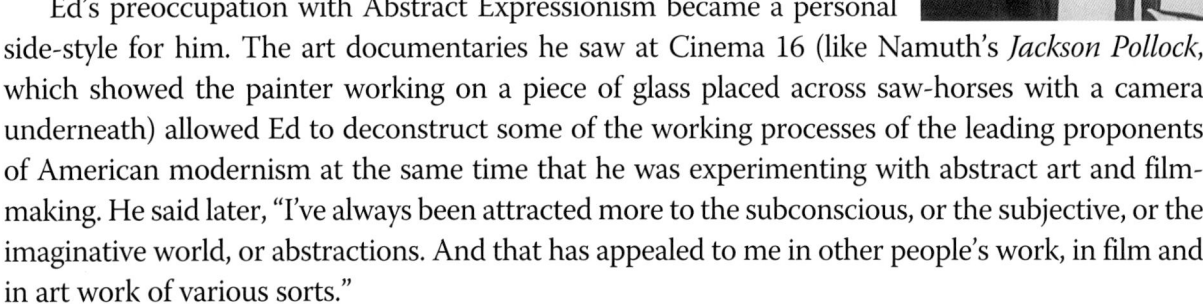

Ed giving a speech at Fancon in the spring of 1955. The oversized art he is holding appears to be by Frank Kelly Freas.

Ed's preoccupation with Abstract Expressionism became a personal side-style for him. The art documentaries he saw at Cinema 16 (like Namuth's *Jackson Pollock*, which showed the painter working on a piece of glass placed across saw-horses with a camera underneath) allowed Ed to deconstruct some of the working processes of the leading proponents of American modernism at the same time that he was experimenting with abstract art and film-making. He said later, "I've always been attracted more to the subconscious, or the subjective, or the imaginative world, or abstractions. And that has appealed to me in other people's work, in film and in art work of various sorts."

Commercial art never captured Ed's undivided attention. In October 1954, Ed saw a screening of *George Braque* at Cinema 16, showing the cubist artist also painting on a glass table, which gave Ed the idea to film the creation of some of his paintings. By the mid-fifties the old Filmo had been replaced by a used 16mm Bolex Leader camera with single frame capabilities, which Ed used to record the evolution of a few science fiction cover paintings and some of his abstractions. "I was really interested in action painting and did a lot of stop motion records of the development of those action paintings…. Those evolving records were like flowers blossoming in slow motion."

Ed later recalled, "When I was an action painter I had the experience a number of times of having painted past the point when a painting worked best. I wished that I could go back to an earlier stage, but I couldn't. Both film and video have a great advantage in having total recall in that respect. Unless you have chopped up the original film, or erased the original tapes, you can reassemble or return to any stage of the work at will, economics permitting."

Ed had built a camera brace over his drawing table; a cable release was connected to a foot pedal, which he would use to trigger the shutter while he would reload his brush with paint. "I worked at what I called doodles, which were film exercises. Almost anything that I had seen done in film I tried my hand at. I'm a great one for making tests. Any time a technical problem comes up that I think in theory should work, then I make a series of exhaustive tests. I think in that way I developed whatever technical abili-

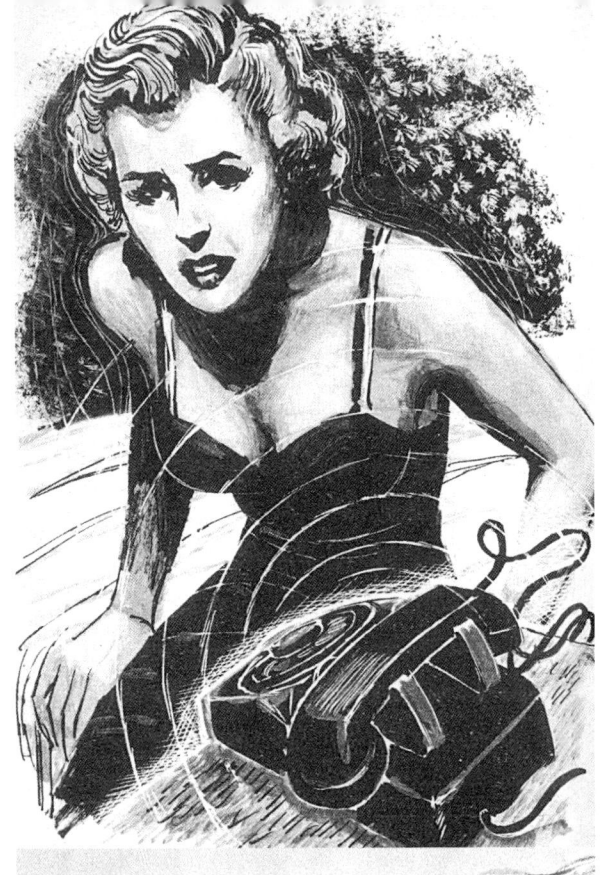
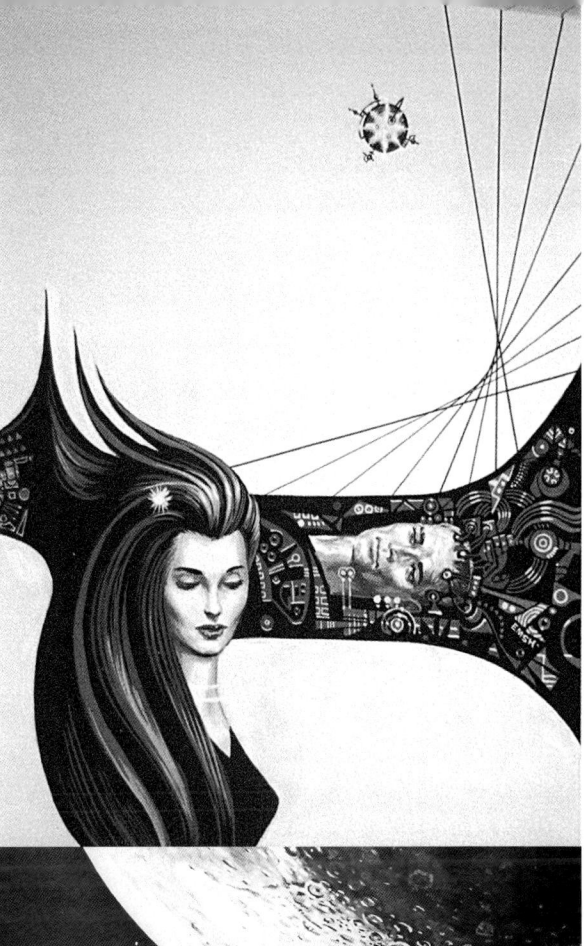
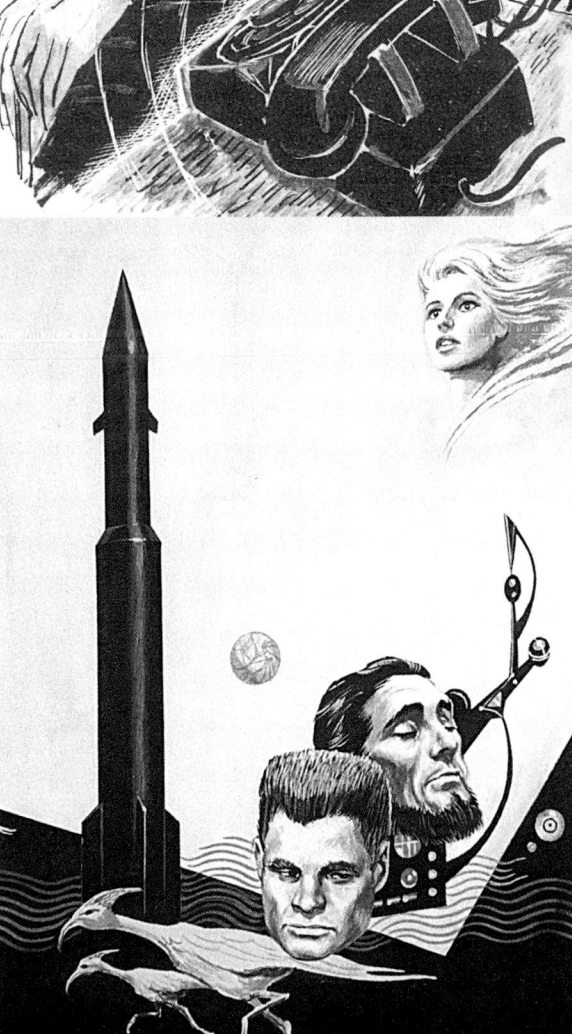
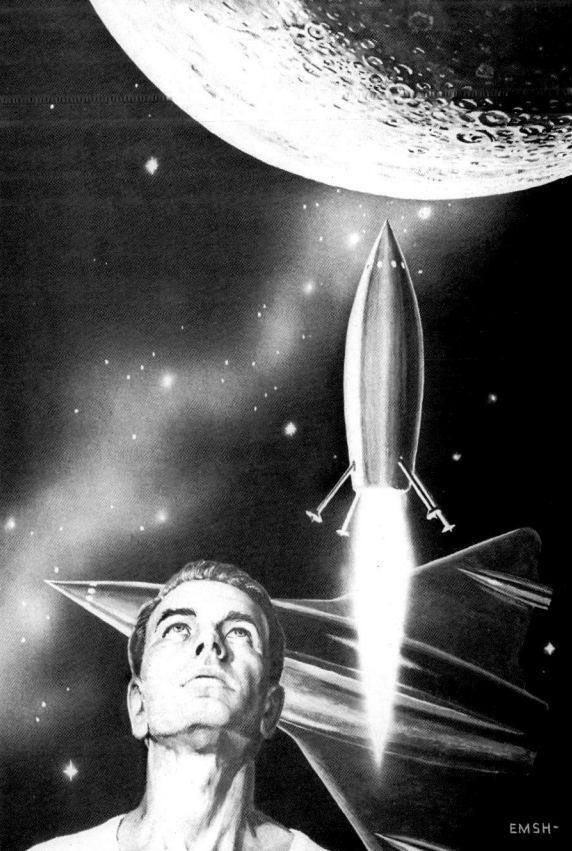

(top L) 25 SHORT SHORT STORIES FROM COLLIER'S. "I'm Sorry, There is no Answer" by Corey Ford. 1953.

(top R) BRIDGE TO YESTERDAY by E.L. Arch. Unk. date. Avalon

(bot R) PRELUDE TO SPACE by Arthur C. Clarke. 1954. Gnome Press.

(bot L) THE MARTIAN VISITORS. By Frank B. Long. Unk. date. Avalon

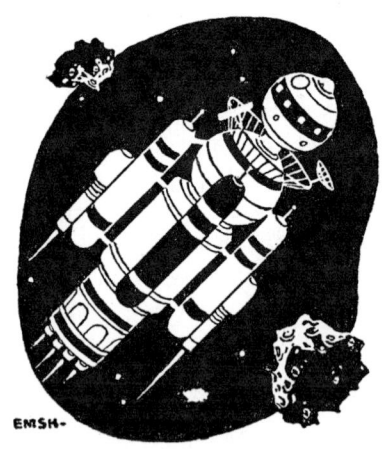

ties I have. That carried over into art. I believe that technique simply helps one to be a better artist. I think sometimes there is a tendency among some filmmakers either to put overmuch emphasis on technique [or] to deride it as unimportant. I think it's essential; but it certainly isn't the crux of the art. Stated simply: the better the technician you are, the more able you are to achieve whatever you'd like to do." Ed also was experimenting with clay animations, animation cels, and additive animation.

Since the drafting table where Ed created art was also an animation stand, he began recording the stage-by-stage development of many paintings. The run-through would usually take two minutes on each film. Most of these early stop-motion studies accidentally caught Ed's paint hand or the shadow of the cable-release wire in the shot before he got used to the setup.

Ed mimicked Abstract Expressionism techniques, with a bit of De Kooning's palette knife smearing, for one of his early film experiments. Pollock was attempting to get at pure abstraction without any representation. Early Dada artist Hans Arp had attempted something similar, during World War I, by creating chance abstractions out of cutout paper shapes dropped and glued down where they fell. It seemed possible for anyone to imitate Pollack's technique: even Norman Rockwell attempted a credible abstract expressionist painting—within a *Saturday Evening Post* cover. "The Connoisseur" presented an *action painted* wall canvas viewed by a perplexed art patron. Of course, Rockwell concentrated on the body language of the art patron (to suit the *Saturday Evening Post*'s audience), but unknown to many his heart was really in the faux abstract art he depicted on the wall before the art patron.

In the silent film Ed made of his abstraction, the painting metamorphoses into the appearance of an "LSD Christmas tree on a yellow background" as remembered by Robert Silverberg. So pleased was he by the finished image that when Silverberg recognized the piece from the film on the wall of the Emshwillers' living room during a visit, he traded a camera for the painting and — as of this writing — still owns the piece.

A group of New York-based artists, including Jackson Pollock, Robert Motherwell, Franz Kline, and Willem de Kooning were having a considerable influence upon the fine art world at this time. When not arguing how much representation is allowable in abstraction, they plotted the equivalent of a modern art coup from Greenwich Village taverns and cheap downtown eateries. Ed was not above taking whatever he could use from this crowd to keep his own interest from flagging on some of his commercial art assignments.

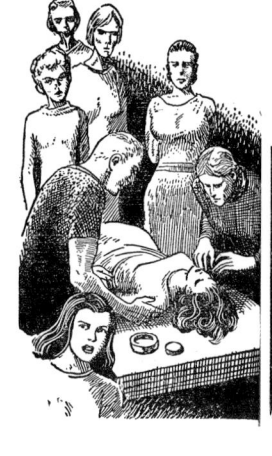
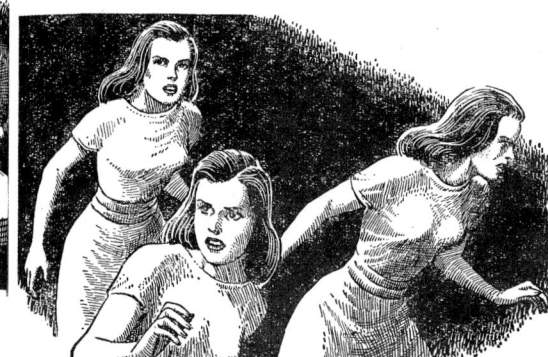

(top L) Spot illustration for unknown SF magazine. C. 1953. Ink and scratchboard.

(bot R) GALAXY SCIENCE FICTION. April 1952. "Accidental Flight."

Five

Science Fiction Boom

HAVING COME FROM A BIG FAMILY, Carol was used to hearing laughter in the house as soon as she awoke in the morning, and would rush to join other people. Levittown's quiet streets were the opposite of Paris and New York, or even Ann Arbor's bustling college town ambience. In Levittown, even if Carol had wanted to, she did not have to cross the street to avoid anyone. The only life on the flat and empty sidewalks was sparrows chirping. For the first few years, before she had her children, Carol found married life—found living in a home with just one person difficult.

The Levittown house had more of an appearance of an art workshop than a Long Island home. The living room had light fixtures that could take photoflood bulbs to allow for indoor photography. Ed felt financially comfortable enough to buy a drafting desk in 1955. Up until then he had used a makeshift tabletop made out of a door as his drawing board. With the addition of a baby's crib the downstairs living area started to look more domesticated – if you use a before and after picture analogy.

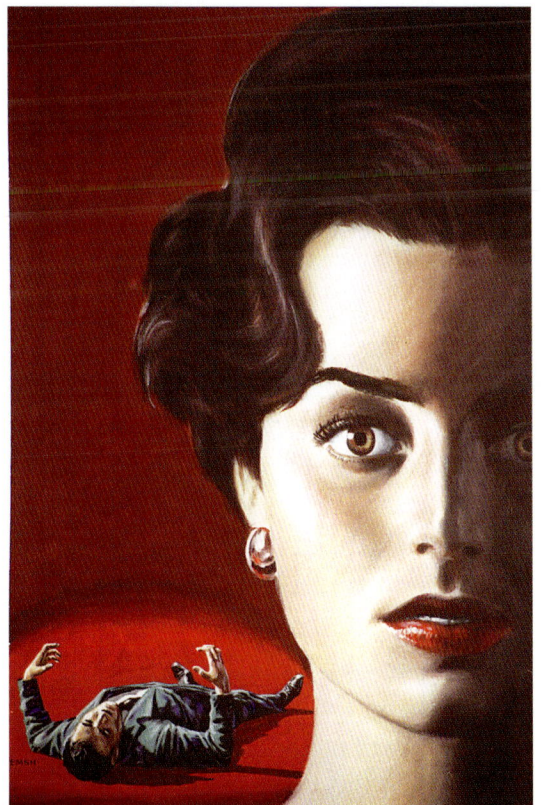

Cover art from ELLERY QUEEN'S MYSTERY MAGAZINE. Aug.1958.

Carol began taking an interest in the contents of the science fiction magazines that came into the house and tagged along with Ed to some of the local science fiction conventions. *I guess what triggered my first stories was wanting to join all those SF people I met through Ed and the fact that they talked about writing as if it was a chess game and a normal person could learn to do it.*

It was sometime between 1954 and 1955, while she was pregnant with her first child Eve, that Carol began writing stories. These first efforts were conceived with science fiction markets in mind and a new attitude. As Carol later recalled, *Something clicked. So this is what writing is all about. It's not at all that stuff in high school or freshman English.*

She showed her work in progress to Ed, who made comments based on his own take on genre fiction. Except for art assignments, Ed was not a big reader of fiction. In his studio could be found copies of "figure study" art reference magazines showing photography of nude models with all hair below the neck carefully air-brushed out, men's magazines including *Playboy*, and *Popular Science, Scientific American* (one of the few magazines he really enjoyed reading). According to Carol, *All the reading Ed did — besides* Scientific American *— was what I read to him as he worked or as we traveled, him driving, me reading.*

In January 1954 Ed produced over $1,300 worth of art, his best month ever. That month he finished four hardcover dust jackets, three magazine covers, and a dozen or more interior illustrations. Ed also learned that he had overpaid his last quarterly income tax for 1953 and had enough credit to cover his first tax payment of 1954. For the first time, he had a sense of doing more than just making a subsistence living. Ed believed that his most recent work had taken a big leap in development and would open new doors once art directors saw it.

In the mid-fifties new SF magazines sprouted like mushrooms in a dank grotto. Any writer of minimum competence who could fill the bill had a better than even chance of selling to the field. It didn't hurt if a writer was already a fan reading the stuff. Most of the field's editors were not looking to transcend the genre—it was hard enough finding writers that weren't trying to turn westerns into SF. Emsh was seen as someone who could give instant visual cachet to a new magazine. Immediately after Larry Shaw started *Infinity SF* at the end of 1955, he snared Ed as the magazine's only cover artist and Ed painted all of the next nineteen issues' covers. Robert Silverberg was one of the primary writer for *Infinity*, under various pen names.

The science fiction boom was as fortuitous for Carol as it was for Ed. Robert Lowndes, perpetually working with a shoestring

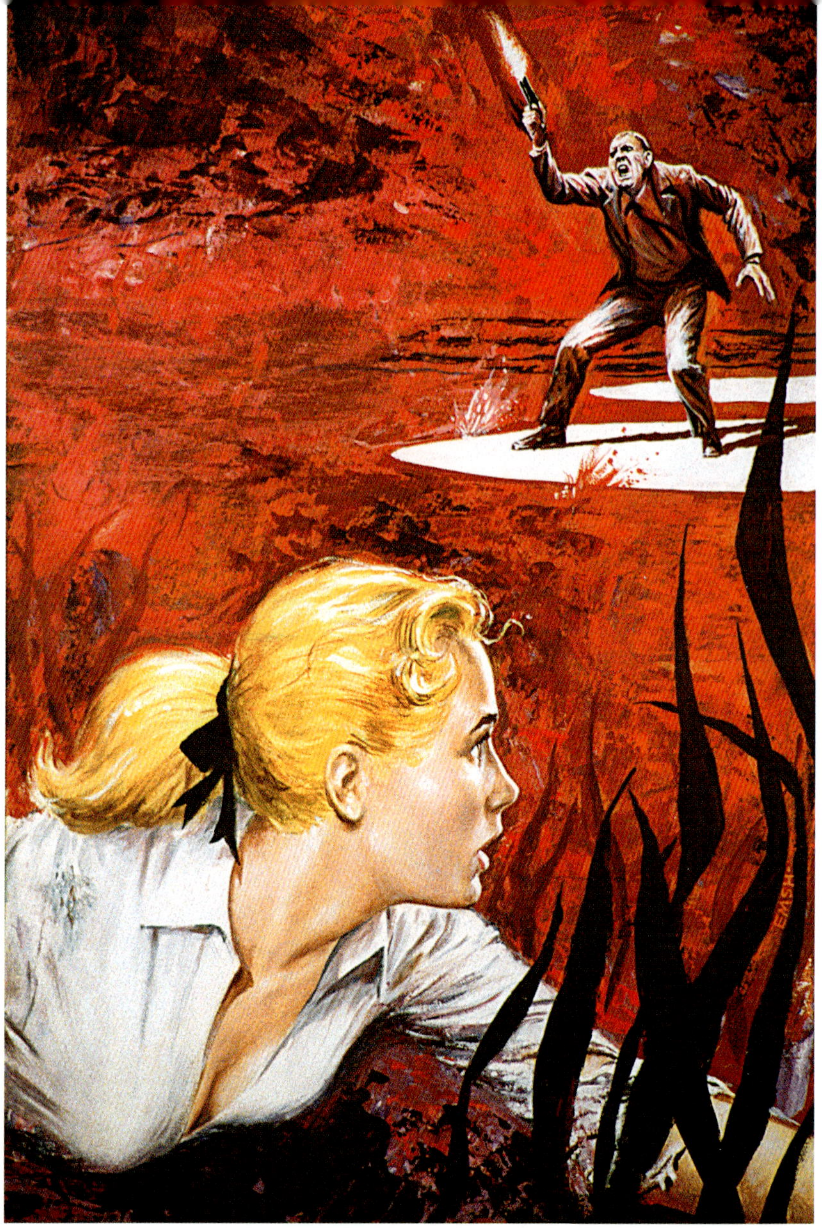

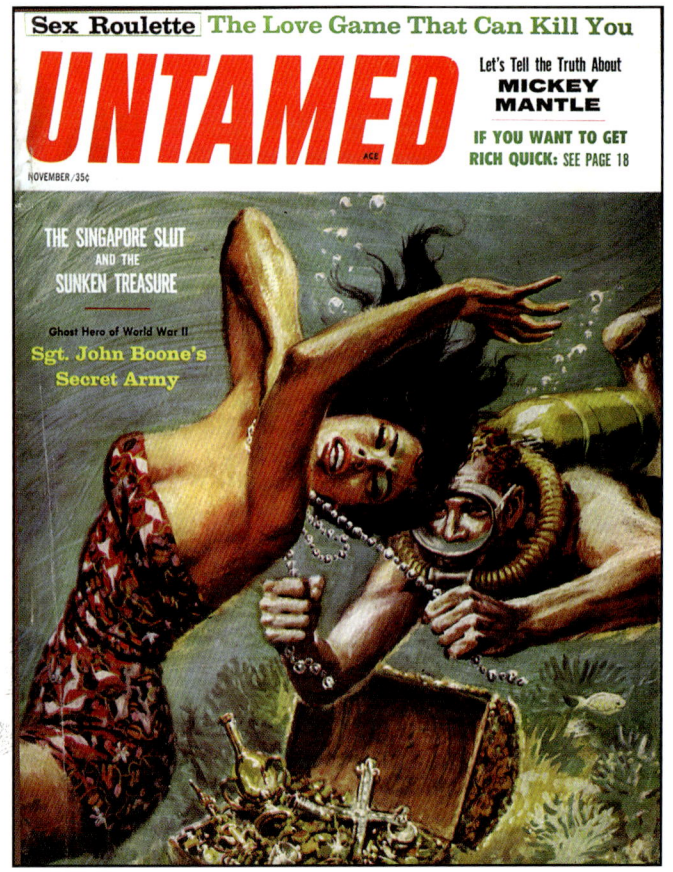

(top R) Unknown mystery magazine cover art. C. late 1950s.

(bot L) UNTAMED. November 1959. "The Singapore Slut and the Sunken Treasure."

budget, bought Carol's story "This Thing Called Love" in the summer of 1955 for *Future SF* at half a cent a word—after publication. (The slight story-line concerns a distracted wife "in love" with robotic TV "actors" and her husband's attempt to break her of her TV addiction by getting her to go pioneering on other worlds.) In the same issue (#28), Lowndes wrote about the maturity of science fiction and the possibility "… for a work of science fiction to appear which could qualify as literature." Lowndes clarified this: "Stories dealing with the 'ideal society' or its obverse."

A story Carol wrote about the same time, "The Victim", which appeared in Lowndes' *Smashing Detective*, September 1955, may have been on newsstands before "This Thing Called Love". "The Victim" was written as a science fiction story, but Lowndes needed to fill a gap in one of his mystery magazines and Carol's story had a murder in it. After this Carol did write a few stories specifically as mysteries for Lowndes.

"This Thing Called Love" was the fourth or fifth story Carol had written. She had sold one early story to a local Long Island magazine, but the magazine went out of business before printing the piece. Many of her early stories would go off to *F&SF*, and after they came back with rejection slips she would send them to Lowndes.

Lowndes was another SF fan turned pro who had been slogging in pulp publishing since 1941 as a jack-of-all-trades for Columbia Publications. Over the interim he had developed close friendships with many SF writers and artists, who he used in an assortment of magazines he helmed: *Famous Detective, Future Science Fiction, SF Quarterly, Dynamic Mystery, Sports Winners,* and *Double Action Western*. Lowndes began working in pulps as a young man and was one of the original members of the Futurians, a New York City kibbutz of SF fans that

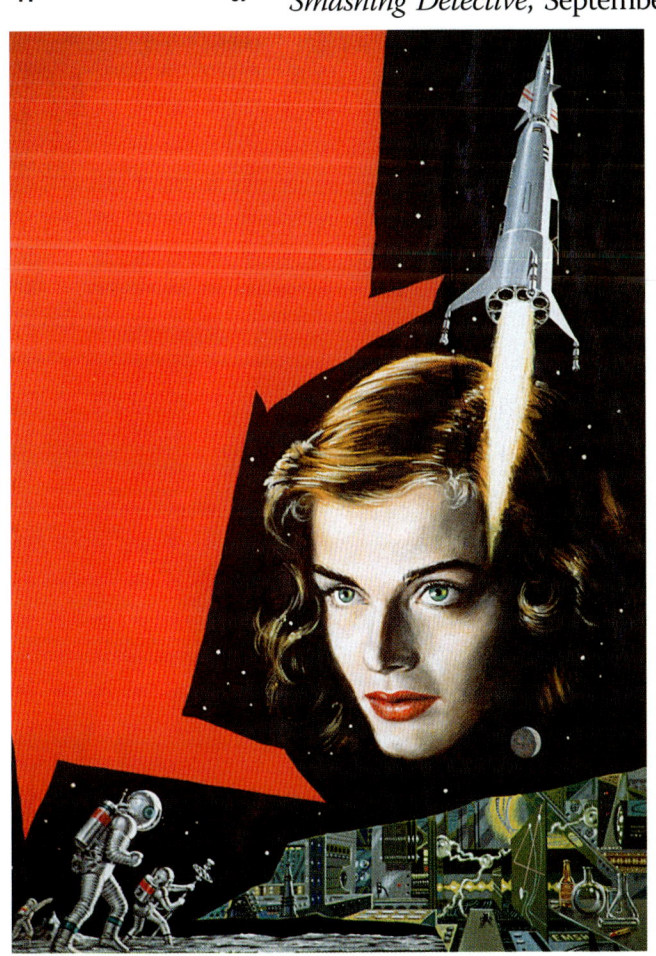

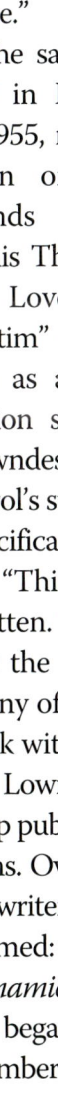

(top R) Unpublished cover art, probably for ORIGINAL SCIENCE FICTION STORIES.

(bot L) VENTURE SCIENCE FICTION. July 1958. "Lady of Space." by Lester del Rey. Ed shows his penchant for fracturing pictorial space to get inside things. A lovely lady…and dramatic view of a lovely and plausible two-stage rocket. The lab is an essay in geometric patterns, and typical of Ed's approach to future technology.

included Damon Knight, Fred Pohl, Cyril Kornbluth, and Isaac Asimov. As Lowndes later reflected, "… my connections, and freedom from some of the more pointless tabus of formula pulp fiction, resulted in my getting many stories which another person might not have gotten at the rates we could pay." But, Lowndes knew he needed new writers, willing to write within his budget, and encouraged Carol to submit more stories.

Ed would have his own bust and boom period, times where he would work 60-70 hours a week and times where he would find himself mowing the lawn midweek. He was doing more mystery covers for Mercury Publications, including *Ellery Queen* and *Mercury Mystery Book-Magazine*, and was considering getting an artist's rep to go after higher paying markets. Digging up new accounts was a "grind" and a rep could do the legwork for him. At this time Ed was doing some experimental color photography as samples to show art directors.

He was hoping to crack the paperback field. "If things go through as hoped I'll get $250-$300 per cover, which is better than I've done to date." He had shown some surrealistic color photos to Van der Poel who was "quite enthusiastic" about them. Ed's aim was to get him to use them for *Galaxy* and *Beyond*, but both magazines stuck to illustrative covers.

He began processing his own rolls of Ektachrome transparencies and bought a 4x5 format camera in anticipation of getting work: "One cover sold would pay for it." The publisher of *Ellery Queen* magazine was dissatisfied with the photo covers they were getting from a NYC studio and asked Ed to try his hand at it. One of his first attempts had him building a waterproof box to allow him to take pictures underwater and Ed shot color photos of a woman in a pool being forced underwater by a killer which he later adapted for a men's magazine cover (pg. 56). He also asked his father to take some pictures of a windshield with bullet holes in it, since with the strict gun laws in Long Island he was unable to manufacture this prop (145).

At the beginning of 1955 Ed heard from the art director of *True Detective*, who was looking to see some current art samples. Ed felt that this was one more "unproductive" going through the motions, but made the trip into the city. Much to his surprise, he got the assignment to do a cover at $300. This was two to three times the amount his covers had been bringing in to date. The same publisher was putting out *Saga*, one of the leading men's magazines and better paying art markets around. Ed had also managed to hook up with *Gun and Rod* magazine.

Carol was still learning how to write stories when she and Ed went to the eleventh WorldCon (now known as Nycon II, after

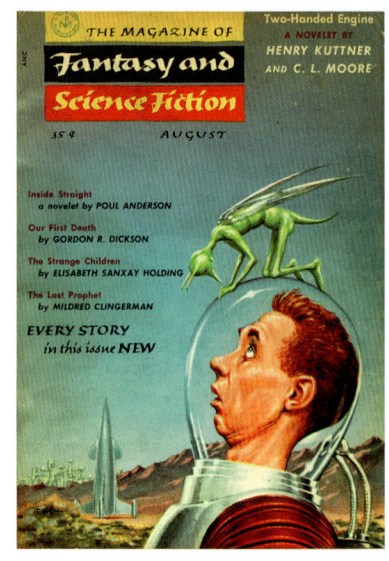

(top) F&SF, Aug. 1955.

(bot) MERCURY MYSTERY BOOK-MAGAZINE. September 1956.

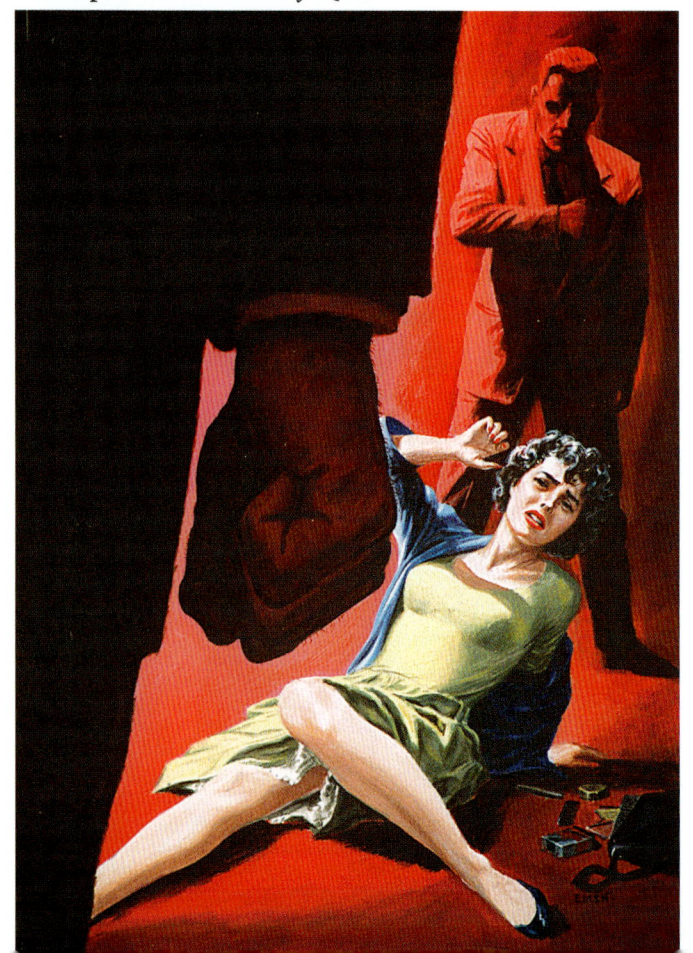

the first New York Worldcon in 1939) in September 1956. Kelly Freas won the best artist Hugo that year. After the convention, Ed and Carol had been invited to a gathering of professionals put together by Damon Knight, Judith Merril, and James Blish, a group of SF writers living in and around Milford, Pennsylvania, a small resort town 80 miles west of New York City.

Twenty-five science fiction personages, including Lester del Rey, Arthur C. Clarke, Theodore Sturgeon, Cyril Kornbluth, Algis Budrys, Fritz Leiber, Katherine MacLean, L. Sprague de Camp, Harlan Ellison, and Robert Silverberg, huddled during the week (when not socializing) to discuss everything from writers' slumps to religion in science fiction, but the intense daily workshop sessions (where unpublished manuscripts were read and dissected in the presence of their authors) were the best-received event.

Ed and Carol were only invited for the first day of the conference, set aside for editors, artists, and others in the SF field, but enjoyed the group so much that they asked to stay for the remainder of the week. Arrangements were made to share a cottage with two other couples. Ed and Carol rushed back to New York to pick up their daughter Eve from the neighbors and were back in Milford by late afternoon of the second day. "It was like camp and college-plus rolled into one," Ed wrote his parents later.

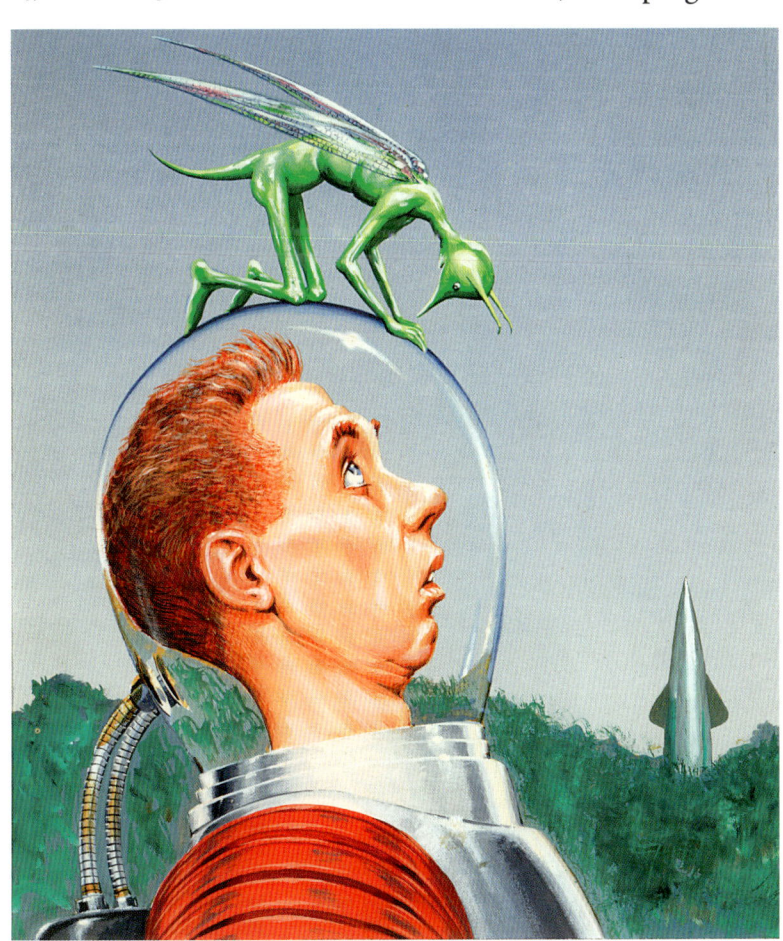

(top R) Unknown publication. C. 1959.

(bot L) Original painting for THE MAGAZINE OF FANTASY AND SCIENCE FICTION. Aug. 1955. A winsome example of "First Contact" between human and alien. Ed later complained about how "they were always changing my art or flopping it." Here they did both …though all modifications were made on a separate overlay, not on the original.

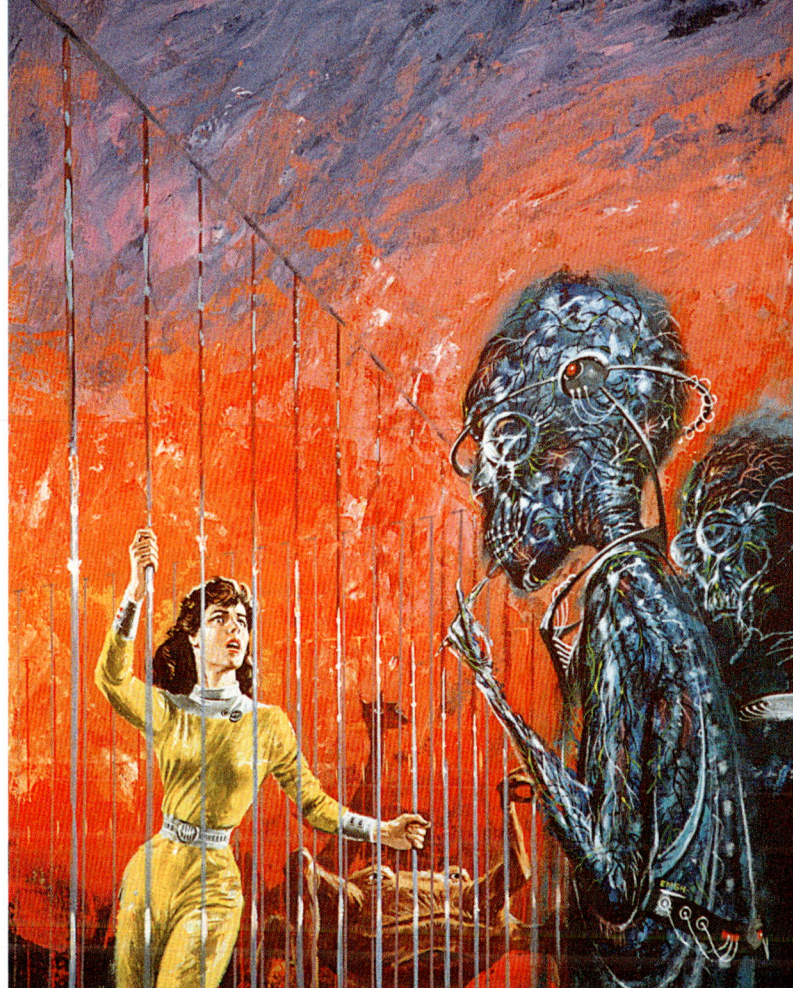

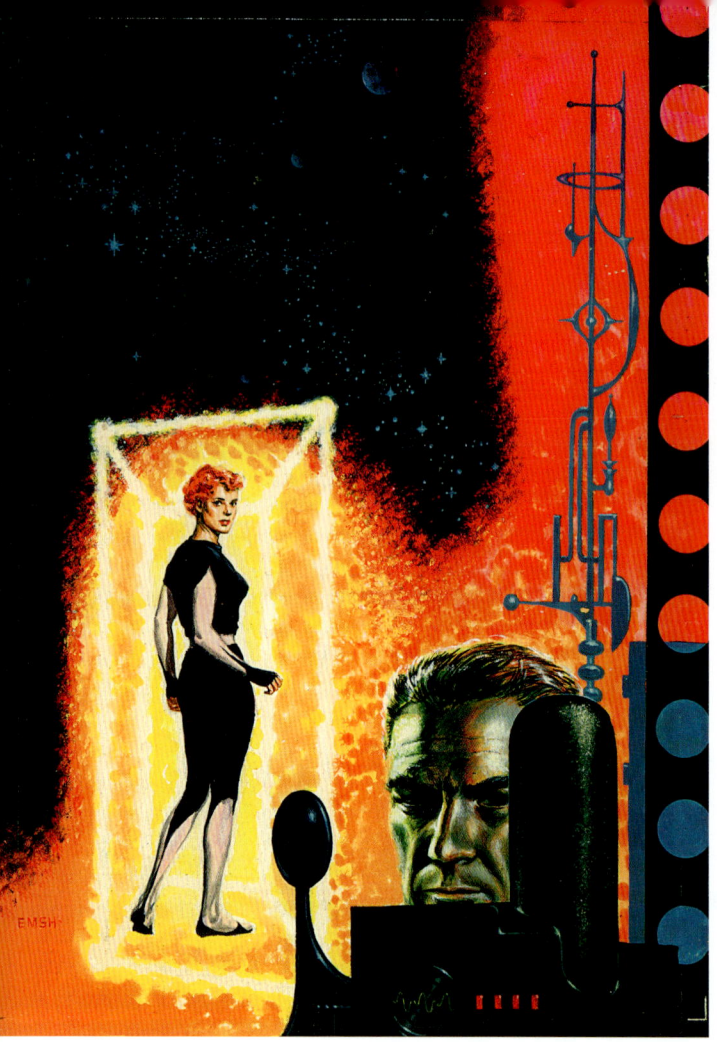 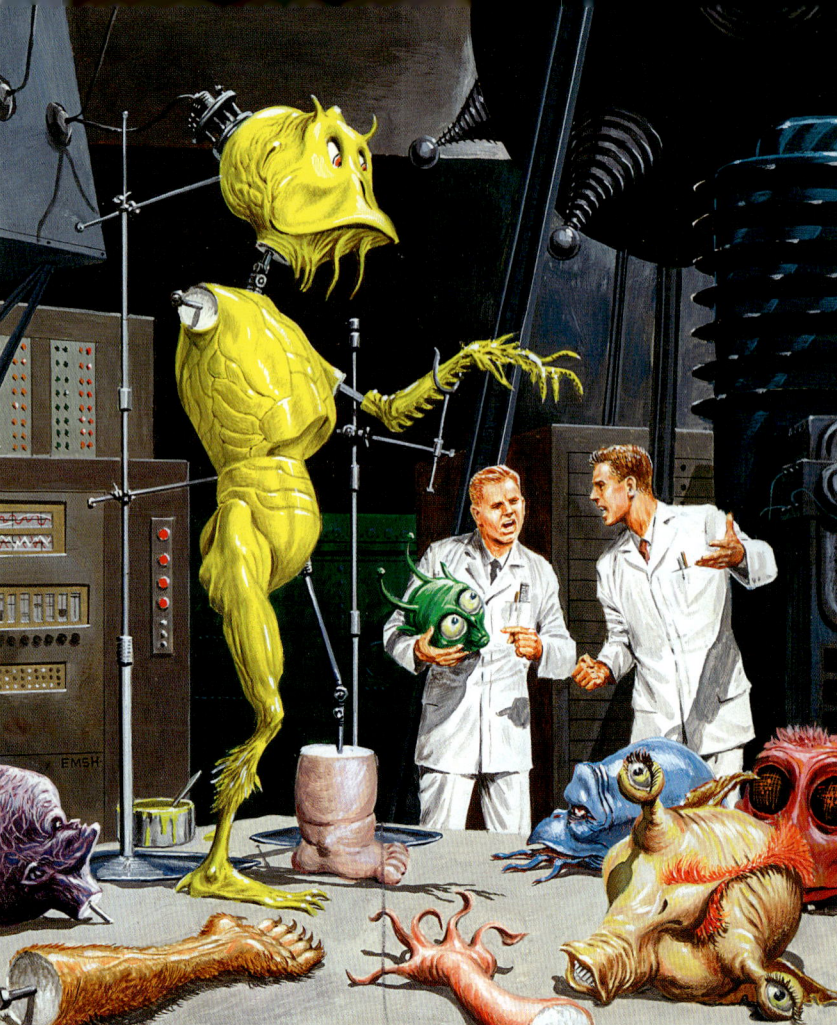

The conference headquarters was at a group of vacation cottages overlooking the Delaware River (the same river where Carol's grandfather had drowned), called the Colony, but many meetings were held in the grillroom of the nearby Dimmick Restaurant due to the large turnout. Ed was the only artist at Milford, but fitted easily into the social group. Many writers came to Milford with half a mind to vacation fun, packing swimsuits and fishing poles, but quickly became so absorbed in the long sessions and discussions that they found little time to enjoy the outdoors.

That first time at Milford I had already sold three stories and that was enough, Carol said, *but it was mostly because of Ed that I got in.* She remembers the workshop sessions: *I was always a very slow reader. At Milford we were sitting around, seventeen people reading a manuscript and we had one copy. I was in the middle of this group and before long I started skipping whole paragraphs because I realized I was the slowest reader there. Pretty soon, even though I was skipping so much out of every single page, people got really mad at me and they made me go to the end of the reading line.*

After a reading people would argue the merits of a story. The author had to remain silent throughout. Unless a story was thoroughly bad there were always defenders. Carol felt intimidated, and had a

(L) **THE MAGAZINE OF FANTASY & SCIENCE FICTION.** May 1956. A figure enclosed by an open-frame box is a recurring subject in Ed's art, film, and video. The fiery version here excites our imagination about harnessing the raw powers of spacetime. That's Carol caged inside the lurid coruscations.

(R) **GALAXY SCIENCE FICTION** April 1956. "Let's Build an Extraterrestrial!", by Willy Ley. The title is made literal in this delightful take on a latter-day Frankenstein lab. The yellow humanoid seems a bit anxious that the two arguing techs may switch his head for one less appropriate. Note the fat pink foot which already doesn't match. With clamps and an armrest, the yellow e-t exudes a Daliesque flavor of the absurd, along with those strewn-about heads and arms. Yet despite the incomplete (even wrong) assembly, his lean tendrily corpus makes him one stunning galactic dude.

THIS PAGE
(top R) INFINITY SF. Oct. 1957.

(bot L) ORIGINAL SF. Jan. 1957. "Strikebreaker" by Isaac Asimov.

sense of dread when one of her stories was being torn apart, but she was encouraged by Judy Merril, who was one of her early advocates. Carol admired Damon Knight even before she met him, but at the conference she found herself in agreement with Merril every time the two conference leaders had a difference of opinion,

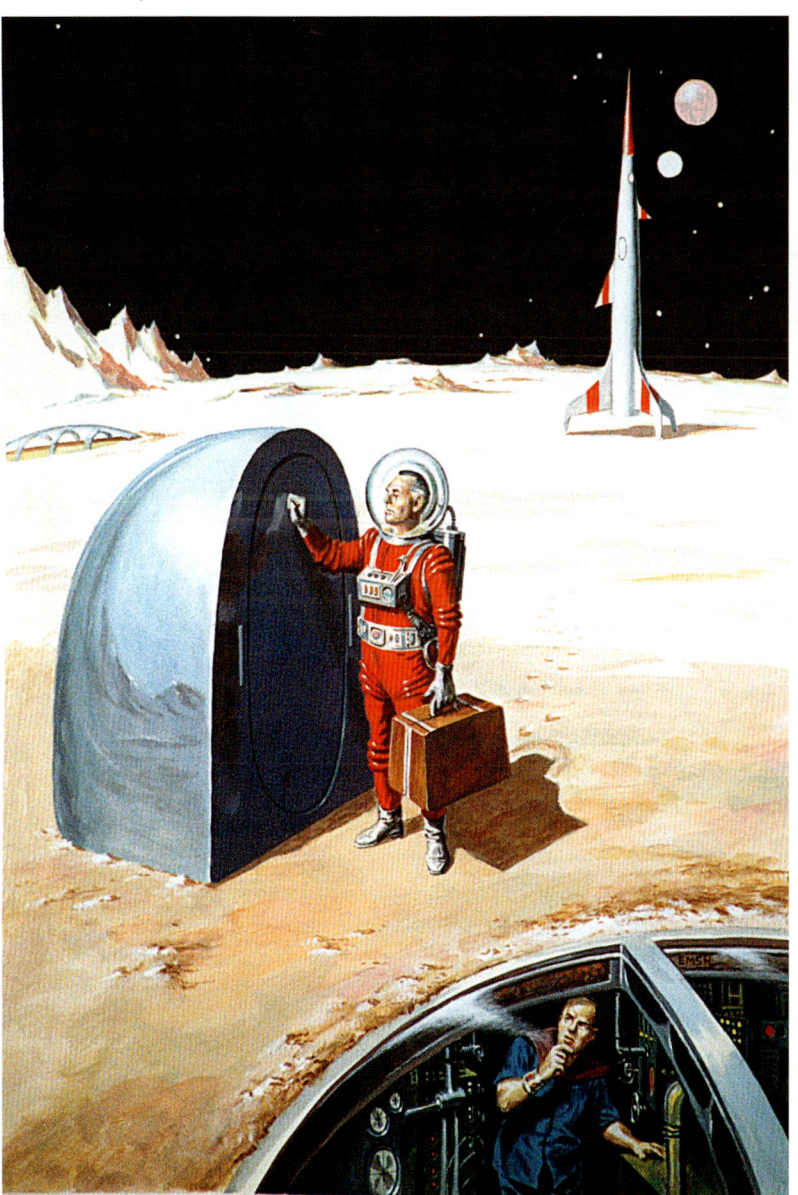

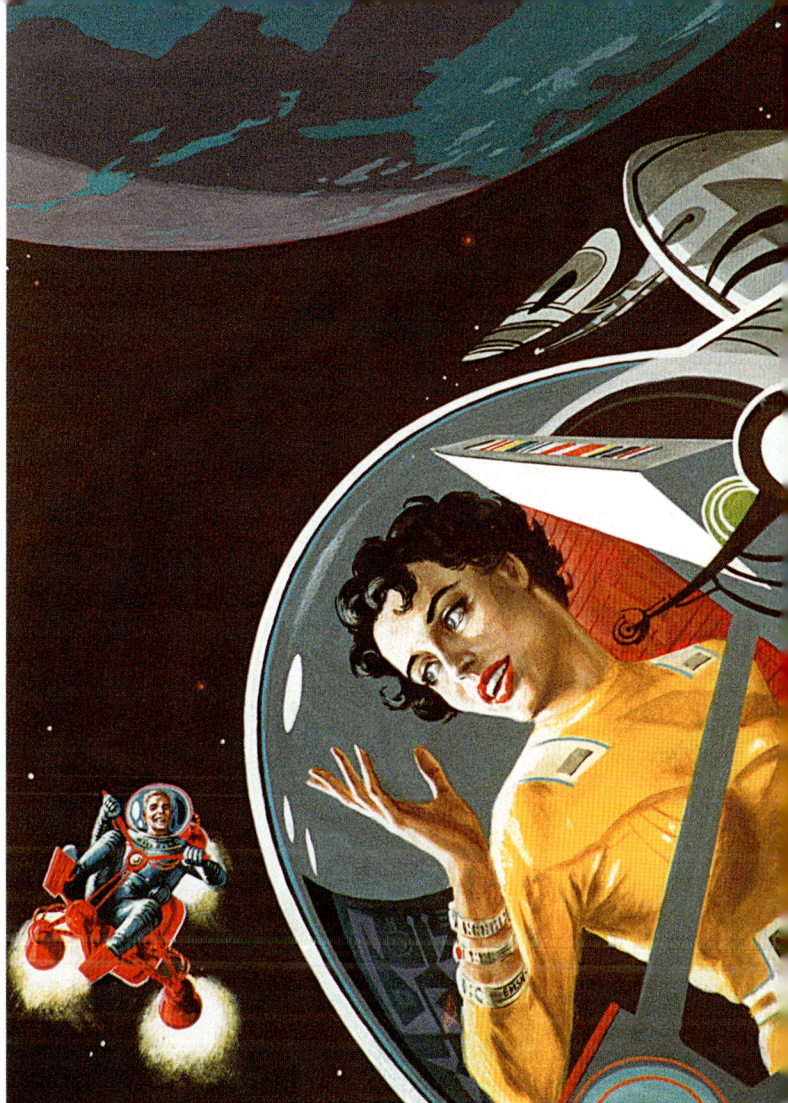

though this would change over the years.

Damon Knight was the real driving force at Milford. It seemed as if he could get away with anything, including once throwing someone's manuscript out the window as a critique. He quickly became one of Carol's favorite people; *He was kinda cute and pixie-like, and funny.* (Knight tagged Carol a "buttercup", and Carol would be the maid of honor at his wedding to Kate Wilhelm in 1962.) Knight once told Carol that new writers meeting established writers was important because that way they could see that they weren't gods, and new writers could also get some validation this way.

Judy Merril, a strong personality herself, was often at loggerheads with Knight (he accused her of campaigning for "diapers and piss" storytelling), and eventually with other commitments (and her ill-received idea to open the conference to non-sf authors), she faded from conference activities. The Milford conference became an annual summer event, even continuing when Knight moved to Madeira Beach, Florida in the seventies. A roll call of Milford attendees would be a who's who of American science fiction of the 20th century.

Robert Lowndes commented about Carol's early stories, "They aren't attempts to swashbuckle so that readers will think she's a man: nor are they heart-throb-and-diapers accounts such as you see in the slicks." Some readers found her fictions, in early years, leaning towards the obscure. These early stories gave the author room to roam through a science fictional scale. Lowndes blurbed her writing as "strange, off trail stories."

Carol had chosen to locate the action around characters of self-centered men and women going through some sort of mental or emotional turmoil. She would also jump into any consciousness that pleased her: a dog ("Pelt"), a gestalt alien-entity lost from its family ("The Piece Thing"). Small-minded men dominate: the dog's hunter owner, the discoverer of the "piece thing." As other critics have noticed, all futuristic fiction is about the present:

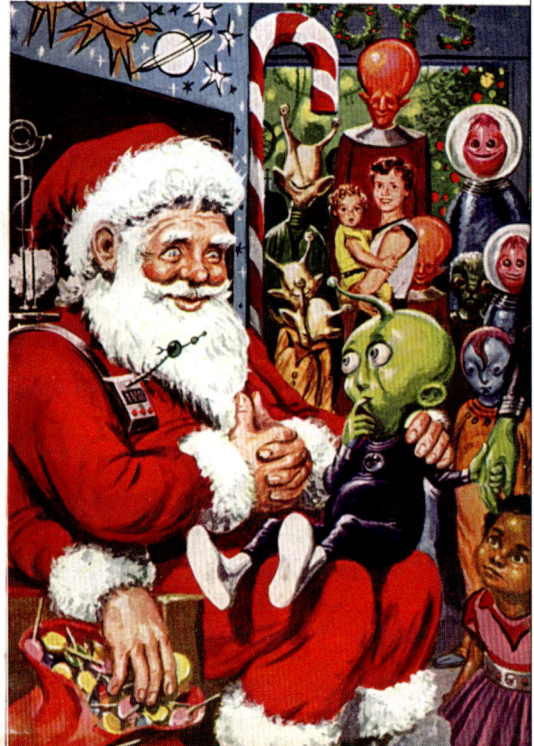

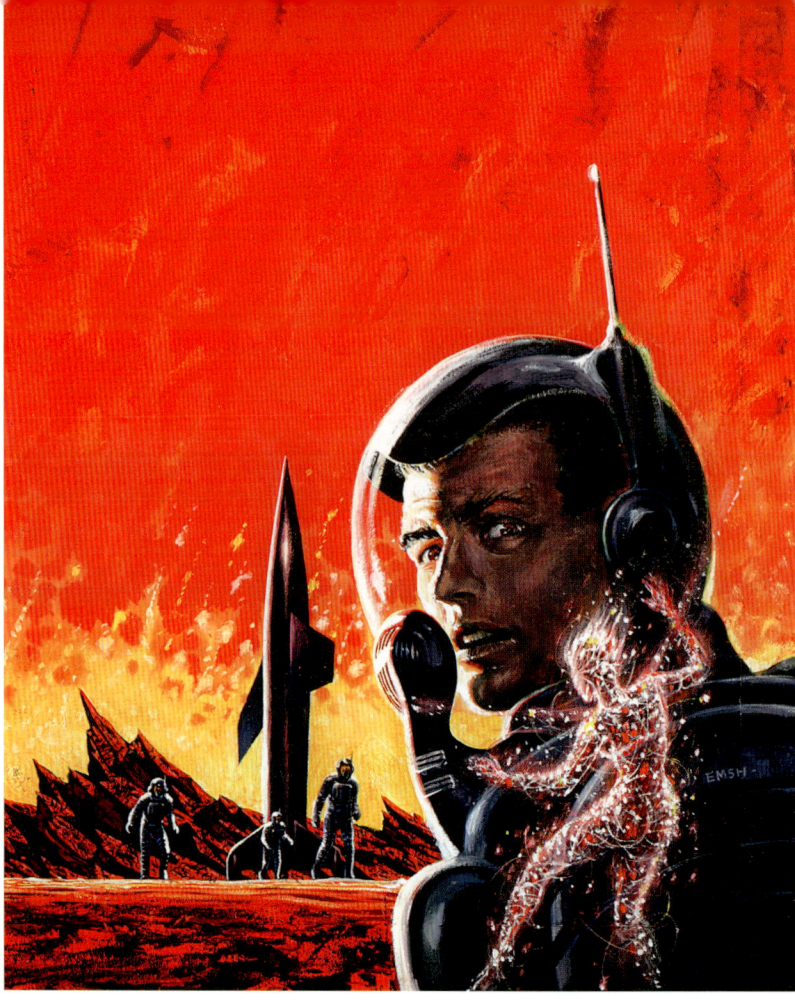

Even on lonely asteroids, we'll have unwanted visitors. The taxman? Fuller Brush? Orkin? The curving horizon gives a sense of the littleness of this outpost, where windows are in the ceiling; but distant crags also lend it an expansive side. The polished airlock bears a reflection of mountains, inducing us to feel that the landscape extends beyond the frame (confirming its reality). What can this intruder want? His rocket is stylish, raked like a barracuda, and so we (and the resident) don't trust him.

THIS PAGE
(top R) FANTASTIC UNIVERSE, December. 1959. "The Answer" by H. Beam Piper. If there's an Answer, there has to be a Question ... and some of those are

Big Questions, which may strike terror in the hearts of men. Molten magma blankets the horizon, as a well-armored Earthman attends the advice of a glimmery pixie. The apprehensive glint of his eye hints that what he learns is something from which no armor can protect him.

PAGE 62
(bot L) GALAXY, January 1957, "Season's Greetings to Our Readers". The merry four-armed Santa, a GALAXY tradition, works a department store. On his lap, a bubble-head kid ponders the Great Question, while children of every color and species wait their turn. A black girl peers up patiently at the greenie kid; Ed was aware of the significance her presence made for readers of 1957. Smiling in the rear is another Earthling: Ed's wife Carol, holding daughter Eve. By Santa's electro-translator and bag of lollipops, one can tell all's right with this world.

THIS PAGE
(top L) THE ORIGINAL SCIENCE FICTION STORIES. Febuary 1959. "Delivery Guaranteed" by Calvin M. Knox (Robert Silverberg).

(top R) VALLEY OF THE FLAME by Henry Kuttner, Ace 1964.

(bot R) FANTASTIC STORY, May 1953, Portfolio Sample Art.

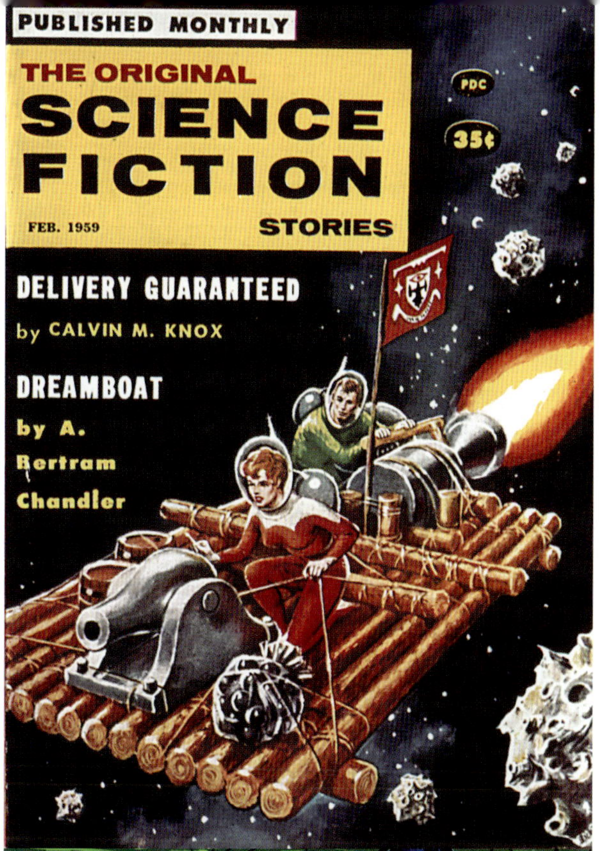

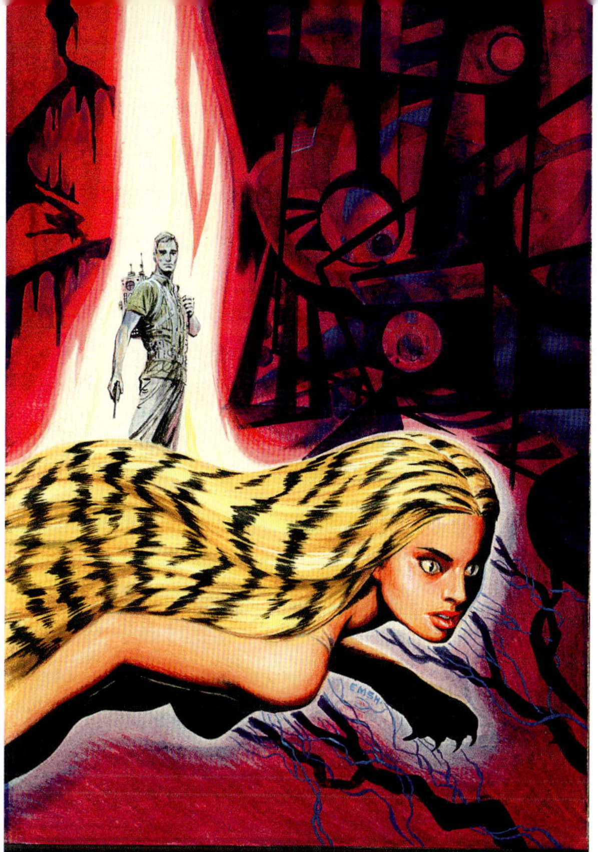

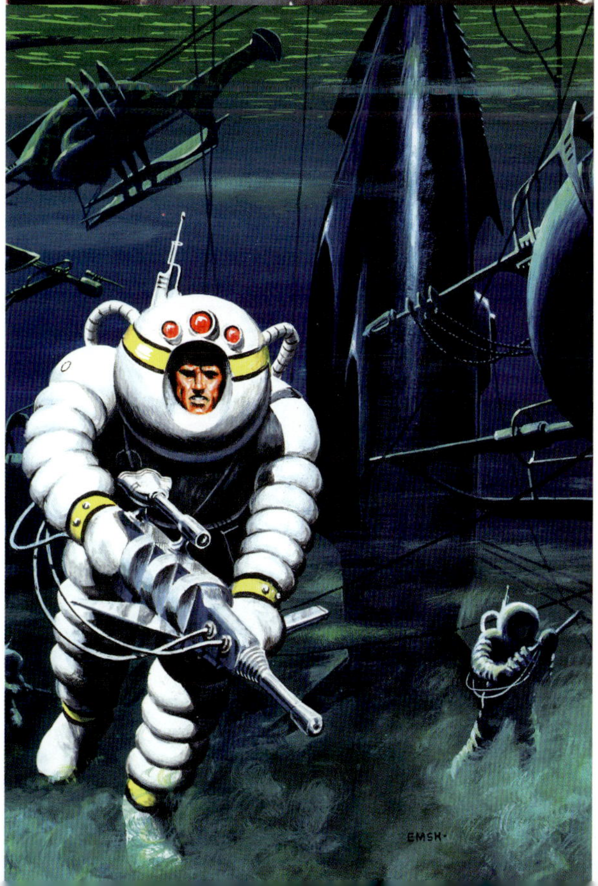

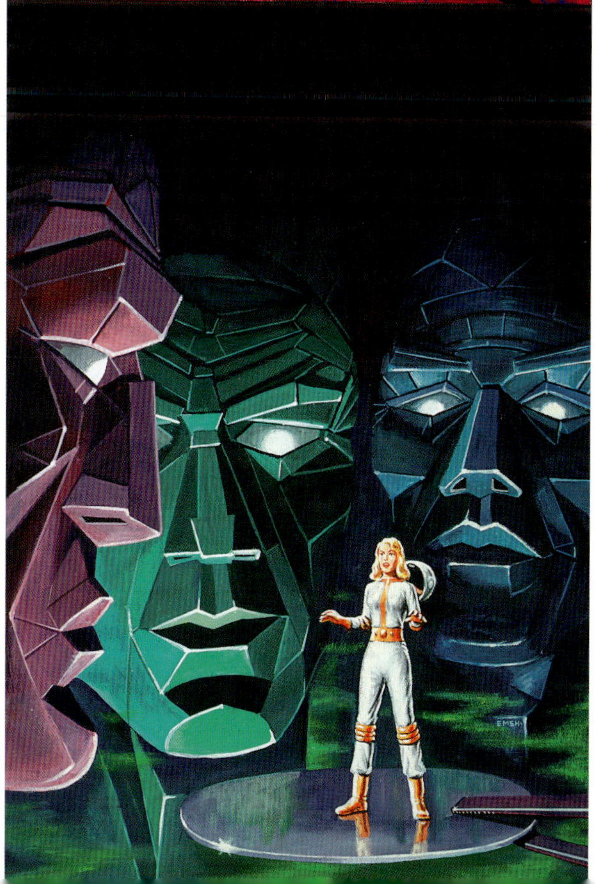

(bot L) GALAXY SCIENCE FICTION, Mar. 1956, SLAVE SHIP by Frederik Pohl (Pt. 1)

the writer's own real-world and real-time topical concerns.

Other science fiction writers influenced Carol's stories, along with some of the major themes prevalent in the fifties: the A-bomb and communists; advertising on TV; racism; women examining their roles in American life. If any theme dominated the fifties, it was paranoia. The government terrorized school children with mock nuclear attacks, telling them to hide under their desks. Drills were nationwide even in isolated rural areas where the likelihood of mushroom clouds looming over the immediate horizon was equal to the chances of surviving a nuclear conflagration. There were demagogues ready to exploit these fears. Vaccinating children against polio wasn't always as interesting as taking down Hollywood actors or screenwriters who were believed to be sympathetic to communism.

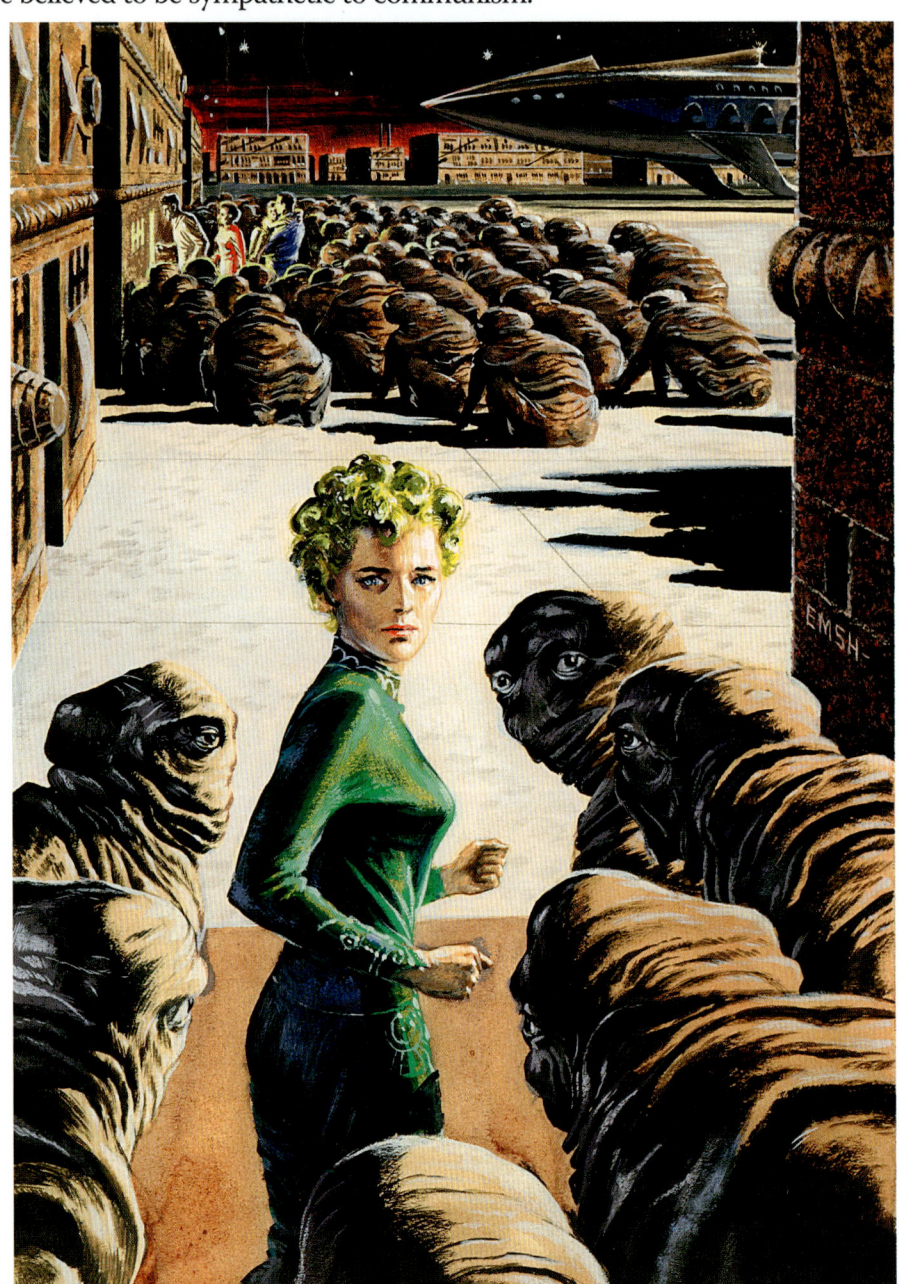

GALAXY SCIENCE FICTION. June 1959. "Whatever Counts" by Frederik Pohl.

Judy Merril, in talking about the bleak McCarthy era and science fiction, said, "The interesting new work tended to emphasize literary qualities rather than philosophic ones. And by 1955, the field had achieved just enough literary respectability to be able to serve a vital function…. It was science-fiction magazines that provided the only widely read medium for protest and dissent in a witch-haunted country." Merril also cited 1955 as a year of "… many conformity/alienation stories." This is a theme inherent in Carol's early work and would become more pronounced during the sixties.

At that first Milford Conference, Ed became friendly with Cyril Kornbluth and Robert Silverberg. Kornbluth, when he found out that the Emshwillers lived in Levittown, wanted to know more about the real estate market in the area. He eventually bought a house near the Emshwillers. Cyril and his wife Mary had a handicapped son who needed special care. Ed was one of the few of the Kornbluths friends who could handle the child and he babysat in a pinch for them.

Silverberg, who at the age of twenty-two, had won a Hugo a few days earlier for most promising new writer, was a native New Yorker with a self-described dark streak, and attended the 1956 Worldcon and Milford Conference while on his honeymoon. He found Ed's affabil-

(top L) MERCURY MYSTERY BOOK-MAGAZINE. March 1956.

(top R) F&SF, Mar. 1958, "The Prize of Peril" by Robert Sheckley. The 24-hour televised world. Even a hunted fugitive is perpetually onscreen wherever he runs. The camera rigs are a marvel of mechanical ingenuity, visioned by Emsh long before the advent of Steadi-Cam®. The ambience is lifted lightly from the title shots of the late-Fifties TV series "Peter Gunn," famous for its cool-jazz background theme. A welter of soft shadows and oddly angular cut-outs lends this a touch of early Fritz Lang, as well

(bot. R) STARTLING, Apr. 1953, "Halos, Inc." Another note of Fritz Lang, adapted to the demonstration of a teleporting device. Now you can (almost!) be in two places at once.

(bot L) F&SF, Oct. 1953, "Letter to a Tiger". Heaven protect the Walter Mitty of our time from the predatory lady of the future, in tiger-stripe pajamas and armed with sleek assault rifle. The nebulous vision of the hillside house lends this the aura of a sinister dream.

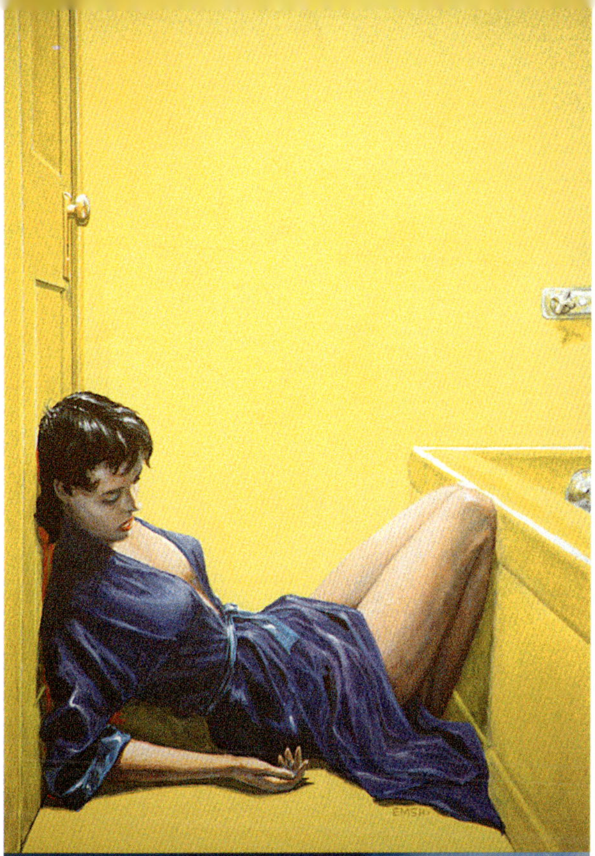

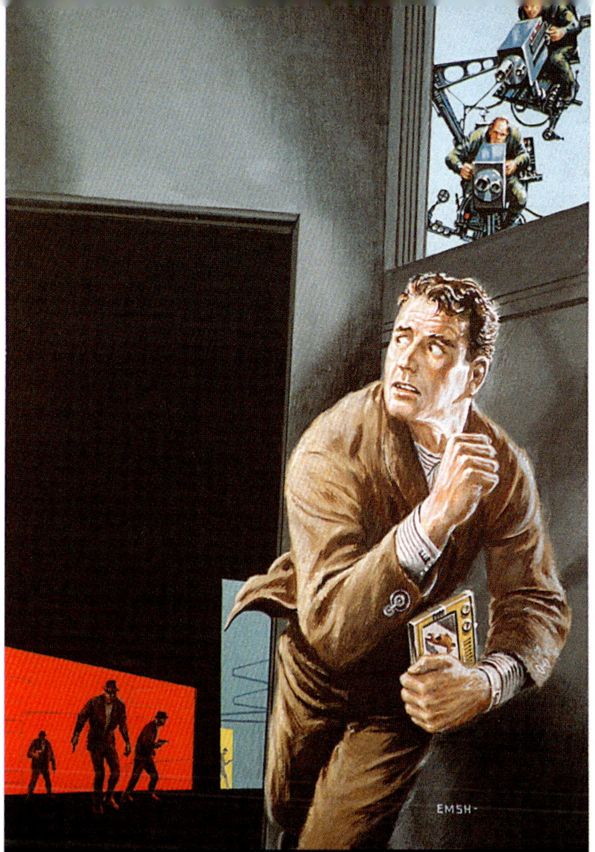

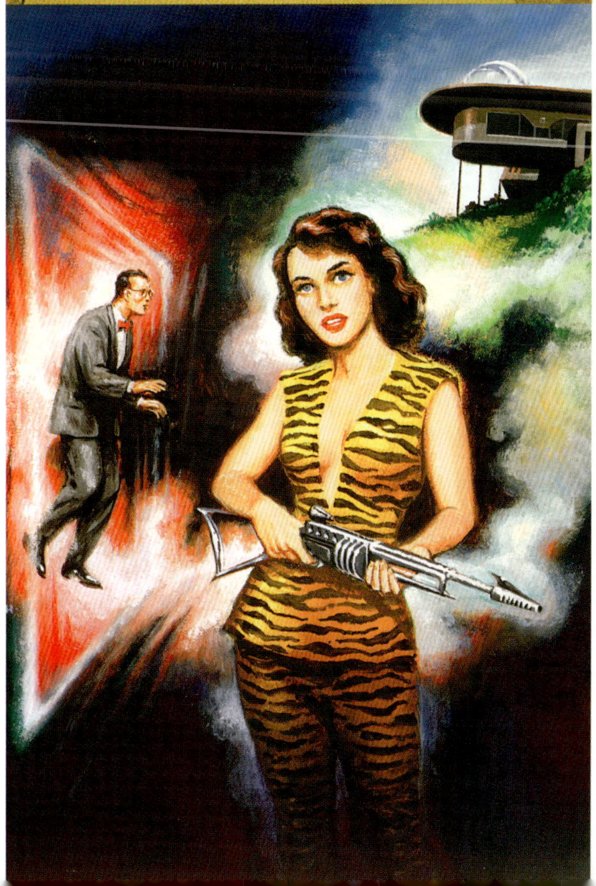

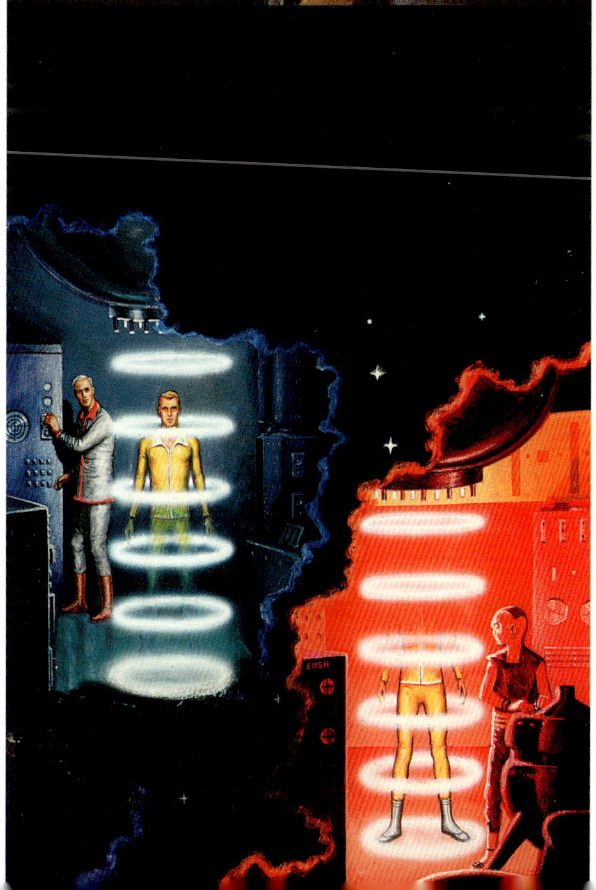

ity a pleasant change of pace. After the conference, the Emshwillers and Silverbergs shared a ride back to New York, with Ed getting a speeding ticket on a rural New Jersey road. This put the usually genial Ed into a foul mood for the rest of the drive.

Back in Levittown, Carol placed a photo taken by Ed at Milford above her desk to keep her inspired, and soon after wrote Judy Merril, *It not only changed my feelings on writing and writing directly, but my feelings about people. In fact, I feel changed all over. I think what did it was the earnest, candid way everyone at the conference opened up to each other. Now I look at everybody differently and better. I hope it lasts.*

SEARCH FOR ZEI. By L. Sprague de Camp. Avalon. 1962.

Talking about that time, Carol stated that she did not want to be a good SF writer—she just wanted to be in with all those SF people. *In those days I wouldn't have aspired to be anything but the worst. I hoped to write any old thing that would sell to F&SF magazine at best.* She thought that there was so much that she had to know to write even at a basic level—plot, craft, and rules—but she could learn little by little. Ed had read her first few stories and torn them apart. Any merits of the work, Carol felt, were overlooked to settle marital scores. It was only after she began placing works with magazines that Ed's petty cavils stopped.

Once Ed began taking her writing seriously, whenever Carol got stuck in a story she would go up to the attic and use Ed as a sounding board to discuss works in progress. In many cases she discovered this helped her solve plotting or structure problems.

Until the fifties there were few female voices in science fiction. Katherine MacLean, Merril, and Carol made up the main contingency of distaff writers at Milford. Some of the men there may have not taken them seriously, and only considered them part-time SF writers—between having babies and taking care of households—but Merril and MacLean viewed themselves the equal of any of the men present at Milford. As they saw it, the only advantage that the male science fiction writers had was the Niagara of words that had poured from them since the time of Gernsback. Merril was quick to quote Ted Sturgeon's theorem that ninety percent of science fiction was trash, but that of course ninety percent of everything was also trash. This also meant that throughout the history of pulp science fiction men wrote most of the trash.

On March 21, 1958, Kornbluth shoveled out the driveway of his Levittown home after a late winter snowstorm, then rushed to the nearby Wantagh railroad station where he had a fatal heart attack. His death at the age of thirty-four would leave a big hole in the SF field. Kornbluth was on his way to an appointment in Manhattan to interview for Tony Boucher's job as editor of *The Magazine of Fantasy and Science Fiction* — the interview was merely a formality. Kornbluth's death foreshadowed some of the hard days ahead for the science fiction field.

Six

Art first, Story second

A FEW MOVIE STUDIOS had begun previewing SF and monster films at science fiction conventions for the publicity. With film programs added to the proceedings, fans began showing up with home movies of fannish interest and Ed decided that this would be a good place to show some of his experimental film "doodles." He had spliced together a few time-lapsed films: one showing the creation of SF magazine covers from rough drawing to color blocking to finished painting, and the second presenting the freeform development of an abstract painting. These went over well with the fans, and for the first time Ed heard audience applause for a film he had made. He also heard for the first, but not last time, the audience question: "Do you always work that fast on a painting?" Ed's answer was always, "No, this was a slow day."

Ed was especially intrigued by the audience's response to his abstract stop-motion film. Isaac Asimov came up to Ed after seeing a screening and said, "Instead of filming the painting of an abstraction, why don't you create an abstract movie?" Ed had been thinking along the same lines himself: "Abstract Expressionism, seemed to me, should exist in time. It would then be truly 'action painting'…. The movies seemed to be a natural solution."

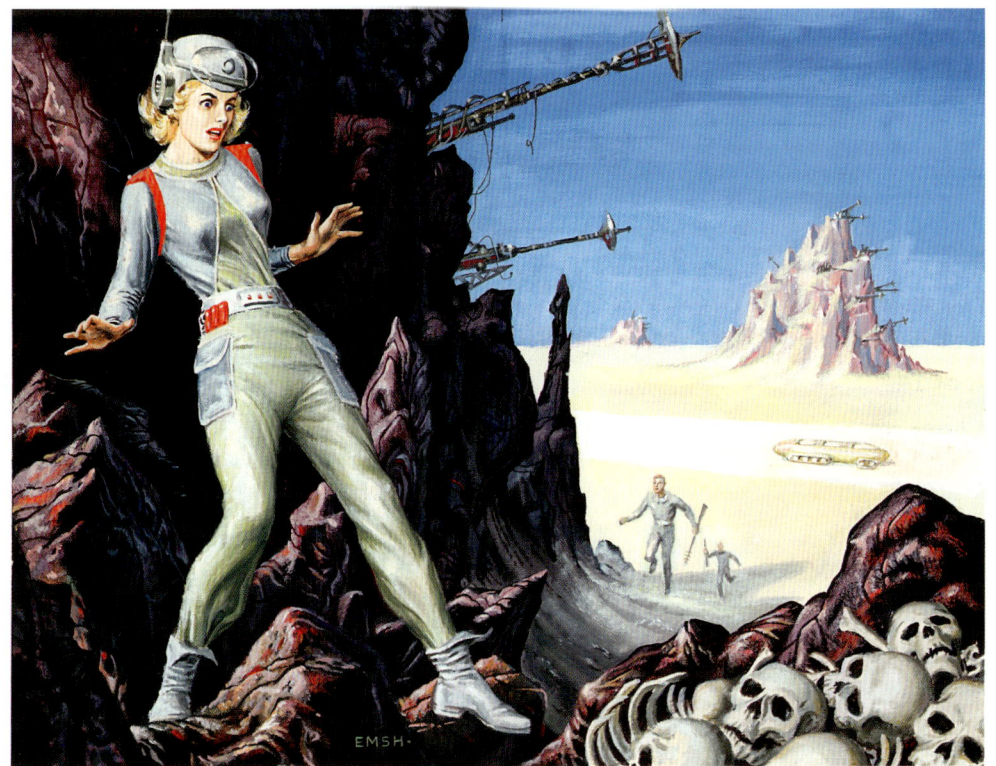

STARTLING, Summer 1955, "White Spot" by Murray Leinster. The shock of discovering a human boneyard. Emsh was fond of novel antennas and beam emitters and putting them in odd places; in the distant future, on other worlds, high-tech devices and natural environs would tend to merge or cohabit. The igneous formation behind the explorer is, in form and texture, almost as lovely as she; while the pile of skulls makes a mute appeal for our pity.

During the fifties, many of the prodigies that would make up the American experimental avant-garde filmmaker movement crossed paths at Cinema 16. Amos Vogel, the director of the film society, "We had…two different audiences—at least two. We had an audience that preferred documentary and nonfiction, social and political films, realistic films; and we had an audience that preferred avant-garde and experimental films." Ed was one of the latter.

The first wave of post-war avant-garde filmmakers included Maya Deren, a Ukraine-born free spirit, sometime dancer, and voodoo priestess. (She was known to put Dahomean curses on her enemies.) Her early eighteen-minute film *Meshes of the Afternoon,* a personal film-poem made in 1946, galvanized a loose group of independent filmmakers in New York. This group of amateurs was attracted to the forbidden. Postwar American audiences were catching up on the European avant-gardists. Pre-war films such as Luis Buñuel and Salvador Dali's *Un Chien Andalou*, Jean Cocteau's *The Blood of a Poet*, were now being seen in America as canonized European avant-garde work. Ed had first experienced audience reaction to abstract films at Cinema 16 screenings, and was surprised to find that these kinds of films could provoke laughter, shock, and even a kind of dramatic tension.

In his attic studio, Ed sometimes watched the slivers of light projected through the window, the reflections of sunlight off cars passing outside, diagonally warping up the same blank wall where he screened his films, before accelerating away. There was no tangible apparition in that light, but some sense of drama was still conveyed. Within his own cinematic Plato's Cave, Ed always thought in terms of creativity and mechanics, learning what to avoid from his failures. He was the opposite of a moviemaker who is deaf and blind to a camera or projector that is working smoothly. In Ed's early film experiments there were more failures than successes, yet he was comforted by the few seconds of images that showed unexpected life. By the late sixties he would joke that seeing his old films was like looking at wallpaper.

In 1956, Ed worked on a short film he titled *Variation on Mondrian*. He reproduced *Painting No. 1,* (1921) by Piet Mondrian, through stop motions stages, altering the color organization and balance. "Though the formal organization dictated by the painted grid remained static, the changes made purely by altering the blocks of color had an emotional effect upon viewers which many expressed spontaneously (gasping and sometimes laughing) while watching the picture."

In a later abstract film, *Sequence in Abstraction,* Ed concentrated on the sequence of changes in the painting. "Time became a factor…in addition to form and color in two dimensions…. I was no

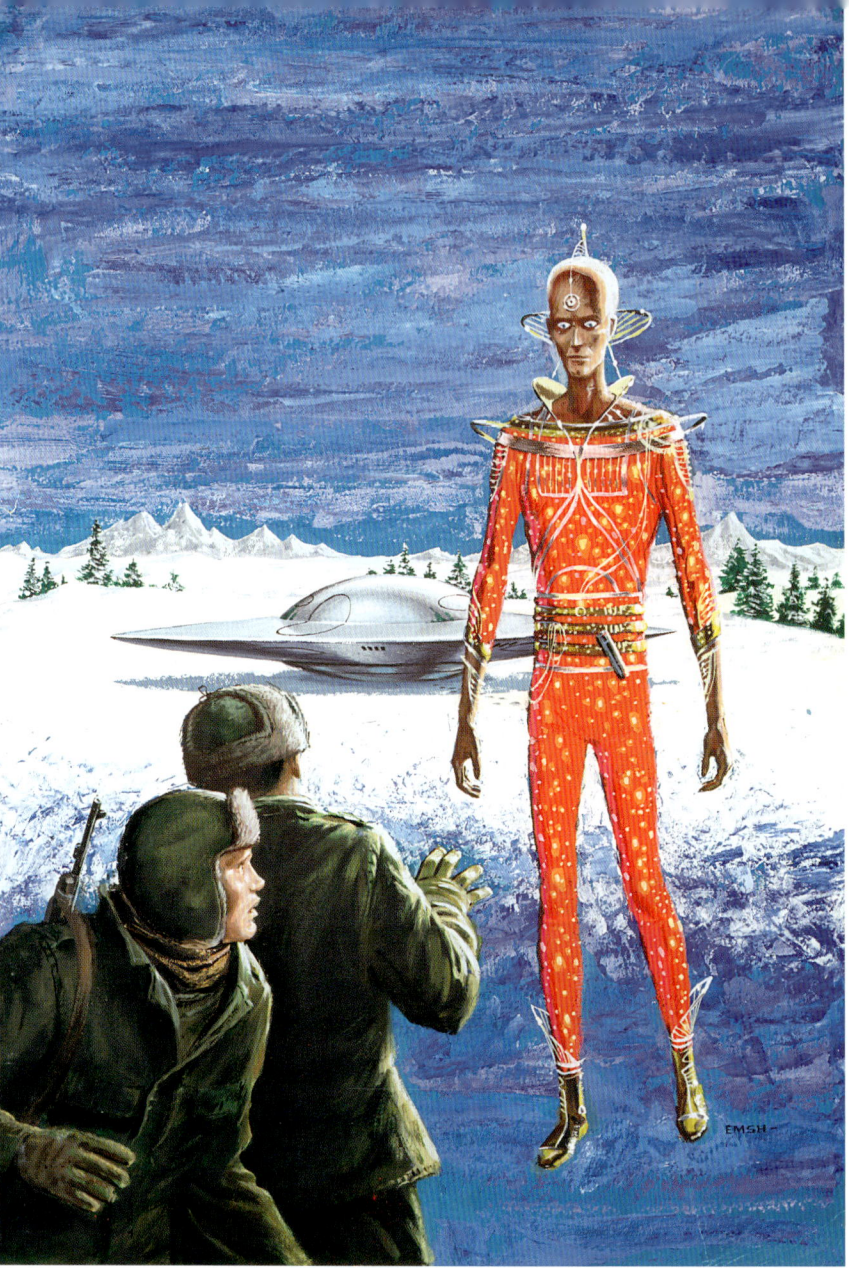

FANTASTIC UNIVERSE. Mar. 1960, "The Mind Thing" by Fredric Brown.

PAGE 69
(top L) ORIGINAL SF STORIES. May 1957, "Sunrise on Mercury." Dali's limp watches were never like this. Planet Mercury's terminator explodes with radiant heat as the sun balloons onto the arching horizon - here exaggerated for effect. Deep reds,

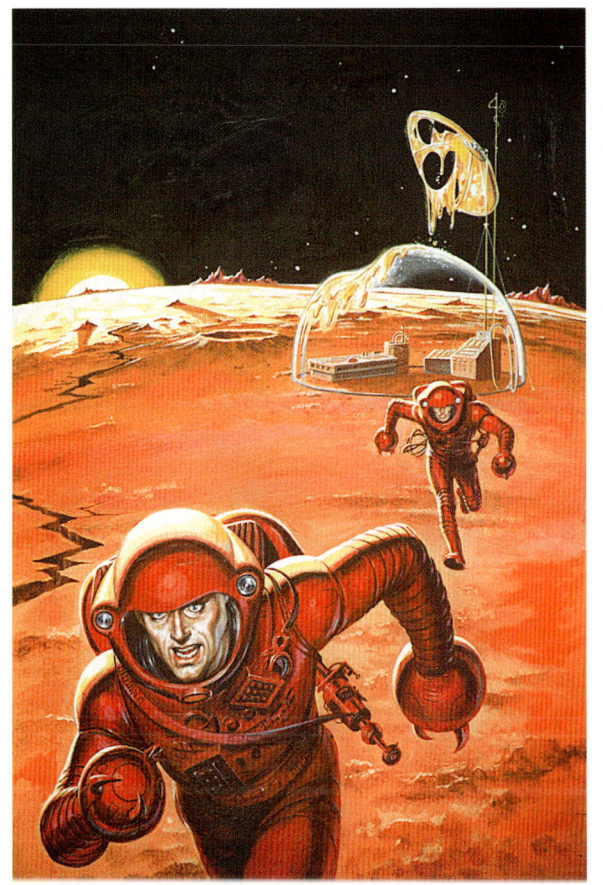

longer recording 'finding a painting' but was 'finding a film,' (although perhaps the word 'film' here is not right because the film is merely the means of giving movement to graphic art)." Ed has recorded that some viewers expressed the feeling that they understood abstract art for the first time through seeing these films.

About this time Ed learned of an animation workshop at the Manhattan studios of John Hubley, one-time animator for Disney, who had worked on *Snow White*, *Fantasia*, and *Dumbo* in the late thirties and early forties. Ed was more familiar with Hubley's UPA cartoons, which by the early 1950s were even influencing Disney. The workshop concentrated on traditional Hollywood animation, but Ed closely studied the techniques Hubley used in the production of commercial animation, and the construction of Hubley's animation stand. Hubley's animation studio, Quartet, became famous for the "I want my Maypo" TV commercials, done with the help of Hubley's wife Faith, utilizing the UPA style of sparse graphics, streamlined characters, and vivid, shifting backgrounds to convey moods.

At the same time Carol took a writing class at the New School for Social Research. When Ed got home late from his evening animation class, they would talk like excited school kids until the early morning about the new ideas and techniques they had both learned. Ultimately, while Ed explored cel animation, he found it too laborious to suit his way of working. Carol was excited by the possibilities of writing—something she would not have believed before meeting Ed and SF writers.

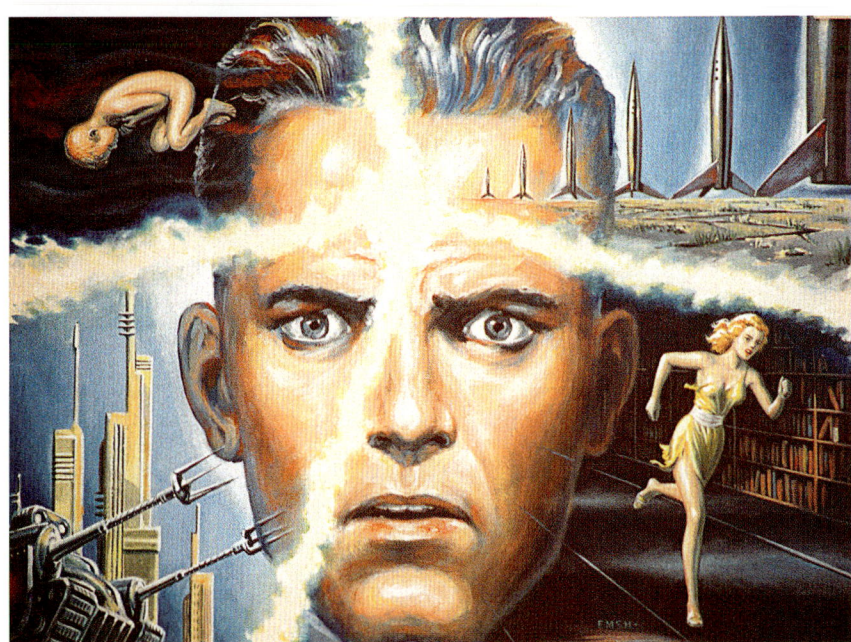

Columbia Publications paid some of the lowest rates in the field for art and fiction, but Ed found Robert Lowndes, who had learned every aspect of magazine publishing from the ground up, one of the more likeable editors to work with and offered to illustrate Carol's early stories published in *Future Science Fiction* and *Original Science Fiction Stories*. This led to Lowndes using more Emsh art. A cost-saving trick that Lowndes used extensively was to have stories written around already purchased cover art.

Magazine publishers could get cheaper printing by "gang printing" covers from different magazines on one sheet (this led to many publishers having a stable of companion magazines to cut cost), but this also meant that covers had to be created well in advance, with stories to match — in many cases written later. (Hugo Gernsback got around this by running contests for the best story written around cover art.)

The *Magazine of Fantasy and Science Fiction* had used Ed's cover art to generate the story "Love" by Richard Wilson in their June 1952 issue (pg. 39). (It had been one of Ed's original Ann Arbor samples and was bought straight out of his portfo-

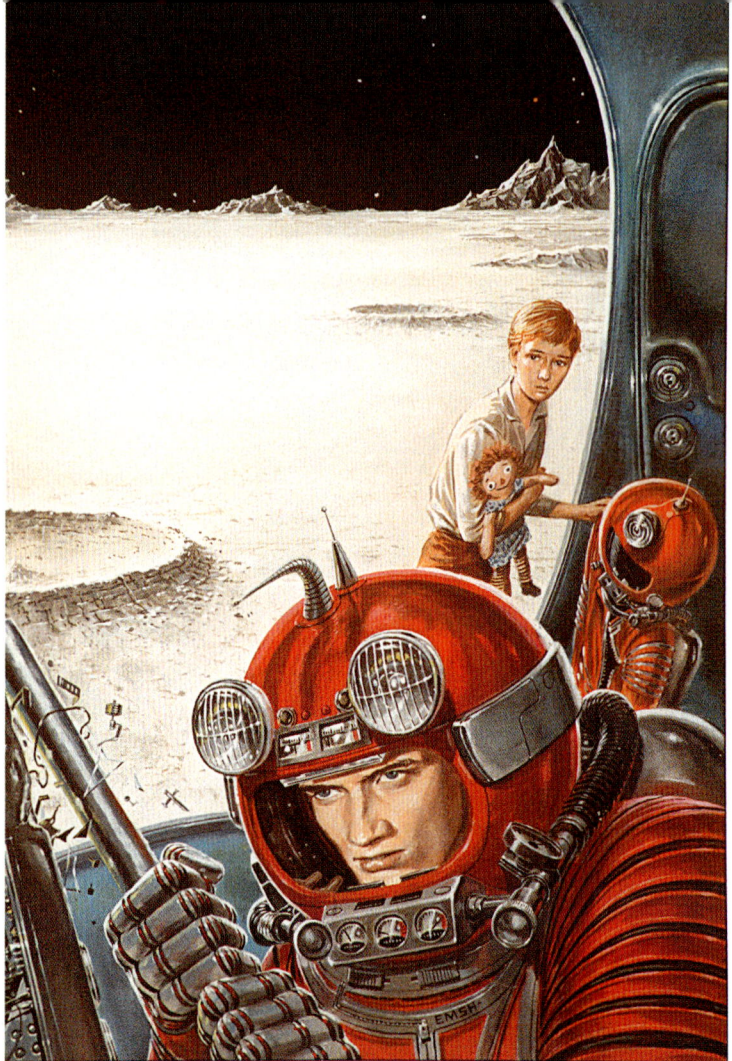

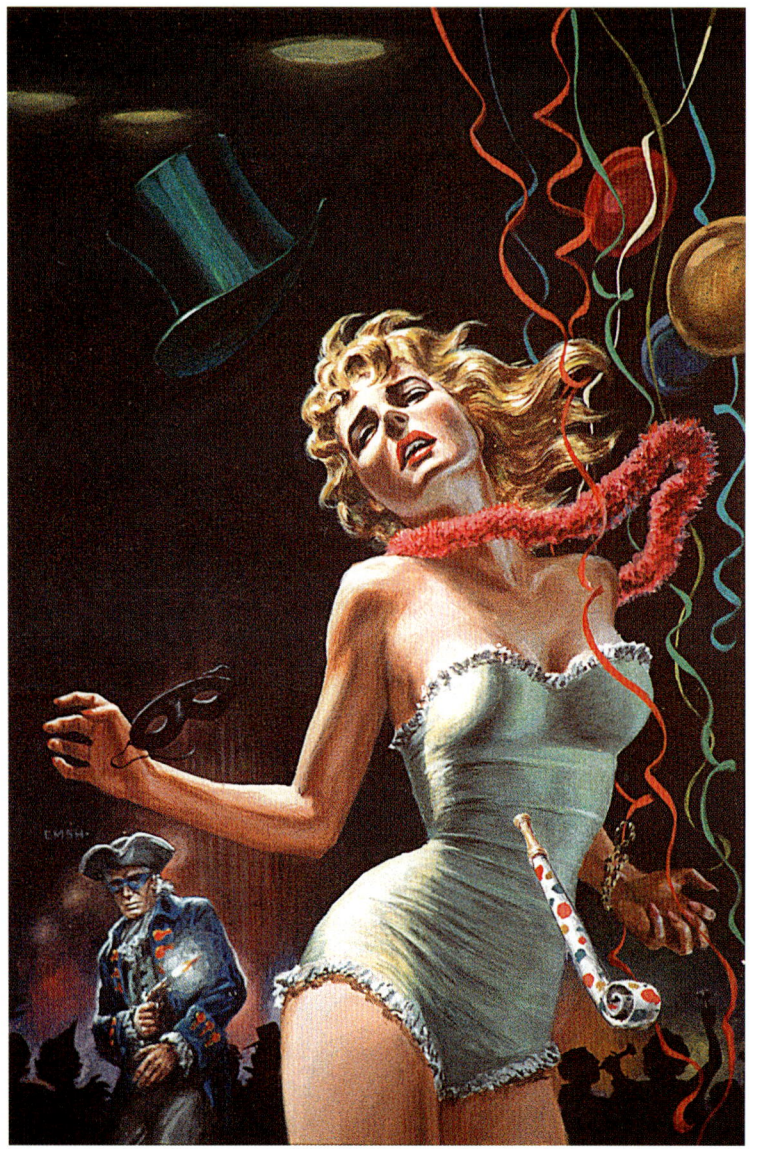

lio.) This practice worked better in theory than in execution, but publishers believed readers looked for stories connected to the cover art in a magazine. All major SF writers did at least one story using this method at some point in their careers. The list includes Sturgeon, Leiber, Merril, Knight, Kornbluth, and Asimov.

Ed was adept at "dreaming up ideas" for his own "story" images, and Lowndes utilized Emsh's paintings as inspiration for authors to write

orange, and salmon pink, plus a sagging dome, convey just how hot and deadly, as stalwart astronauts flee their collapsing station.

PAGE 69
(bot L) STARTLING STORIES. Fall 1955

THIS PAGE
(top R) F&SF, Aug. 1958, "Have Space Suit - Will Travel" by Robert A. Heinlein. Emsh achieves a remarkable degree of depth in the lunar landscape. Kip's space suit is a bonanza of well-researched technology: gauges and gaskets, flex airhose and sealbeam headlights. Silver highlights sparkle along the curvilin-

ear hatch and window, leading our eye around the composition, while also teasing us about the nature of this alien ship. The steel bar in Kip's hands has a luster and heft that speaks of the damage it can inflict. Meanwhile, the open plain of the Moon calls out: Escape across this wide expanse, flee!

(bot L) ELLERY QUEEN'S MYSTERY MAGAZINE. Jan. 1957.

THIS PAGE
F&SF, Feb. 1957. "Collapse of a Field Force" Another concept cover, and one with visceral impact. We feel the slap of the shockwave hitting the young brunette, and we almost want to reach out and break her fall. The whole background is an abstract palimpsest of angles and atmospheric pastels, with a foaming brightness erupting in its midst. Human figures in the distance provide a sense of the background's colossal scale

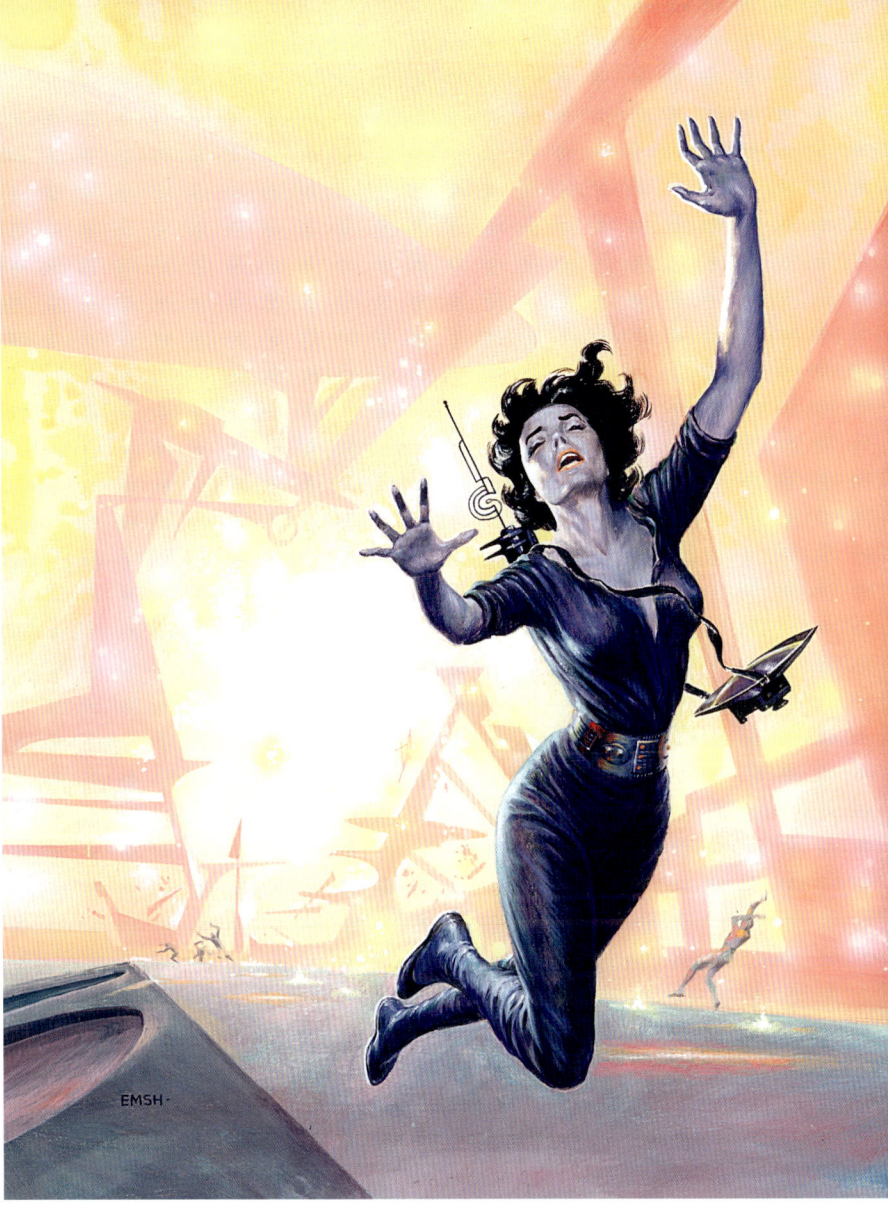

catch-up stories later. Lowndes assigned stories based on art to various authors, but was unhappy with the results—until he began using Robert Silverberg.

Lowndes would supply Emsh sketches or a cover proof to Silverberg—sometimes Ed would be in the office and give a verbal description of his next cover, or do a quick sketch for Silverberg. "Ed's cover ideas were always clever ones, with a clear narrative line visible in them, and I had no difficulty turning them into stories."

Silverberg, who did quite a number of Lowndes' art first, story second science fiction assignments, remembers: "[In] one situation Ed Emsh and Bob Lowndes presented me with: a log raft, moving through space with a kind of rocket engine clamped onto the back, with two people sitting upon it. Well, I brooded about that for a while and I worked out what I thought was a convincing enough explanation for how a log raft would be going through space, how it would hold together, and how they would ever get it off the ground. I had them leaving an asteroid where there wasn't much of a thrust problem." (Pg. 63.)

Silverberg saw these cover assignments as "amusing challenges". The space life raft was "…more fun than usual because of the oddball imagery of the painting."

Another author, Randall Garrett, invented the Remshaw Drive for a story after he was given a black and white photostat of a painting showing a strange gadget. Ed had placed his signature on the circular band of a vacuum tube and Garrett saw it as the partially visible brand name of this piece of electronics.

Ed thought of these narrative paintings as "… poster[s] which [had] a gimmick [….] There have been covers where I have tried to do a little bit more; tried to imply a little sequence of events; but I think that a painting is a very limited medium in that sense. It can, at most, imply and sometimes tell a story. But most of the time, despite the Chinese with their painting that equals a thousand words, the statement that can be made with a painting is only sort of a one-shot, whereas a story is an evolution. I never try to tell that evolution in a painting."

During the summer of 1957, Ed brought in a cover showing two men in spacesuits on a dismal planet racing away from a glass dome station melting in the first rays of sunrise. Lowndes gave Silverberg a photograph of the art and the author quickly worked out an explanation for the unexpected fiery sunrise by setting his story on the planet closest to the sun. He wrote "Sunrise on Mercury" in a day (pg. 69). Another time in Lowndes' cramped, dingy Church Street office near the pointed tip of Manhattan, Ed joined Silverberg to work out an idea for a cover and story. The three hashed out ideas till they settled on one, and Ed and Silverberg walked out to the street—each reassured that they had the story concept well in mind. A week later, artist and author were surprised to see that their finished work appeared to have nothing in common.

Harlan Ellison remembers that a day would be set aside for the viewing of cover art at *Amazing Stories*. On that day authors would arrive at the magazine's office to see the paintings already set up on chairs, and select one to write a story around. There would be nine or ten paintings, and if you got there late, as Harlan once did, you might be stuck with a painting of a giant praying mantis watching a girl sunbathing nude on a rooftop. Most SF authors preferred working from Ed's art, which always used plausible scientific principles. Though Ed stated in a panel at Pittcon in 1960, "I've been encouraged to do…flagrantly wrong ideas on covers simply for the effect…. I believe in doing scientifically accurate work in many cases…[but] I will do jobs, gladly, that have an effect which I know full well is not supportable scientifically."

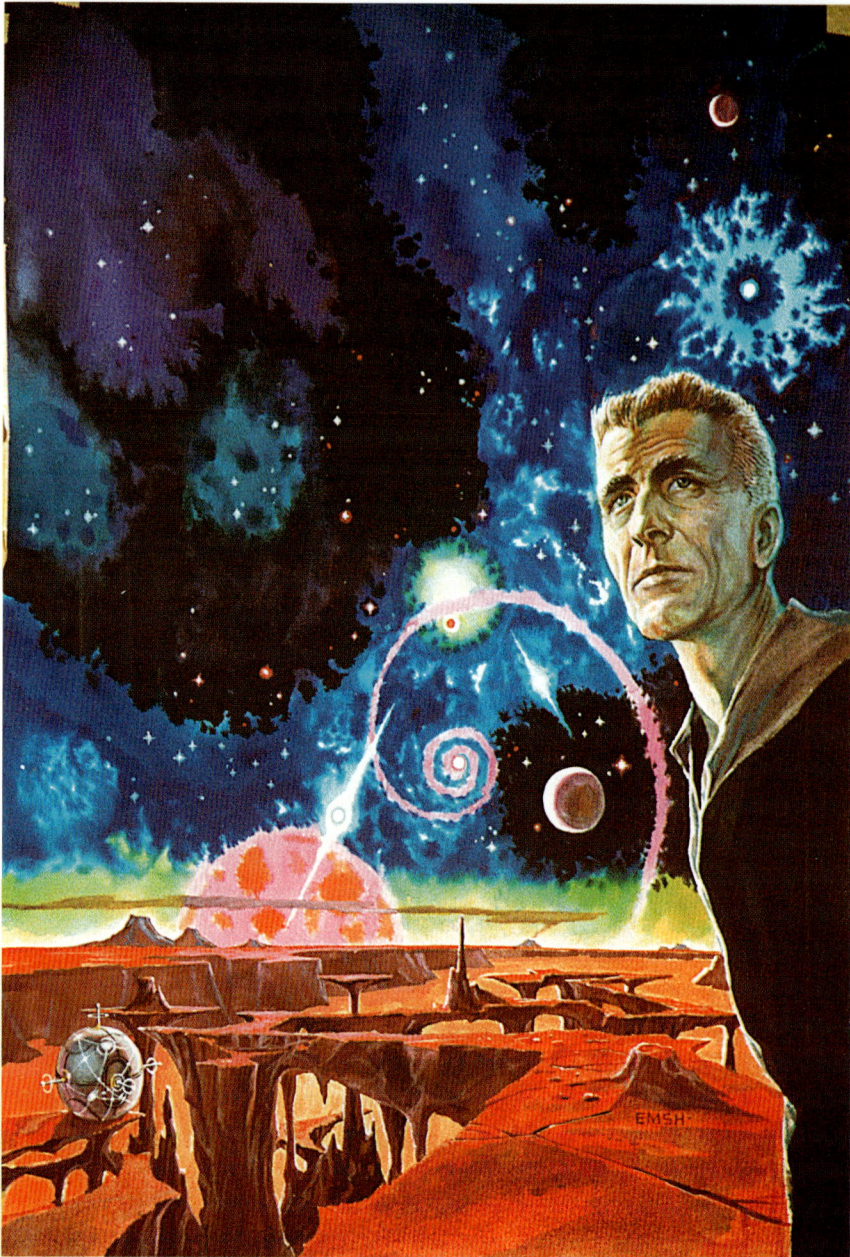

THIS PAGE
VENTURE, Nov. 1957, "It Opens the Sky" by Theodore Sturgeon. This may be Emsh's only watercolor, and one of his most metaphysical cover paintings. The sacerdotal man may have reached the end of time: moody badlands, a poisonous orange river flowing down the chasm, a tie-dyed sky of eerie nebulae, an exhausted sun on the horizon. The man gazes upward, to some-

thing above and beyond, while behind him the skies are crowded with ghostly entities. See the eyes of The Watcher within the spiral coil?

THIS PAGE
(top R) SUPER-SCIENCE FICTION, Feb. 1959. A moment of terror for a quick-change artiste. Looks like she's doffing the humanoid skin, but she may be donning it. Probably this mag's most revealing cover art, though the bottom line here is danger among the primitives.

(bot L) UNTAMED. June 1959. "Death Orgy of the Doomed Vice Queens" One of Emsh's more action oriented men's magazine covers.

Ed's SF machinery looked like it could work in the real world. The cover to *Infinity Science Fiction* for October 1957 showed a woman (with Carol the model) in a sleek space-bubble craft waving to a man in a spacesuit riding an open tri-rocket-chair that looks perfectly functional — and *fun* (pg. 61). His robots were not Mr. Machine toys, but show honest thought on how they would function in the real world.

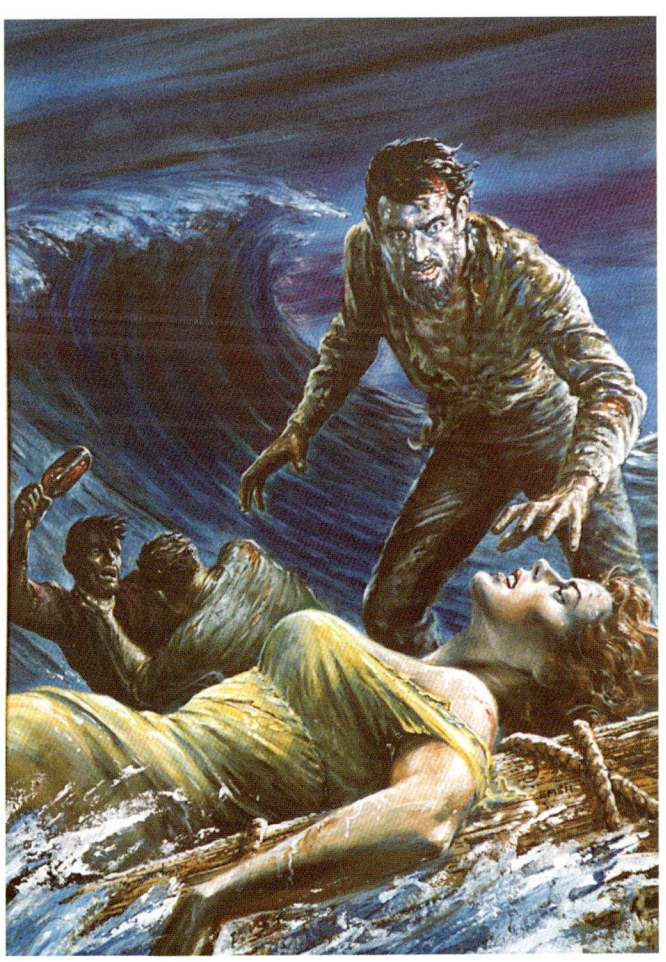

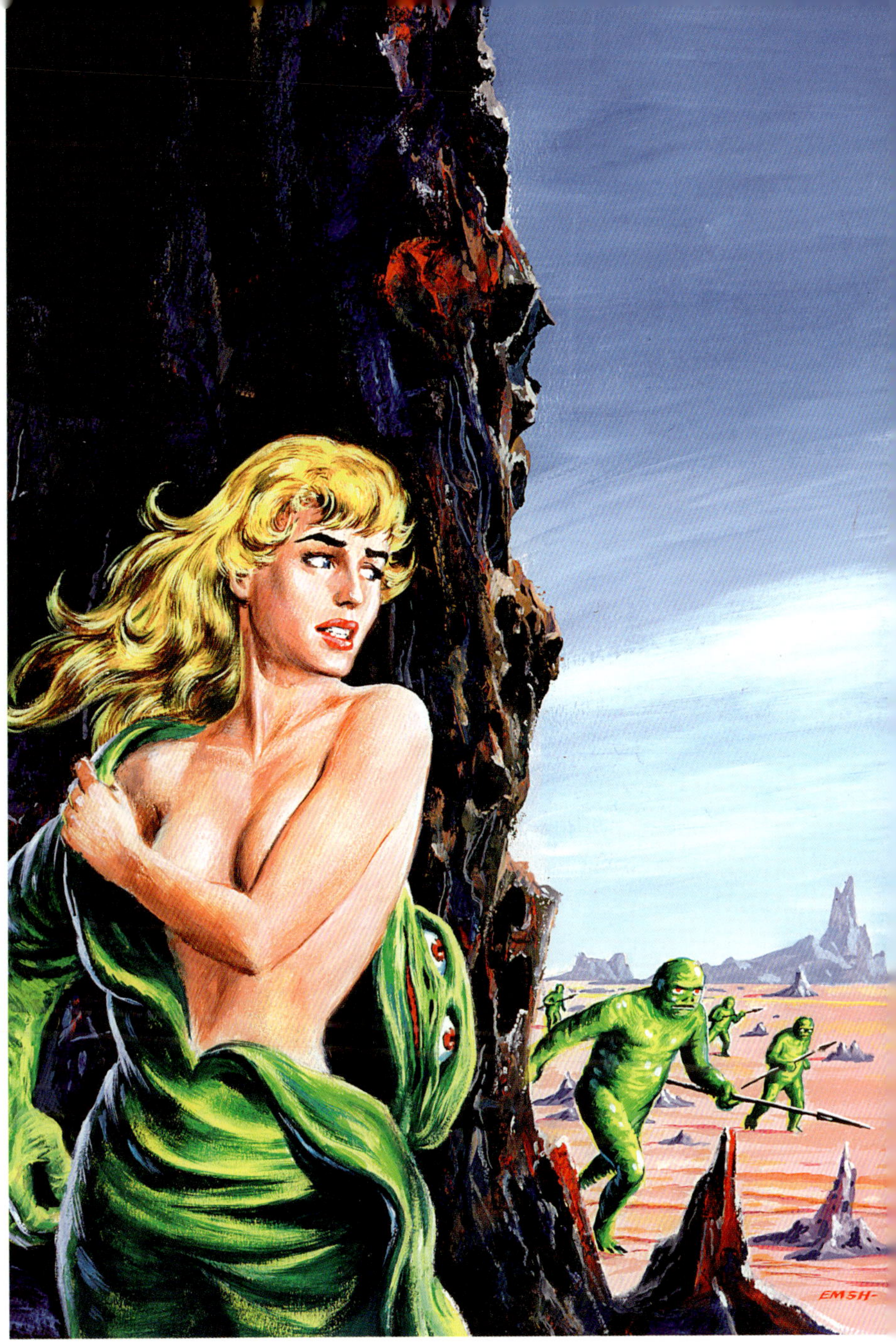

An arbitrary publishers' quirk that Ed was subjected to more times than he liked to remember, was changes made to his art without his knowledge. In one instance, Ed had painted a scene of a spaceman in profile with an alien flying insect alighting on his bubble helmet for the *Magazine of Fantasy & Science Fiction*. His original art showed foliage behind the spaceman, with the nose of a rocket peeking above the treetops. Without informing Ed, the magazine had some unknown artist paint out the foliage and render in its place a sparse environment with purple mountains and a futuristic city in the distance. A space-rocket with fins is now fully shown in the middle ground. The changes were done either on a separate piece of illustration board, that was removed when the art was returned to Ed, or on the film pulled for printing. Even the distortions and reflections visible in the spaceman's transparent helmet were redone. There seemed to be little rhyme or reason for these changes (pg. 58, 59).

In other instances, Ed's art would be changed to censor parts of it. This happened for the June 1957 *SF Adventures*, which showed a future time wherein a woman succumbs to some unknown force that has already killed many in the distant background. In the British edition of the magazine, all the dead bodies on the killing fields have been removed and replaced with a barren landscape—only the woman is left, half standing in a cryptic pose.

On October 7, 1957, a metal ball called Sputnik was launched into orbit from the Soviet Union. Its sole function was to transmit a continuous mocking radio beep back to non-Soviet regions of earth. McCarthy was gone, but the Red Menace continued. American could now read about the future in the newspaper instead of a SF magazine. Throughout the fifties the country was turning its back on American scientists with leftist leanings, driving them underground or out of the country, while embracing rocket scientists snatched from Nazi Germany, although even Wernher von Braun and his V-2 rocket collaborators were having trouble getting American rockets off the ground. "KAPUTNIK" was one typical headline after a series of failed launches. Ed seemed to have anticipated this scenario: a minor theme that he used in the mid-fifties was rocket ships blowing up on their launch pads.

IF: WORLDS OF SCIENCE FICTION. Dec. 1958, "Rat in the Skull" by Rog Phillips. The title does say it all. The cyborged rat pilots a mannequin that looks more like a doll than a store dummy. Not only do we get a cutaway view, Ed also adds a transparent plate bolted down with Phillips screws. The careful design of the cranial cockpit heightens the sense of reality, so we wonder more how the rat perceives the startled couple than what they make of him.

Seven

So be a Camera

CAROL WROTE AT THE DINING ROOM TABLE or at a small desk in the bedroom. A blurb for her first story for *F&SF* mentioned that she had small children and set up her Smith-Corona manual in the playpen to get any writing done — this being the last place the kids wanted to be. In reality she had taken apart the side-rails and used them to fence out the kids from her desk. This way she could watch them and still type. *They were happy. I was the one who wasn't*. For a long time she felt powerless to resist her father's opinions, the allure of music, marriage, being a mother and wife. When her sense of suffocating in everyday minutiae grew too strong she would steal time to write.

Ed was self-absorbed much of the time, lost in his projects and artwork, though not quite oblivious to money or supporting his family. Carol believed they had taken vows of poverty in the name of Ed's homemade movies, though they were somewhat better off financially than many of their neighbors in Levittown.

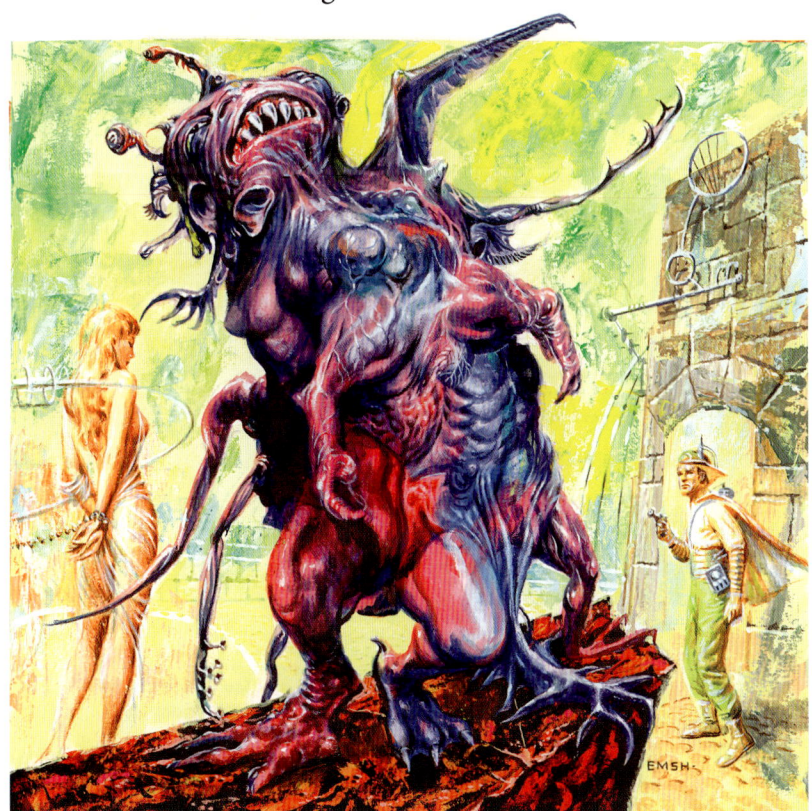

INFINITY. Nov. 1958. "Space-rogue" by "Calvin M. Knox" (Robert Silverberg). The cover that has almost everything: sexy slave-girl in chains, castle doorway and guard with raygun…and at center stage the all-out monster to-beat-the-band, so hideous it scales the heights of a new and awful beauty. Like melted-wax figures, every imaginable being seems amalgamated in its protean carcass, including a nude female torso beneath a fringed tentacle. Dr. Frankenstein might not approve, but Dali should be green with envy.

In June of 1957, Carol brought her story "Baby" to the second Milford Conference. "Baby" is set in a future time where people have disappeared off the face of the earth due to a vaguely described war. A few parents had left their babies in the protective care of robot servants. Damon Knight pointed out a spot in the story and said, "This is where you learned how to get deep down inside yourself, into your subconscious." The grown up "Baby" climbs onto the head of a three-story statue after temporarily escaping his caretaker robots. Carol was not sure why that particular scene worked as Knight said it did. The story was published in the February 1958 issue of *F&SF*, sporting an Emsh cover (pg. 79).

Her story "Pelt," published in the November 1958 *F&SF*, came about when someone told her, "Never tell a story from an animal's point of view." Carol had read Saki's cat stories and thought *I'm going to write one from the dog's point of view* — in this case a loyal hunting dog tracking alien creatures on another world for her human master. The creatures turn out to be sentient, a fact first sensed by the dog when the creatures communicate with her. Until the very end of the story, the hunter is oblivious to the true nature of the creatures he hunted, and the dog must make a choice. This is a theme that would be amplified later in her 2001 novel *The Mount*. Carol work-shopped "Pelt" at Milford that summer.

After its magazine publication, Judy Merril picked up the story for her anthology *The Year's Greatest Science Fiction and Fantasy* (Gnome Press, 1959), and would reprint the story again in 1967 in *SF: The Best of the Best*. Carol's original title for the story was "Fur," but *F&SF* editor Bob Mills changed it, and Merril also preferred the new title even though Carol tried to talk her into going back to the original title.

Almost as soon as she began to learn plotting, Carol was looking for a "cooler" feeling away from narrative building blocks in her work. She was reading John Cage's writings, and the the poems of Frank

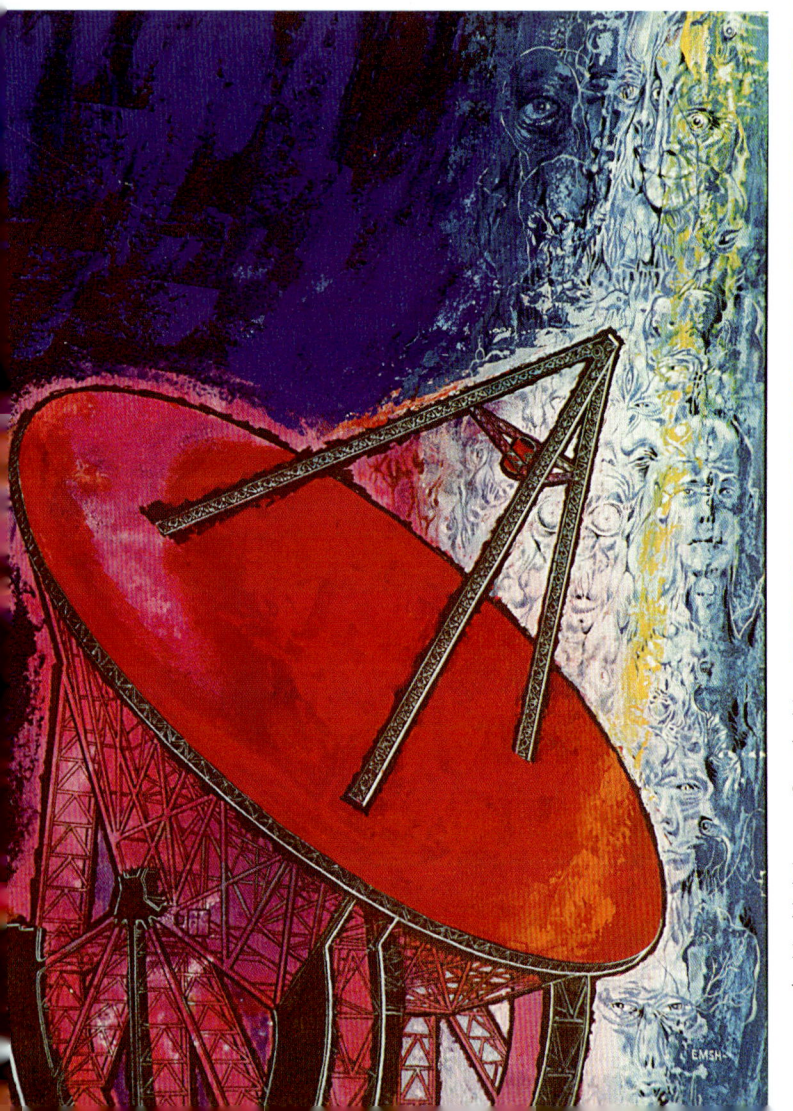

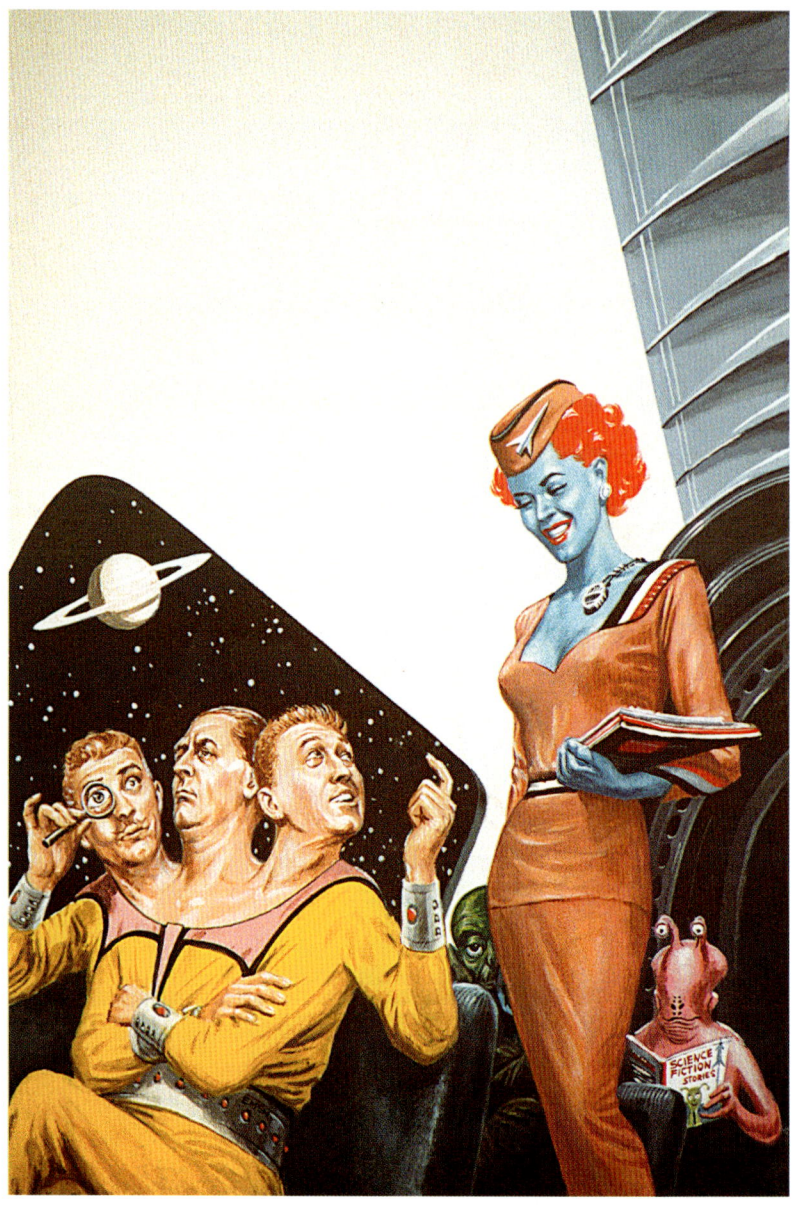

(top R) SCIENCE FICTION QUARTERLY. August 1957

(bot L) F&SF, Sept. 1960, "The Word to Space" by "Winston P. Sanders" (Poul Anderson) (top R) F&SF. Nov. 1955. A decade before UFO abductions, Emsh painted this tableau showing a woman bound like Gulliver while little lizard-men, reacting in varied ways, document their "specimen." The scene harks back to gremlins and pixies, transferred to the Fifties saucer mania. Later, Spielberg would produce a kinder, gentler E-T who only wanted flower samples and would never stoop to rifling a lady's purse.

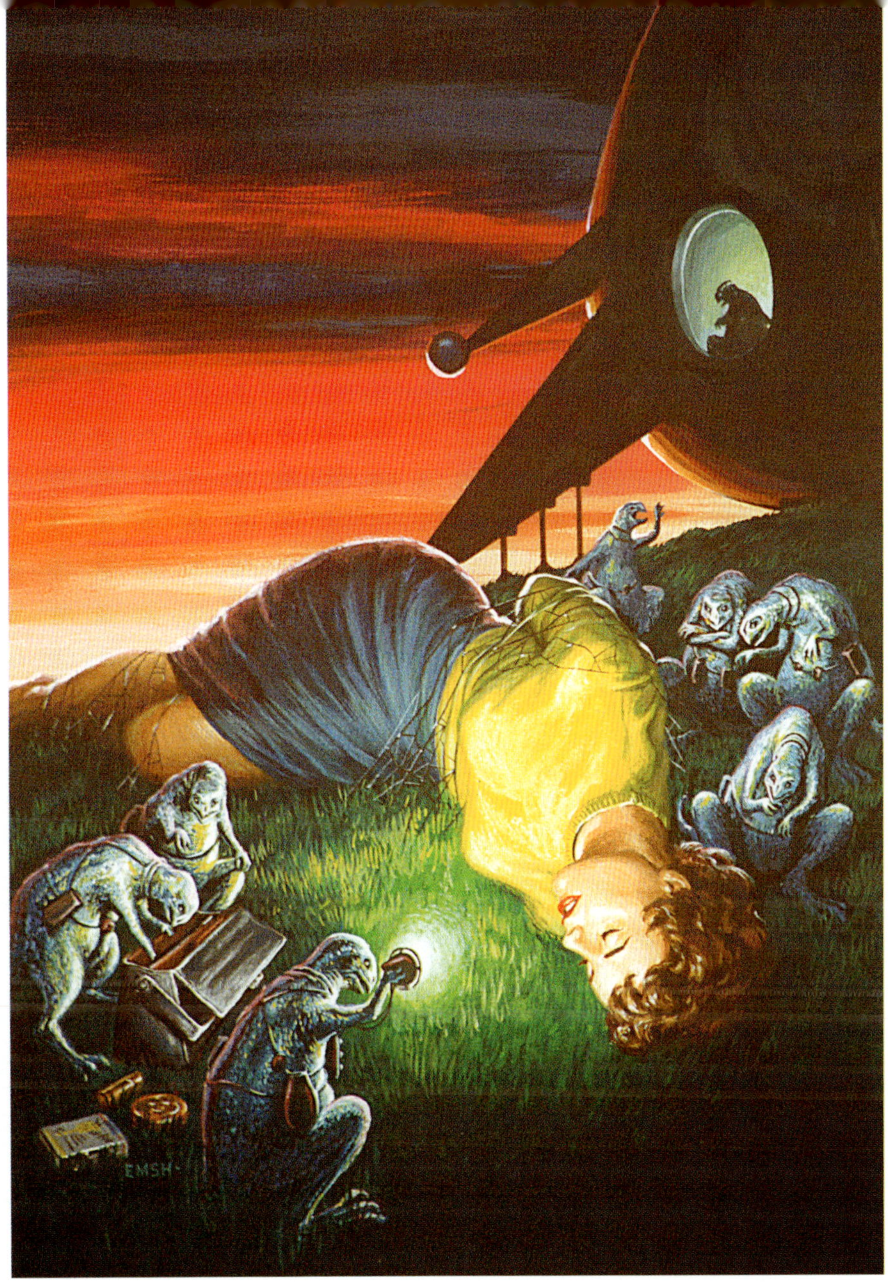

(L) F&SF. December 1953. "Marooned on an Asteroid"

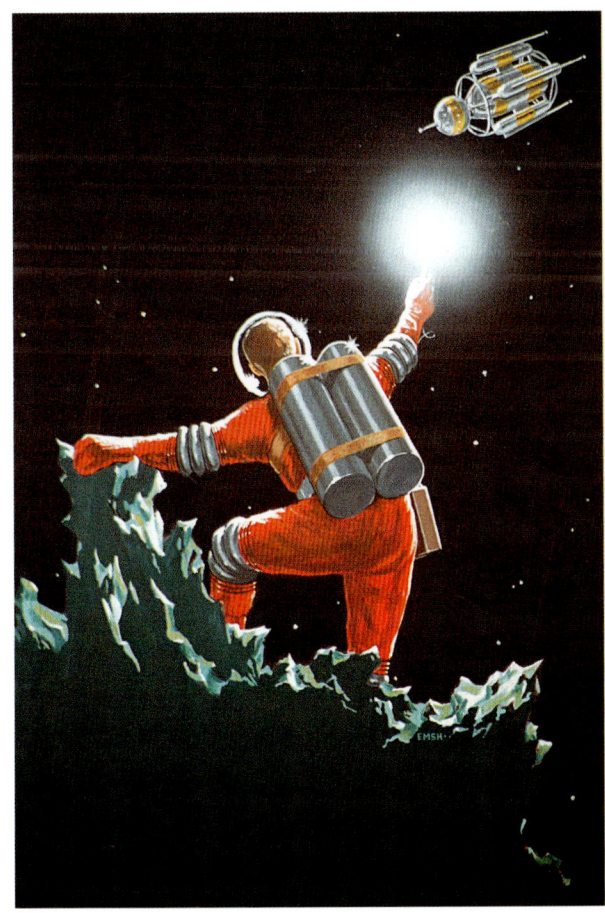

O'Hara. Getting away from conventional fiction meant more anxiety when she sat at her typewriter and tried to mesh her imagination to a story. *I think that instead maybe I will manipulate the rhythms, the styles, the organization of paragraphs or the words, or maybe sometimes just deal with little bits of fun or little bits of reality.* Carol and Ed were beginning to influence each other. *Can you write a story that looks like a Robert Rauschenberg painting?*

One quirky SF editor (in a field fraught with eccentric editors) who gave Ed and many writers pause during the fifties, was John Wood Campbell Jr. at *Astounding Science Fiction.* Campbell spent endless hours tucked away in his cell-like office situated above the printing plant of his publisher Street & Smith. The two things he seemed to like best were

77

smoking and talking — usually done together. In outward appearance, SF was a marginal and disposable literature, mostly alive in magazines from 1926 through the 1950s, but beginning in 1938 Campbell single-handedly gave SF a gravity heretofore unknown by forcing his writers to work harder for their penny a word. He expected his authors to know their science as well as to be able to write to his standards. It is a testament to Campbell's despotic vision that he did shift the field, single-handedly, onto a new path.

Science fiction may have been on an evolutionary fast track after John W. Campbell, but book publishers still lagged behind, afraid to publish what they considered absurd fantasies. (Up until this point only detective-mystery pulp writ-

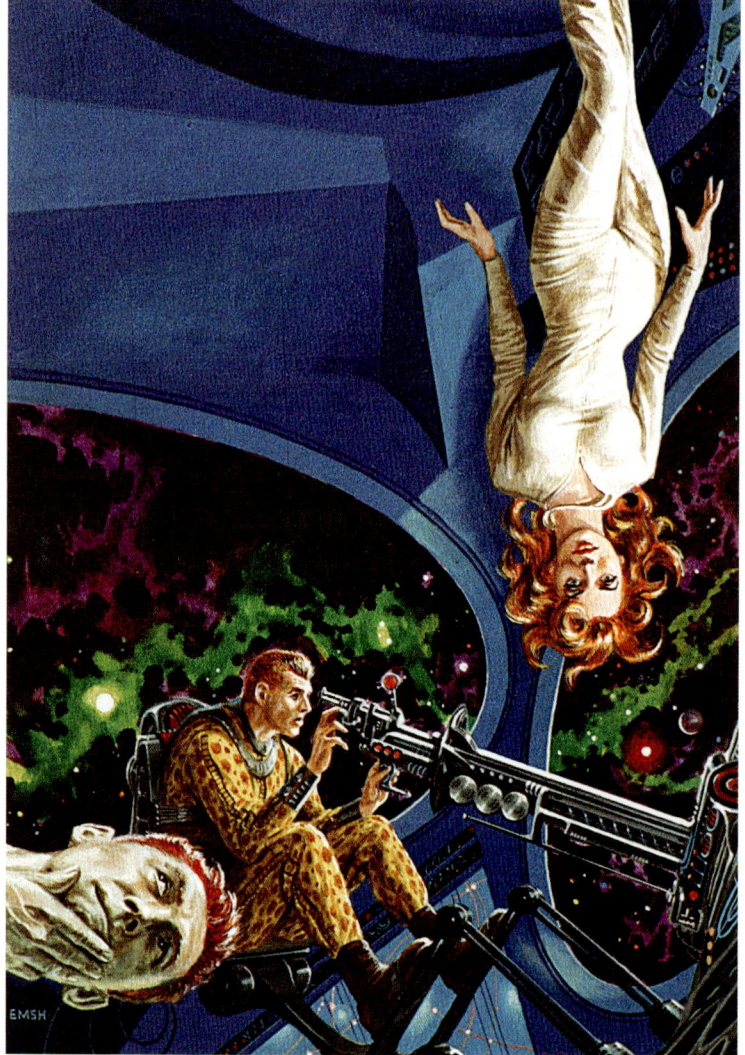

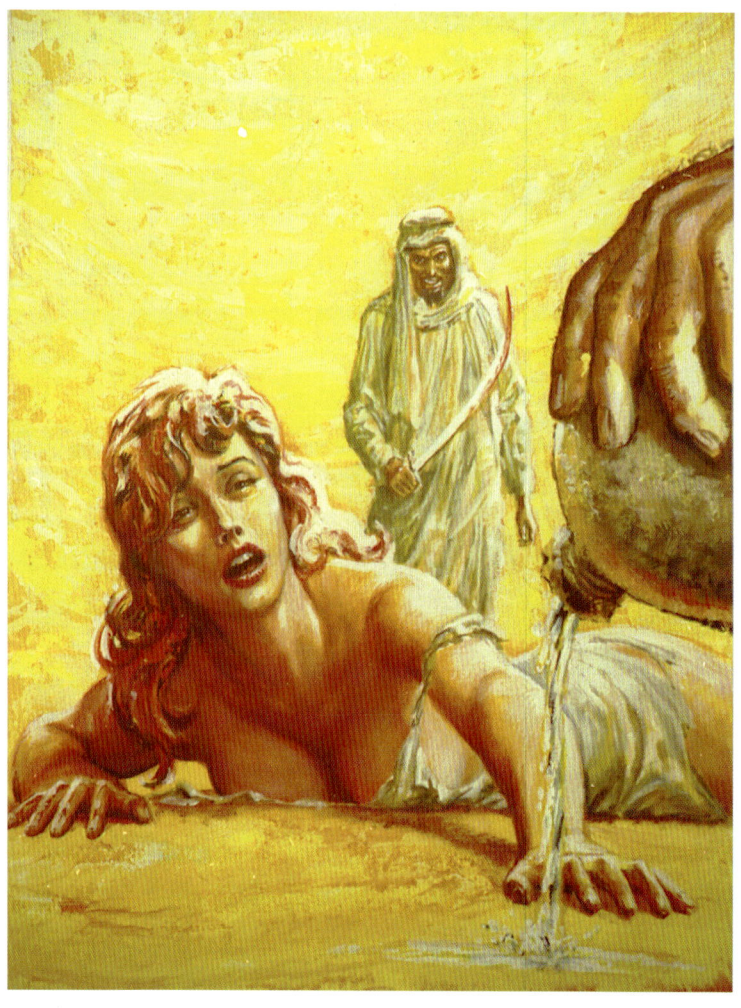

ers like Raymond Chandler and Dashiel Hammett had made the transition from pulp pages.) It took two 1946 anthologies, Random House's *Adventures in Time & Space*, put together by J. Francis McComas and Raymond J. Healy, and Crown Publishing's *The Best of Science Fiction*—both books culled most of their stories from Campbell's magazine—to alert non-pulp purveyors to some of

(top R) INFINITY. Feb. 1957. "Hunt the Hog of Joe"

(L) UNTAMED. July 1959. "Bessie Darling's Thirty-Hour Ordeal"

(top R) ASTOUNDING. June 1958. "Pastoral". The grass is always greener on the other side. This one is in the "double-take" school of normalcy; we know it's not a rustic SATURDAY EVENING POST cover when we notice two moons in the sky. Yet all remains bucolic: a blissful cameloid lapping up "daisies," a stick-figure Huck Finn trotting down the road with fresh catch for supper. All that's missing is a chorus of crickets to complete this peaceful, down-home scene - that is, if one can ignore that stubborn, stunted, revenant thorn tree.

(bot L) F&SF. Feb. 1958. "Baby" by Carol Emshwiller. Ed only did cover paintings twice for stories by Carol, including this one. Robot minders for the innocent "baby" appear to control him via a flesh-pink umbilicus (a symbolic element not literally in the story). The taller one tilts anxiously toward Baby, as if the naked man's maturity and livid strength might become a problem. Though raised by them from the marvels available at dime-store newsstands. In a post-atomic world, both hardcover science fiction collections sold over 30,000 copies at $3 a book, surprising their respective publishers.

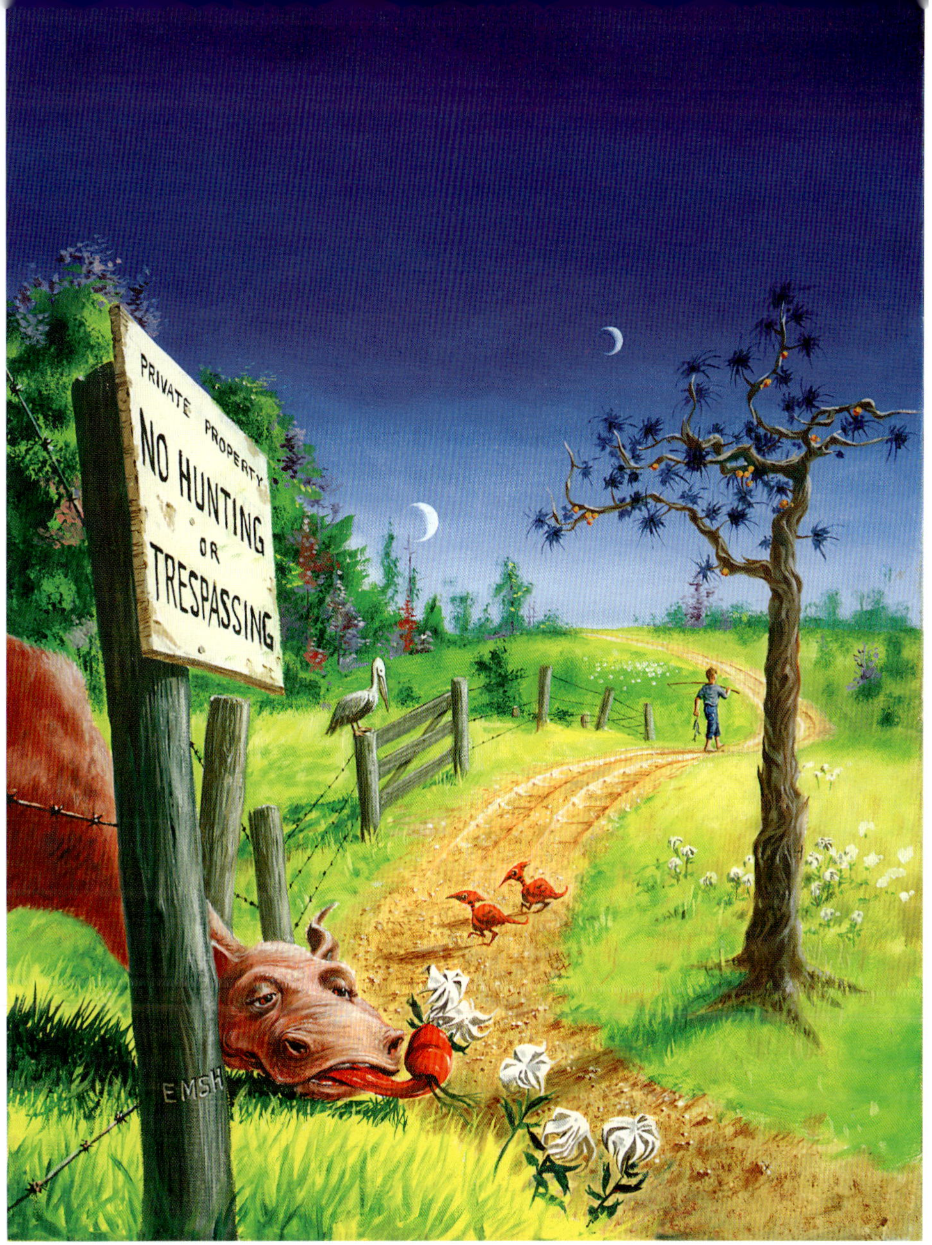

On February 14, 1955, Ed met with Campbell in his Manhattan office. Their previous meeting four years earlier had led nowhere. This time Campbell was more receptive, and Ed left

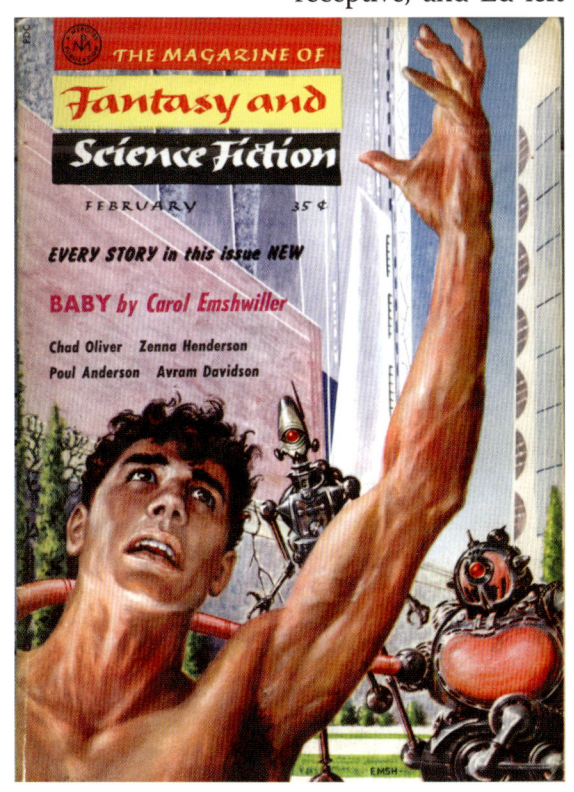

with a cover art assignment. *Astounding* had the best rates in the SF magazine field and Ed was glad to get the work.

For a long time Campbell *was* the field, but by the fifties *Astounding Science Fiction* was showing some chips and cracks along its edges. Campbell's zealous espousal of Dianetics, then the Dean Drive (an antigravity engine), followed by advocacy of the advantages of a future society having a rigorous class system (including slavery), and the pushing of psi sciences of the mind, alarmed and drove away some readers.

Robert Silverberg remembers: "Campbell put everybody who entered his office through an intense philosophical inquiry, grilling them in the Socratic manner about whatever subject was uppermost in his mind that day, and I think Ed felt a little intimidated by that. Sometimes when we left John's office together, Ed would say, 'Did you have any idea of what he was talking about?', or something similar. But Campbell admired Ed's work and probably didn't give him a hard time as an artist, just as someone on the receiving end of the day's interrogation. I'm sure Ed enjoyed his visits with the kindly, twinkling, soft-spoken Lowndes much more, even though Lowndes didn't pay as well."

In *John W. Campbell Letters, Vol. I*, Frank Kelly Freas recalls the limits of Campbell's art appreciation: "He was perfectly willing to admit that he knew nothing about art, but he knew storytelling and he knew what it took to illustrate a story. John had no use whatever for abstraction, very little for stylization, and barely tolerated anything that approached the fashionable." Freas records Campbell saying, "Look … if I could send a camera to Mars, or into your bloodstream, or into the future, I'd use a camera. But you're all I've got. So *be* a camera, OK?" Ed never felt comfortable around Campbell and only did a handful of covers for *Astounding Science Fiction*. Freas' work fitted in with Campbell's idea of art, and he became the signature artist for *Astounding*.

Ed's *Astounding Science Fiction* covers were not illustrations for interior stories, but freestanding art. He often appeared in Campbell's office with ready-made cover sketch ideas that would sell or not. One of the first paintings that Ed did for Campbell's *Astounding Science Fiction*, for the March 1956 issue, showed a bear defending an exploration team from a weird-looking dragon creature. Campbell had Murray Leinster write "Exploration Team" around Ed's painting. Ed once told a science fiction convention audience, "It's fascinating … to see what ingenious ideas the writers come up with…." Campbell usually worked the other way around — giving manuscripts to artists he trusted and letting them have a free hand.

Campbell's attitude was not unique among SF magazine editors. Ed remembers, "… having many battles about the response (of editors) to modern styles of artwork. The more literal, realistic, docu-

birth, he has grown apart from them. Usually the eros in an SF cover is focused on a woman, but here it blossoms in a strong male form, and in the beautifully marbled pinks in the flesh of this dark Adonis. We feel the amazing vitality in this last son of Earth as, with yearning face, he reaches for the sky.

THIS PAGE
F&SF. Sept. 1961. "The Monster in the Park" by Gerard Klein. Irreal colors and a tessellated sky establish the dominant mood of alien-ness, and alienation. Beyond a thick haze, soldiers

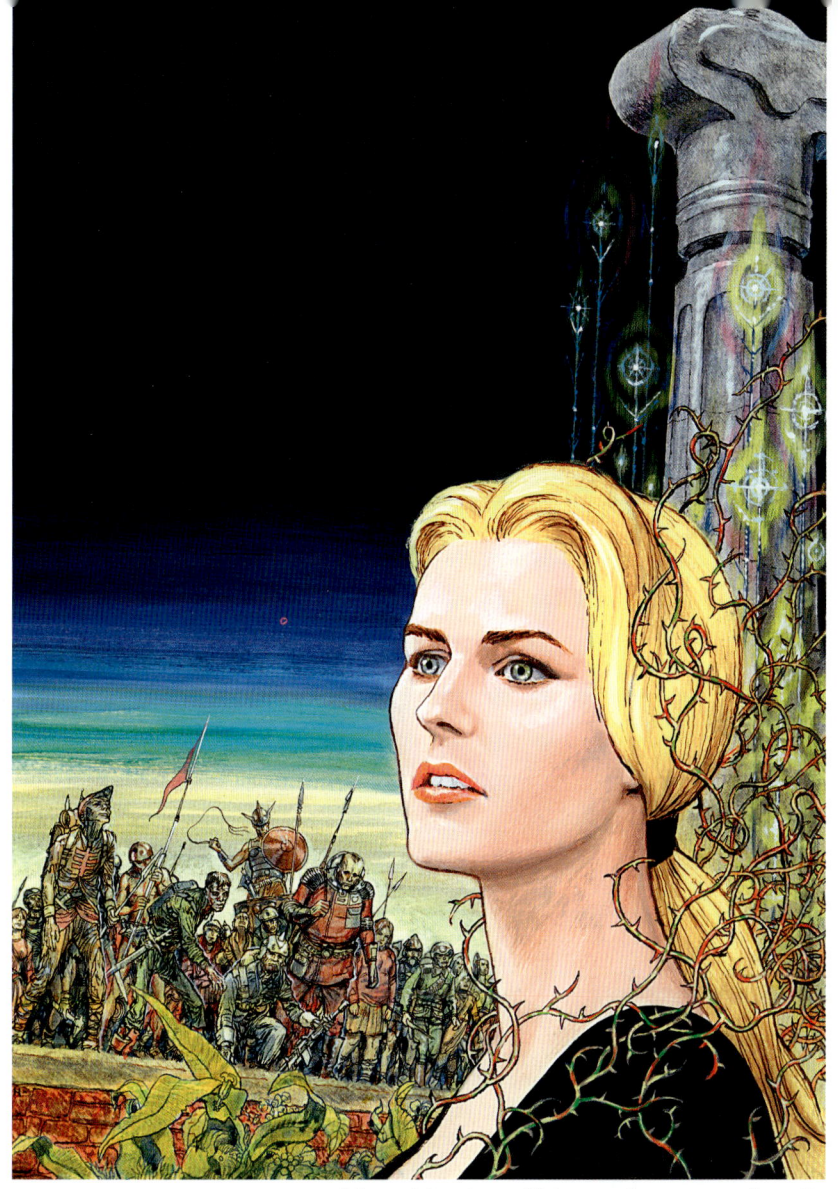

stand ready to kill the bubbly slug-thing with eyes and mouth like precious gems. The blonde woman - is she afraid? Concerned for herself…or for the monster? Look close and you'll spot the entity within: the dark figure of a man. This image is like a discolored newsphoto - except that the sky is spread not with rainclouds, but a psychic storm.

THIS PAGE
F&SF, Febuary 1962. "The Garden of Time" by J.G. Ballard. A classical beauty, in quasi-classical setting, stands transfixed by a tangle of art nouveau vines. The motley

mentary (approach) was what many science fiction people thought was the only valid way." Richard Powers may have been the most influential science fiction artist of the twentieth century, and the most modernistic with his covers, splicing together Tanguy, de Chirico, and Franz Kline with science-fictional motifs to create his own lucid style, but Powers' art was little seen on SF magazines.

Powers created fine art abstractions for the Rehn Gallery in New York, but made a living from commercial illustration, including his giddy, surrealistic-tinged work for Ballantine and Dell SF paperbacks. The preponderance of Powers' SF art shows arrangements of elongated figures, alien landscapes, organic spaceships, and planets linked by elaborate fluid lines and haphazard splashes of colors. Yet each painting was a new experience to readers. Powers never painted an uninteresting piece of book cover art. To readers looking for science fiction in bookstores, it may have seemed as if he was everywhere — the same was not true on newsstands. (Berkley Books came out in the late fifties with a series of paperbacks collecting stories from *Astounding* using Powers art, but here Campbell had no say in the choice of artist.)

Powers' surrealistic semi-abstractions helped set the style of many book publishers' science fiction lines during the late fifties and early sixties. The out-of-this-world ambiguity of his work was perfect for the genre, and Powers' graphic appeal remains strong today — something that cannot be said of many of his contemporaries. Throughout the fifties, magazines were the heart of the SF field. Yet it was almost as if there were two different audiences for SF. Powers' art rarely turned up in SF magazines, except for a few early issues of H. L. Gold's *Galaxy* and *Beyond Fantasy Fiction* (published between 1953-55 as a companion to *Galaxy*), and Fred Pohl's one-shot digest *Star Science Fiction* (1958), but Powers was to become a big influence for many of the younger science fiction artists, including Ed.

A science fiction fanzine writer describing the cover art by Richard Powers for the first issue of *Beyond* wrote in 1953: *The little freebles floomped blurrily along while the tendrils of light blue flangle crinched grayly to and fro. The petrified altapoge leaned faumly against the trews as the rope from red looped down over it and the kluum balls. Blood twisted sinuously from a stature-hand and worked*

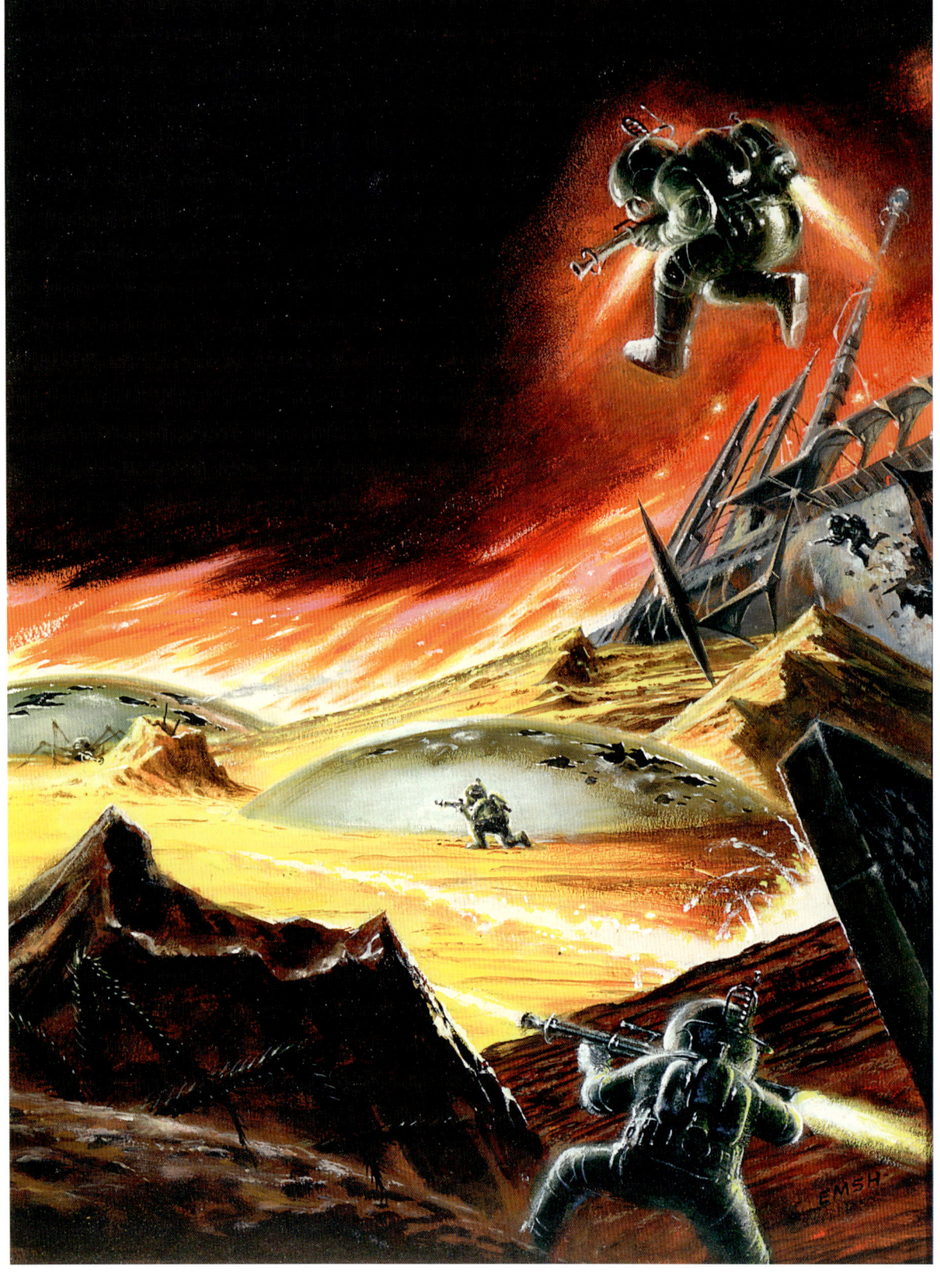

soldiers of history, a zombified army, clamber onto her garden wall; yet the haggard men seem restrained at the wall's edge; it's as far as they can go. Perhaps the twisting vines protect the regal blonde, along with the leaf-point lights dancing about the pillar. This is the Garden of Time, where one may be insulated from the ravages of the world, and time, yet have no assurance of happiness. The picture is like an etching, with outlines and filigree: everything old, yet eternally young.

THIS PAGE
F&SF, Nov. 1959, "Starship Soldier" by Robert A. Heinlein. The artist's later (1977) title was "Battle on a Burning Planet." It has to be some kind of ultimate in depicting red-hot war - in this case, the middle of a nuclear firestorm. Supersonic blowtorch flame-winds scream past shock-slammed buildings on the ragged horizon, while the surface glows a fierce (if runny) yellow. Well-armored troops do their damndest to blast the remaining "bugs," malevolent spiders with cockroach legs. The chaos of war and the searing incandescence leap off the page, engulfing the viewer. Because Ed Emsh went there mentally, so, too, you are THERE.

(top R) VENTURE SCIENCE FICTION. Jan. 1958. "The End of Winter" by Algis Budrys. Possibly Ed's weirdest SF cover: the really mech-tronic man. Ed knew the painting would be flopped, so he signed it backwards. (!)

(bot L) Mystery cover to unknown magazine. Stealing dough from some dame. A study of humanity in the raw, with wonderful movement and design. The sensuous creases in their clothing enhance and twist the tension of the robbery tighter, as the anonymous suit plucks his quarry clean.

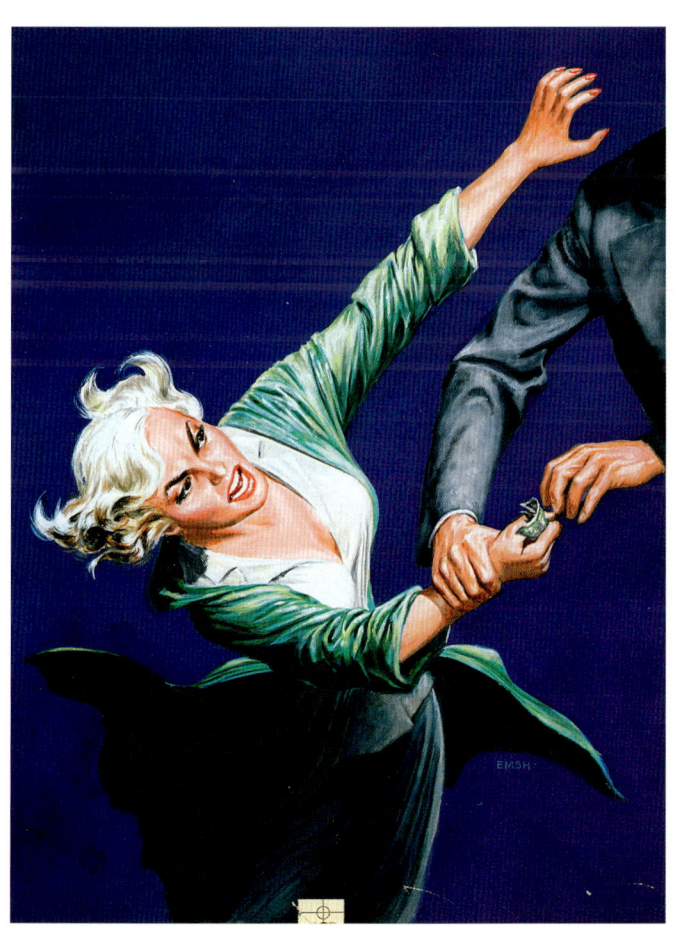

its way avidly into the mught vault... [These type of] artists had to be coaxed and encouraged over long periods of years — mostly finger-painting in kindergarten — before they finally made their appearance. Takes a lot of courage to take some multicolored paint, slosh it around a little, and leave it that way. It is possible that H. L. Gold was dissuaded from using more Richard Powers art by fan reactions like this.

Some of Powers' influence can be seen in the covers Ed did for *Original SF Stories* Aug. 1956 (pg. 49), *F&SF* for June 1963 (pg. 94), and the 1959 paperback anthology *The Macabre Reader* edited by Donald Wollheim (pg. 112). Ed had already introduced abstractions (with few SF fans noticing) into some of his SF art as outer-space debris, alien backgrounds, or representations of energy. It was a short hop from Pollock's abstract expressionism to Powers' blend of surrealism mixed with humor (pg. 88).

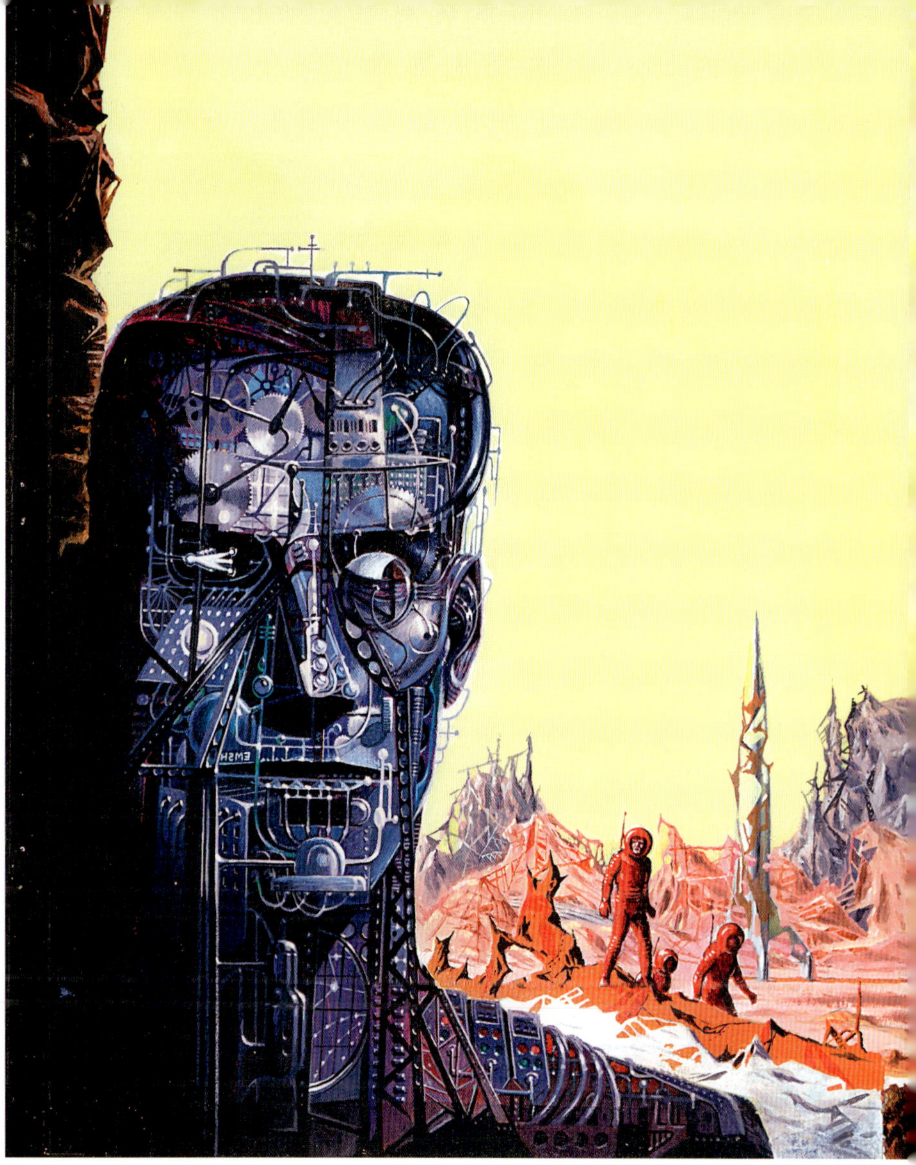

Ed once asked John W. Campbell if he would ever use Richard Powers' art on *Astounding Science Fiction*. Campbell replied, "No, I would not. I wouldn't use *that* technique. Now, if he has another technique, fine." Emshwiller thought that the science fiction and

83

fantasy field should "stimulate and broaden" and allow for "growth" and present abstract art along with realistic art. Campbell believed that cover art had very little to do with newsstand sales, and cited a study done by *Astounding* that appeared to corroborate his thinking.

Symbolic covers may have annoyed some long-time SF fans, but they sold to many non-fans who were attracted to the strangeness of the art, and wondered what was going on inside a book with such a cover. Ballantine and Dell were routinely doing 180,000 to 200,000 copies of their SF titles — most 1950s SF magazines' print runs averaged 55,000 copies. (*Astounding*, at the high end, figured at around 100,000.) For book publishers, this had been a constant number through boom and bust periods. While there are different factors involved in selling books compared to magazines, the one selling point they have in common is cover art.

One also has to consider the premise that science fiction magazines were becoming too insular — appeasing their old audience while ignoring a new one, with the corollary of diminishing readership. Or as one publisher put it: "We found if we do not call a book science fiction we can sometimes come out in the black."

Another SF fan, Bob Tucker, noted what he called SF fans' "pulp's disease" in May 1950. "Speaking generally, knowing there are many individuals contrary to the rule, it appears that the fan field was weaned on magazine fiction, grew up on magazine fiction, thrived and will die happily with magazine fiction because they have never known or never bothered with any other. Apparently this type of fan reader is so completely educated to and dependent upon magazine fiction of pulp quality, that

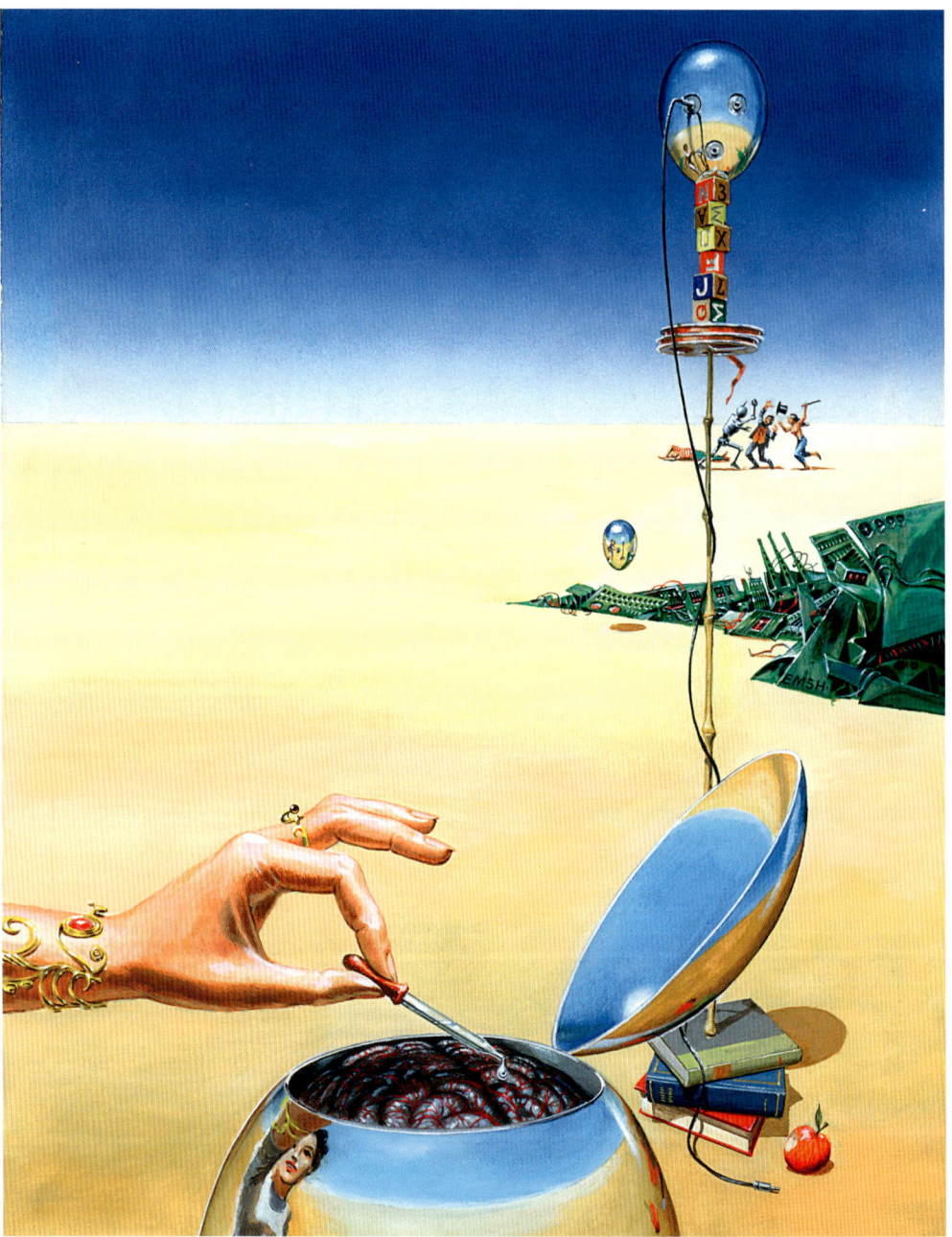

F&SF. Jan. 1959. "The Silver Eggheads" by Fritz Leiber. In a serene desert, mundane and surreal elements recede toward a hazy horizon: mirror eggs, schoolbooks, techno-ruins; skirmishing figures; an apple with a bite taken out. An array of objects almost beyond comprehension; a cryptogram or catechism, for which the story is the nominal sacred writ. Are these eggs visitants from a higher dimension? The foreground one may be the key, for it seems to contain a mass of worms ... or else a human brain, which a pretty woman is feeding with an eyedropper. Another egg perches atop alphabet blocks on a pole made of bones. Imagery as challenging would grace Ed's video and film. Though far from his last SF cover, this was probably a turning point of sorts.

THIS PAGE
(top R) THE ATLANTIC ABOMINATION by John Brunner. Ace 1960. The purple tyrant-god on its palanquin. The slaveys of the world heave forth to sustain him, filling a crevasse with their bodies. No better image of enslaved masses can be imagined. The particolor rock merges with the seething figures. A truly despairing image, of humanity reduced to the status of ants

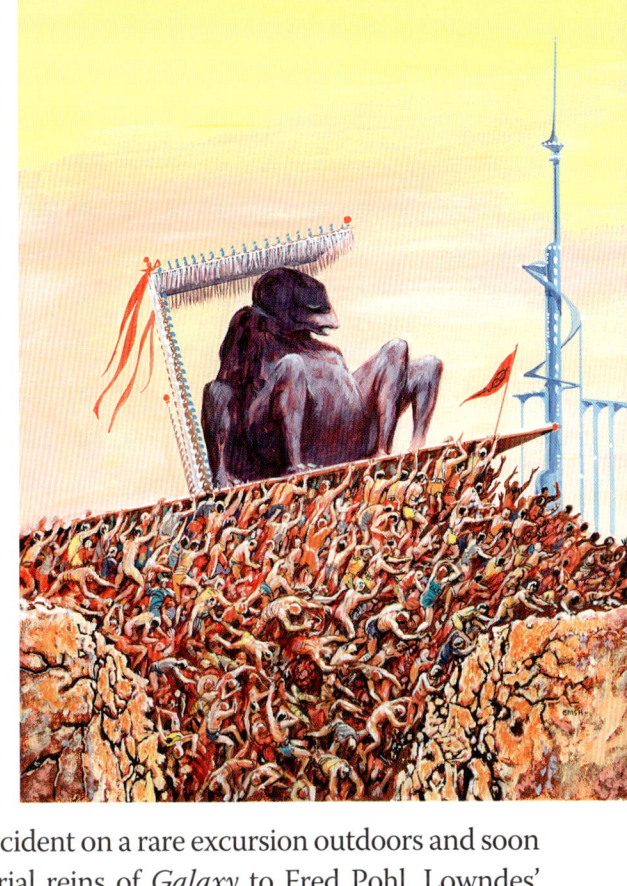

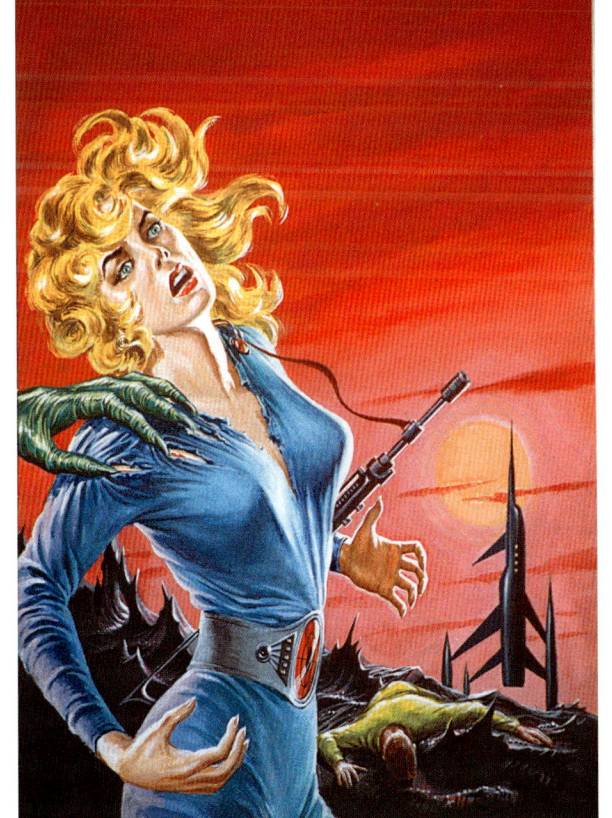

an original novel not intended for a magazine and not written down to magazine standards, is consequently not understood by him. Meaning that the long-held taste for magazines is so thoroughly ingrained that the new taste of a book is unappreciated." This pulp disease seemed also to apply to the SF art on book covers.

By the late fifties there were other tribulations for science fiction. Most detrimental of all: American News Company, one of the main independent magazine distributors, was dissolved, putting many marginal SF magazines out of business overnight. Those magazines with better sales, such as *Galaxy* and *F&SF*, or linked to a stable of better-selling periodicals like *Astounding Science Fiction, Fantastic Science Fiction* and *Amazing Stories,* managed to survive. Close examination of the field shows no signs of editorial exhaustion, except perhaps for Horace Gold, who was involved in an automobile accident on a rare excursion outdoors and soon after relinquished the editorial reins of *Galaxy* to Fred Pohl. Lowndes' group of SF magazines limped along and saw their last issue in 1960. Of course, Campbell still had his plow in the same pseudo-science rut.

As good an editor as he was, Gold did have his blind spots. He let two of the best all time SF stories get away from him through sheer ignorance: Walter M. Miller, Jr.'s "A Canticle for Leibowitz," because he did not know how Catholics would respond to it (Boucher, a Catholic in good standing, quickly bought the story for F&SF); and Daniel Keyes' classic story "A Flower for Algernon" because Gold wanted to change the ending to an upbeat one — a change Keyes refused to do. (On the other hand, it was Gold's editorial prodding that got Alfred Bester's classics *The Stars My Destination* and *The Demolished Man* written.) Carol and Ed read Keyes' manuscript at Milford in the summer of 1958 and both loved the story. Keyes easily sold the story to Bob Mills, who had replaced Boucher a year earlier at *F&SF*, and Ed got to illustrate it for the cover of the April 1959 issue of *F&SF*. He wound up giving the painting to the author as a gift when Keyes' first child was born that September.

On a spring day in 1958, Kelly Freas and Robert Silverberg were in

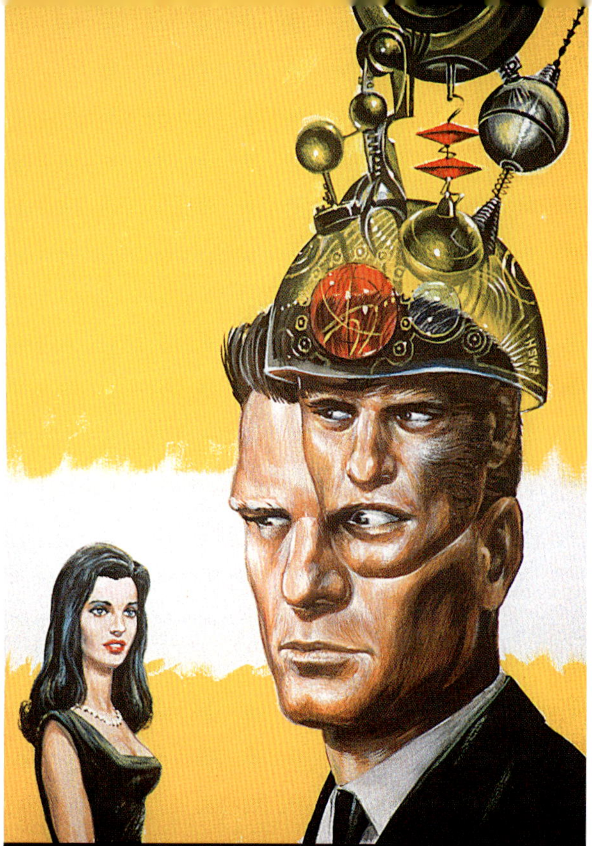

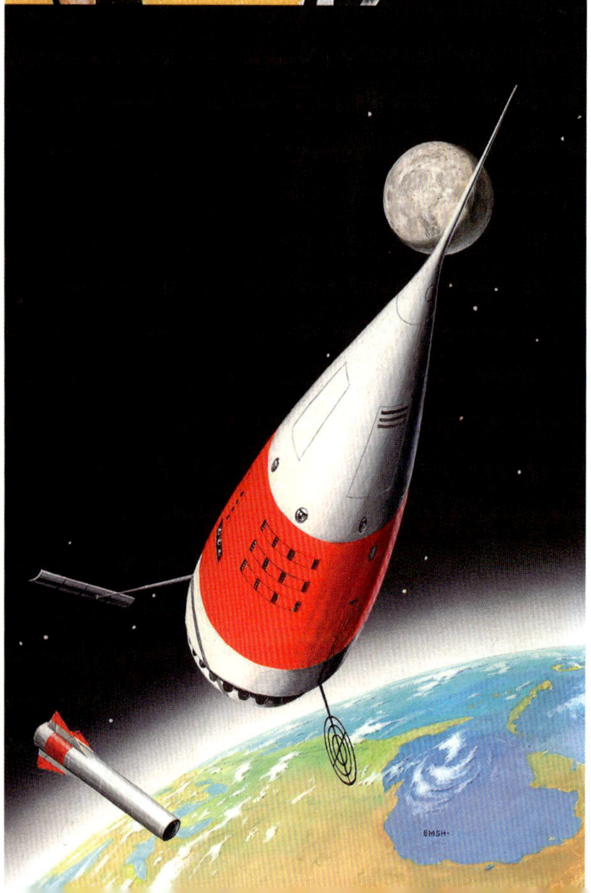

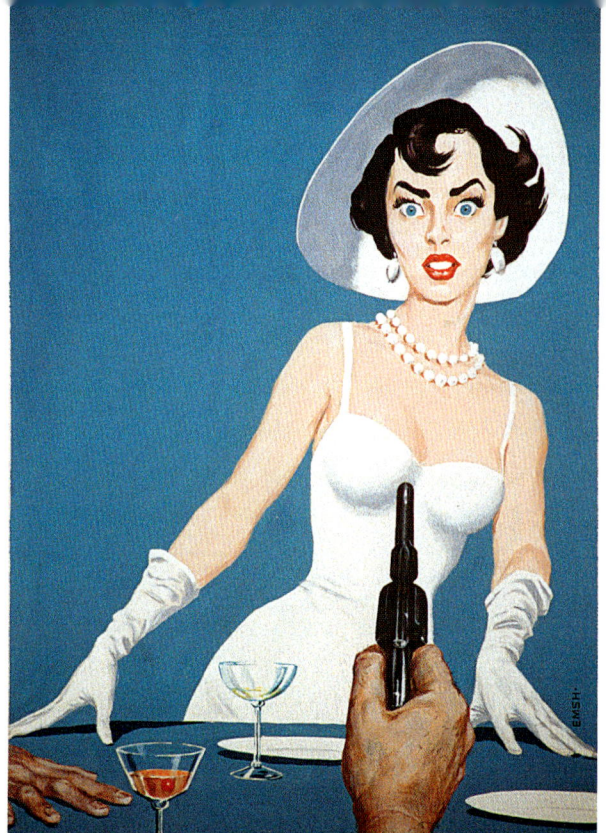
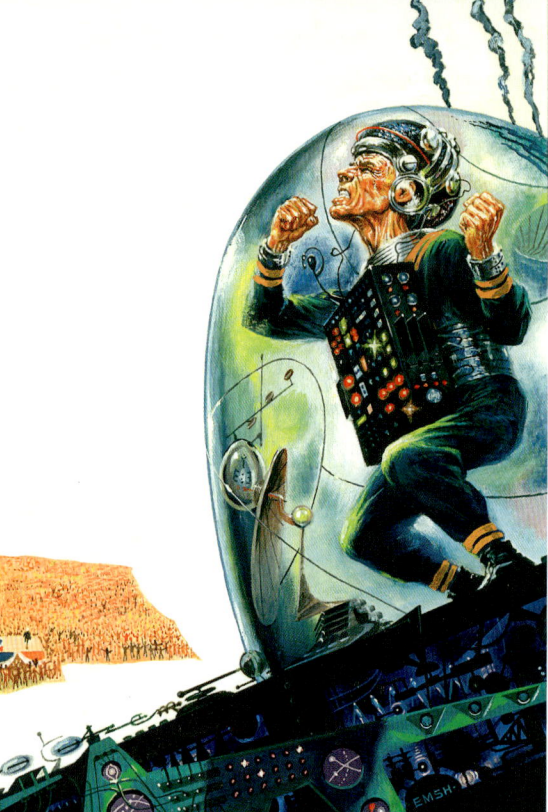

PAGE 85
(bot L) SUPER-SCIENCE. June 1957. An uh-oh moment with the Green Clutching Claw. This is one of those garish ones, where the best things are the landscape and the needle-nibbed spaceship. (But hardcore pulp-fans dig it.)

THIS PAGE
(top L) AMAZING SCIENCE FICTION. July 1964. "Mindmate" Ed used the likeness of his brother Mac for the man in this piece of art.

(top R) MERCURY MYSTERY BOOK-MAGAZINE. October 1957

(bot R) INFINITY SCIENCE FICTION. June 1956. "The Guests of Chance" by Charles Beaumont & Chad Oliver

(bot L) INFINITY SCIENCE FICTION. April 1957. "Friends and Enemies" by Fritz Leiber.

PAGE 87
(top L) INFINITY SCIENCE FICTION. April 1958. "Wings of the Phoenix"

(R) VENTURE Jan. 1957, "Virgin Planet" by Poul Anderson. The red and the black: redheaded amazon pride meets (Earth) male wariness. The black of the cage glimmers and shivers, as if quasi-real, reflecting the tension of her Touch-me-if-you-dare stance. The amazon was modeled on Anderson's wife, Karen.

(bot L) INFINITY SCIENCE FICTION. Mar. 1958. "She Was Made for Love" by Robert Sheckley.

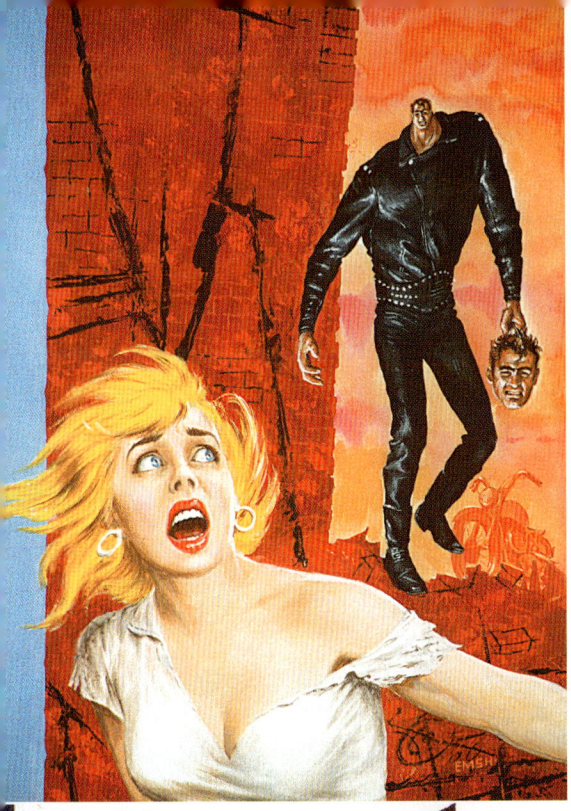
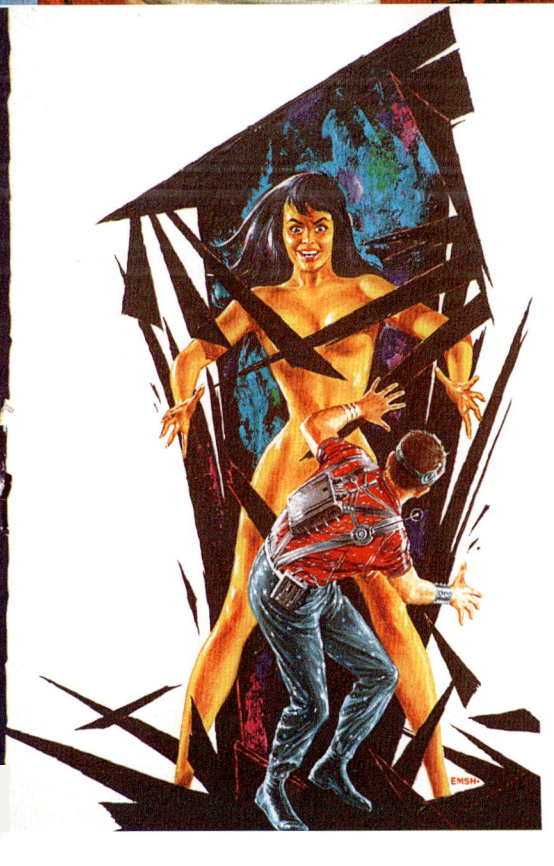

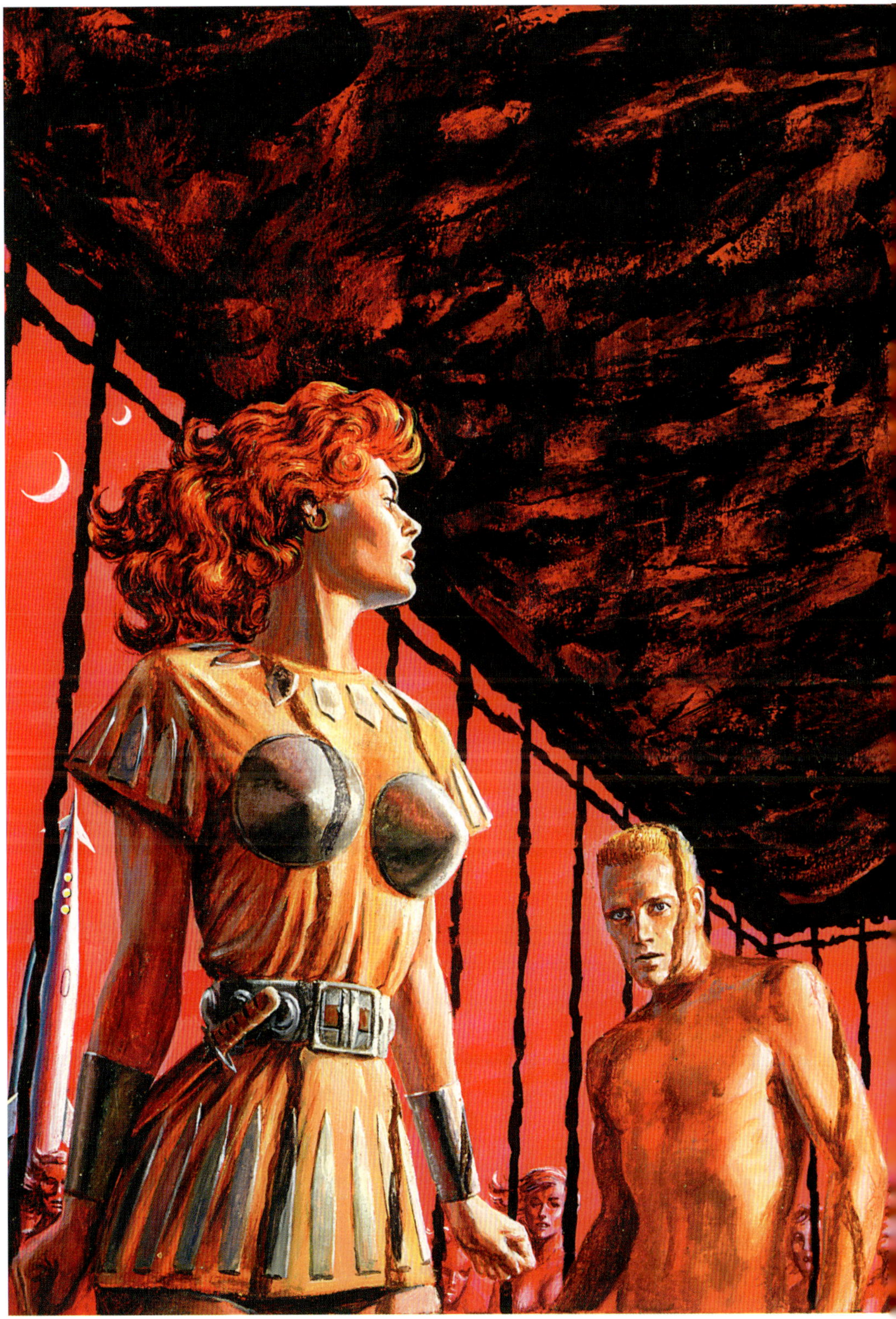

John Campbell's office when Ed came in. Freas had his sketchbook with him and did a quick sketch of Silverberg and Emshwiller with Campbell, which became the basis for the July 1958 *Astounding*'s interior illustration for Jack Vance's "The Miracle Workers," showing Silverberg as a young wizard and Ed as the older mentor. A few SF convention-going readers recognized the bearded pair.

By 1959 science fiction, as a field, was experiencing a morning-after moment. The high of 1952-53 had subsided into a sullen fatalism. In early 1960 Chicago fan Earl Kemp put out a fanzine called *Who Killed Science Fiction?*

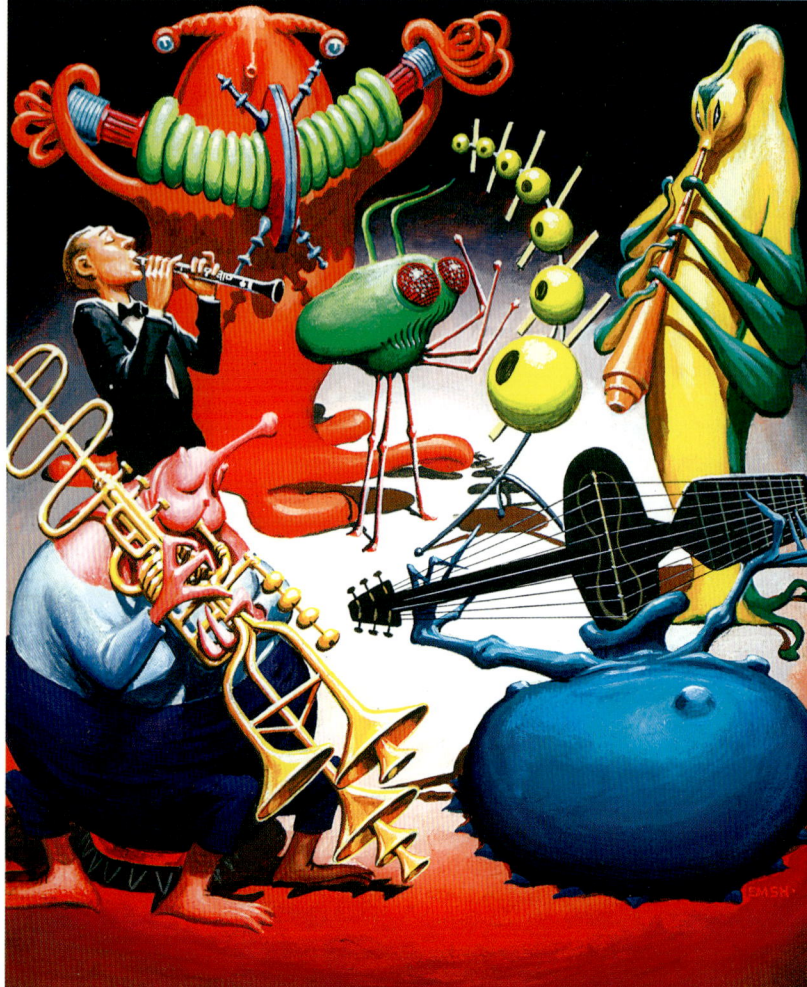

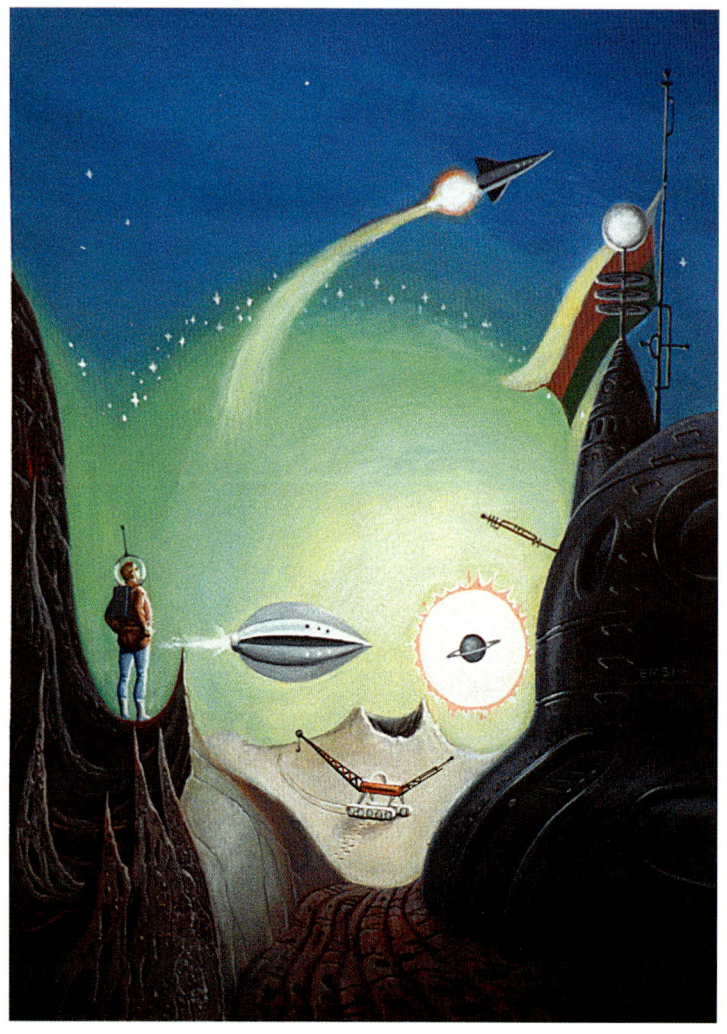

with an Emsh cover showing various SF archetypes gathered at a grave for the genre (pg. 100). Kemp had gone around asking SF professionals the headline question and gotten back many responses, quite a few taking issue with the reported demise of the field. Still, people like Silverberg and Freas were getting out of science fiction (although both would return in the mid-sixties).

While the SF magazines and small specialty book publishers had devel-

(top R) GALAXY. Feb. 1955. "Chamber Music Society of Deneb" Chamber Emsh indulges his penchant for delightful yet plausible aliens. Actually, this sextet is more of a cool-jazz combo, the Earthling clarinetist being the main clue. A genuine Daliesque chord is struck by the blue whatzis at bottom right. Some of these instruments, though rare in mid-century America, have a suspiciously authentic look. Clearly, all are playable, and the players well-suited to their instruments. Their jam session radiates a rousing sweetness and joy.

(bot L) Unknown publication, showing the influence of Richard Powers.

(top L) F&SF, Jan. 1961. "Time Lag" by Poul Anderson. When deep space beckons, the call to duty will of course be answered by women as well as men; who may also be (by current standards) multiracial. The tangle of glowing filaments that is her hair speaks - along with the false-color reds - of confronting hard radiations, magnetic fluxes, and the warp and twist of hyper-dimensions on her journey to the stars. Not to mention the "far look" in her quicksilver eyes. By rendering it in "hot" primary colors, Ed lends this vision a startling rawness and vital beauty.

(top R) VENTURE SCIENCE FICTION, Aug. 1963, "Turn Off the Sky" by Ray Nelson

(bot R) ASTOUNDING SCIENCE FICTION. Aug. 1956, "The Healer". A space traveler has been hauled out of the burning wreck of his ship by a passing country doctor…not from any colonial or Amish culture, but still a horse-&-buggy milieu. The alien humanoid, clearly a trained physician, can check a pulse and listen for a heartbeat; even so, he cannot save the dying astronaut. The sadness in the healer's face may be over-obvious - or else members of his race simply look that way. The observant viewer may detect that the doctor's arms have three joints, though his sallow hands are expressively human

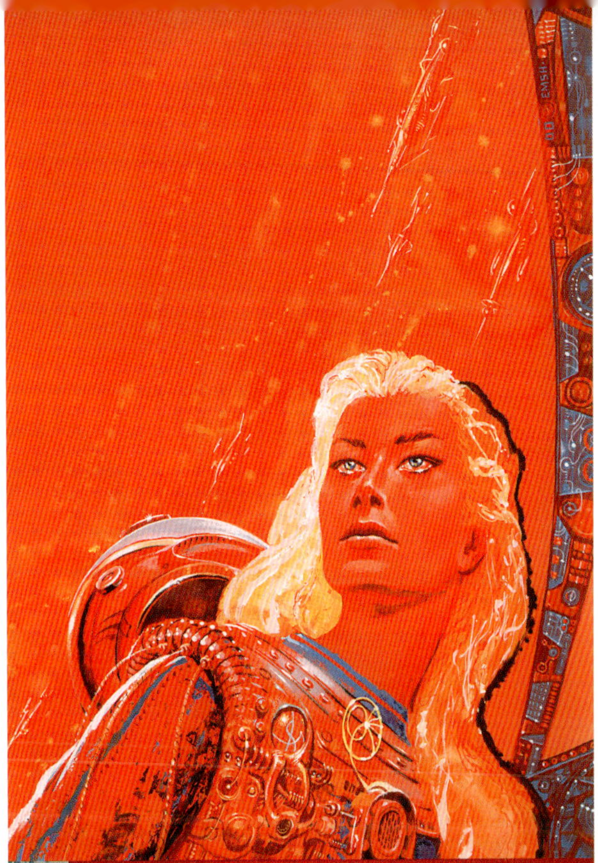

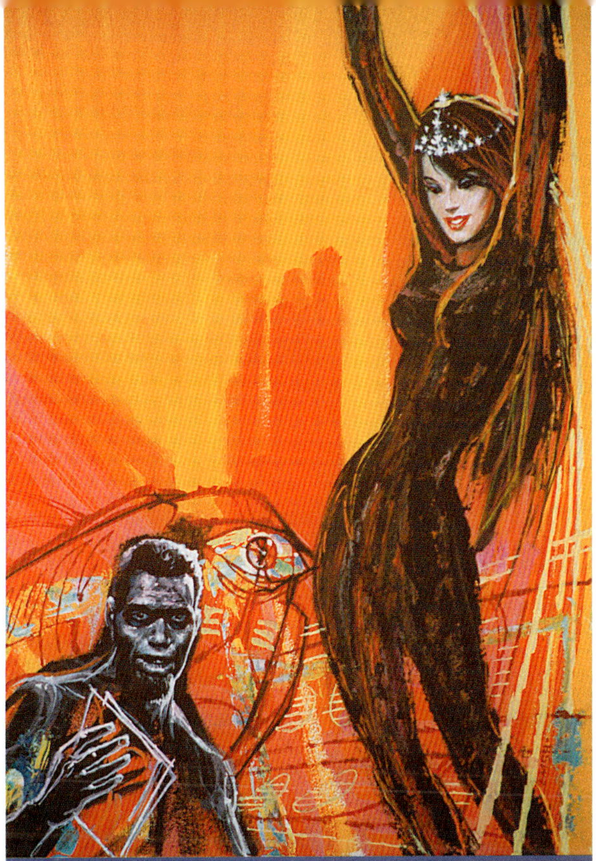

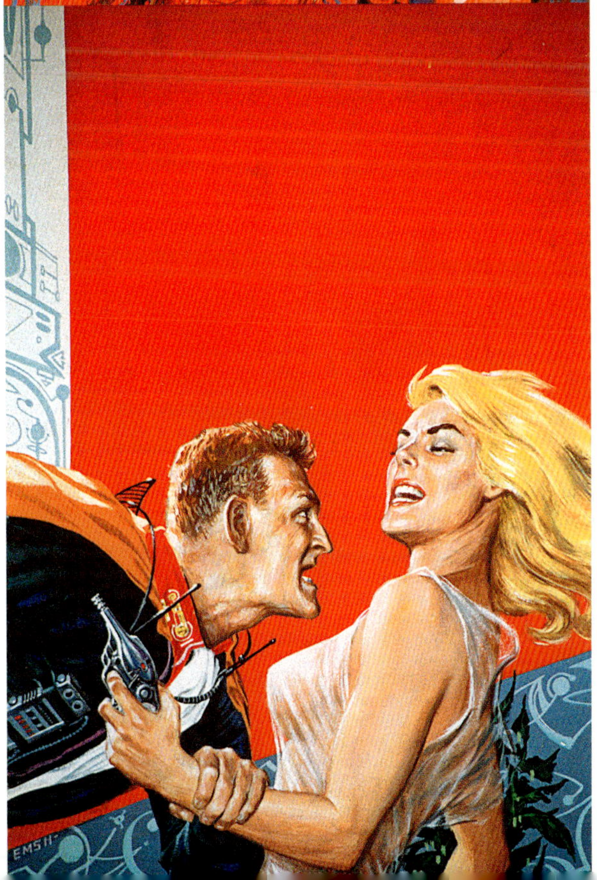

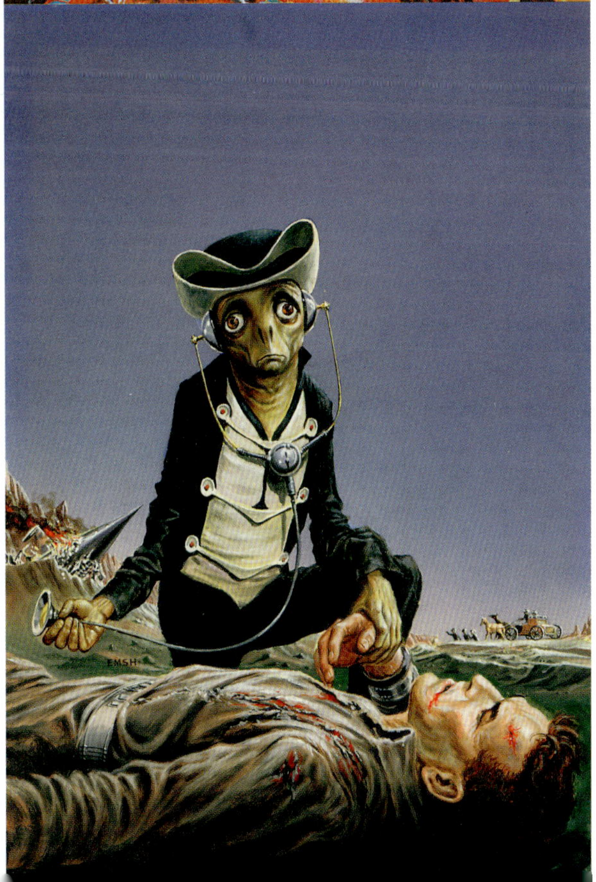

(bot L) INFINITY, Oct. 1958, "The Silent Invaders" by "Calvin M. Knox"

oped the field, the major publishing houses were now muscling in, and in a way helping to kill them off. Although not done deliberately, it was, nonetheless, more flowers on the coffin. Book publishers were mining the magazines for story collections and novelettes that they could expand into novels or use, in the case of Ace, for the unique format they had of putting 30,000 word "novels" back to back for their line of SF paperbacks. Science fiction authors found they could make more money from doing paperback originals.

Gnome Press and Avalon, like Ballantine and Ace in paperback, were bringing out one science fiction book a month. Avon published eight to twelve SF paperbacks a year, Bantam six, and Signet five. Ed had cracked most of these markets.

Even with many SF magazines folding, technically accomplished art with narrative content and a contemporary feel was still selling. Emsh had enough of a reputation to continue pretty much as he had throughout the fifties. The artistic rear guard, which still clung to its pulp palettes, went into other fields of commercial art, including what were then referred to as men's "sweat" magazines. These were adventure magazines geared to manly endeavors informed by war, hunting, and the encountering of willing women in exotic areas of the world. Ed, keeping his options open, did burly art for *Sportsman, Untamed, Lion Adventure, Man's World, See for Man,* and *True Action.*

Ed's style would change depending on whatever commercial art jobs came his way. "I received assignments from a wide range of people. These would run from a specific assignment where I was told practically where to place the people, and how and what they were to be dressed like and so forth, through the case where I was given a manuscript and given a free hand, and other cases where there's a discussion, give-and-take, an expression of ideas, to cases where they say: 'We want something different from last month. We had a black cover last month, we want a red cover this month.'"

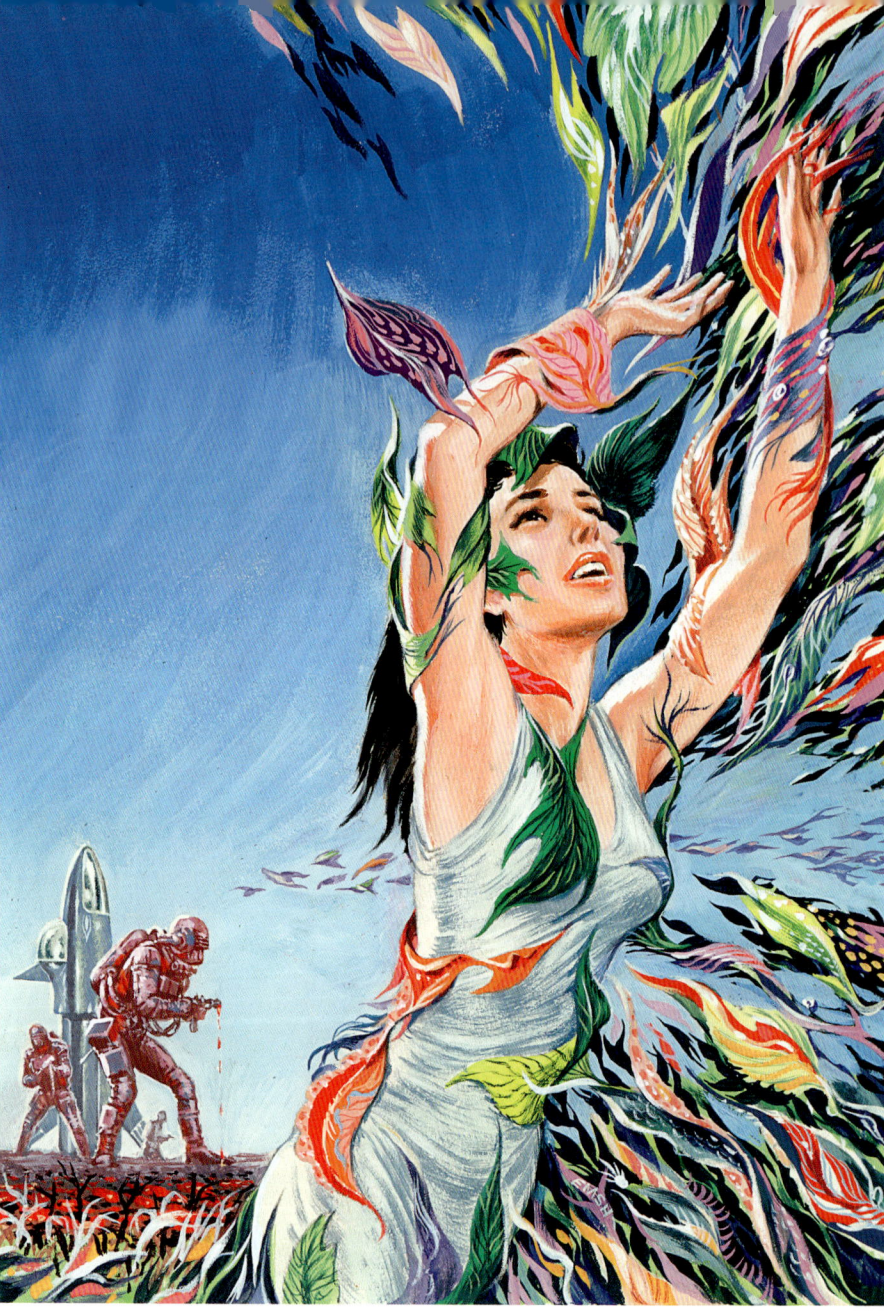

F&SF, Mar. 1963, "Hunter, Come Home" by R. McKenna. The eternal woman merges with the natural world. Sentient leaves swarm about her, possibly to absorb her into their mass-mind; rather than resist, she yearns for apotheosis, while the heavily armed men clearly don't. Poignant, thrilling, creepily seductive, portraying a radical transcendence, the scene is also layered with the profoundly sensual and erotic.

Eight

"Oh, there he goes again"

IN THE SPRING OF 1959, Ed was sitting in his studio chair in the semi-darkness. A film projector clicked and whirred beside him. The unedited Kodachrome film flickering on the opposite wall showed a young dancer (fourteen-year-old Nancy Fenster, the daughter of a Levittown dance teacher) superimposed over one of his animated "action-painted' abstractions. Ed had no idea how things were going to turn out while he was filming. Sometimes he photographed the art first, in his studio, sometimes the dancer, in her home — juxtaposition was done *in-camera* using the Bolex rewind function and frame counter to "sync" the two disparate scenes together. Ed wound up using Carol as a stand-in for Fenster when she was unavailable for filming. (Some time later when choreographer Alwin Nikolais saw the film he told Ed that he should have used Carol throughout the film. Her movement was much better than the teenage dancer.)

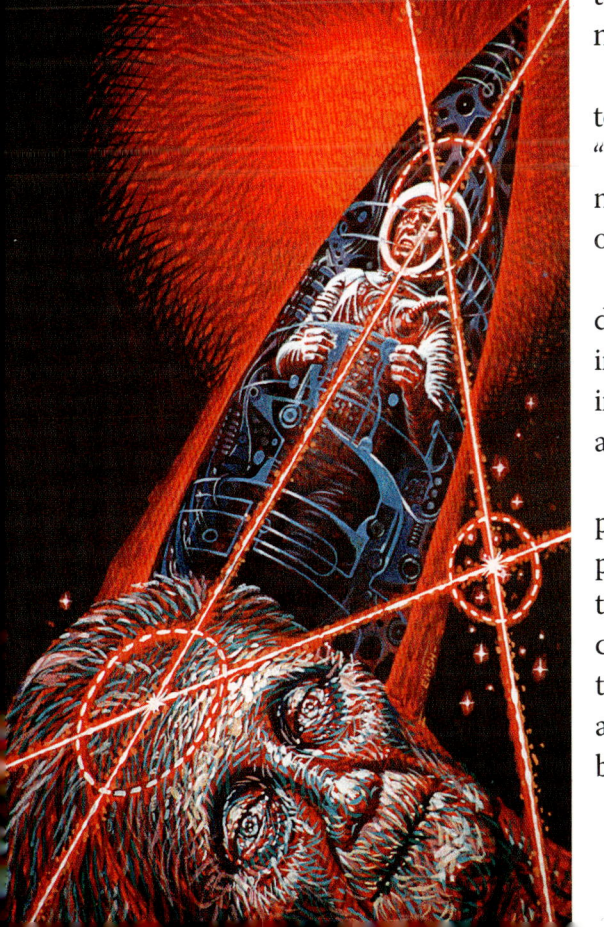

THE MAGAZINE OF FANTASY & SCIENCE FICTION. Nov. 1964, "The Third Coordinate".

He made some notes of frame counts to help him tie drawn and live scenes together, but already had the aesthetic structure of the film in his head. "…There were to be three stages: first, monochromatic and classical movements; second, polychromatic and agitated movements; and third, solid blows of color and bold sound and movement."

The film had the "gut" feeling he was always talking about when he described a particular abstract film he liked to non-artistic people. He was trying to pull off an emotional response on a kinetic and sensual level by mixing incompatible images to show "… an experience in the sense of the unfolding of a small universe." Ed re-ran the film all afternoon.

All artists claim a certain "vision" when they talk about their work. As Ed put it himself, "I was interested in making almost pure visual abstractions with practically no allegorical implication." Ed noticed at Cinema 16 screenings that there is a tendency for the mind to give order to anything lacking it and that a crowd's audible response to an abstract film would reinforce certain moods throughout the whole audience. But he was afraid of doing a fully abstract film, and knew that without some point of reference viewers of abstract art can become miffed at the intent of the artist.

With the introduction of a live figure, Ed undermined some of his own abstractionist theory and even the title, *Dance Chromatic*, gave the show away by avoiding the usual avant-gardist's love of cryptic movie titles. The editing went quickly (some of it already done *in-camera*) using an editing block made of wood with nails hammered through it to fit the film's sprocket holes. Later a percussive musical soundtrack, *Canticle #3*, by composer Lou Harrison (a John Cage colleague) was added and the film was ready to exhibit (pg. 102).

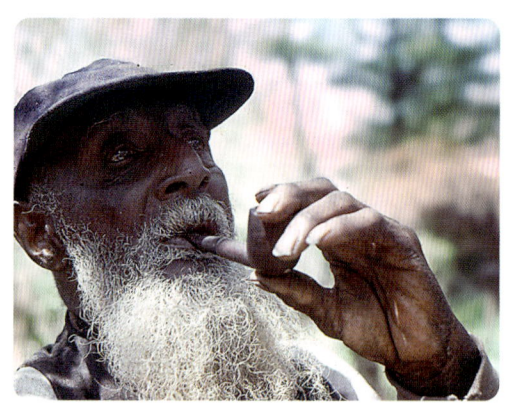

There was only one person to take *Dance Chromatic* to—Amos Vogel at Cinema 16. Vogel's own aesthetic judgment was final for the avant-garde films he chose to exhibit. The film society co-sponsored an annual experimental film award with Maya Deren, and after seeing the seven minute original print (spliced together with Mylar tape and with a separate rough-sync, quarter-inch tape soundtrack), Vogel said he would present *Dance Chromatic* to that year's jury, if Ed created a dupe of the film with a sound track in place. The jury included Deren, art critic Clement Greenberg, writer Parker Tyler, Barney Rosset, publisher of Grove Press, poet James Merrill, and Vogel himself. *Dance Chromatic* impressed the jury enough that it was given the Award of Exceptional Merit (the foundation's highest award). The film premiered on January 6, 1960, as part of that year's program for the Creative Film Foundation.

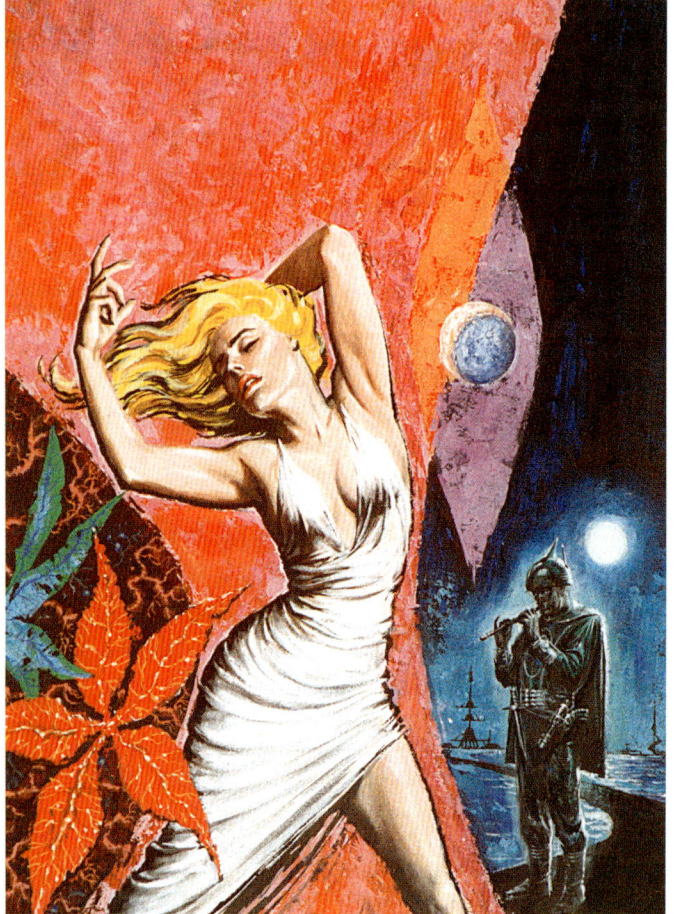

Cecile Starr, the cinema critic and educator, was in the audience: "I remember that when [it] was shown on the screen in the huge Needles Trades High School Auditorium, it took my breath away. The entire audience of several thousand people seemed equally impressed. Here was a dance film that was innovative and exciting in concept and execution, mature in both its technical and its artistic achievements." The grounding in commercial illustration and years of experimentation had turned Ed into a proficient filmmaker. Emsh was elated with the response to his film and rushed out and bought a new reflex-view Bolex 16mm camera to reward himself. (All his personal films throughout the sixties would be done wholly or partially with this camera.)

Avant-garde filmmaker Stan Brakhage

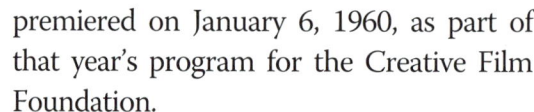

(top L) GEORGE DUMPSON'S PLACE. 1965. 16mm, Color, 7 min.

(bot L) FANTASTIC UNIVERSE, Jan. 1960, "A Twelvemonth and a Day" by Poul Anderson.

THIS PAGE
(top L) THE CURRENTS OF SPACE by Isaac Asimov, Lancer Books

(top R) F&SF, Jan. 1960, "A Little Girl's Xmas in Modernia". The gaunt threadbare android, playing at being both Santa and Daddy, is imbued with exquisite pathos. He even appears arthritic as he reaches up to fix the star on the tree.

(bot R) F&SF, June 1960, "Emsh's Version of a Soft Landing." An incredible "first encounter" moment between human and alien; in this case, an entire world. Using the body as landscape is a venerable notion in art, but never quite like this, disassembled and then reordered into a new topographic/organic whole. Emsh captures the moment just before the shock of recognition, as the explorer turns to meet a new-risen planetary eye. And giant hand, index finger raised to point, to hail…or conceivably, take exception to the proceedings

(bot L) FANTASTIC, Oct. 1963, "The Screen Game" by J.G. Ballard.

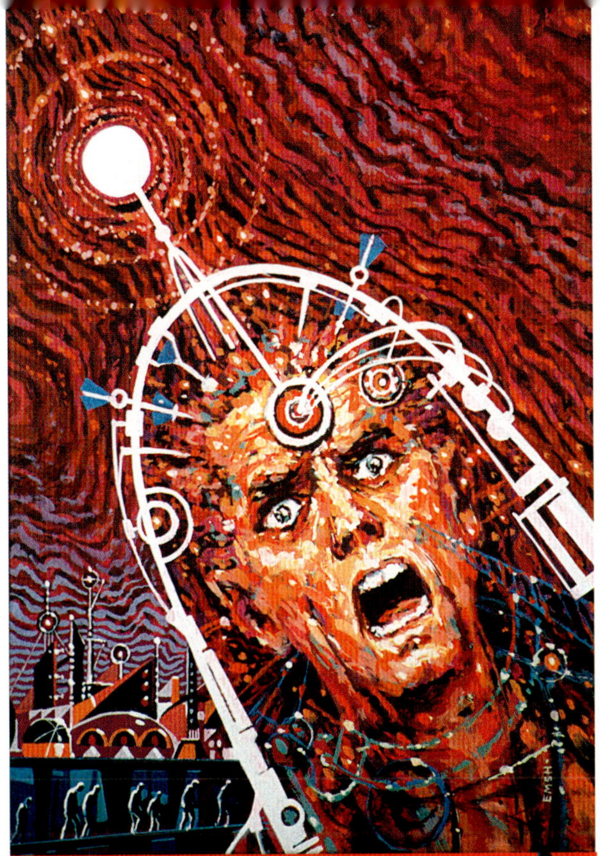

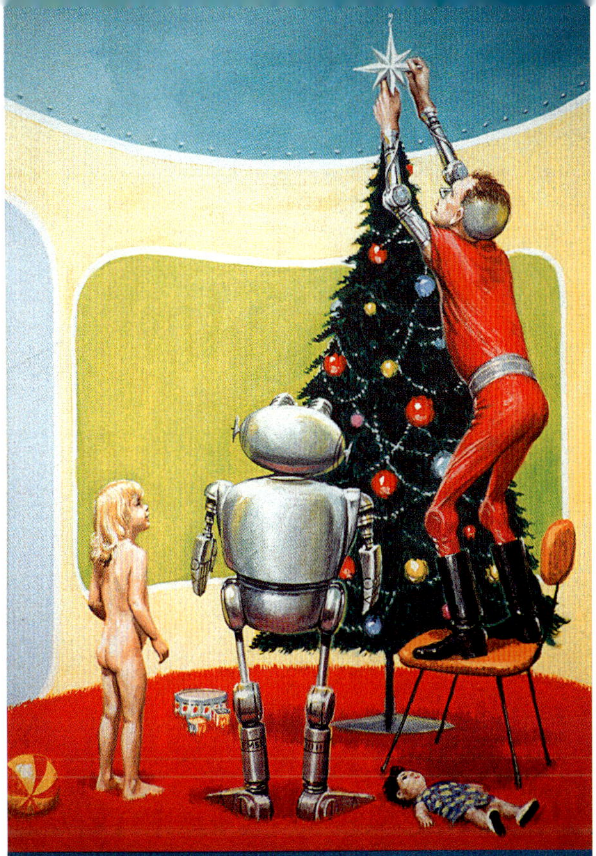

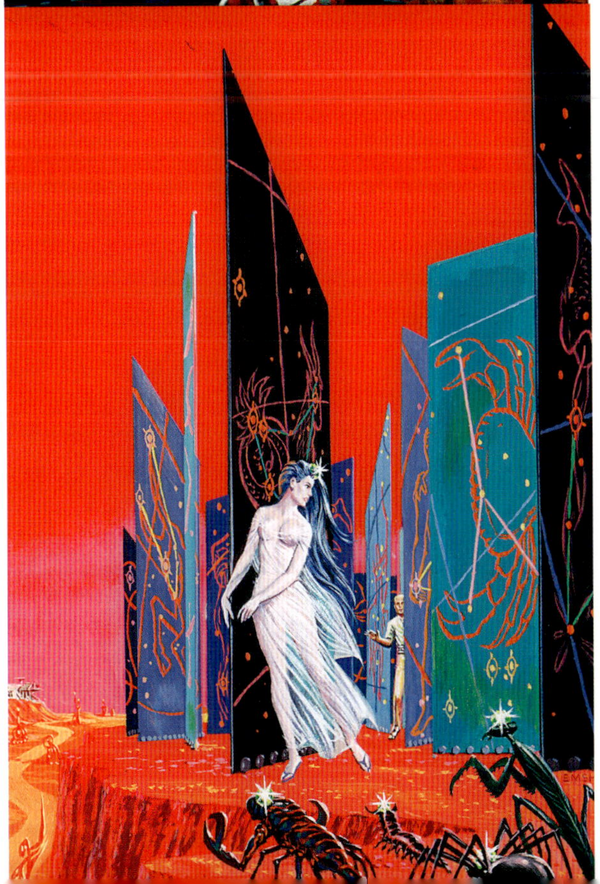

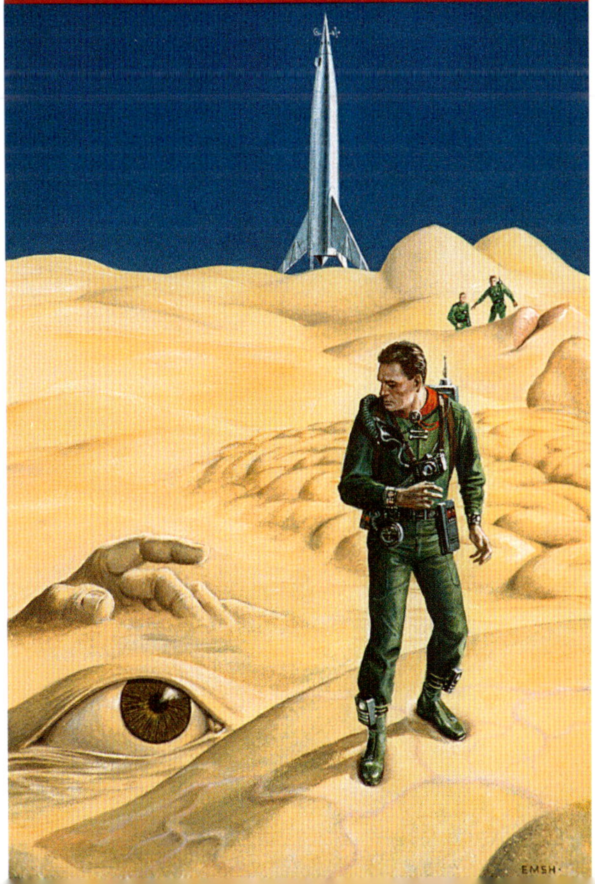

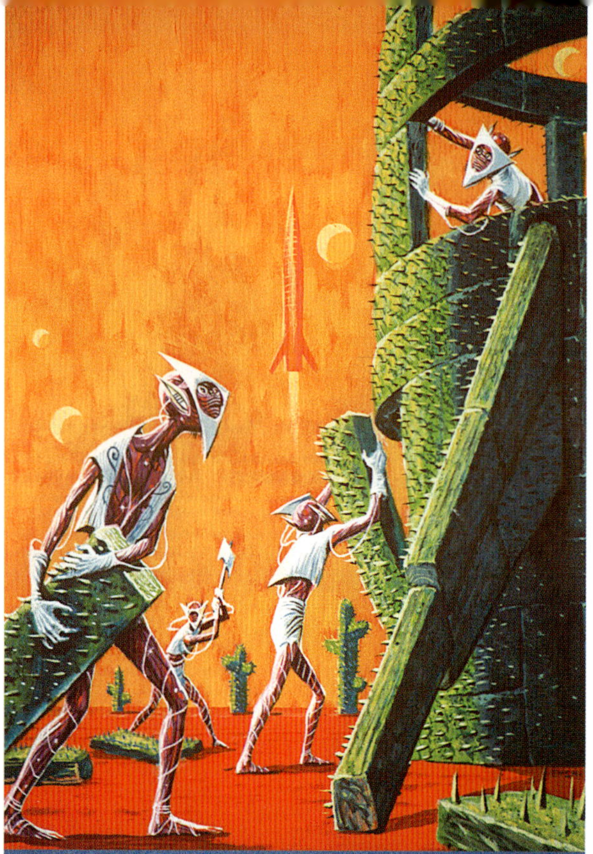

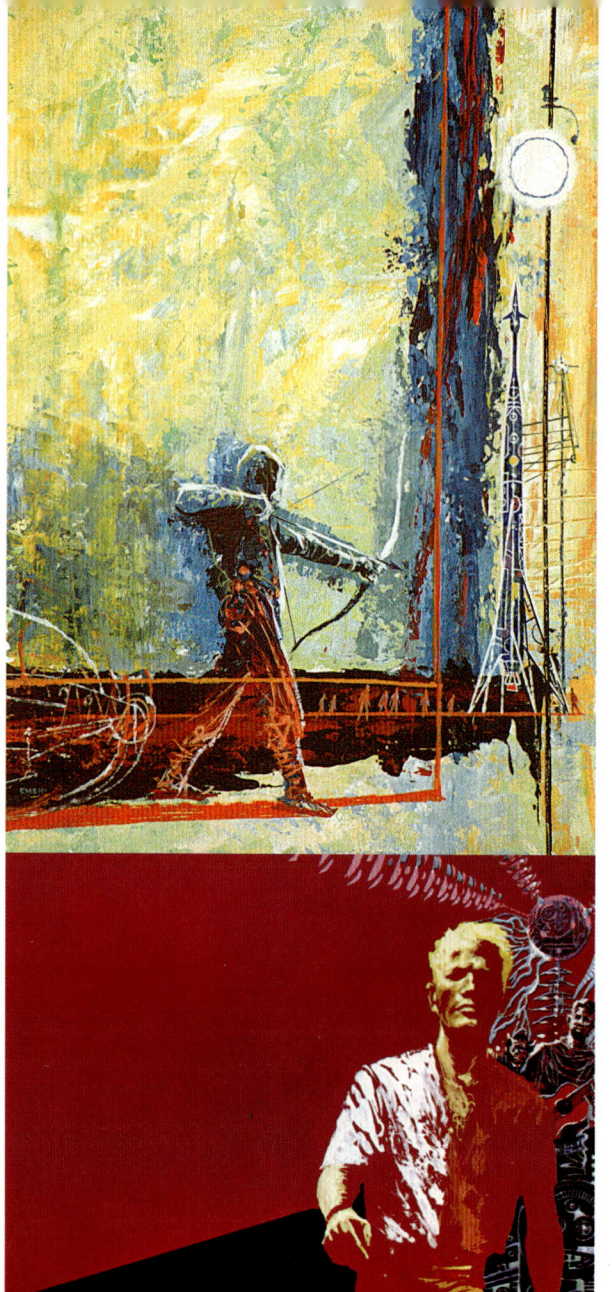

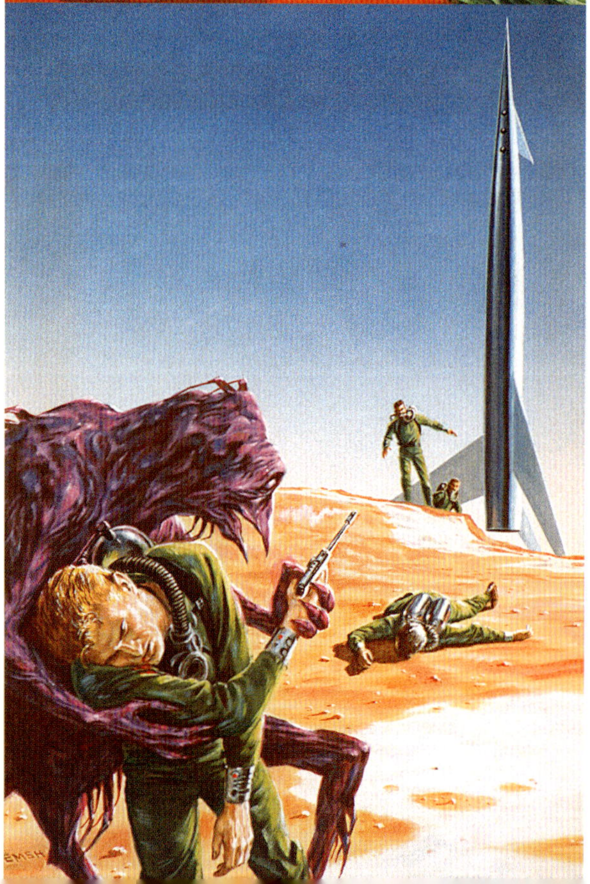

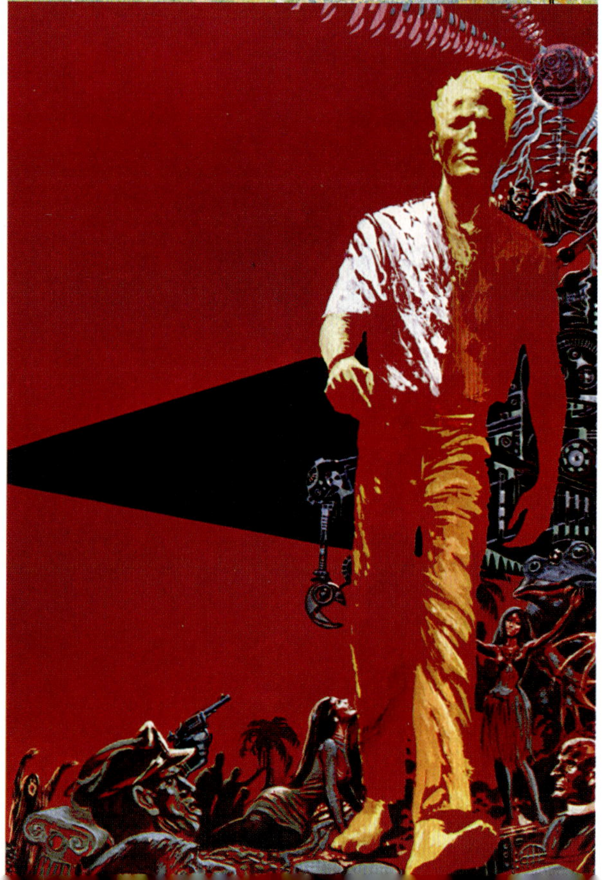

THIS PAGE
(top L) AMAZING SCIENCE FICTION. Dec. 1963.

(top R) F&SF, June 1963, "No Truce with Kings" by Poul Anderson

(bot R) F&SF, Oct. 1962, "The Journey of Joenes" by Robert Sheckley

(bot L) Unknown publication.

wrote to Ed after seeing the film, "What a perfectly wonderfully perfect experience…. The girl, Nancy Feinstein [sic]…comes thru as an incredibly (I might almost say indelibly) distinct personality created entirely out of film in (almost) opposition and/or inter-relation to paint. She is a non-painted (and non-dramatic-and/or — dance) personality portrait if ever I saw one."

From the beginning, Ed was outstripping everyone else in both technical knowledge and the elements without which any avant-garde cineaste can be dismissed as merely an "experimental filmmaker" — he had a fine artist's standards and skills. Only Norman McLaren and John Whitney matched or exceeded Ed's technical skills as independent filmmakers. Ed quickly produced *The Big Vacation* using animated cutout figures, and exhibited it, along with *Dance Chromatic*, at the 1959 WorldCon in Detroit. The films together made a strong impact on the midwestern fans who were not used to seeing avant-garde filmmaking.

In his films, Ed was fusing the motifs of science fiction, experimental film, and abstract expressionism. He had briefly considered using Alfred Bester's 1956 novel *The Stars My Destination* (which he had illustrated when it first appeared in *Galaxy*) as the basis for a film. The bleak, claustrophobic settings of the novel — a crippled spaceship and underground prison — would have involved an inventive adaptation. Ed thought the story would make a "fantastic film" if the elements could be worked out. This project was never realized— to many SF fans' regret, though there are visual elements of the story that appear in *Relativity* (pg. 126).

Filmmaking had a tremendous pull that drew creative polymaths like Emshwiller. The braiding of the technical aspect of movie-making and visual manipulation has attracted artists as disparate as Oskar Fischinger and Andy Warhol to film. Warhol was beginning to make a name for himself with pop art canvases that broke the post-war dominance of abstract art.

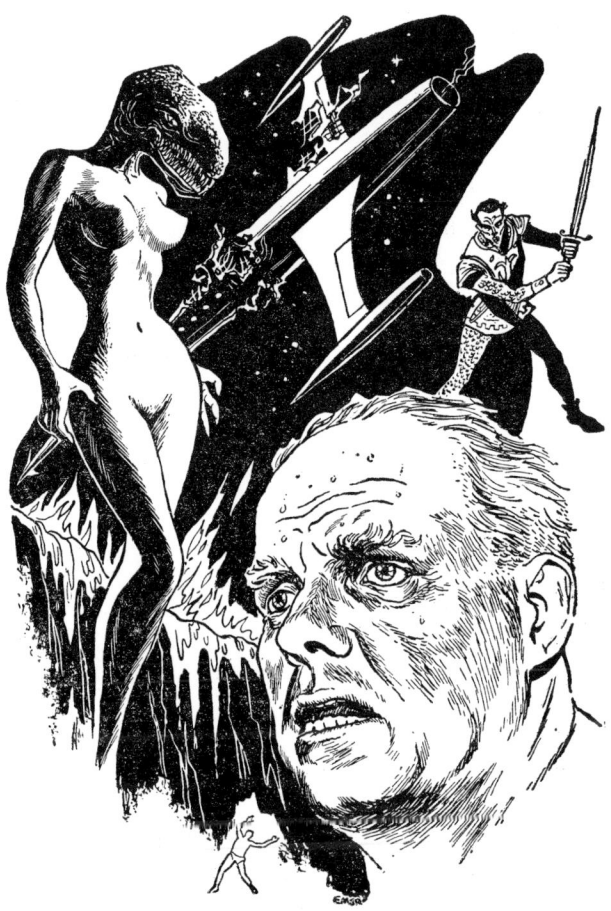

(top R) INFINITY SCIENCE FICTION, Oct. 1956, ink and scratchboard. "The Silver Corridor" by Harlan Ellison.

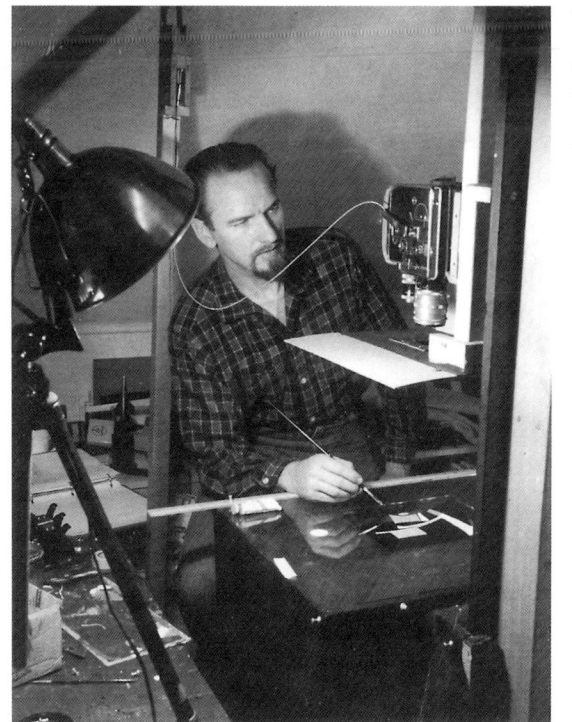

(bot L) Ed in his attic studio. Dec. 1960.

Warhol's early, deliberately static films (*Sleep* was a six hour film of a man sleeping) provoked controversy when shown by the FilmMakers' Cooperative at the Gramercy Arts Theatre in New York. Like Ed, Warhol was selling commercial art and paintings to finance his early films.

By the sixties Ed's movie-making equipment was taking over his attic studio. His homemade film editor and 16mm film rack, and pillowcases filled with various film stock clips would sit side by side with his art materials. Sometimes, when he was working on a film, he would laugh his head off at some weird relationship he saw coming together in the editing stage. Ed would tell interviewers that Carol must be downstairs saying, "Oh, there he goes again."

Ed took to carrying the Bolex wherever he went and would shoot whatever took his fancy. In this way he built up a personal film library that he would use to make later films. His son Peter's earliest memory of his father is that of a man holding a movie camera to his eye.

Almost immediately after *Dance Chromatic,* Ed was developing the images that would become *Transformation.* He was attempting a "found film," using every technique of animation

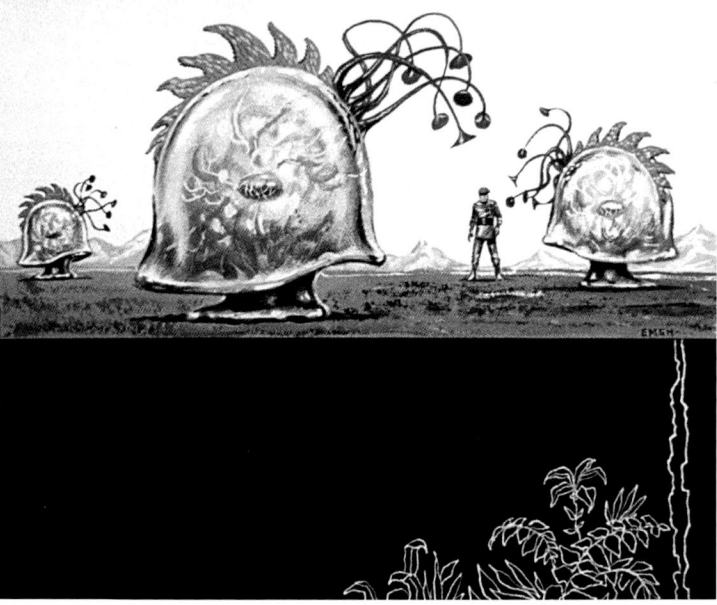

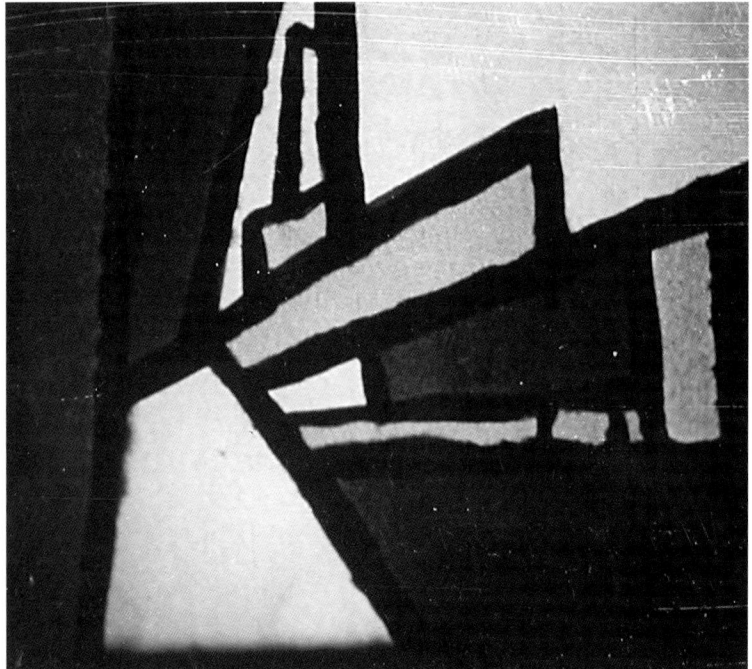

he could think of, letting each "spontaneous" scene suggest what followed. *Transformation* proved to be a mélange of Ed's abstract art made with crayons, paint, cutouts, and ink. "I just went on with it until it was done." While he was editing *Transformation,* Ed heard music composed by Gunther Schuller played on the New York radio station WBAI. Emshwiller visited Schuller and projected a cut of *Transformation*; after seeing the film Schuller pulled a reel from his music library and played it as the film ran a second time. Ed and

(top R) THE DARK DESTROYERS by Manly Wade Wellman. Unk date. Avalon

(L) TRANSFORMATION. 16mm, 5 minutes, color, 1959. Here his animated abstract paintings pass through evolving styles and techniques.

Schuller were delighted to find that the music fit the spirit of the film, and gave the abstract images a sense of relationship.

For his next film Ed began thinking about the definition of the word *lifelines*, "The lines in your hand, procreation, drawing a live nude, life drawing." Ed had his own score composed for *Lifelines*, but scrapped it after he decided that it did not fit the mood of the film, and a friend improvised a new musical soundtrack. Later on he would work on his own scores before or at the same time as he was creating a film. Although Ed had not planned to use a live figure in *Lifelines*, he thought of literary associations with the title and decided that a nude would emphasize the idea. This time he combined the dancer with his art, in this case integrating the drawn lines into radiating networks giving shape to the anatomy of the dancer. When it premiered, *Lifelines* received an award of distinction at the fifth annual Creative Film Foundation competition in July 1960 (pg. 118-119). On the same program, *Transformation* was given a special citation.

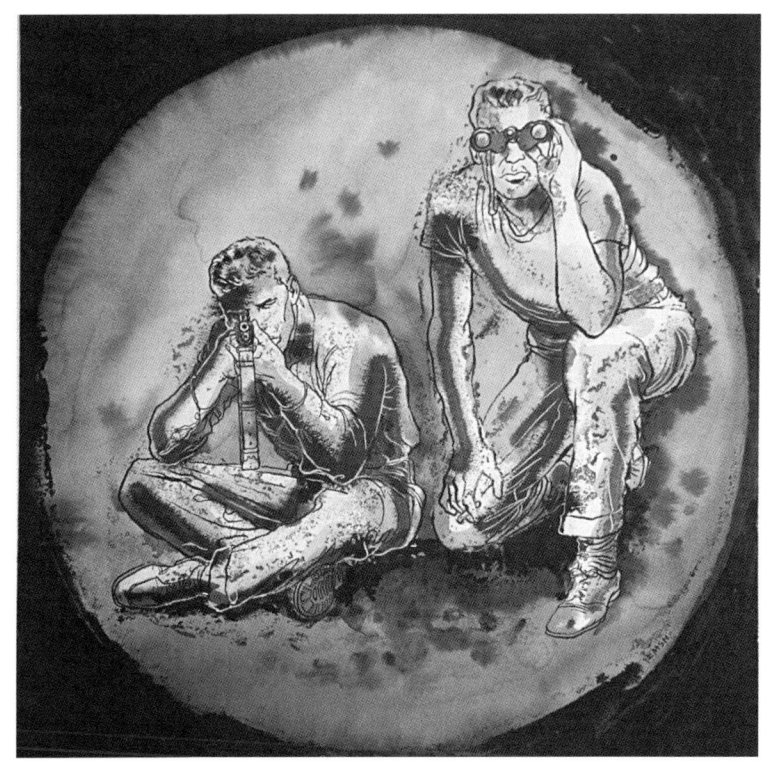

(top R) Unknown publication c. 1959.

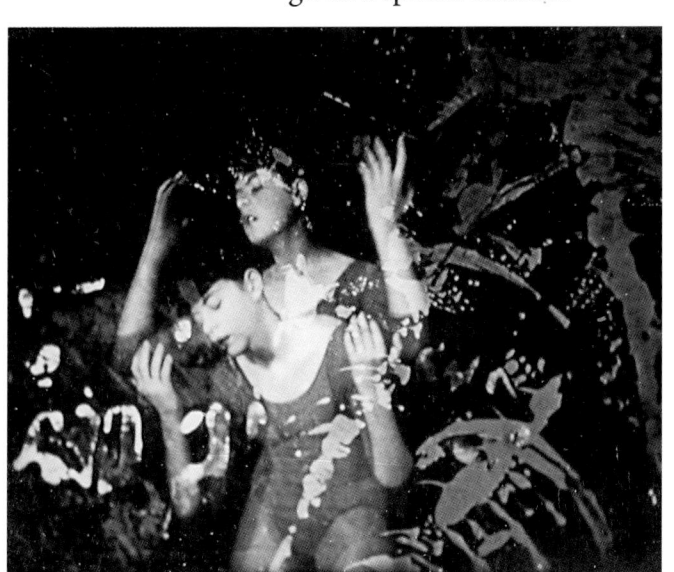

(bot L) Fifteen year old dancer Nancy Fenster in DANCE CHROMATIC. 16mm, 7 minutes, color, 1959.

At this time, the public reflexively associated underground and avant-garde films with nudity. This would bring larger audiences to some avant-garde film showings, but irked some filmmakers. While Ed used a nude figure in *Lifelines*, this nudity was presented in a demure manner that would have been in keeping with the increasing acceptance of naked flesh in mainstream American films.

In New York at this time independent filmmakers were chafing at what they believed was Vogel's imperial control of the exhibition and distribution of independent and avant-garde films. Cinema 16's side business of distributing independent films was akin to an aesthetic blessing, and within the dictates of independent cinema Vogel held a rather commercial view, taking only films he thought would generate an audience big enough to elicit multiple rentals.

Ed was still producing some striking SF art, especially for *F&SF*.

His approach to assignments had changed. Working strictly from stories and art directors' instructions, rather than coming up with his own narrative ideas, he introduced a decorative, brighter palette to his canvases; more ochres, oranges and crimson pigments, less umbers and burnt siennas to go along with a modernistic quirkiness he had developed. At one point Ed painted a half-eaten banana floating in the void of space. This peculiar bit of pre-Warhol Pop-ism was thought up by someone at *F&SF*, most likely Ed Ferman (pg. 109).

Oddly enough, with less demand on his creativity, Ed reached a popular peak as a hired hand. In 1960 he won the Hugo award for best artist, and would repeat the win in 1961, 1962, and 1964. Ed was constructing his paintings like a film director, most times he began by first daubing in a

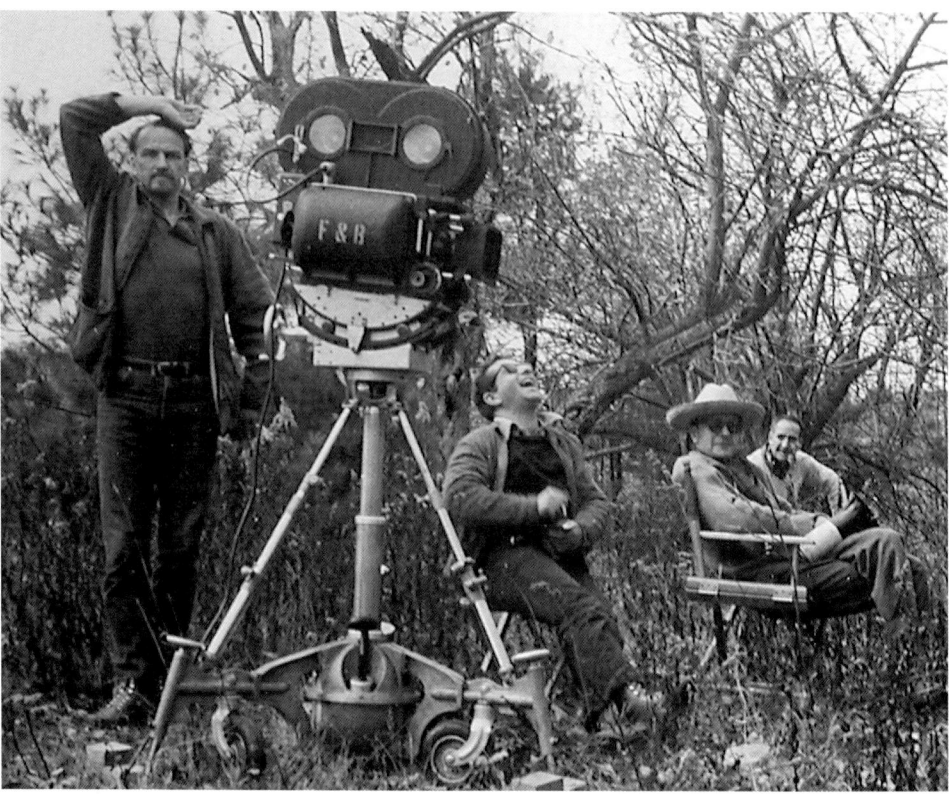

(top) Ed as cameraman in Vermont for HALLELUJAH THE HILLS (1962). Adolfas Mekas is sitting in chair with hat. The film was the American entry at the first New York Film Festival, and played at film festivals in Cannes, Montreal, Lodarrno, Mannheim, and London.

semi-abstract backdrop, then setting up his characters with one dominant figure or face in the foreground. When Ed was painting, Carol or their children would go up to watch his progress. They never lost their sense of fascination while watching a picture develop.

In many cases an editor would only give Ed a quick run-down of the scene to be illustrated. Ed preferred reading the manuscript "…to get my own feeling for it, feeling for the characters…and maybe know what they look like, rather than just get a couple of lines, which happens all too often in some places…. I've done many, many jackets…many illustrations where to this day I've never read the story."

Don Wollheim, the editor-in-chief of Ace's science fiction line, was an ex-boxer and another fan turned pro. He also had complete control of what appeared on the covers of his SF paperbacks, and believed strongly in having every one of his SF book covers showing a spaceship or at least one alien—preferably both. Ed quickly became one of Wollheim's main cover artists, alternating on front and back covers of Ace Doubles with Ed Valigursky. His first Ace art was for Phillip K. Dick's *The Man who Japed*, (pg. 123) a story about a terrorist in a future dystopia using mockery as a weapon. Ed captured the moment after the anarchist decapitated a statue of the tyrant and is running through a nighttime futuristic city with the head tucked under his arm.

Ed would do two or three sketches for a particular assignment, making each as different as possible in style, content, or action. At times he would do one purposely-bad picture to get a client to pick the one he actually wanted to paint. After a painting was accepted, Ed took rejected sketches and modified them enough so they weren't so obviously derivative from a published story or book, and attempted to sell these elsewhere. "Sometimes I think [the rejected ones] are *better* than the ones that have been selected — that happens frequently these days."

Ed was the first science fiction artist to break the $100 barrier for a painting sold at an SF convention auction. This was at the 1963 Discon where the cover to the July 1963 *F&SF* (for Robert A. Heinlein's *Glory Road*) sold for the high bid of $110 (pg. 107). Usually these early science fiction convention auctions were full of paintings that publishers had sold or given away, few came directly from the artists. Wollheim at Ace had the policy of not returning original art. In the fifties, Ace classified art as a service and not a product to avoid paying a sales tax, but the IRS didn't believe in this sort of having your cake and eating it philosophy, and Ace was forced to buy the art outright and pay the sales tax.

Except for the *Magazine of Fantasy and Science Fiction*, fully representational art was all that SF magazine editors wanted. It didn't matter that the subject depicted might be impossible to represent visually. Crystal clear

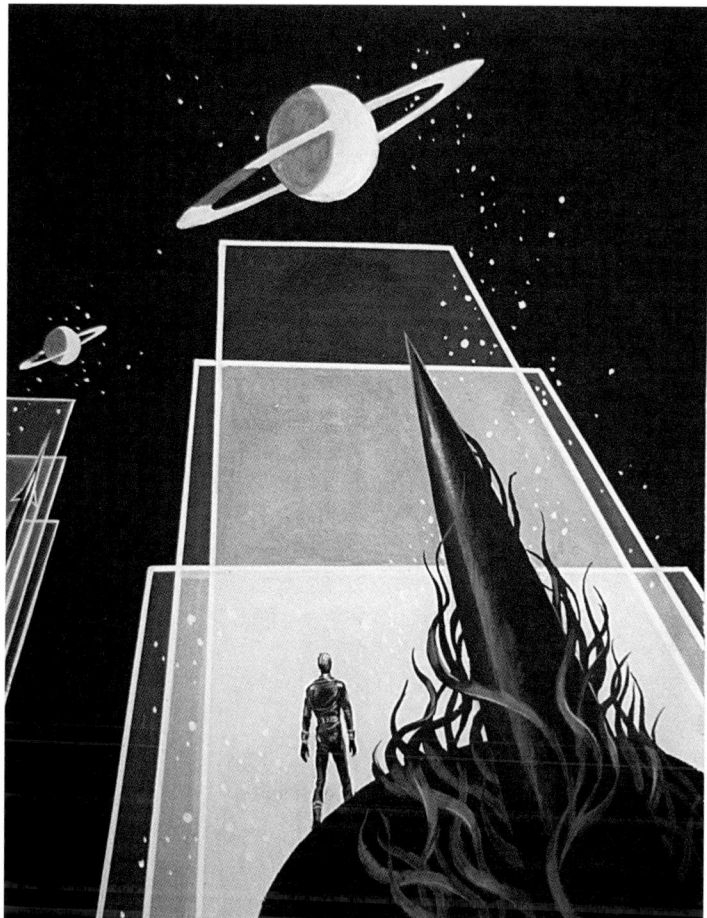

(top R) THREE STEPS SPACEWARD by Frank Belknap Long. 1963. Avalon

(bot L) THE MEN FROM ARCTURUS by Russ Winterbotham. Unk date. Avalon

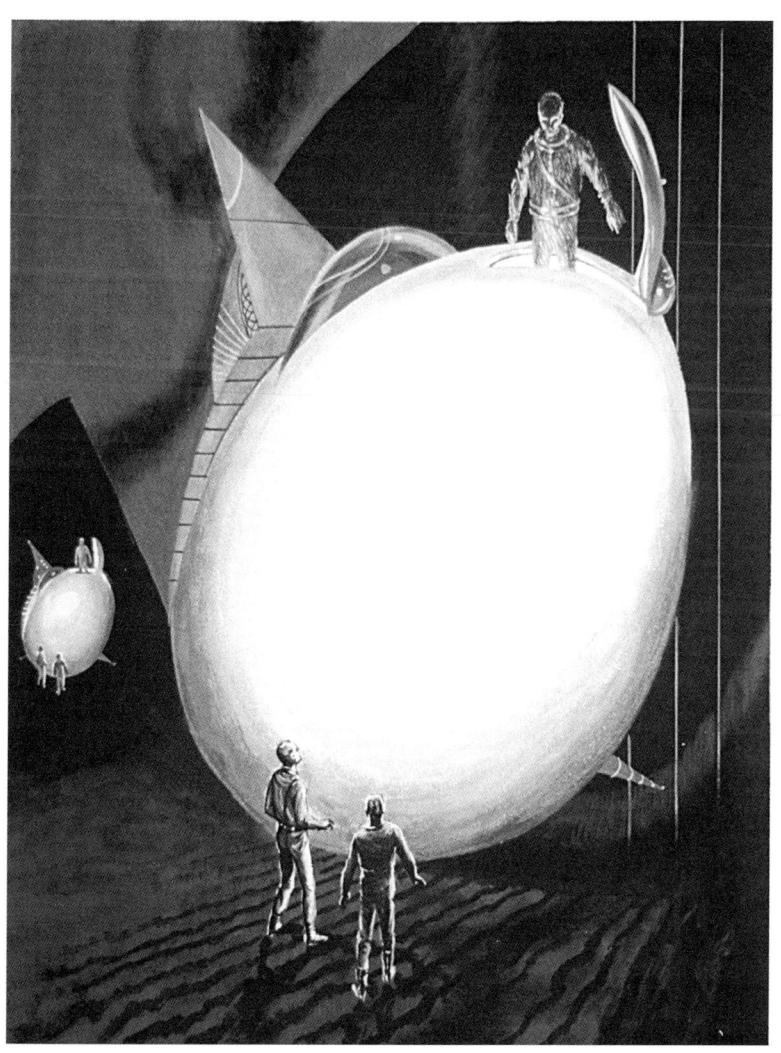

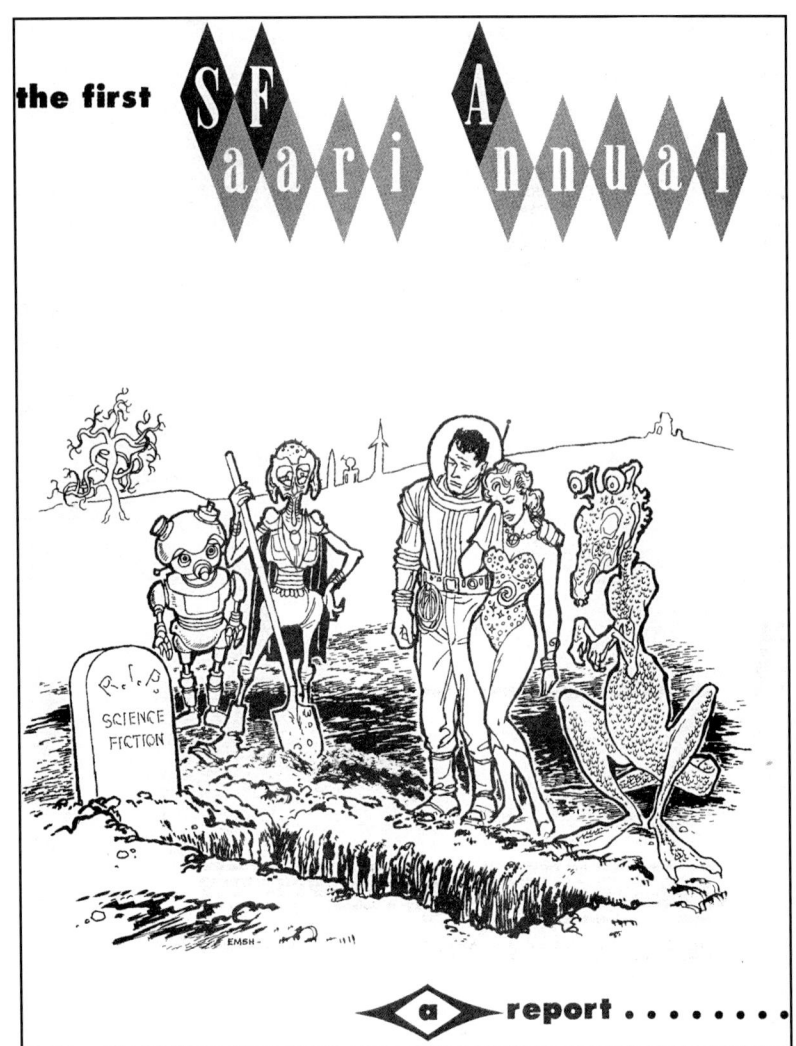
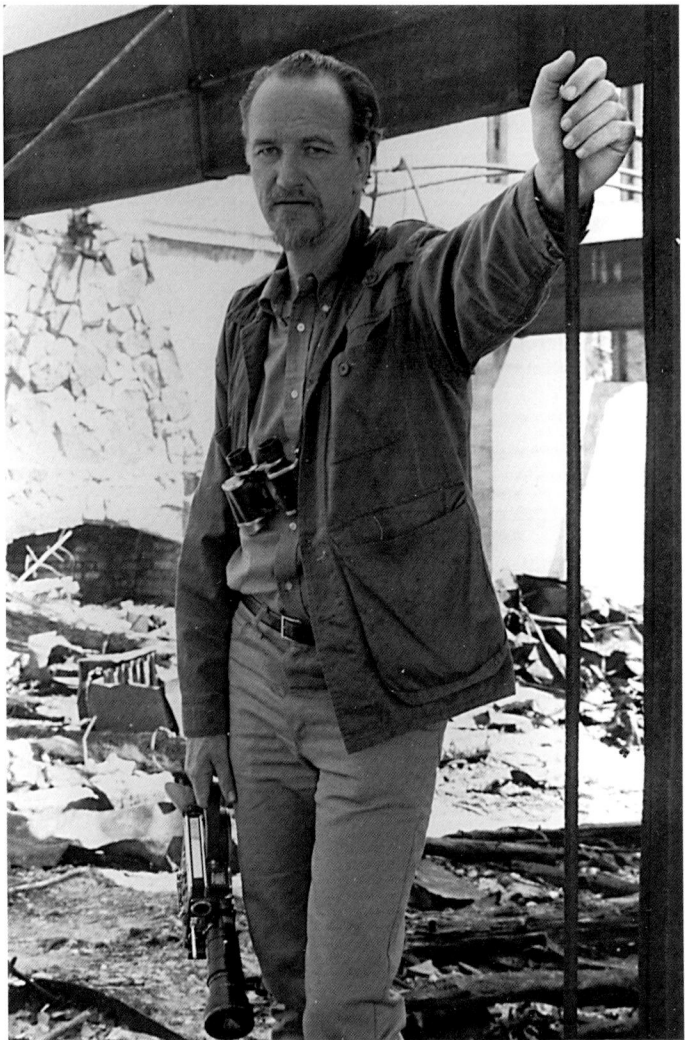

renderings of sights and scenes familiar to SF fans and readers were expected, in the same way some patrons of regional, small museums expected to see landscape paintings of the world immediately familiar to them. Ed saw each art client as a brand and used a slightly different style for each. His own natural style of art helped set the look for the *Magazine of Fantasy and Science Fiction*.

Ed's cover art for the 1960 Ace Double Novel Book edition of *Earth's Last Fortress*, by A. E. van Vogt (pg. 139), shows rocket ships, but Ed painted a frantic dogfight in the pale-red sky, using explosions of color, dots, and swirling exhaust contrails to give an abstractionistic bent to the nightmare battle. A pile of bodies seen in the receding background barricades a ruined city. In the foreground fresh soldiers are ready to sacrifice themselves in the ceaseless war of van Vogt's novel. Ed painted a brick wall behind the soldiers—who are lined up as if before a firing squad. In one 6" by 10" image (printed on a 3" by 5" paperback) Ed managed to capture much of van Vogt's story.

(top L) WHO KILLED SCIENCE FICTION?. SaFari Annual. 1960. Edited by Earl Kemp.

(top R) Ed on film set. C. 1962.

VENTURE SCIENCE FICTION (the companion magazine to F&SF). May 1957.

After Eve came along in 1955, Susan was born in 1957. In February 1959 Carol wrote to Judy Merril, "By next month we'll have 3 babies! I must rush back to writing. I've got a kind of frantic feeling it's my last chance — hope not." Peter was born early in 1959. Ed was the sole support of the family, and used this fact to get away from many domestic duties. Carol was once asked if she was happy to have a technically minded husband around, but she responded that just because Ed knew how to fix machinery didn't mean he could use the washing machine.

Ed was handy when he wanted to be. He once went to have some film developed and was told that the automated processor was broken — Ed talked the owner into letting him look at the machine, and after pulling some ribbons of film from the interior, and making some adjustments, got it working again.

It seemed like Ed was always working on some piece of art or taking a long trip in connection with some film — Carol was left alone with the kids and a balky automobile. They had not planned on having a bunch of children so close together. Carol was grateful that ... *Ed's work ... made the money that kept us going.*

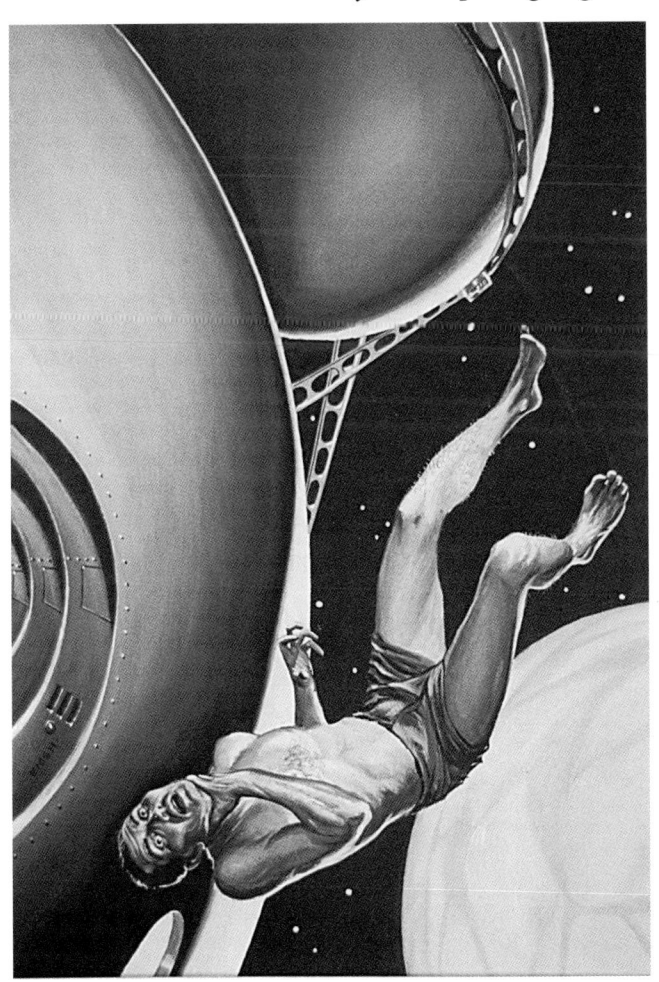

Even with his many long absences, by all accounts Ed was a good father. A very young Peter once had a nightmare and woke up screaming. He remembers a very tall man gently singing: "I'm Quacky! I'm Quacky! I'm Quacky the little white duck!" while doing a silly little dance. "He was ... not necessarily the finest improvisational dancer." Later on, Ed made a little stop-motion animated film for Peter of "Quacky the little white duck" using cardboard cutouts. Peter would sit on Ed's lap while he painted. "I could watch as— right in front of my eyes — people, monsters, robots, space ships, entire *worlds* were slowly born."

A teenage Levittown neighbor, Bill Griffith, who would grow up to become the syndicated cartoonist of *Zippy the Pinhead*, remembers Ed as a "man's man," tooling around on a motorcycle, working at home as an artist, and making films unlike any Bill had seen before. Bill called Ed a beatnik, a misnomer for the artist. Ed used Bill as a model for his August 1955 cover for *F&SF* (pg. 59), and the September 1957 issue of *Original Science Fiction* (pg. 44), which showed young Bill hijacking a rocket ship while an army general threatens him on the view-screen. (Bill's father was the model for the general.) Ed also took the time to make a professional-looking sign for Bill to use in his neighborhood lawn mowing business.

Carol knew that the few pennies a word that she received for her stories were little more than an ego boost now that she was putting an

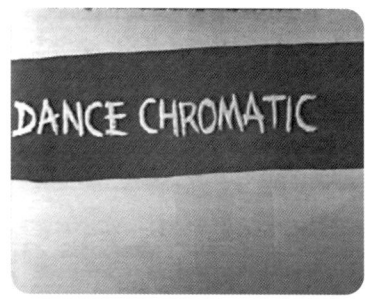 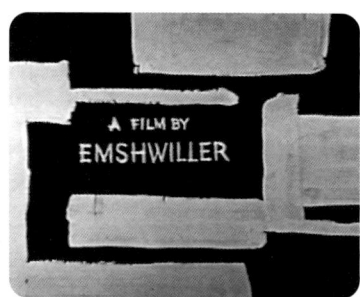 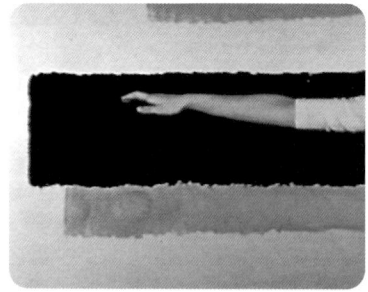
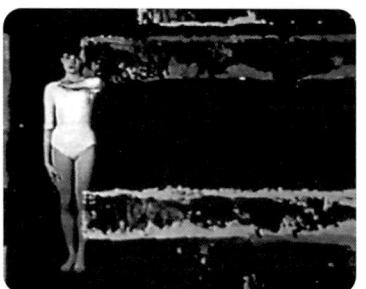 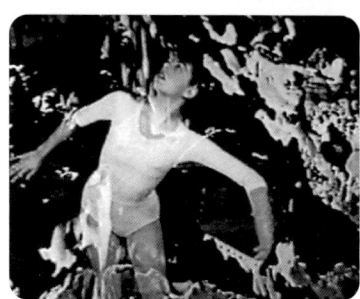 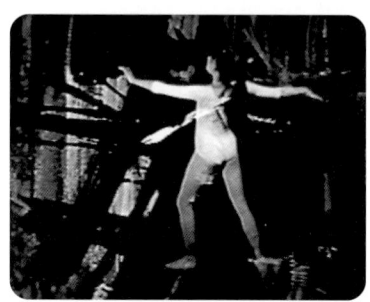
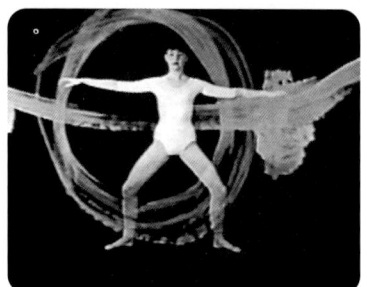 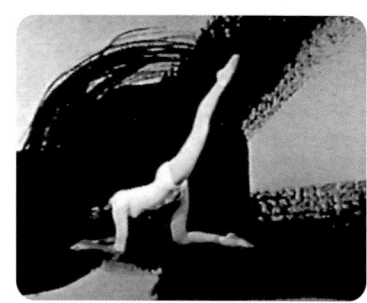 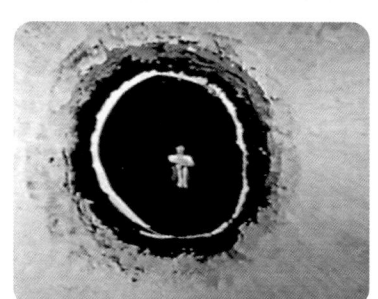
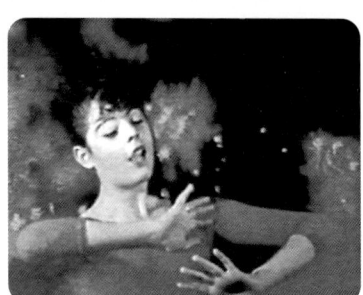 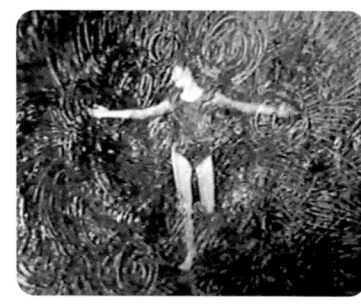 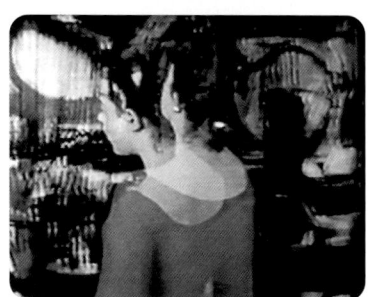
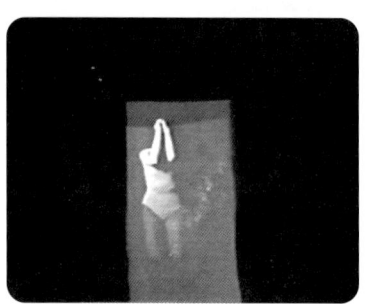 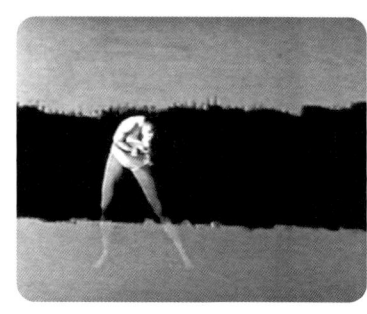 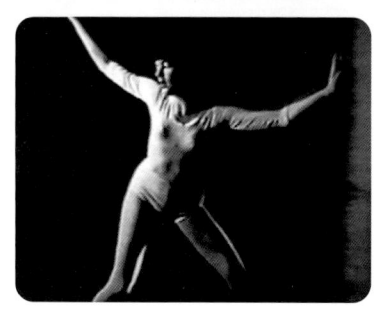

DANCE CHROMATIC. 1959, 16mm, 7 minutes, color.

"The first serious film I made, DANCE CHROMATIC, was cine-dance. For a few years I had been making cinematic doodles. Then, around 1957-1958, started recording the development of some of my abstract paintings. Their permutations on the screen were sometimes as interesting, if not more so, than the final paintings. I decided to make a film involving my painting, but the film was to be the end product, not the paint of the canvas. I'm not sure why, but I wanted to include a dancer. Perhaps it was because the paint seemed to flow and dance. Perhaps, because the dancer would add a human element, a basic appeal. In any case, I knew I wanted to combine the two.... I made DANCE CHROMATIC, combining images of the dancer Nancy Fenster with my animated, abstract paintings. This was done by double exposing the two in the camera. Although sometimes I did the artwork first, I found that by filming the girl first, then following my notes carefully as to where her movements occurred, I was able to do the artwork so that the two functioned best together." — EE-

PAGE 103
(top R) F&SF, Nov. 1962, "The Secret Flight of Friendship Eleven"

(bot L) F&SF, Aug. 1959, "Day at the Beach" by Carol Emshwiller. A future Madonna and child, post collapse of civil society. The norm is now hairless, so the little brown kid with Keane-like eyes and coal-black mop is the mutant. We intuit he has a strange brain. Note emblematic decorations nailed to cathedral-style window, and suburbia gone awry.

avant-gardist slant to her writing — when she could find the time to write. Carol wrote Judy Merril, *I've always wondered if the other writers were doing their laundry? Washing dishes? Painting walls? I mean Samuel Beckett, for example? Or Kay Boyle? Anne*

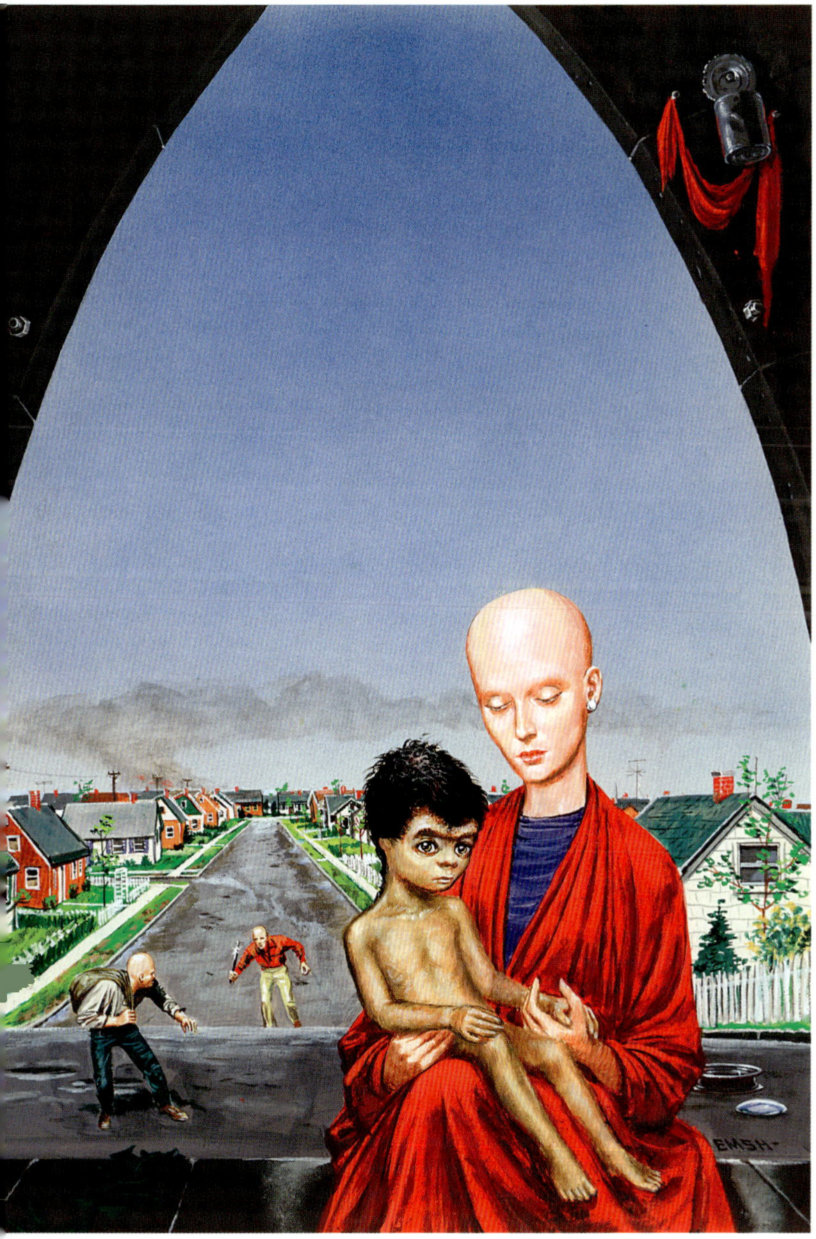

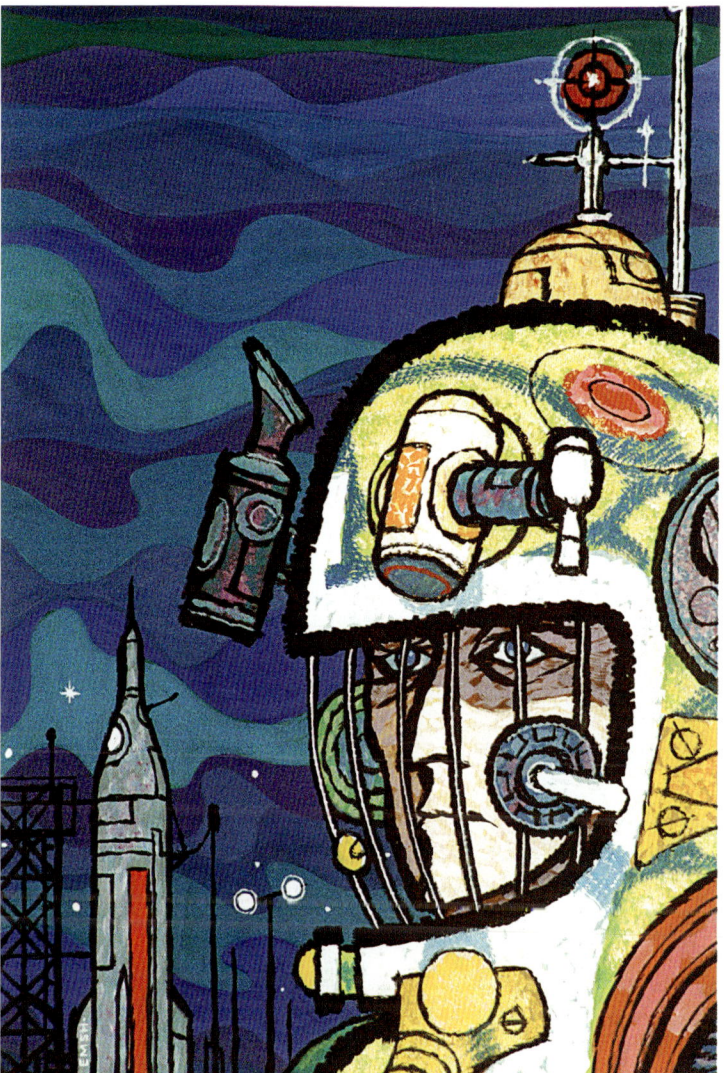

Waldman? Anaïs Nin? Of course, Ed's films were not making any money either. (It would take many years of rentals for them to even make back their production costs.)

Ed, a demon perfectionist with verifiable details in his art, would send Carol into Manhattan to get photo reference shots from the Bettmann Archives (typically of things mechanical). She would also lend a hand with Ed's films, but never got any credit unless she wrote material. *If I helped him it was the same as if he was doing it. He didn't think that someone else is doing it. I remember I once got mad at him, and I said, "I worked on this, and this, and this...." So on my* next birthday he made a little plaque listing everything that I had done, all very nicely written out.

Writing may have seemed a subconscious act of creative defiance to Carol. *I do know that I was very frustrated back [then].... I got a lot of that out of my system through stories.*

Ed began working as a cameraman on other people's projects. He called these "external" projects, to differentiate them from his "internal," or self-generated films. In October 1960, he was introduced to Peter Kass, a New York theatrical director. Kass told Ed about a 35mm experimental feature film he was planning with the working title "Into the Arms of Fallen Men." Neither had worked on a feature film before and Kass said, "Why don't we do one together?" Ed did not like parts of Kass' script.

"Well, could I change it so that you

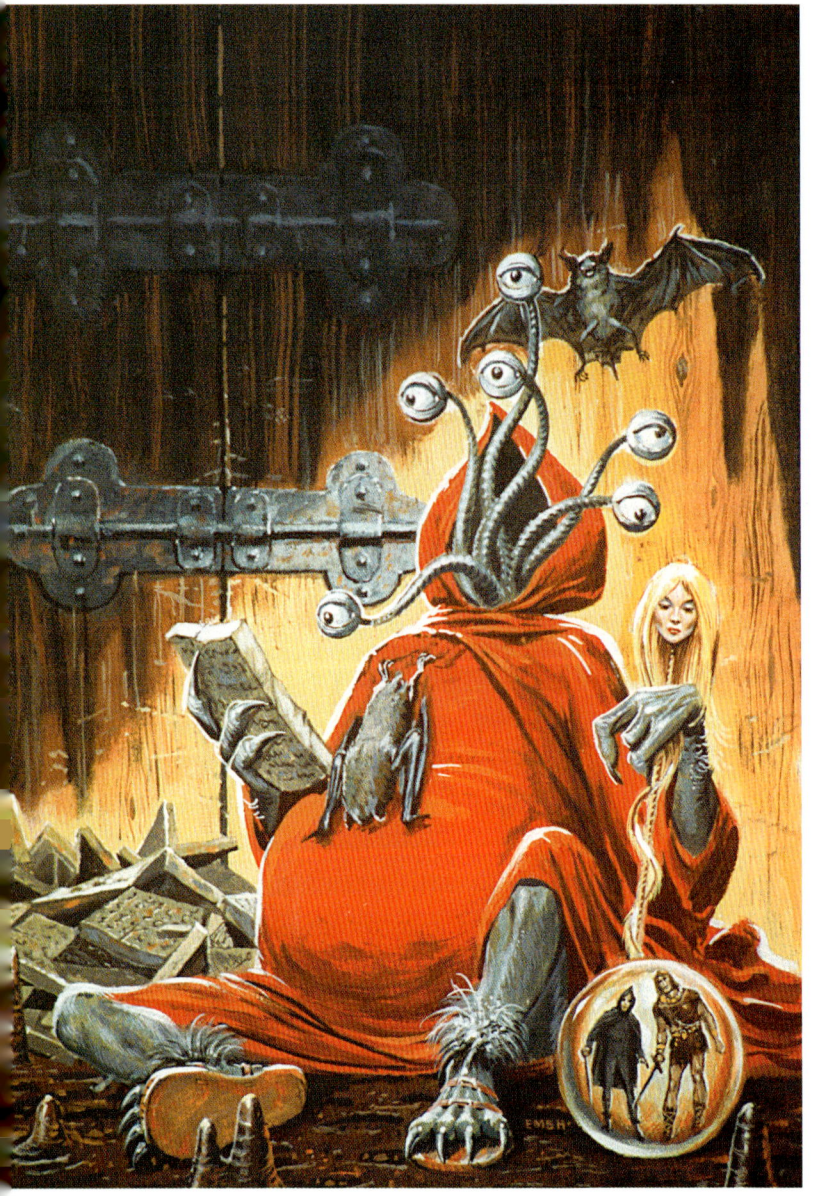

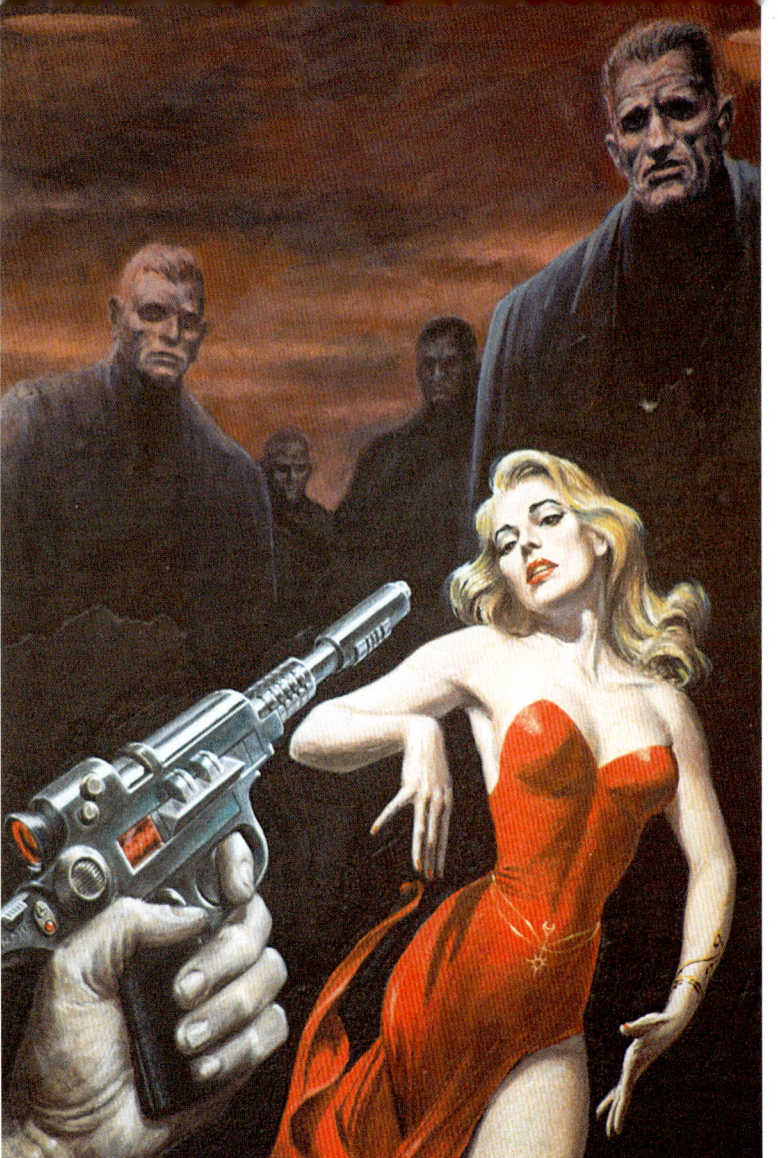

(bot L) FANTASTIC STORIES OF IMAGINATION. May 1964. "Adept's Gambit" by Fritz Leiber. The blurb for this story in the previous issue informs the reader: "Once again Fafhrd and the Grey Mouser roam the magic-haunted lands that spread outward - and down - from Lankhmar. This time, guided and guarded and appropriately bedeviled by Ningauble of the Seven Eyes (the undescribable [sic], who for the first time has been visualized in a superlative cover by Ed Emsh) our heroes experience excruciat-

would be interested?" Kass asked.

Ed and Kass spent a week together arguing over the rewrite until both were satisfied, if not happy. Ed became the cameraman and co-producer on *Time of the Heathen,* a murder mystery with eccentric characters. Besides helping with the script, photography, and doing animation for the film, Ed invested $4,000, out of the $20,000 total budget, for a quarter interest in the picture. He expected that before completing the movie he would have put into it a total of $10,000 in time and cash.

The final script combined a racial subtext with French New Wave storytelling techniques. The north shore of Long Island substituted for the New England setting of the story and Broadway theater actors filled in for most of the roles. Ed's main contribution to the film, along with camera work and story elements, was a surrealistic, animated delirium sequence switching *Wizard of Oz*-like from black-and-

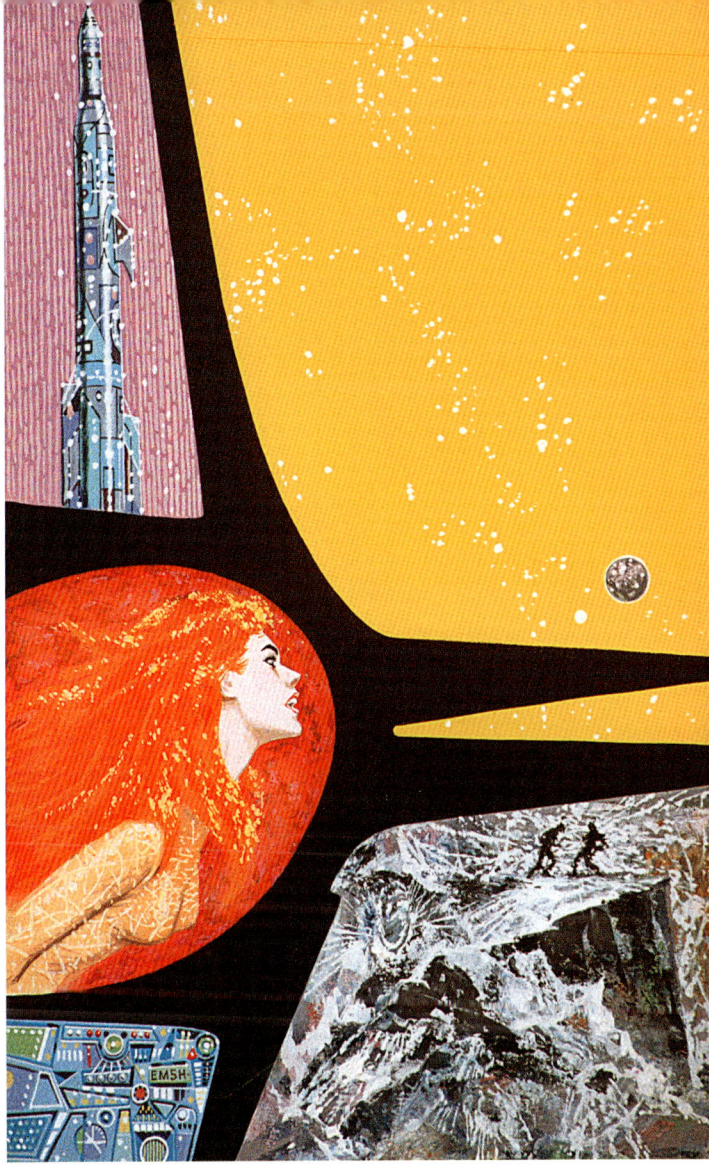

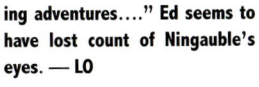

ing adventures...." Ed seems to have lost count of Ningauble's eyes. — LO

PAGE 104
(top R) VENTURE SCIENCE FICTION, Sept. 1957. "Executioner No. 43" Emsh took rayguns seriously and made them look very real and deadly. This one's a good example, and stiff competition for the lush dancing girl.

THIS PAGE
(top L) THE STARS LIKE DUST by Isaac Asimov. 1963. Lancer paperback.

(bot L) Abstraction by Ed. Unk title. 1960.

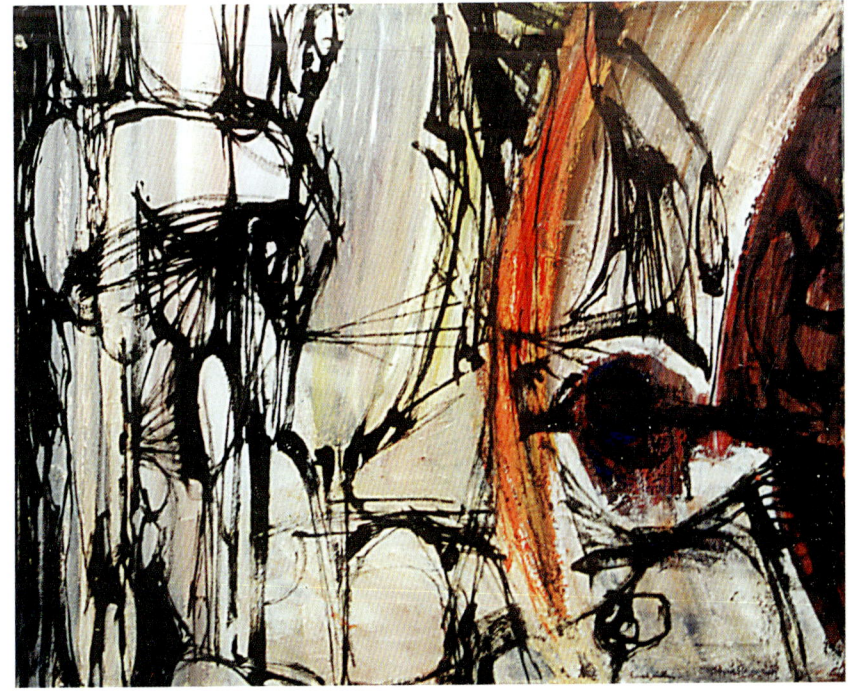

white, stock to garish color scenes, and utilizing drawings, maps, and flashbacks of people and events. The three weeks of filming was an exciting time for Ed. He worked from 6:30 in the morning until midnight the whole time. The family Plymouth was also enlisted into the production and Carol had to do her shopping on foot.

"All my films up to that point were very personal. In a way, very selfish, where I thought, 'It's mine, it's mine!' Then I found that Peter and I, coming from very different backgrounds, made a work which I think was different from anything that either of us would have done on our own. The collaboration wasn't just an averaging; it was somehow a combination which had its own personality, like a new being, or a new perception, that infused the work. It was a combination of a lot of pluses each of us could give, and a few of the minuses each of us gave. And I found that I had broken through that need to be the sole author." The finished film won the $4,800 top prize of the Grand Prix at the 1961 Bergano International Film Festival, but languished at the box office.

While filming *Time of the Heathen*, Ed met George Dumpson, a reclusive Long Island gardener and scavenger. Dumpson lived in a house surrounded by a "junkyard" of garden ornaments, sculptures, and found bric-a-brac. Ed was fascinated by Dumpson's "Natural inclination … to remake his world — which is, I guess, what artists generally do … but, this man, with a very limited opportunity in our society, had taken his experiences as a gardener and helper, and … had created such a wonderful, personal world. I thought it was beautiful." Dumpson had created his own personal Gardens of Babylon from the effluvia of civilization.

George Dumpson's Place deconstructed the typical biographical documentary, as the film presents scenes of inanimate objects, then quickly moves into a fluid, gliding camera, like a fly buzzing through Dumpson's grounds. Ed moved his body like a dancer for these tracking shots, using a camera with a wide-angle lens to minimize the apparent bobbing of the image. Through objects, Ed managed to capture Dumpson's private world, seemingly outside of time, without showing Dumpson. Faces of statues, broken dolls, and framed photo that may be found object, gave fleeting allusions to a familial life. At the end of the film we finally glimpse George Dumpson — by this point Ed has already bared Dumpson's spiritual soul. "I wanted to paint a portrait of him through his work, and film is the medium that I am happiest to paint."

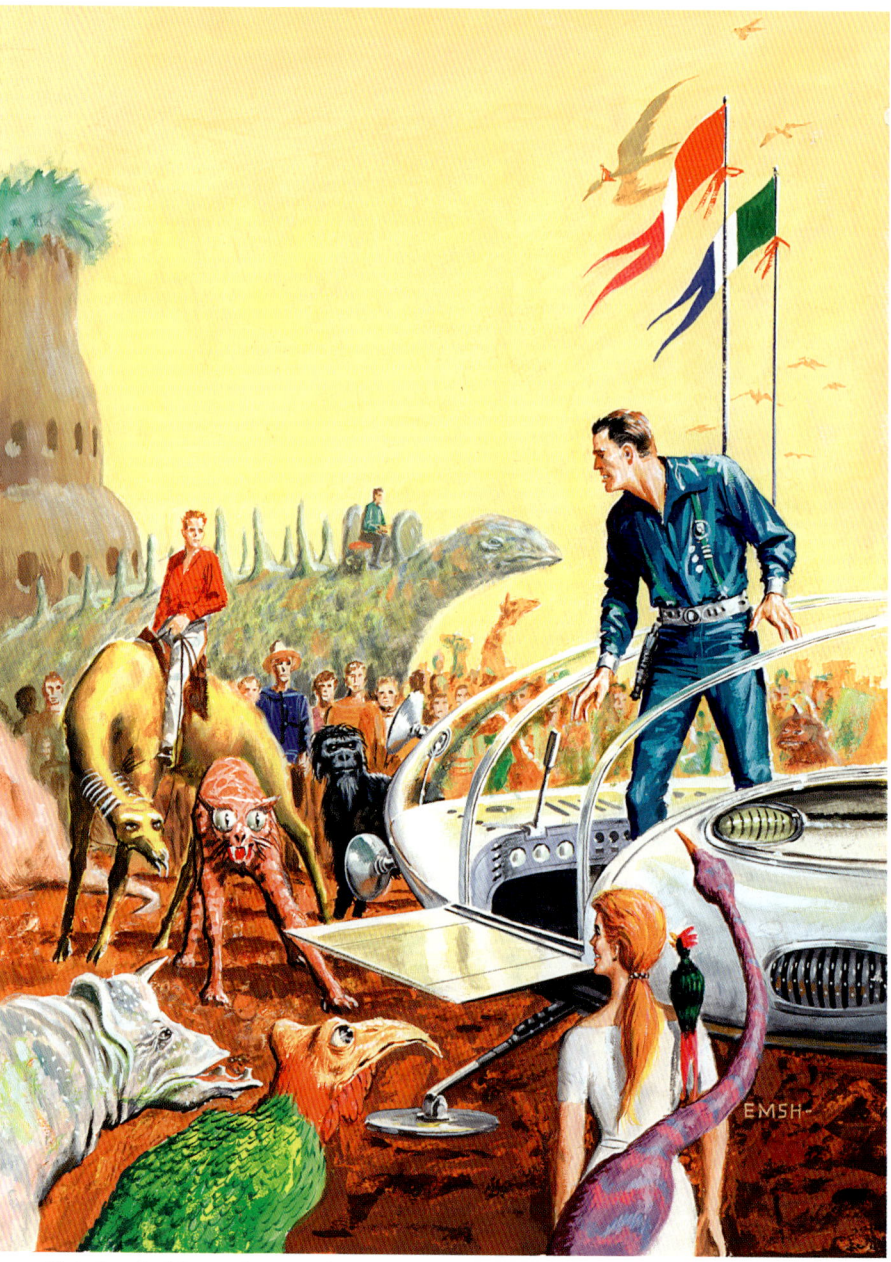

MASTERS OF EVOLUTION by Damon Knight. July 1959. Ace.

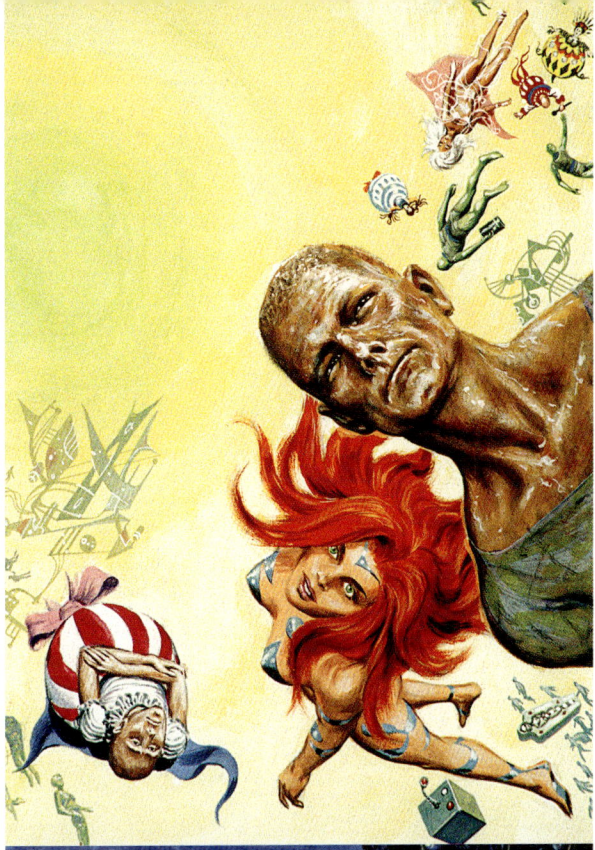

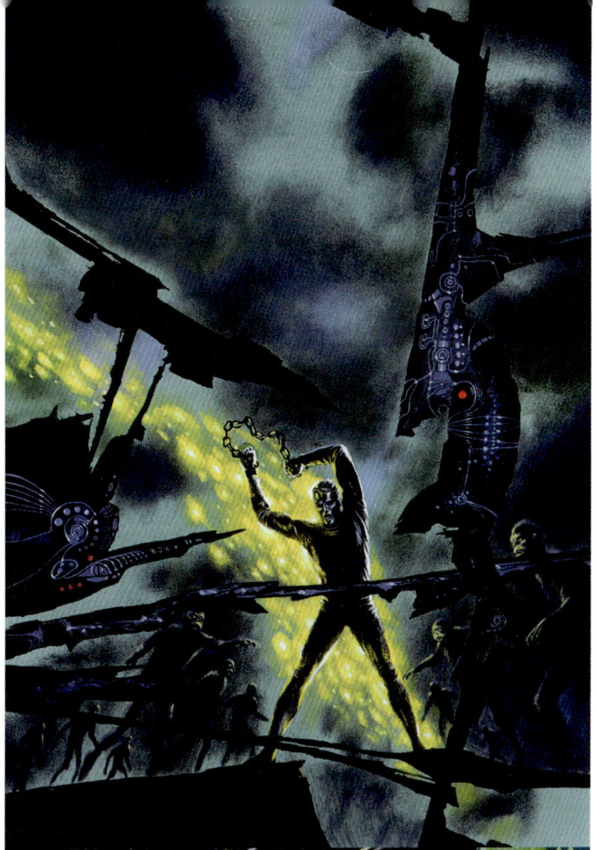

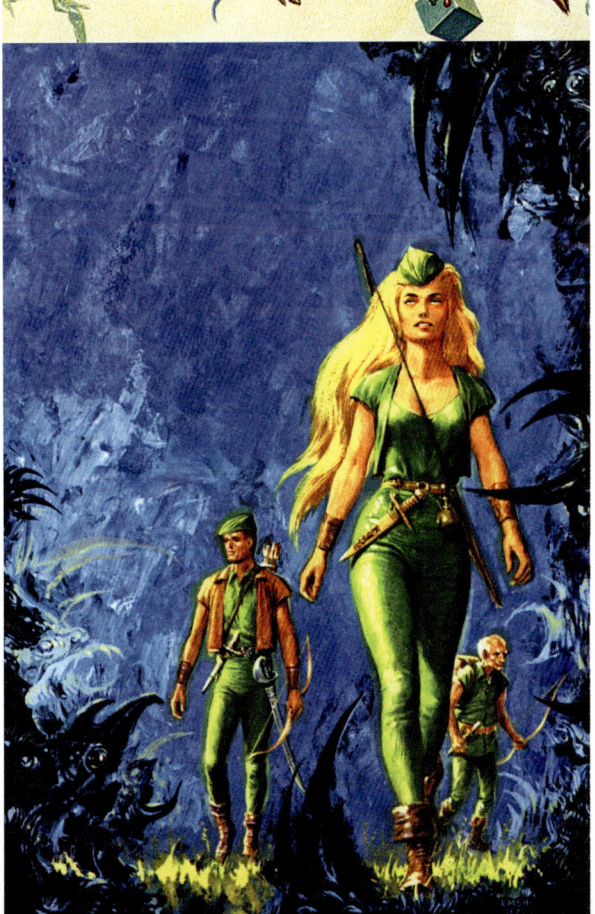

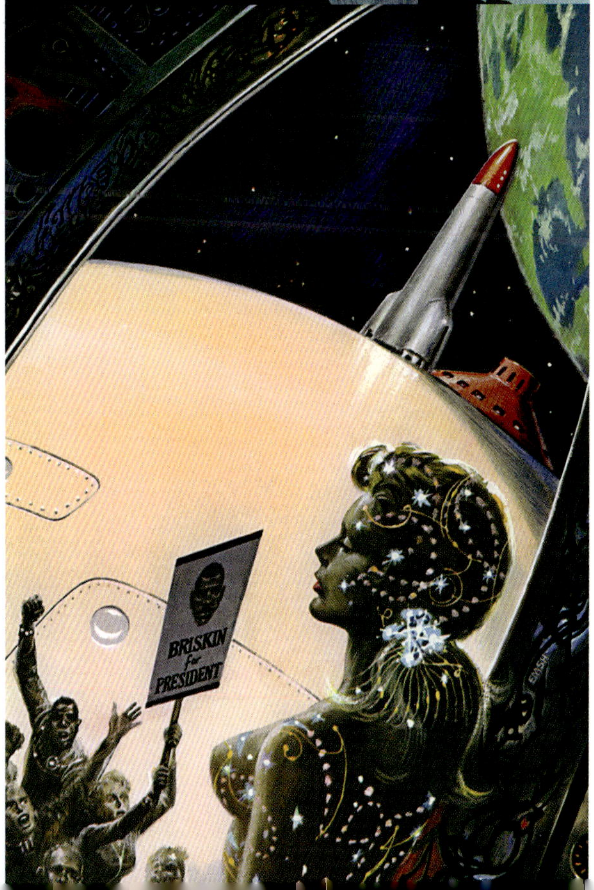

THIS PAGE
(top L) THE MAGAZINE OF FANTASY AND SCIENCE FICTION. Jan. 1964. "Beyond the Barrier" (Pt. 2) by Damon Knight.

(top R) THE NEMESIS FROM TERRA by Leigh Brackett. Ace 1961. A struggle in an underwater kingdom of jagged wreckage and wild electronic circuitry. The ocean gothic of Poe and the techno-weird of super science clash to produce high visual drama, aided by the beauty of the "abstract" in service of technological magic. The frogmen add something, too.

(bot R) THE MAGAZINE OF FANTASY AND SCIENCE FICTION. July 1964. "Cantata 140" by Philip K. Dick.

(bot L) THE MAGAZINE OF FANTASY AND SCIENCE FICTION. July 1963. GLORY ROAD by Robert A. Heinlein.

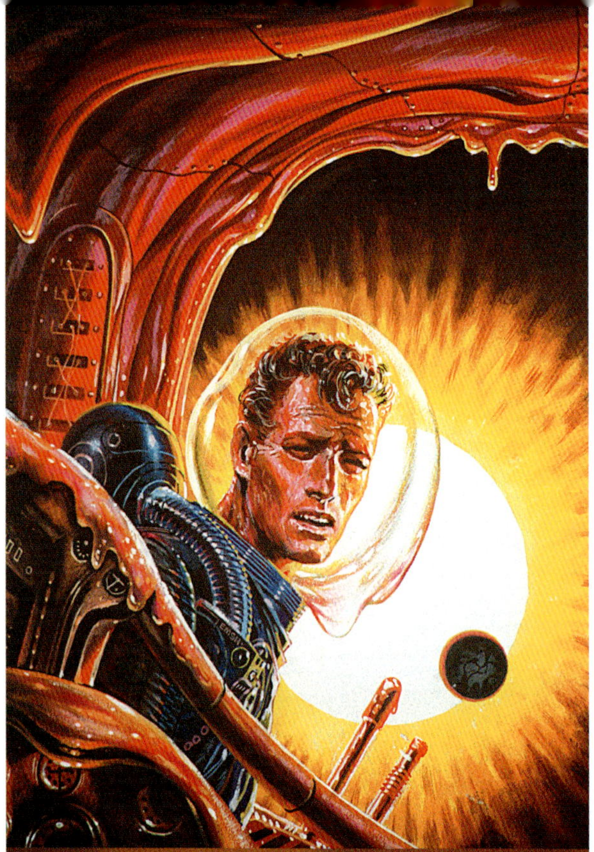

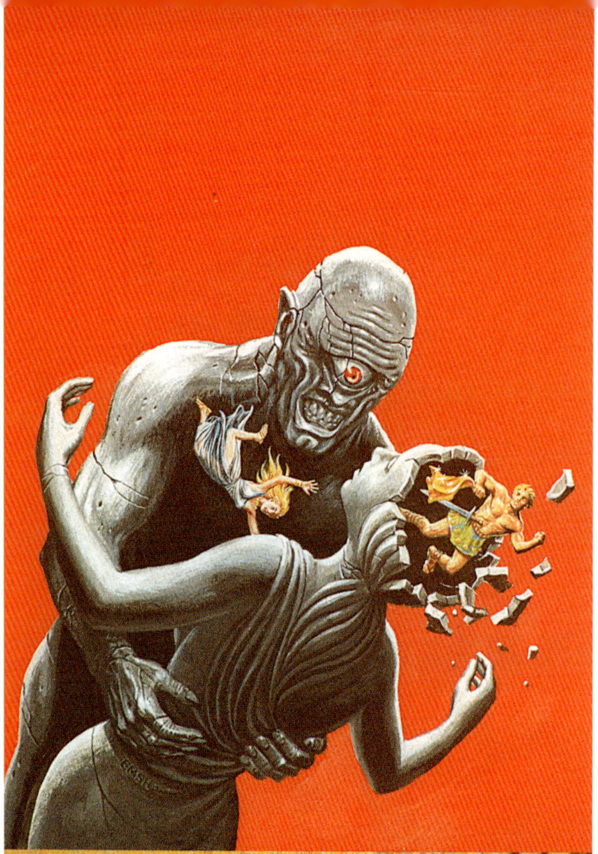

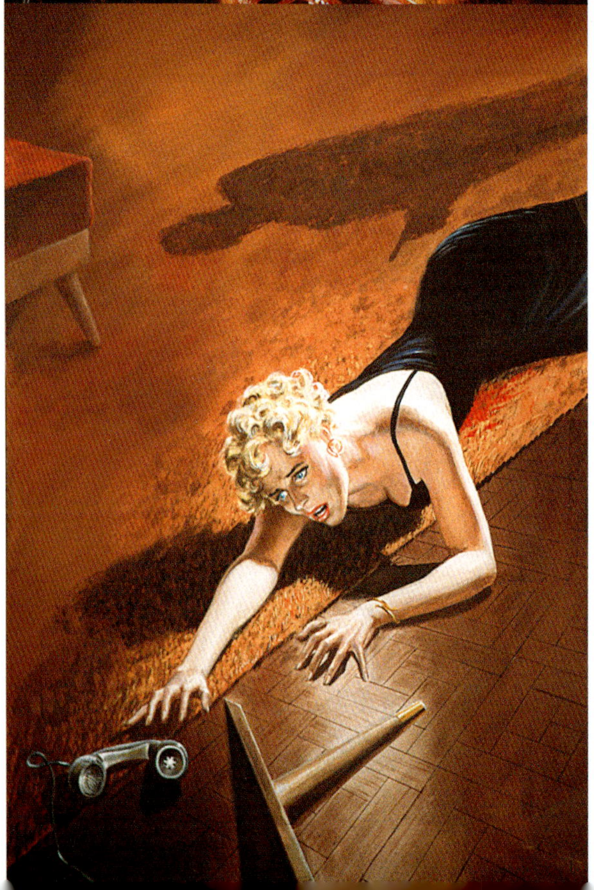

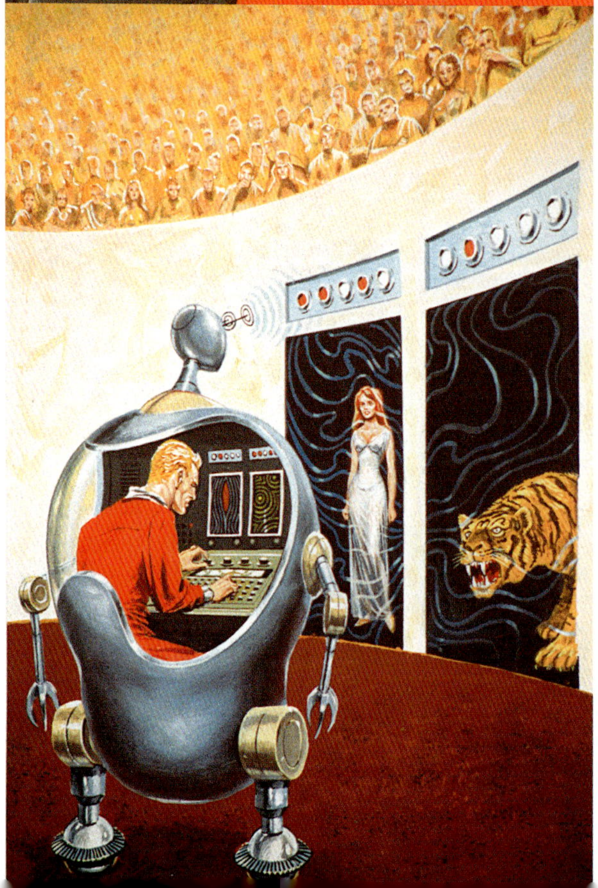

THIS PAGE
(top L) AMAZING STORIES. May 1964. "Boiling Point" by Lester del Rey. Eat your heart out, Mr. Dali. A number of stories dwell on the topic of getting too close to the Sun, and Emsh also had a certain fascination with the idea. Remember "Sunrise on Mercury"? Here is an even better essay on the theme. Everything in the control room is softening like hot wax, oozing and flowing, turning into syrup in the fierce solar glare. The yellow feathers of the Sun's corona lick at the cockpit, creating a candy-colored realm of death. The spaceman's coppery face registers, in every lurid highlight, his exquisite anxiety and discomfort, and even his helmet has begun to sag like chewing gum. Every surface has gone cherry red, except the cooling system of his air supply, which keeps his suit icy blue. But not for much longer.

(top R) FANTASTIC STORIES. August 1964. "When the Idols Walked" by John Jakes.

(bot R) AMAZING SCIENCE FICTION. March 1964. "Arena of Decisions" by Robert F. Young.

(bot L) Unknown mystery magazine cover art. One of the sharper mystery covers, in which we see the world of the helpless victim sliding toward death: the whole scene slants toward the pool of darkness in the lower left. Everything is honey-warm, except the chalk white of her back and forearms, and the pewter phone just out of reach - the chill colors of death. The killer's shadow, with its obscenely close gun, parallels her across the carpet, the thin barrel aiming at her head. Hope fading in her desperate eyes....

Nine

Rainy day scenarios

On January 7 1962 Ed was invited to a gathering of independent filmmakers at the Manhattan work/living space of Jonas Mekas, who had an idea for a new film distribution service. Many of these filmmakers were having a hard time getting Vogel to exhibit or even distribute their films. Vogel's rejection of Stan Brakhage's film, *Anticipation of the Night*, served as the catalyst for the creation of the FilmMakers' Co-operative as a new distribution center for independent filmmakers. Vogel saw the co-op as a personal attack and thought the existence of two distributors would weaken both rather than strengthen the entire field.

Ed tried to talk Vogel into co-distributing his films with the FilmMakers' Cooperative, but Vogel wanted no part of this. For one thing, he had already seen the effects of customers "bargain-hunting" for independent films between the two distributors. Vogel's real concern was the co-op's open door policy to all filmmakers. He believed this would flood the market with new works of dubious quality and told Ed, "I feel that I cannot be a party to this kind of regrettable 'diffusion.'"

Although Cinema 16 continued to distribute Ed's films, the FilmMakers' Cooperative offered a non-exclusive, non-discriminatory venue for underground filmmakers. New film societies, college film screenings, and art theaters were springing up and welcoming programs showing some of the new independent films — Vogel now found himself with competitors using Cinema 16 as a model. Within a few years Cinema 16 would be out of business. Vogel's success had created the means for his own demise.

Jonas Mekas and his brother Adolfas were film nuts. They arrived in New York from a European displaced persons camp in 1949, and one of the first things they did was go to a Times Square screening of silent films with English subtitles, including *The Cabinet of Dr. Caligary*. (The brothers' smattering of English was learned from reading Hemingway.) Within the month, they had borrowed $300 to buy a 16mm Bolex camera and began making a documentary of their Brooklyn neighborhood. The brothers haunted Cinema 16 screenings. When they did not have funds to pay for tickets, Marcia Vogel would take pity on the broke pair and allow them to enter the theater.

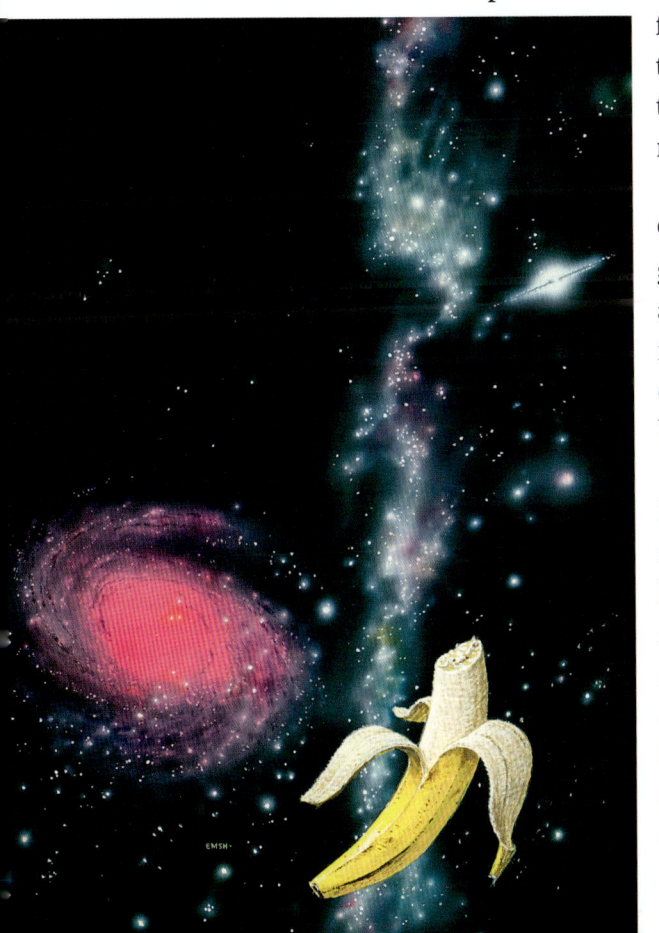

F&SF, Apr. 1961. The cosmic banana, half-peeled and half-eaten, beautifully rendered against a backdrop of phosphorescent star fields and galaxies. Does it drop a hint of God? Or of space-going litterbugs? Who can say; but its incongruity prompts a laugh from almost everyone who sees it.

Jonas began publishing *Film Culture*, a magazine advocating independent films, in 1955. Adolfas Mekas had been working on a feature-length film scenario, which paid anarchic homage to Mack Sennett and Jean-Luc Godard. Ed had met the Mekas brothers at a Cinema 16 screening and liked them. It didn't take much for them to talk Ed into becoming the cameraman on their production *Hallelujah the Hills*. The spirited film, made for $25,000, became a favorite of international film festivals in 1963, and was written up in *Life* and *Time*.

Everyone on the production took it as a lark, even during the wintry Vermont part of the shoot where the crew used jeeps to get around, and seemed to enjoy the improvised gaiety of the production. The rented 35mm camera and truckload of film equipment

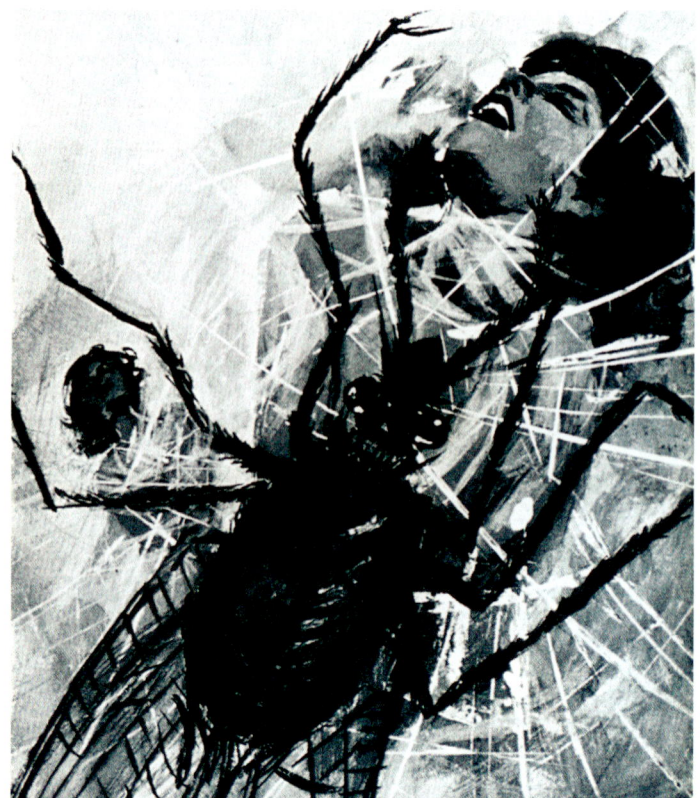

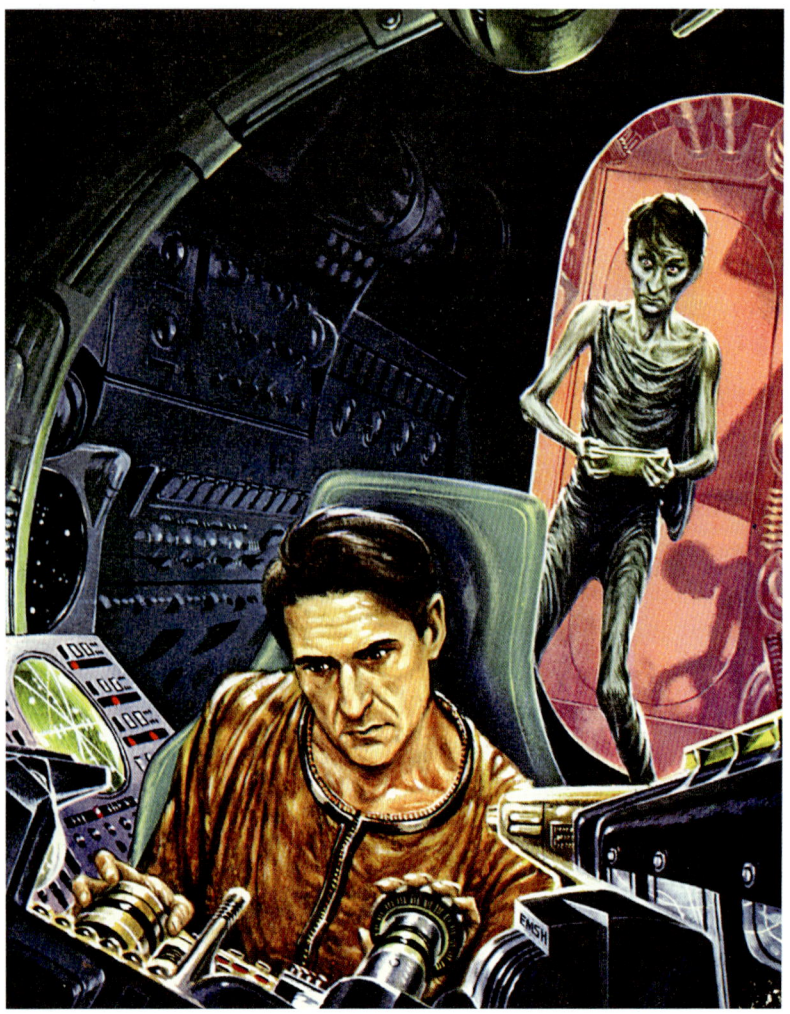

had been delivered without any instructions to the group masquerading as a professional film production, and Ed spent the better part of the first week figuring everything out. Toward the end of the shoot, Ed shouted out, "It's great! See what this camera can do? I wish I knew about it eight months ago." For a couple of spirited scenes, Ed took the 135-pound camera off its tripod and lugged it around on his shoulder.

The story, what little there is of it, revolves around two buffoonish city guys who go to the country planning to marry the same girl. The film was better

(top R) ORIGINAL SF STORIES. Nov. 1959. "The Impossible Intelligence" by Robert Silverberg.

(bot L) F&SF, Apr. 1963, "Fast Trip" by James White. Weird, chilling image of space travel, implied even in the color scheme - warm ochres in foreground, cool cyan-&-teal-blue to the rear. Though replete with high-tech detail, the ship's cabin has a sepulchral aura, and the starveling with beggar's bowl exudes a clammy death-camp vibe: a spaceship endlessly speeding to the stars, its passengers trapped in a half-life limbo. The odd likeness between pilot and beggar evokes gothic doppelgangers and time-warped paradox. Filmmaker brothers Adolfas and Jonas Mekas were the models.

PG 111
(top L) Carol posing for Ed.

(bot L) EE Nude study. 1950s.

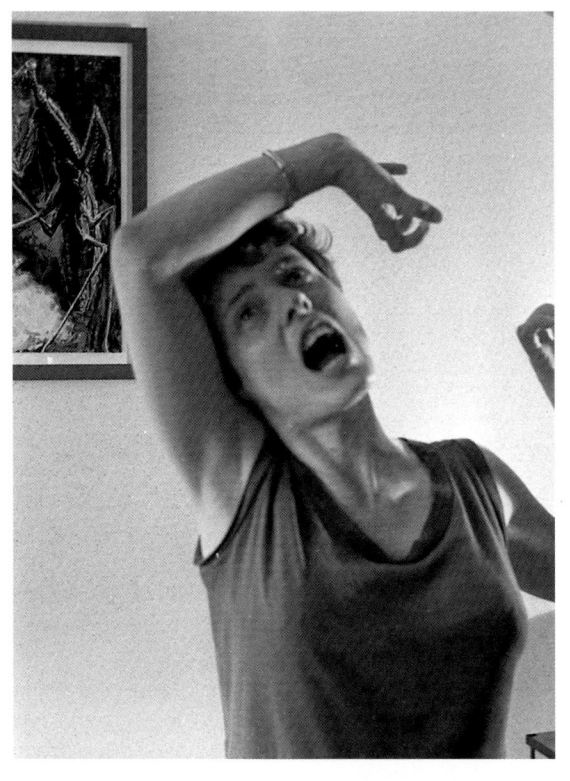

received abroad than at home, but most critics praised Ed's photography if not his brief acting as Gideon, and the movie became a big hit for Filmmakers' Cooperative.

On April 11, 1963 the Museum of Modern Art presented a program of independent films, that included Ed's work in the Animation and Abstraction part of the show. "I always thought it would be nice to be in the museum but I hadn't expected to get in via the movies."

Ed's "external films" branched out into documentaries when he met Jack Willis, a producer/director for the Canadian Broadcasting Company. Willis talked Ed into going to Greenwood, Mississippi, to work as a cameraman in a film about black voter registration during the oppressive June of 1963. Under the sweltering Mississippi sun, Ed again struggled with an unfamiliar camera, a converted Auricon borrowed from folk singer Pete Seeger. At one point, he filmed Bob Dylan singing "Only a Pawn in their Game" at a rally on Silas McGee's farm outside of Greenwood. (This clip turned up in Pennebaker's Dylan film *Don't Look Back*.)

This was early in the civil protest of the sixties and people in the town were willing to speak their minds openly, not taking into account how their words sounded outside Jim Crow territory. At one point a local sheriff confronted the filmmakers in a tense situation at a white political rally. To decompress the situation, Willis put a microphone in the officer's face to get his side of the story—even though Ed's camera had run out of film. They missed twenty minutes of racist rant.

Before *The Streets of Greenwood*, Ed had not been very politically involved, but during the sixties, and with his interaction with young radical filmmakers, he marched against the Vietnam War, stood on peace vigils, took part in films made for or portraying social causes, and was at Martin Luther King, Jr.'s "I Have a Dream" speech in Washington, D.C. in 1963.

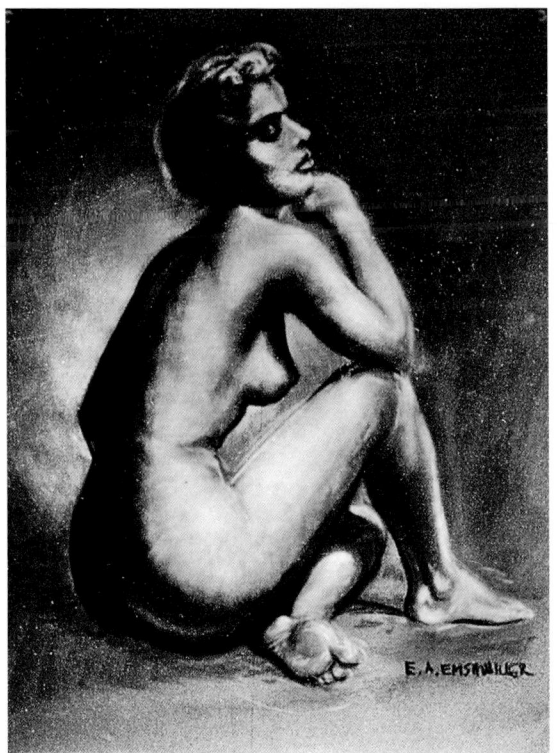

Carol's fiction was one thing, her children another: making organic peanut butter sandwiches for them, trips to the dentist, shopping or pulling up dandelions in the garden during the summer — there were only so many hours in a day, and she took to sending her kids to bed early every night, then writing for a few hours. In this way she was able to write two or three stories during the year. Carol would take one fantastic idea and develop a mostly straightforward story from that premise. "A Day at the Beach" could have been written as a literary piece about a family living in a war zone—if we put the images of the hirsute baby and bald mother out of mind.

"A Day at the Beach" told the post-apocalyptic story of a young couple and their strange offspring. The story is in the details: a trip to the beach, fixing an improvised dinner, and the slightly out-of-kilter mothering of the child. Carol sold the story to the *F&SF* — and Merril selected it for her Best of SF collection the next year. As usual Ed contacted the magazine and offered to illustrate the story, and with Carol's input created a Madonna and child portrayal. The background setting for the painting was their Levittown street (pg. 103).

In 1966, Carol began taking writing classes with Anatole Broyard, a writer once linked to the Beat Generation, and he helped her sell one of her better non-SF stories to *Cavalier*. (She felt she wasn't really learning much in Broyard's class, but had fun there anyway.) "Chicken Icarus" was a small breakthrough for her, and in the central character, a man without limbs living in one room, Carol managed to present an inner life deprived by more than freakish particulars, and her character, through self-actualization, built a bigger prison for himself.

"Icarus" can almost be read as a continuation of Judy Merril's classic story "That Only a Mother", where a radiation-damaged baby, born without arms or legs, is seen as normal by his mother. In Carol's story, however, the limbless adult has a mother that barely acknowledges her son. This was one of her first stories to take a straight-on look at sex.

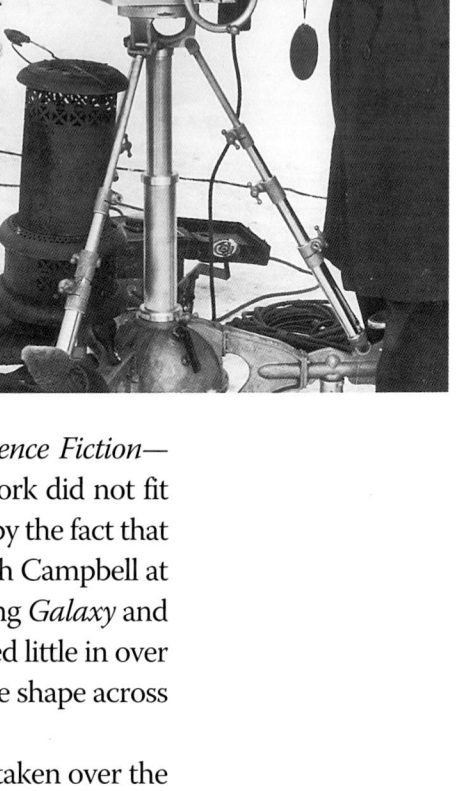

By the sixties, her work was only appearing in the *Magazine of Fantasy & Science Fiction*— and then at greater intervals. At heart, her work did not fit neatly into the SF genre, and this was proven by the fact that she had little chance of placing her fiction with Campbell at *Astounding*, or even Pohl, who was now editing *Galaxy* and *If*. The basic SF magazine formula had changed little in over a decade — but something was starting to take shape across the Atlantic.

A young editor, Michael Moorcock, had taken over the moribund British SF magazine *New Worlds* in 1964. Moorcock realized that a firmament of British authors writing in a science fiction vernacular was doing something just a little bit different. By the mid-sixties *New Worlds* was staging a direct attack on SF's literary immaturity. Moorcock used modern graphics and fiction to develop a new voice for *New Worlds* and J. G. Ballard was his star.

Judy Merril was living in England at this time, working on various projects, including something called *England*

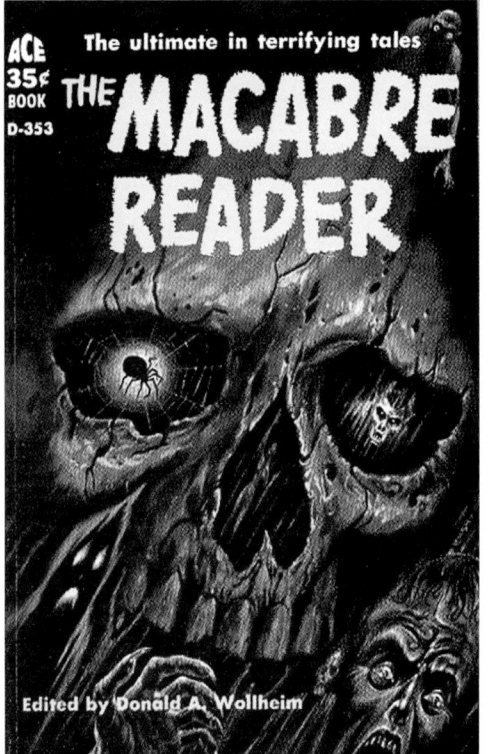

(top R) Ed as cameraman on the Vermont set of HALLELUJAH THE HILLS. 1962.

(bot L) THE MACABRE READER. Edited by Donald A. Wollheim. 1959, Ace.

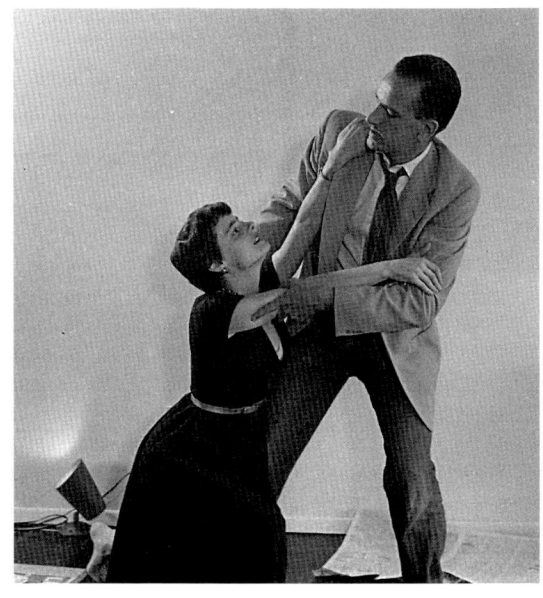

Swings SF. This anthology became the opening salvo in what was to be called New Wave science fiction. (One New Wave author, Tom Disch, referred to it as science fiction without rockets.) Although Merril focused on literary stylists, including international writers who wrote borderline SF, the larger question hovering over all the writers of the New Wave was: how different was their work from what came before? Certainly authors such as Theodore Sturgeon and Alfred Bester were writing at a level indistinguishable from New Wavers. SF traditionalists saw things as black and white, old and new. From the start, it was an internal struggle between revolutionary and counter-revolutionary forces.

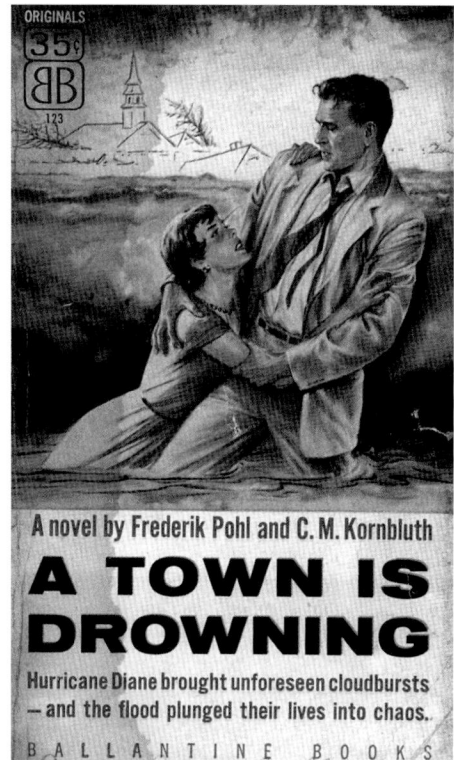

(top) Carol and Ed in photo study for cover to A TOWN IS DROWNING by Frederik Pohl and C. M. Kornbluth. 1956. Ballantine Books.

(bot) Line art from GALAXY SCIENCE FICTION. Feb. 1963. For "Comic Inferno" by Brian Aldiss.

In America, Harlan Ellison became an advocate of the New Wave movement (or his take on it), and in October of 1965 was goaded by Robert Silverberg into doing a collection of stories equal to the standards he was espousing. Ellison began putting together an anthology of "…new writing styles, bold departures, unpopular thoughts." As a Milford regular, Ellison was familiar with Carol's work from the start and asked her to contribute to *Dangerous Visions*.

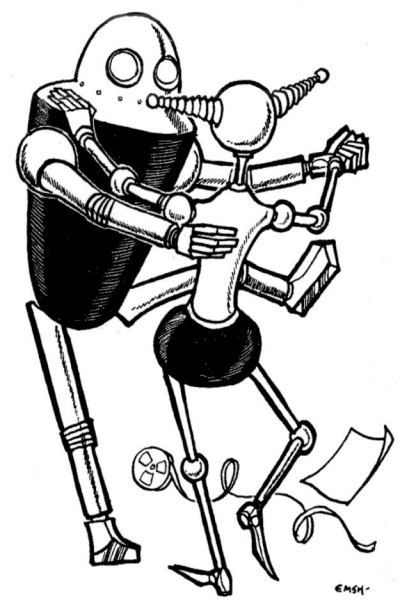

She had finished "Sex and/or Mr. Morrison" shortly before Ellison's request and sent him the typescript. Carol's story fell under the rubric of speculative fiction, a term coined by Robert Heinlein and adopted by SF people during the sixties for anything mixing SF, fantasy, and realism with plots as a secondary consideration. The story seemingly begins as "secret aliens among us" SF, before shifting into an excursion into the realm of Freud and Kafka. The "alien" is an elephantine, shy, gentle neighbor that the middle-aged woman protagonist is obsessed with. One day the woman hides in his apartment, a peeping tom intent on directly observing her obsession: "Well, what would you think if you saw them wearing their suits that were supposed to be bare skin? Naked suits…."

"I am thin and small, almost child-sized," she thinks as she makes a nest out of gargantuan socks and underpants in the closet and waits. It doesn't take long for Mr. Morrison to appear in all his immense bulk.

Carol gave "Sex and/or Mr. Morrison" the sense of an adolescent's discovering the secrets of sex—the discovery of the secret parts of the body through the closest person in

113

an adolescent's world. The story is about a doomed love. In the scheme of things, as a child grows up, the father become smaller — in Carol's story he becomes larger, larger than life, and can only be seen in parts like the proverbial blind men touching an elephant.

Ellison, in his introduction, called the contributions to *Dangerous Visions* a revolution. The book did reflect the new wave ferment of the times. A few critics (including Algis Budrys in his famous review in *Galaxy* urging readers to buy the book *now* even if they have to take a taxi to get to the bookstore) saw Carol's story as one of the best things in the book. Budrys gives his take of *Dangerous Visions* as "…a 'credibility gap' between this generation and the past." He goes on to say, "…we have now matured the first complete generation born into a world that could be winked out, and knows it."

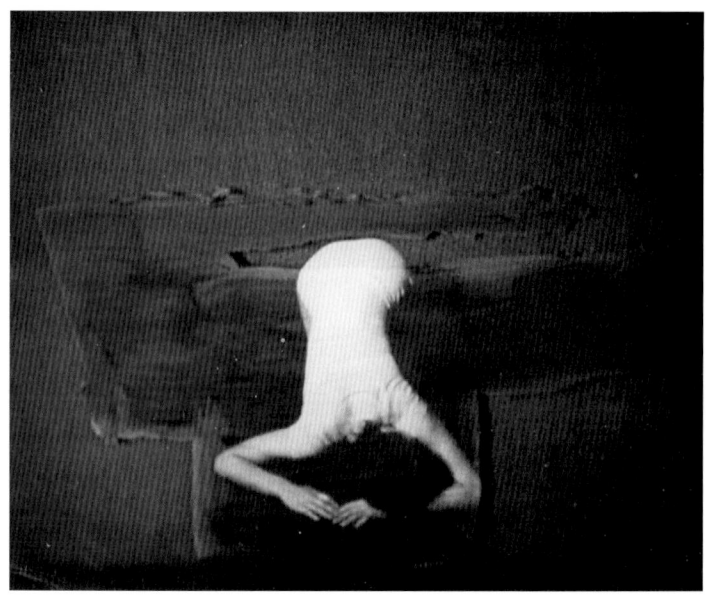

Carol's fiction up until "Mr. Morrison" had been quietly received. Long time readers of F&SF may have remembered "A Day at the Beach" from several years earlier, but the *Dangerous Visions* story came as a surprise to many SF people. While stories like "A Day at the Beach" displayed a tough wisdom and a forward momentum that glides along with sporadic pugnacity, "Mr. Morrison" reads almost as a complete change of genre. Of course, the fact that the story can be interpreted in slightly different ways makes it an inimitable invention, or as much of a unique invention as any author can muster when pulling ideas from his or her subconscious.

Ed's interaction with avant-garde filmmakers was influencing Carol indirectly. She took writing classes with Kay Boyle at the New School for Social Research and attempted some mainstream writing without much success. (Boyle taught writing as almost a free form of expression.) Carol went four years, during the mid sixties, without publishing anything and found that once you learn how to plot, it is hard not to plot. *I had to reject plot little by little by little.* She could only do this by substituting something else in its place and used a more self-analytical approach that included sex. While some of the work was experimental, she still believed in having some sort of structure. *Each story was different, but still had a rounded-out end.*

Carol placed a story in *New Worlds* magazine at the height of the SF New Wave tide. The English magazine was a panorama, in its isolated way, of SF New Wave, and published the more outré SF of Americans like Tom Disch, Carol, Harlan Ellison, and Norman Spinrad when these authors could not find a publisher in their own country receptive to their experimental work.

Science fiction New Wave was more a bunch of writers thinking in the same way than a school of literature. In America the SF New Wave debate may have been reflected less in any particular piece of fiction, but in an advertisement that appeared in the March 1968 issue of *F&SF*, and the June 1968 issues of *Galaxy* and *If*. It was an all-type listing of the names of SF writers against the U.S. involve-

(top R) DANCE CHROMATIC. 1959.

THIS PAGE
THANOTOPSIS. 1962, B&W,
7 minutes, 16mm.

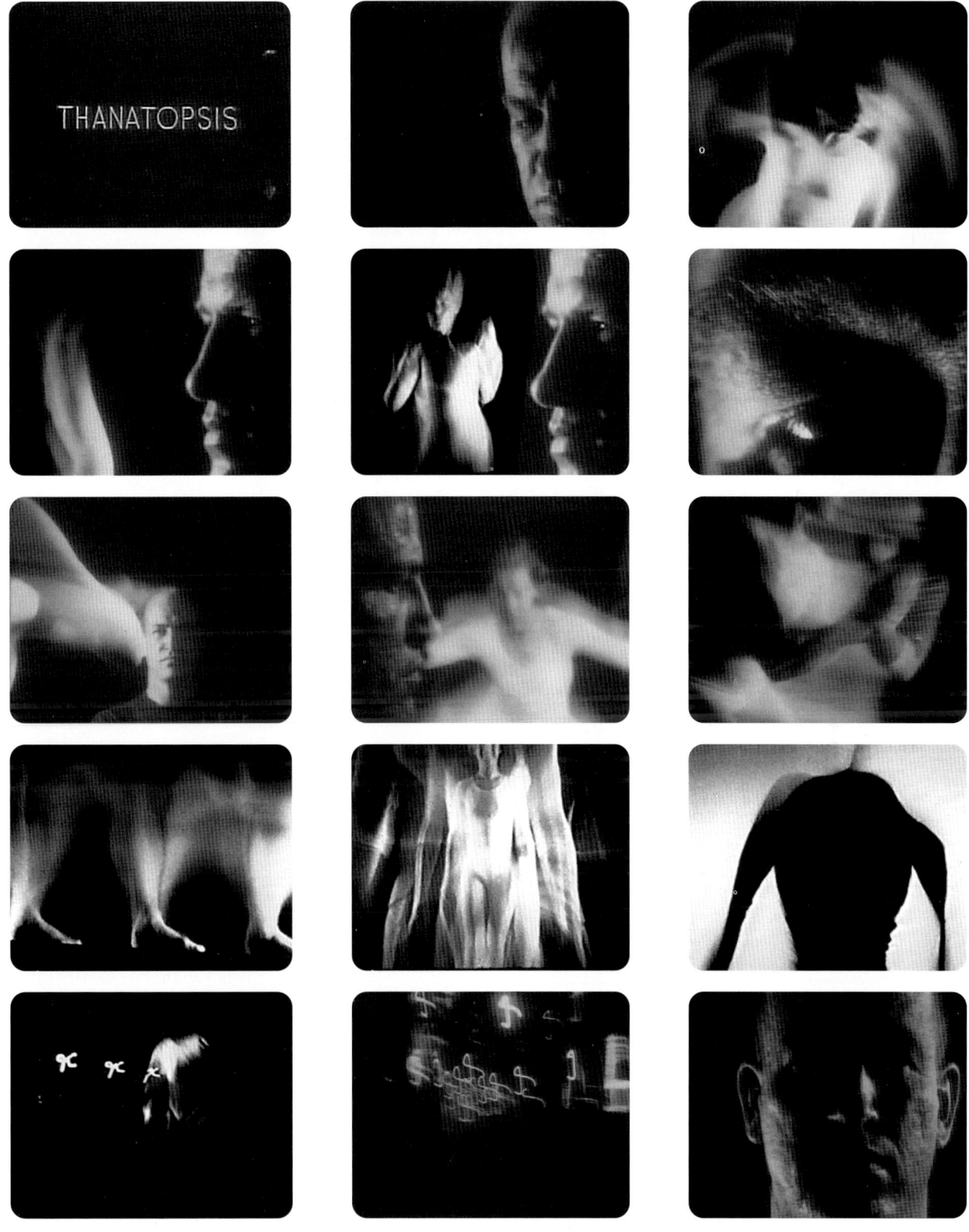

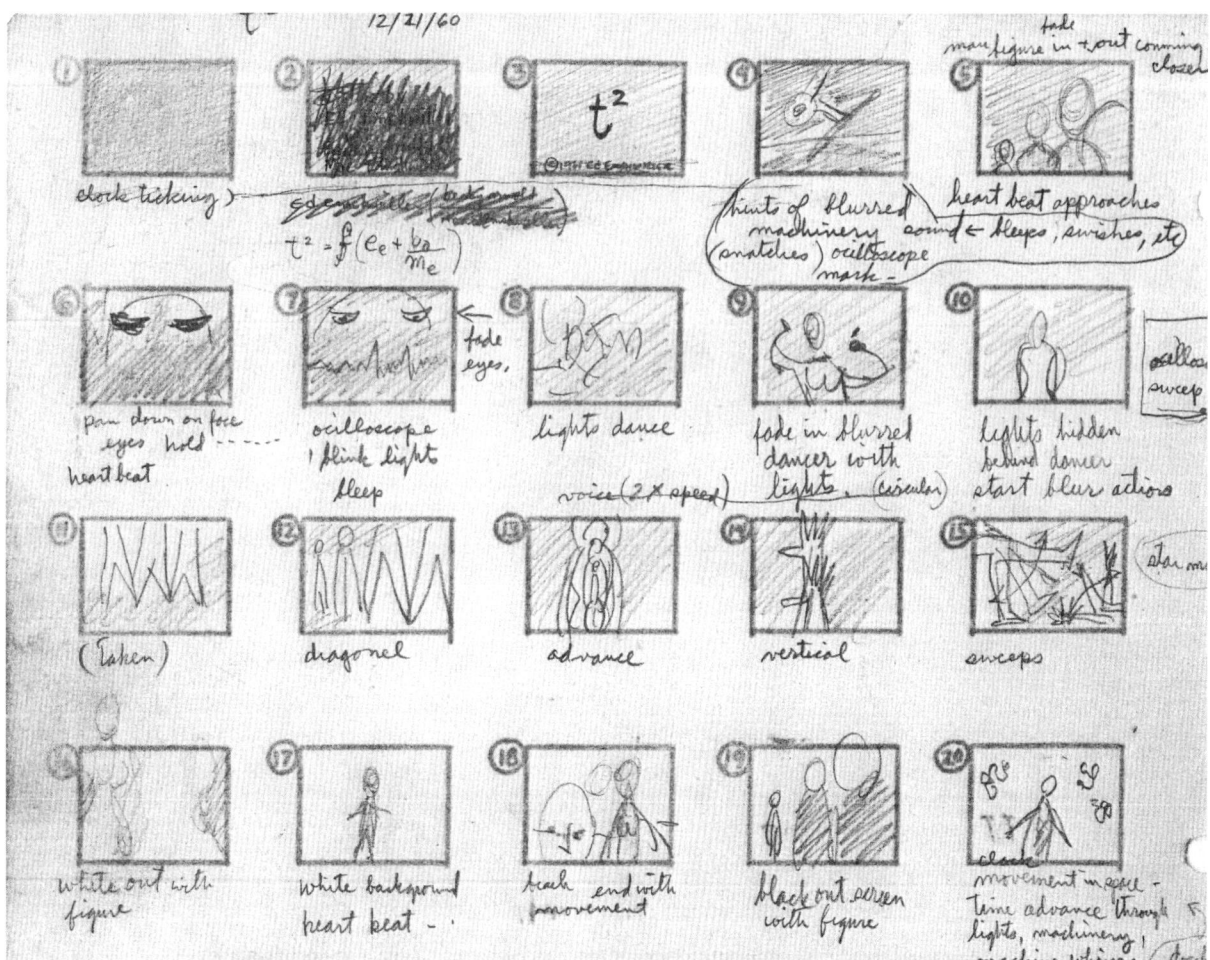

THIS PAGE
Storyboard for T². Some of the ideas from this unrealized film was utilized in THANATOPSIS. December 21, 1960.

ment in the Vietnam War. The original idea, thought up by Judith Merril and Kate Wilhelm, was leaked (most likely by *Galaxy* and *If* editor Fred Pohl) before the ad appeared and a pro-war faction ran their own advertisement in the same magazines. Many writers that had written New Wave were in the ad's anti-war list of 82 SF authors, including Carol Emshwiller, Harlan Ellison, Robert Silverberg, Judy Merril, Norman Spinrad, Barry Malzberg, Philip K. Dick, and Ursula K. Le Guin.

In America, SF New Wave was published in original anthologies, not in SF magazines. Damon Knight's *Orbit*, Samuel R. Delany and Marilyn Hacker's *Quark*, and collections by Merril were some of the few places where it could be found. As much flak as the SF New Wave got at the time from within science fiction, in the long run it may have saved SF from inbred imbecility.

In his next film, *Thanatopsis,* Ed went back to a dance theme. Using $1/3$ to 1 second timed single-frame exposures, he filmed his brother Mac sitting in a chair while his wife Becky Arnold, a professional dancer, moved about him in a gradually modified, repetitious manner. (Carol filled in for Becky when she was not available.) This movement appeared on film as a fluttering, blurred image when projected

(top L) GEORGE DUMPSON'S PLACE. 1965.

(bot L) TRUE ACTION. Apr. 1960. B&W wash interior drawing.

in normal 24 frames per second. Ed described his grueling technique, "It was very exhausting because we were both in essence dancing throughout the whole night's shooting; it was all single framing by hand-held camera, or most of it was, and it was very slow going.... This [was] all done intuitively, I'd say, kind of gut oriented." Ed added a soundtrack of heartbeats and band saws to give *Thanatopsis* a sense of internal anguish and growing tension.

"I wanted to create maximum tension with abstract or non-literal minimum means (as in music). Also, I wanted to use time exposure blurs in a movie, something I had never seen done."

Thanatopsis was an instant hit in New York's avant garde circles when it played at Cinema 16 and later at the Museum of Modern Art. It showed people like the Mekas brothers, Stan VanDerBeek, and Stan Brakhage that Ed was more than a cinematic technophile. (VanDerBeek wrote to Ed, "I think your meditation on death is brilliant.

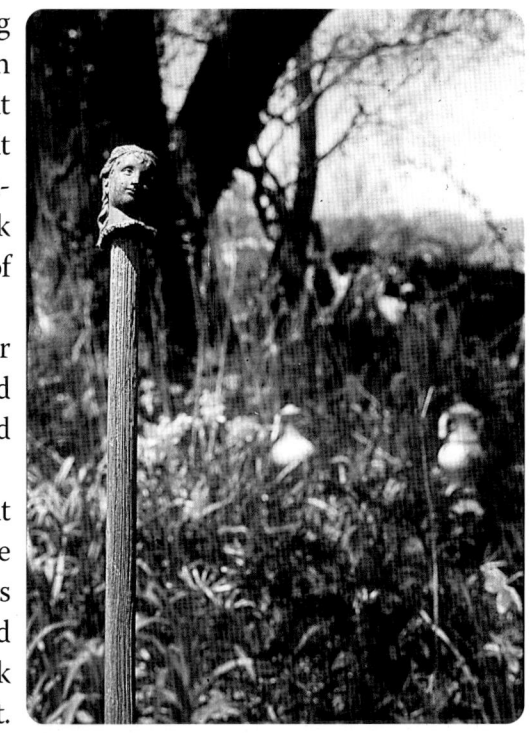

I too am interested in the blurred life form, working particularly with hands...") These film people were passionate about the avant-garde, and drew Ed and Carol further into the fold. Carol remembers: *We both felt that you could say something different — than has ever been said before — through the avant-garde.*

It is curious that many of the experimental filmmakers at this time were well into their thirties. Where earlier avant-garde film movements during the 1920s and 1930s had been a young person's faction,

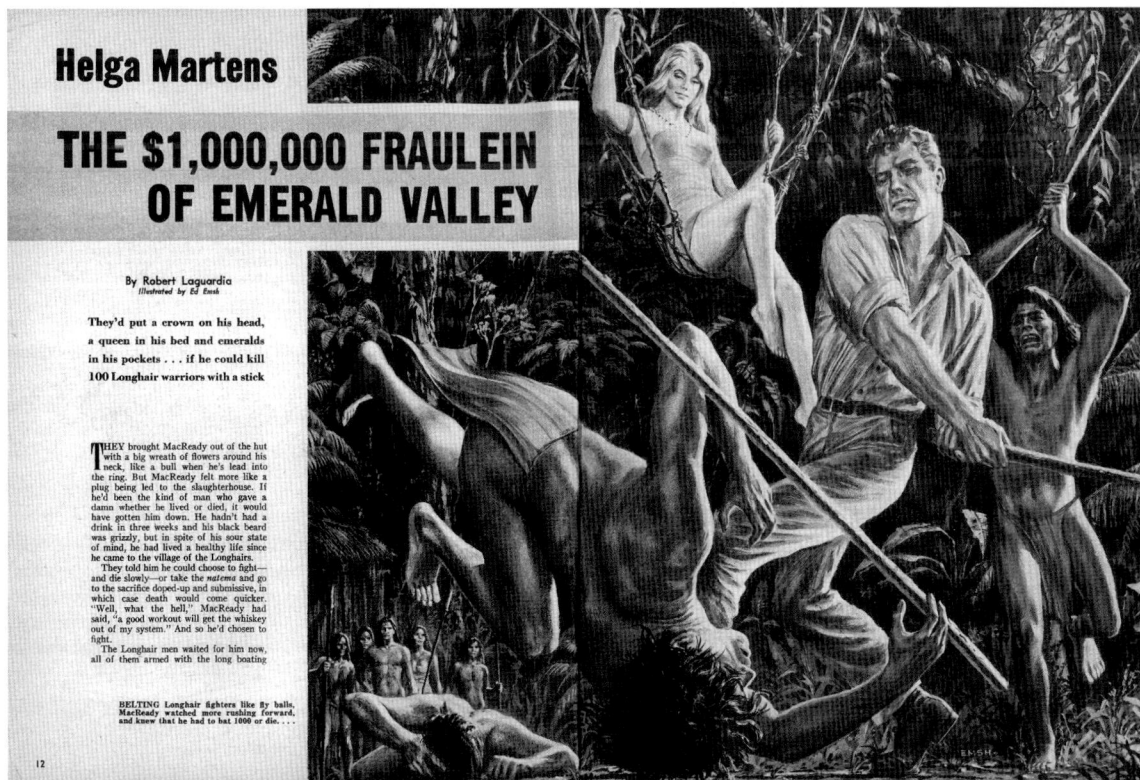

117

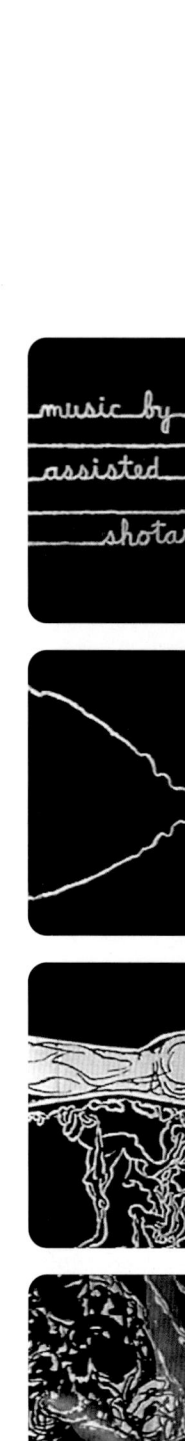
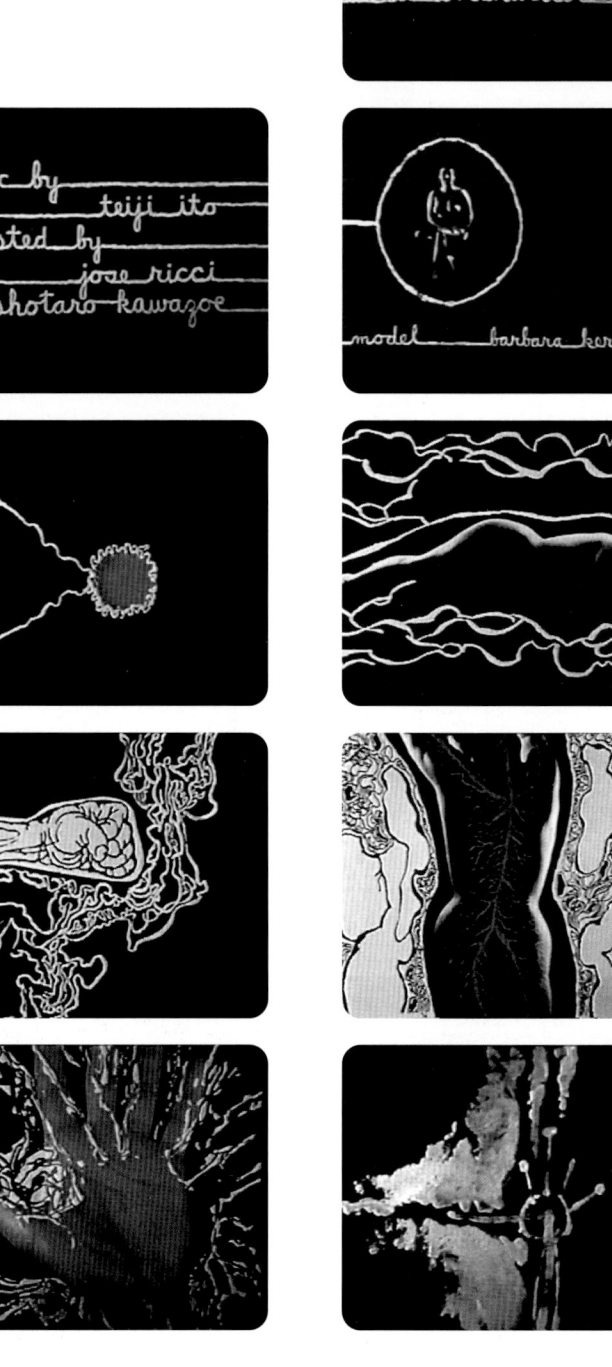
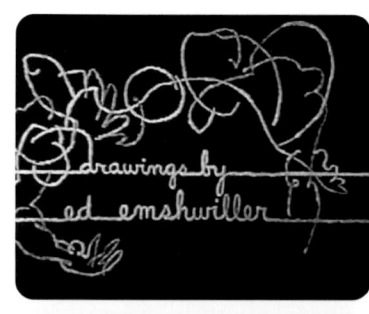
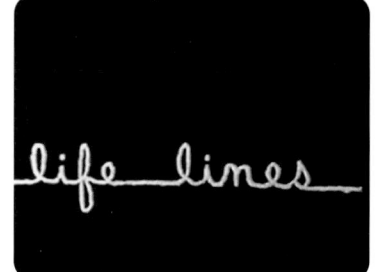
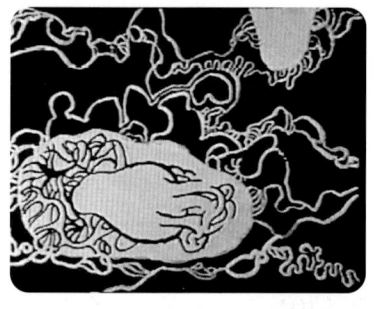
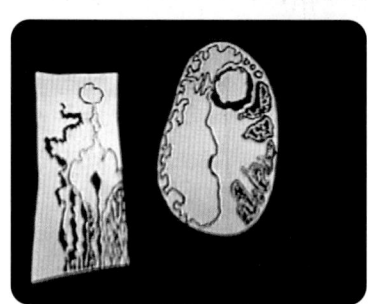
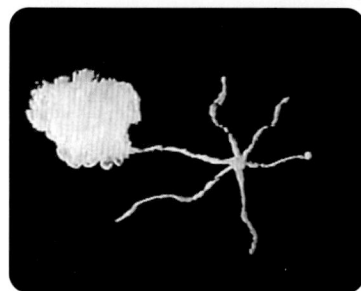

**TWO PAGE SPREAD
LIFELINES.** 1960, 16mm,
7 minutes, color.

"The whole concept of LIFELINES was more literary in the sense that it had a number of ideas playing on the words 'life' and 'line' ... life-lines, line drawing, life lines of the hand, procreation, Mother Earth ... a wild series of things done with an increasing complexity of line. It started out flat, then became more and more three-dimensional, more and more from monochromatic to polychromatic, from flat space to deep space, etc. It's a simple progression actually. Most of these abstract films, and I think most abstract films in general, tend to use a fairly firm structural development, kind of a musical thing."
— EE

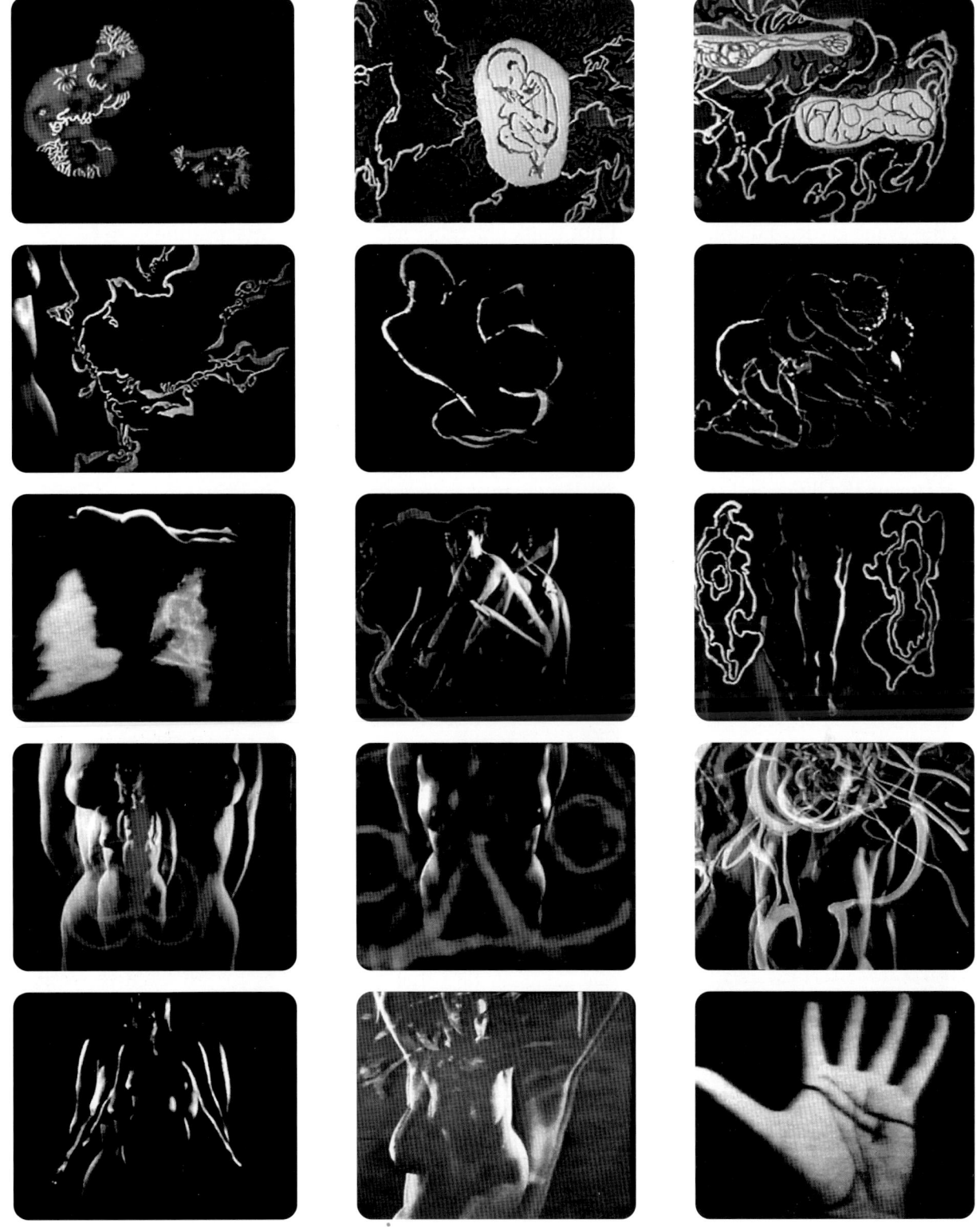

the war years had delayed many filmmakers' educations and careers. They all seemed intent on making up for lost time — squashing learning and creativity together. This group brought to the sixties avant-garde a real-world maturity and outlook. It seemed as if Manhattan's street grids were a utopia for a myriad of artists, filmmakers, and writers throughout the late fifties and sixties. There was a "make it new' zeitgeist in the air.

Carol remembers, *We would use up every penny we had to do Ed's films.* (This money was from illustration. There was little fame — and less fortune — in being part of the avant-garde.) Ed and Carol did not think like other suburban parents: putting money away for their children's college, paying down the mortgage, or having something to cover rainy day scenarios.

Ed's films would pay off much later when, according to Carol, he became the *grand old man of the avant-garde* and this name recognition allowed him to teach and lecture—certainly the derisive amounts he received from rentals or sales of his films were not a spur to creativity. Indeed, when the American Film Institute was formed in the late sixties, he became (as Carol puts it) *their token avant-garde filmmaker.*

During the fifties and sixties, under many names — including new American cinema, underground film, art film, personal cinema, anti-films, experimental, expanded cinema, etc. — artistic quirkiness and the idea of progress outside of commercial features flourished and began receiving mainstream press attention. A groundswell of lessons learned from one another drove the avant-garde community, along with a mixture of iconoclasm, homage, naiveté, eclecticism, a demand for seriousness, and a certain amount of flippancy and prankishness. Avant-garde wasn't: commercial, committee-run, or Hollywood. It was not something that had to be understood — you either "got it" or didn't. This applied, of course, as much to literature as to films and paintings.

For some filmmakers it was out-of-control film making. As an artist, Ed liked to explore serendipitous tangents and by-ways. In many cases his film experiments just seemed more controlled than those of his peers. Ed's habits remained out of sync with many of the experimental filmmakers working at the time, to the extent that his early films were equal parts art and professional technique.

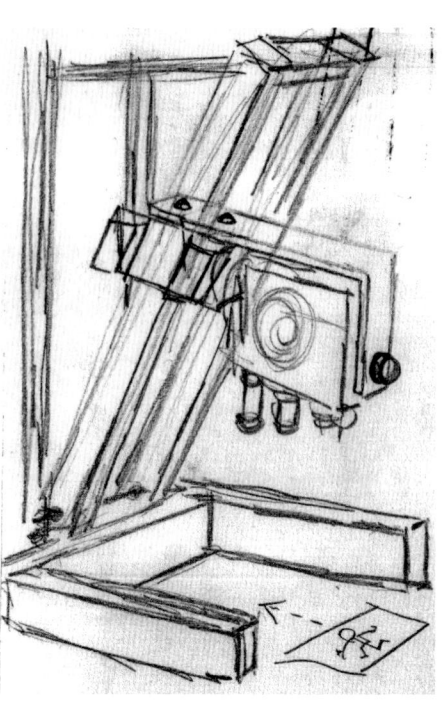

THIS PAGE
(top R) Design by EE for a portable animation stand from the early 1960s.

(bot L) Ed, self posed Polaroid for a painting concept. Sept. 1962.

Ten

Take a Number

ED WROTE, EARLY IN 1963, "My principal project now is a long 'experimental' film, untitled as yet, which attempts to express the state of an individual in the physical universe as we understand it today, and his psychological responses to that state." Ed had Asimov's writings in mind, dealing with the limits of our knowledge in time and space. At that year's Milford Conference, Judy Merril saw *Thanatopsis,* and in a letter to Richard Powers wrote about the connection between SF art and the avant-garde: "[It's] probably the only field of illustration that is both popular-commercial and also open to experimental art."

Ed wanted to do something more substantial than the little films he had created up to this point. He was intrigued with the idea of how far you could carry a long, plotless film. "Warhol and others have made long films, but I wanted to make a film of my own type which has its own requirements and its own limitations. ... A long film, which would carry without conventional plot or drama."

In 1962 at Chicon, during a midnight film program, an early rough-cut version of *Relativity* appeared along with *Lifelines*. At this point, most of the more harrowing elements were still missing from *Relativity*. Ed was curious to see the audience's response to various scenes, and this would affect his later edits of the film. As usual at these venues, Ed also brought the time-lapse build-ups of science fiction covers. He would gang up a dozen or more, each of one-or two-minute duration, on one reel. The fans always got a kick out of viewing the paintings magically creating themselves. Some of the covers demonstrated in this manner were "Get a Horse," done for *If, Worlds of Science Fiction*, August, 1958, and "Have Spacesuit, Will Travel" for *F&SF* (pg 70).

Ed once stated that from about 1955 to around 1959, in the normal course of his work, he filmed the painting of most of his art on 16mm except for rush jobs. He must have filmed the creation of hundreds of illustrations in that time frame.

Ideas were coming together from bits and pieces of projects Ed had worked on over the previous years. In June 1963 the

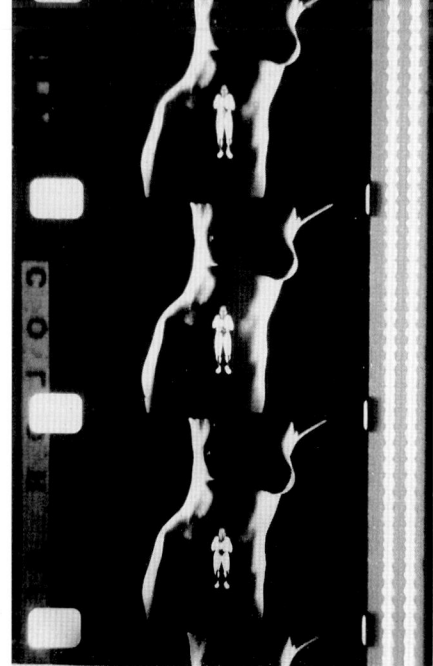

Frames from RELATIVITY.

Ford Foundation announced that it was giving out one-year grants to filmmakers. Producers, directors, critics and other film professionals were asked to nominate candidates for consideration. Stan VanDerBeek, a previous Ford Foundation grant winner, was one of the people to put forward Ed's name.

The foundation contacted Ed and asked him to write a short proposal. Ed outlined a film showing a subjective perception of reality through time and space, life, death, sex, and consciousness. He gave his theme as the relationship of individuals to their environment:

Man alone; isolated in hole, in empty space, separation of walls. Man as animal; insect eating insect, fighting rhinos, romping kids and monkeys. Man to woman; at mother's breast, courtship dance, sexual embrace. Man to society; marching en masse, *piling bricks, nude in marketplace. Man in time and space; life span in 24 frames (one second), the life span and size of a microbe, life of a star.*

It would start as the probings of an individual in what seems to be a deep underground pocket. He seeks clues to his identity and location. As the film goes on, he seeks contact with others. He mentally travels, searches, tries to communicate, enters into relationships with individuals and groups. All the while he is isolated. Then his fantasies take off from the few artifacts confined with him. A doll's arm, a page from a magazine, a broken hammer. He is an artist who molds his dream companions, a dancer who moves through the love and pain in life, a scholar who works with pieces of the knowledge of man. He tries to find, from his blind viewpoint, where he fits in the universe.

Ed had been through this dance before with the Ford Foundation when he applied to their fellowship program for a grant-in-aid for creative and performing artists in November

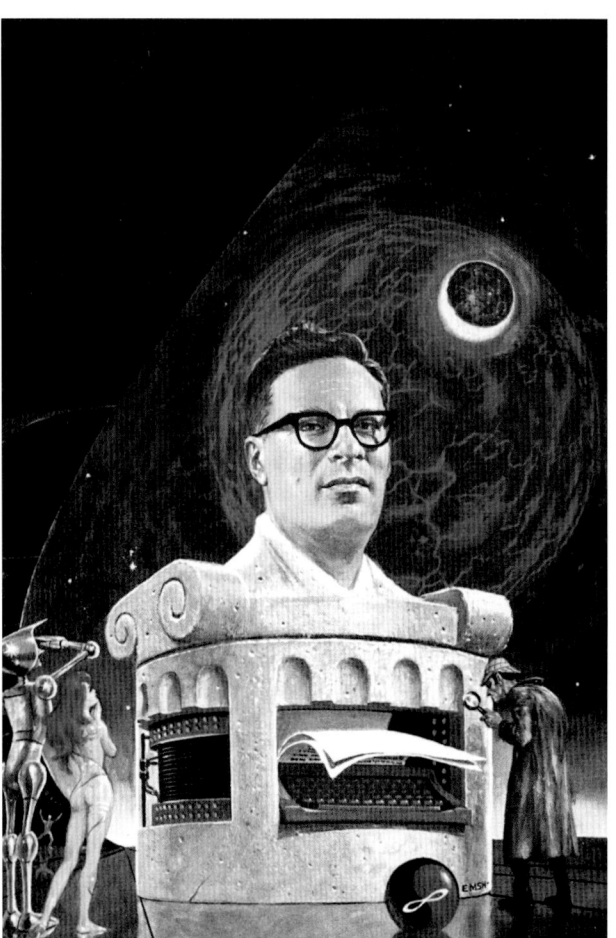

(top R) Ed in his Levittown studio Jan. 1964.

(bot L) MAGAZINE OF FANTASY & SCIENCE FICTION. Oct. 1966, "Special Isaac Asimov Issue."

1960. The Foundation did not deem the three films he had done up to that date as worthy enough, and turned him down.

In the early spring of 1964, Ed learned that he was part of a group of twelve filmmakers selected to receive a grant of $10,000 from the Ford Foundation. That summer Ed informed all his art clients that he was taking a year's break, and threw himself wholeheartedly into filmmaking.

He had decided to finish *Relativity*, which had been more of a collage film, without any two-dimensional artwork, utilizing a motley collection of images and ideas percolating in his head, including leftover material from other projects. While working on the CBC documentary *The Quiet Takeover* in 1964 (a film about computers invading the business world), Ed had filmed hand-held sweeping shots of the mainframe computer's consoles, capturing the pinpoints of light zooming into view like a star field in a science fiction movie, and these clips made their way into *Relativity*.

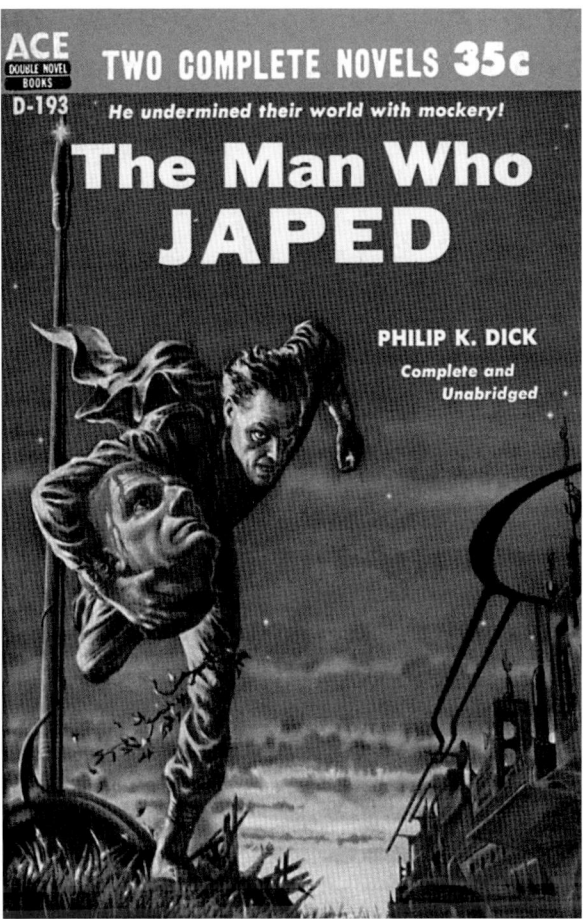

Jack Willis, the director of *The Quiet Takeover*, remembers, "Ed, during our breaks, taking the lens, and swooping that camera over the giant computers, pushing it in and out, swish panning, winding the film back, shooting again, creating multiple exposures." On the same shoot, he came across oil derricks in the California desert and captured their pumping movement in tight close-ups. Ed used these shots in *Relativity* to suggest sexual thrusting.

One can get a sense of the long gestation of *Relativity* by noticing the film stocks and film gauges used in the film: Kodachrome I, Kodachrome II, Anscochrome, Ektachrome Commercial and Ektachrome High Speed. The film can be seen as the quintessence of everything Ed had seen and read, at once serious and comical, of images found and manufactured, and metaphysical and scientific ideas.

As in *Dumpson's Place*, Ed was also thinking in terms of "penetrating space in a kind of flying camera." This was a dream of his since childhood. (John Campbell would have gotten a kick out of this camera lens of the mind, if not the film itself.) The ideas in *Relativity* were ones that were cropping up more and more during the sixties: the individual's insignificance in the scheme of nature's abundance, the scale of infinity, and man-woman relationships. It was as if Ed was saying that the

(top R) THE MAN WHO JAPED by Philip K. Dick. 1957. Ace.

breadth of human awareness and imagination is not up to the sheer plethora of the cosmos. In an interview, Ed stated that he could have dreamed *Relativity* instead of using a camera to film it.

Ed took a break from working on *Relativity* when the United States Information Agency (USIA, an ad hoc propaganda agency of the USA) asked him to work on a documentary titled *Faces of America*. For two months in the late summer of 1964, he became a "… sort of traveling bum, rambling around the country shooting pictures of people."

During the first half of 1964 Ed had made $400 from his own films. He made $40,000 for the rest of the year mostly from his USIA work. The one catch to doing USIA projects was that the finished film could not be legally exhibited in America, although Ed did show the film at a few out-of-the-way film festivals in Vermont and New York.

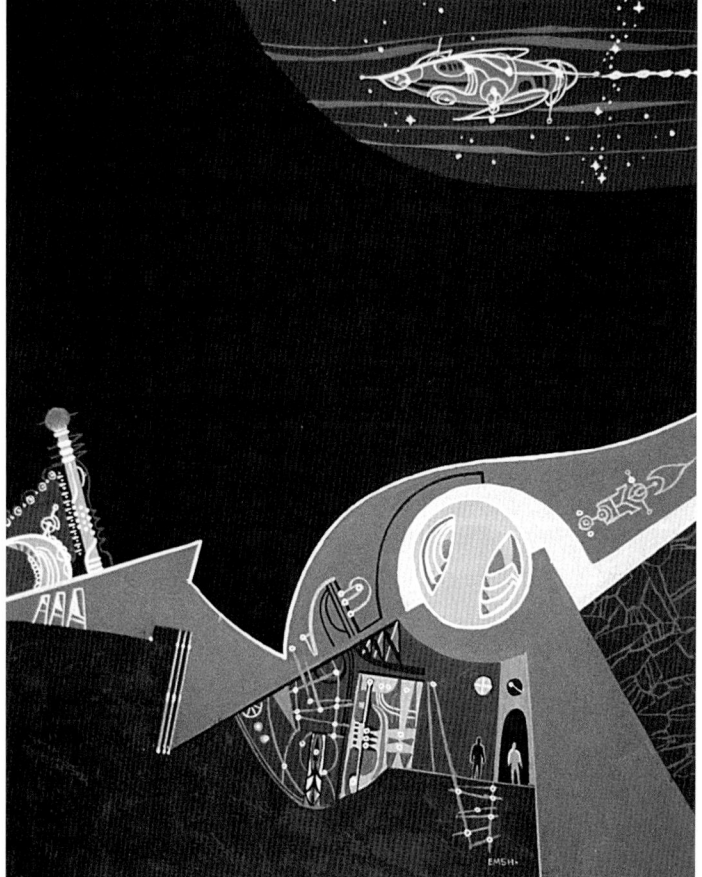

Many reviews of *Relativity* were laudatory. Richard Whitehall of the *Los Angeles Free Press* wrote, "Shot largely in long, smooth, hand-held tracking shots, *Relativity* is the miracle of creation, of life and death, of man's striving both to understand and conquer himself and the universe of which he is part—a flowing, sensuous movie of pattern and form, color and texture, integrated into a joyous homage to nature, to the strange fantasies of scientific fact … and to the irresistible forces which have shaped the world of which we are part…. Ever since he came to movies, Emshwiller has been interested in clashes and dislocations meshed together to create new meanings; his art—and I think him to be one of the finest artists in the movies—is an art of

(top R) TOTEM, 1963. 16mm, 16 minutes, color. Featuring Murray Louis and Gladys Balin and the Alwin Nikolais Dance Theatre. Choreography, costumes, and music by Nikolais. Direction, camera, and editing by EE. "A cine-dance in which the choreography often comes as much from camera movement and film editing as from the dancers. A mysterious, primordial, and ritualistic sequence of movements."

(BOT L) THE DARK PLANET by J. Hunter Holly. Avalon.

revelation, an inter-sensory exploration of textural forms."

For the first time, Ed used a narrator in a film. He explained his use of a speaking voice in *Relativity*, "Many filmmakers seem to have come to the medium from the world of literature. They were storytellers first — writers who later seem to have discovered images. For me, filmmaking was the other way around. I came to film as a creator of images and only now am I discovering the word. But my use of the word is not to give structure to the work. It serves, rather, as another element in the composition, a texture, an aspect of the environment…. For example, the human voice giving forth bits from the library of human knowledge, as in *Relativity*, can be symphonic in its emotional impact."

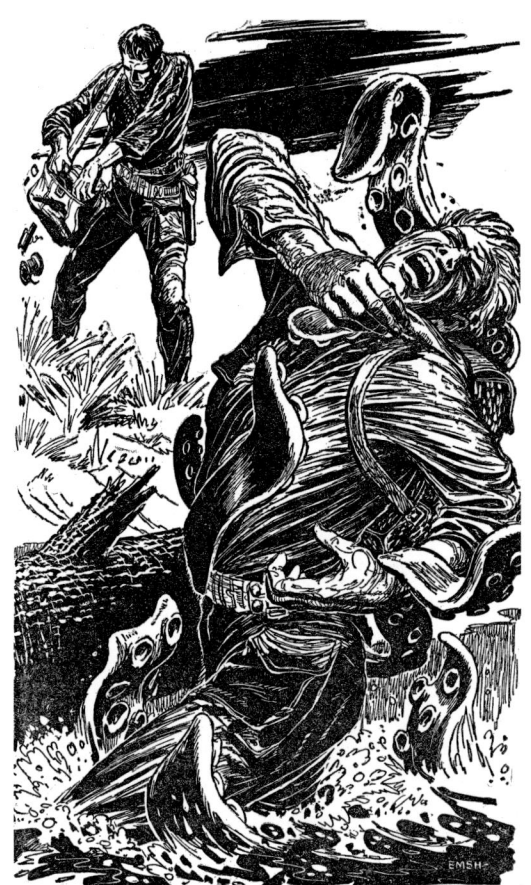

PLANET STORIES. Mar. 1954. "Morley's Weapon" by D. W. Barefoot.

WORLD WITHOUT MEN by Charles Eric Maine. Ace.

Take a number. Make it round. It is estimated that there are 100 billion galaxies in the observable universe. Our galaxy contains more than 100 billion stars. On our planet there are over a billion male humans. On our planet there are over a billion females. A man ejaculates over 200 million sperm during intercourse. A woman releases over 400 ova during her fertile period. Take a number. Make it one. Which one? The age of the universe is estimated variously to be from 6 to 15 billion years. The age of life on earth is estimated between 6 and 15 billion years.

The earliest man lived 1 million years ago. Early civilization began 60,000 thousand generations of man. There have been 560 generations since the Egyptians invented writing. Man's life expectancy has increased to 70 years. Seven years equals 2,208,990,000 seconds. One second is to a man's life span as a man's life span is to the age of life on earth.

The subatomic particle E_0 disintegrates in one-quintillionth of a second. The approximate diameter of a proton is one ten-trillionth of a centimeter. Eighteen quadrillion two hundred and eighty-eight trillion protons laid end to end would form a line equal to the height of a man. A proton is to a man as a man is to the distance of earth to Alpha Centauri.

Human sperm are one-thousandth of an inch long, or 25 microns. The smallest free-living cells, pleu-

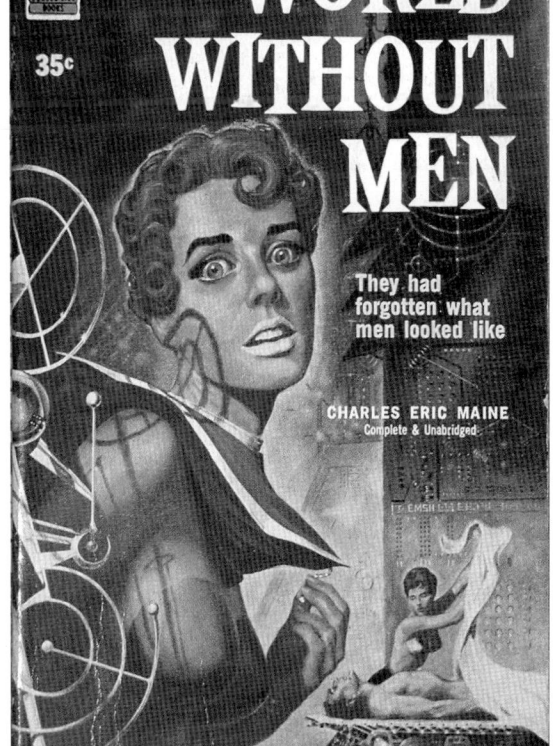

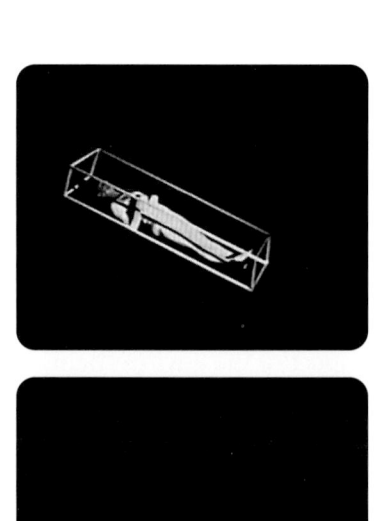
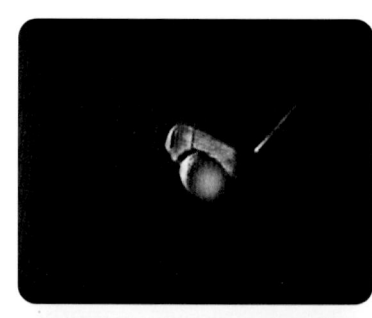
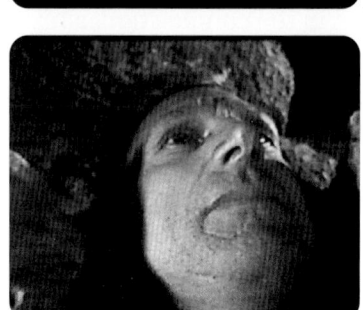
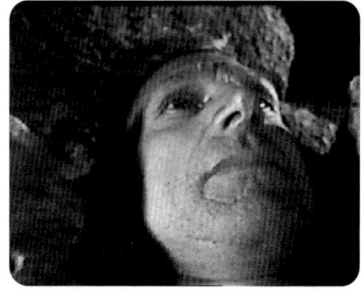
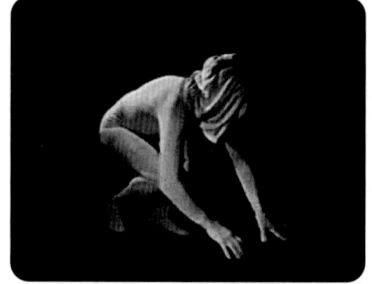
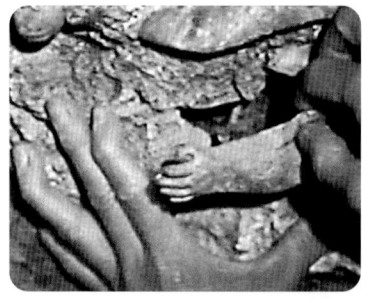
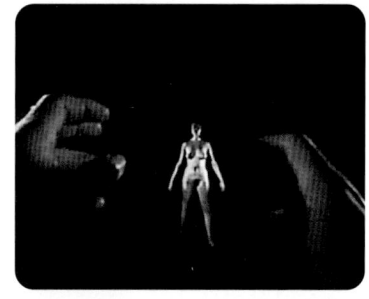
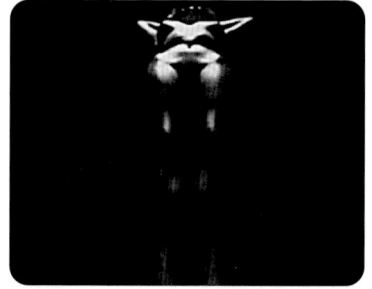
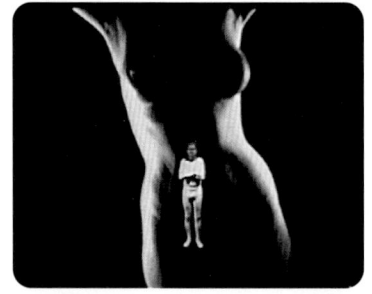
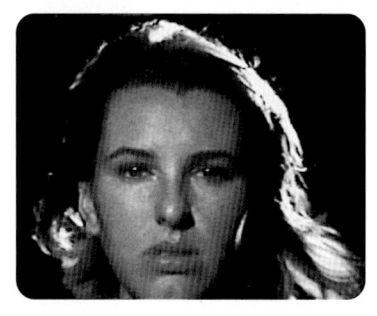
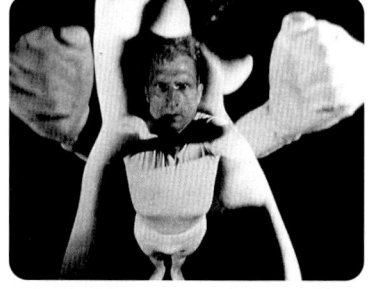
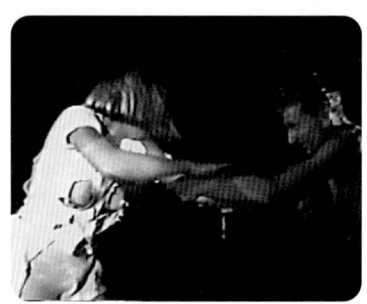
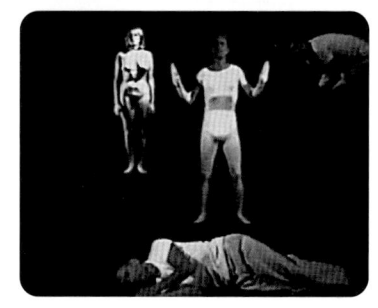
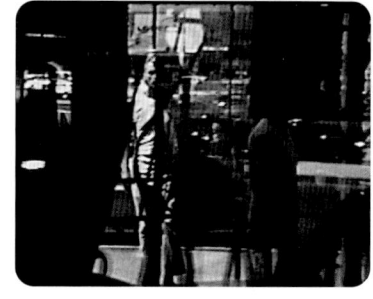

TWO PAGE SPREAD
Frames from RELATIVITY.

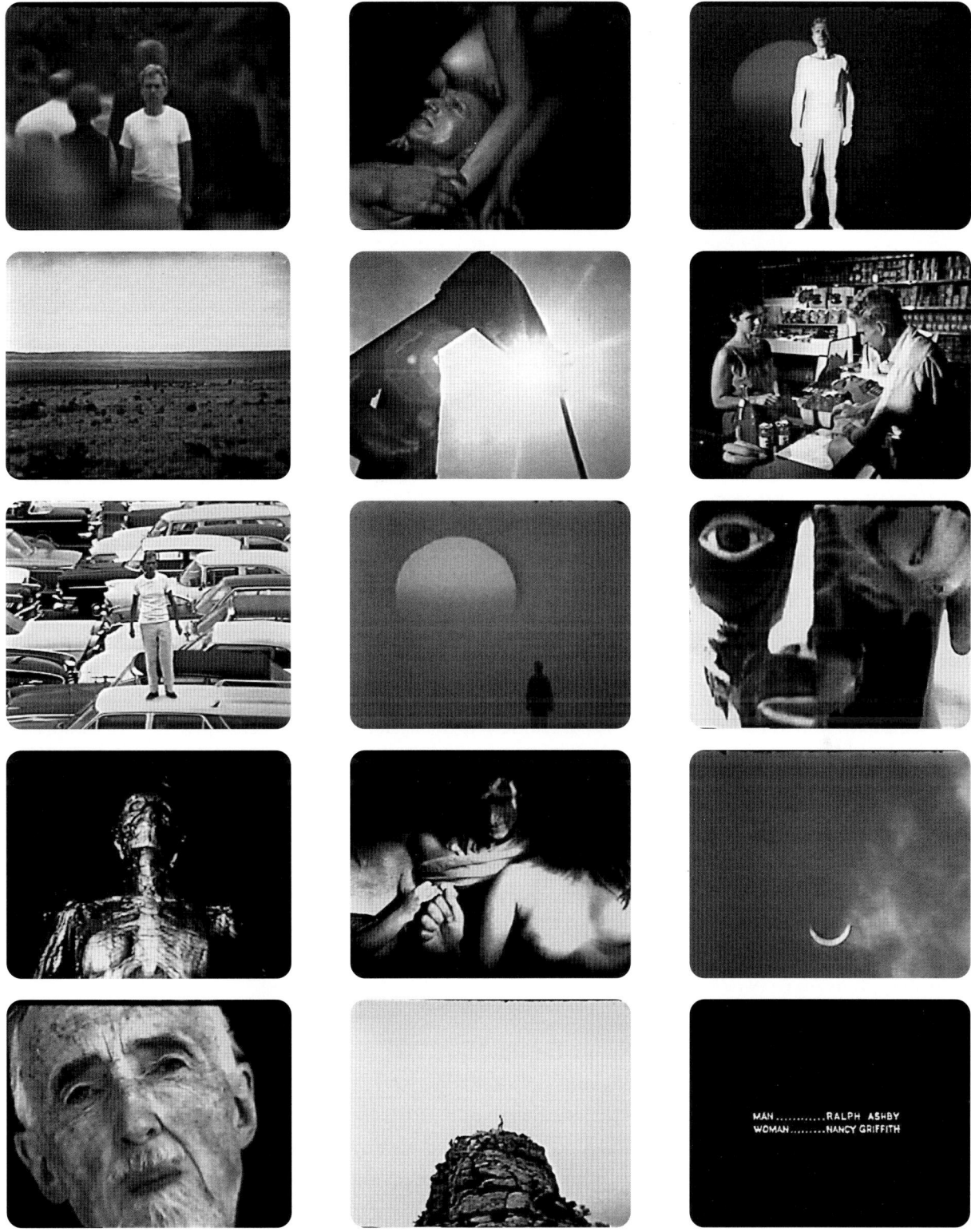

ropneumonia-Ue organisms or PPLO, are one-tenth of a micron in diameter. A life cycle of the PPLO is 5 days. A life cycle of a fruit fly is less than two weeks. The life span of a giant sequoia is 4,000 years. The age of the earth is 5 to 6 billion years. In 7 billion years the sun will be a white dwarf. The temperature of the earth will be 300 degrees Fahrenheit below zero.

This dialog was all Ed's, written and spoken by him in the film. It showed his fondness for hard facts and figures — and his reading of *Scientific American* and Asimov's science articles in *F&SF*. Until *Relativity* Ed's films had been mute in using the human voice, now Ed had moved further away from the silence inherent in painting or the sound effects in *Thanatopsis*, which replaced a musical score and were a more direct way of linking visuals and emotions.

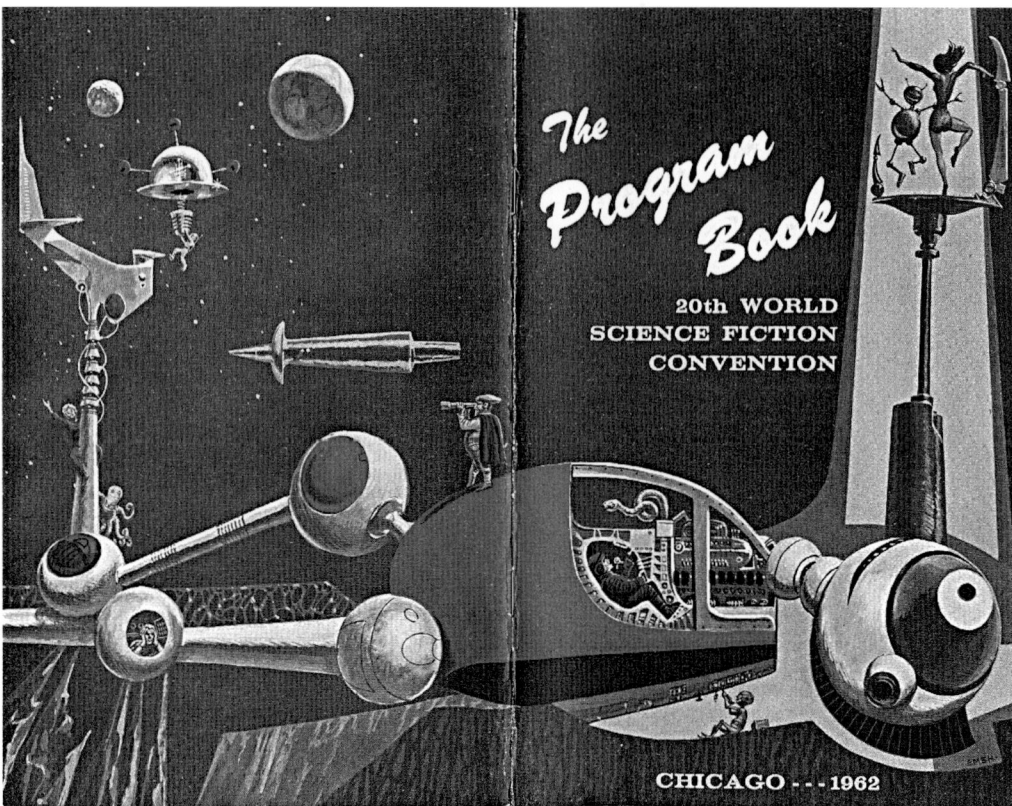

For *Relativity*, Ed built a cave environment out of papier-mâché in his attic studio, a sort of mole-hole the underground man of the film crawls through. An early version of *Relativity* ran twenty minutes longer and had a different ending including a three-minute scene showing a man walking up a hill and standing there while a giant sun goes down in the sky.

Ed's screening of *Relativity* at many SF conventions always caused a stir. At the Eastercon in Bristol, England, *Relativity* was shown after the French experimental short SF film *La Jetee* (later remade into the feature *12 Monkeys*) with the warning that it was "bloody, very bloody." *Relativity* generated so much talk that there was a repeat showing a day later for those who had missed it the first time. *Relativity* went on to become a keystone of sixties avant-garde filmmaking.

By 1967, Stanley Kubrick was well into the filming of *2001: A Space Odyssey*. He had seen a private screening of *Relativity* in England (United Kingdom censors had banned public showings of the film) and was taken with Ed's technical élan. On a visit to New York, he made the side trip to Levittown, and was surprised that Ed could have created his films using the limited facilities he saw in Ed's attic. Kubrick asked Ed to join his special effects production team at the MGM Studio in England and assist with the timegate end sequences of the movie.

(top) Program book for the 20th WorldCon in Chicago with art by EE. 1962. That year Ed won a Hugo Award for best professional artist.

Ed wrote later, "I read the script [Kubrick] and Arthur Clarke had written. The problem obviously was to create an overwhelming alien world experience." (Clarke had adapted and expanded his 1952 story "The Sentinel" for the movie.)

Ed was already committed to other film projects (including a USIA documentary of NASA's Apollo program), and may have been intimidated by the scale of the *2001* production. He turned Kubrick down. It is possible that had Ed accepted Kubrick's offer he would have been drawn further into commercial filmmaking. Instead, he made a conscious decision to have as much control as possible over the films he would work on.

Ed would have loved working at MGM's state-of-the-art filmmaking facilities, but did not like the idea of being subsumed into Kubrick's technical team. Like many creative types, he also had the fear of performing. "I suppose it's the old proving yourself thing and you constantly have to do it over and over and that's a terrible drag. Filmmaking is a little bit like sex in those terms…. Oh, of course it can also be just pure joy…just an easy thing, too," Ed once explained to Carol. "Actually, when I'm shooting there's a tremendous amount of anxiety because even though I'm also regarded as someone who is very competent with equipment and so forth, I constantly have a feeling as though I don't know what the hell's happening behind this piece of machinery … and I hope that it's going to come out right." In hindsight, Ed probably made the right decision not to yoke himself to Kubrick's vision.

While Ed generally liked *2001: A Space Odyssey* when it came out, he also thought that it fell short of its potential. He saw the movie as too "stylized": "There don't seem to be any wrinkles or grease spots on either the people or the machines. I mean this mostly in a figurative sense. I realize the film is stylized, but the manner of conveying 'human' touches, even when ironic, seems studied and unreal."

He had just spent six months creating the impressionistic documentary *Project*

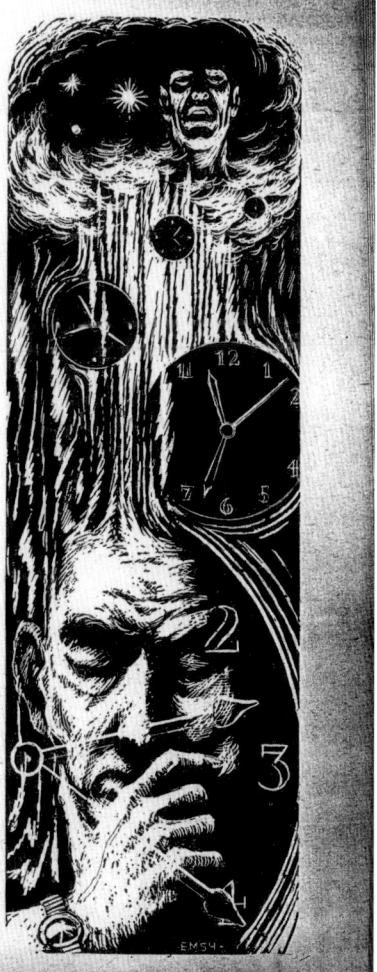

EE illustrated the short story "Relativity" by John Christopher for SPACE SCIENCE FICTION, Feb. 1953. The story has no relationship to the film RELATIVITY, and it is likely that EE had no memory of it while making the film.

Apollo (pg. 137), and had been in close contact with real astronauts and spaceships, "... somehow [they were] more textured than their counterparts in *2001*." He was glad to see avant-garde and experimental film techniques brought into a commercial movie. "Of course, it also means that the cutting edge of the avant-garde is being pushed by an ever-growing sophistication and has to keep moving in new directions to stay in the game."

During the moon landing of Apollo 11 in July 1969, Ed was at the Toronto Planetarium where he hosted a screening of *Project Apollo*. The science fiction writer Samuel R. Delany was at the showing and remembers, "...Despite its conception as propaganda, [*Project Apollo*] transcends that conception brilliantly to provide an astonishing experience of something other, as much as any work by [Leni] Riefenstahl." Ed justified using muffled sound during one technical meeting as a "little bit of humor" that was not appreciated by the literal-minded people at USIA.

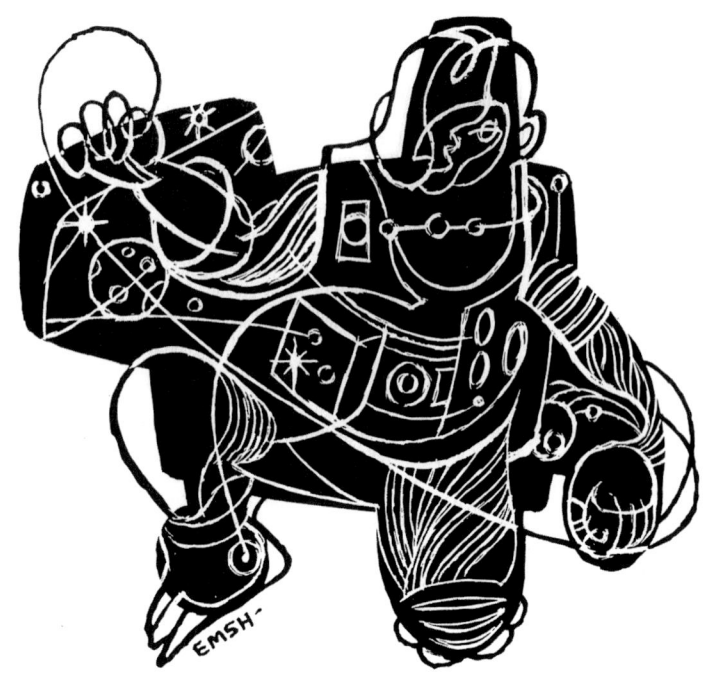

Throughout the sixties, Ed was asked many times to direct feature films, but was not interested in doing plotted stories. "If I'm going to spend the kind of time involved in directing someone else's story. ... I would much rather make a film in the manner in which I normally do, which is to say that I deal thematically in formal terms, almost musical terms, in choreographic terms.... I make film[s] as a living experience, a growth exploration for myself."

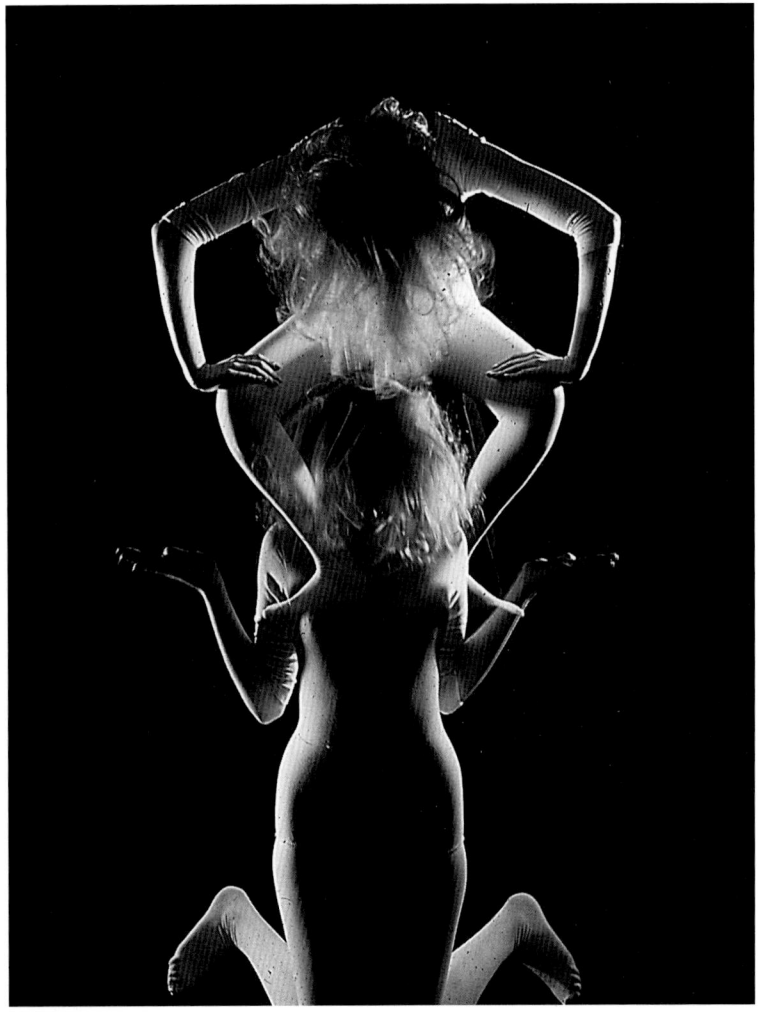

(top R) Spot illustration. C. 1962.

(bot L) Photo study by EE. Model Nancy Griffith. C. 1964.

Eleven

All kinds of branches

ED WOULD ONLY APPLY for art grants when he had a clear project in mind, but preferred to work with his own money. "That way I don't have to satisfy anyone but me. I think that grant people always want something that is successful and that creates a psychological pressure on me." Ed liked "walking the tightrope" of independence and always eschewed mass-marketed films, though he would sometimes get involved in documentaries or other people' film projects that interested him. "I have turned down several requests," he once told an interviewer. "People in the experimental films of the late 50s and 60s had a lot of stuff lifted by advertisers and feature films. They produced ideas which were absorbed into [the film] language. Unfortunately [the filmmakers] were little fish in the game and never got anything. The sharks got it all."

Soon after completing *Thanatopsis*, Ed met dance choreographer Alwin Nikolais, who was working on a new dance he called *Totem*. Ed watched the rehearsals and suggested that a short film could be made of the ballet. He had in mind some film he had shot three weeks earlier, and realized that the two elements could work together. Ed worked out a storyboard using elements from the dance, and shot a series of sessions. Later, he combined three separate shots, superimposing dancers into his prefilmed clips of textural patterns and natural images. After editing the film, Nikolais added his own original electronic score.

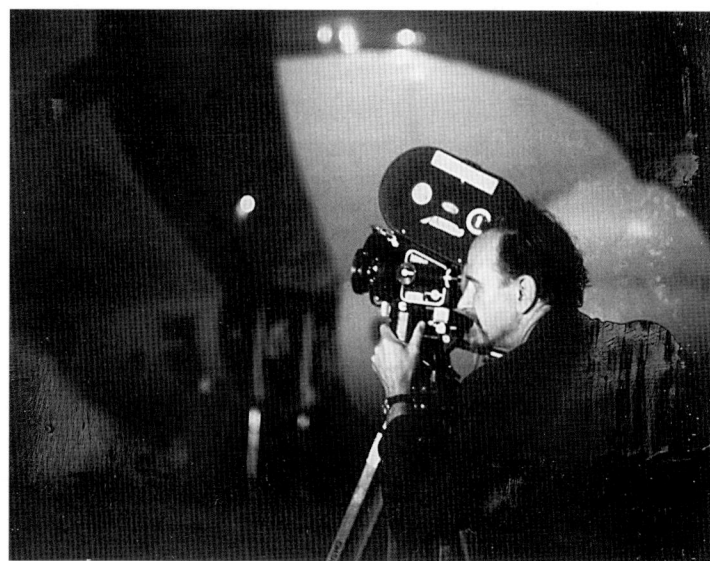

Ed described *Totem* to a dance magazine, "The dancers are first seen as parts of a frieze; then as strange subterranean, headless creatures; then as random beings appearing and disappearing. [Dancer] Murray Louis does a solo, which is interrupted by brief images of his [partner] Gladys Bailing quickly fading in and out. The two dancers become superimposed and interchangeable. A

Ed in front of the "Guppy" (the aircraft used to transport sections of the Apollo rocket) at Cape Kennedy. Nov. 24, 1967.

sextet moves rhythmically through images of water and waving weeds. A hoop duet culminates in a crescendo of flames and massed figures. The dancers form highly textural patterns in mirror images, ending in a kaleidoscopic series of implosions."

Many cine-dance filmmakers seemed more concerned with obliterating dancers on screen, or trying to create a cinematic narrative different from a dancer's or choreographer's intent. Cine-dance, by its very nature, breaks the notion of linear sequences and relationships, the time limits and shifting angles of images create a form of non sequitur. Nikolais worked closely with Ed, and they managed to create a unified vision. The music helped to bridge Nikolais' choreography with Ed's cinematic contributions into a new creation.

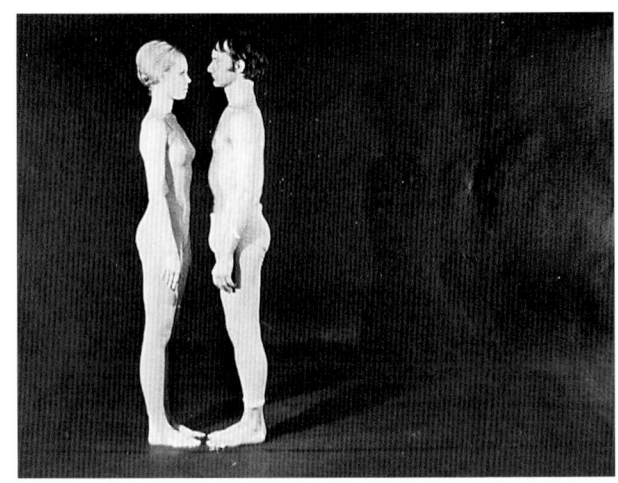

In many of his films, Ed seems to be attempting to present human movement through a dancing, hand-held, point-of-view camera. One of the best scenes in *Project Apollo* is his running, hand-held shot of the take off of Apollo 9. The same can be said of the fly-through scene in *Dumpson's Place*. Ed saw cine-dance as a point of departure for his own vision. He would utilize someone else's choreography in the same way a Pop artist would appropriate a panel of art from a comic book to create a painting.

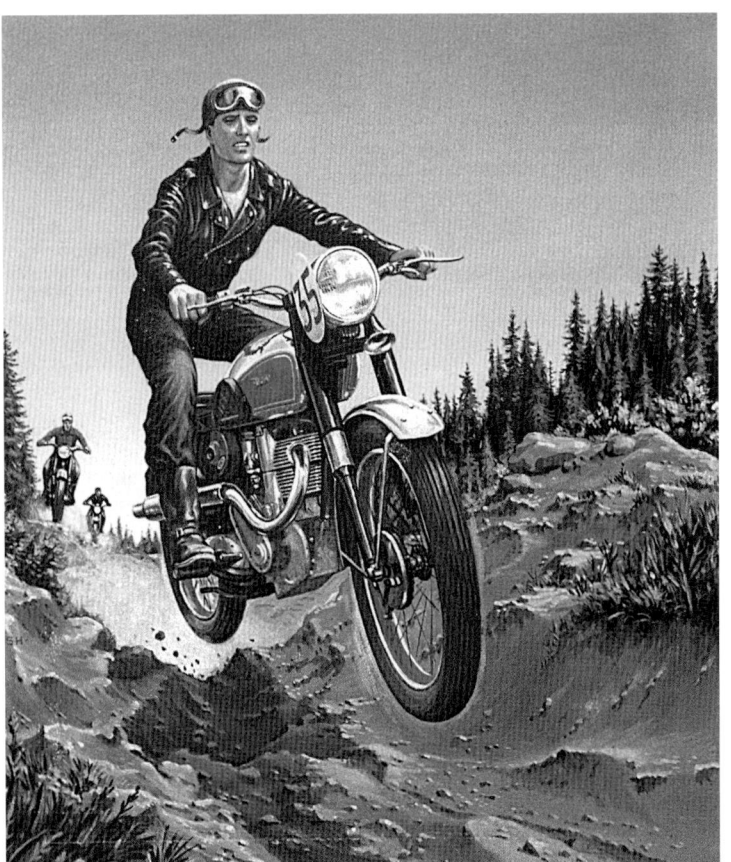

Ed was never interested in documenting a dance. "When the dancer is used in filmic terms, rather than dance terms, space and time are flexible. The images projected on the screen may seem to move forward and backward in time, may be discontinuous, in fast motion, slow motion, frozen, repetitious, or simultaneous. The dancer can appear to shift instantaneously from one location to another, can be compressed, elongated, distorted, or seen from widely varying perspectives…. So, in some cases, two choreographies are united in one film—dance choreography and film choreography. In other cases, dance choreography in the usual sense is practically non-existent. Then the camera and editing techniques

(top R) FILM WITH THREE DANCERS. 1970, 16mm, 20 minutes, color. Dancers: Carolyn Carlson, Emery Hermans, Bob Beswick. "Dancers are seen in different ways. They are seen in formal movements combined and transformed by cinematic techniques. They are shown in semi-documentary fashion, in surreal fashion. They reveal themselves, their aesthetics, their method of working together." - EE

(bot L) Art for unknown publication. C. 1960.

provide the movement, contrasts, and suggestions in the dancer's image. ... I can make films with dancers that satisfy my need to work in abstract, visual terms, yet ... seem more meaningful than pure forms and colors."

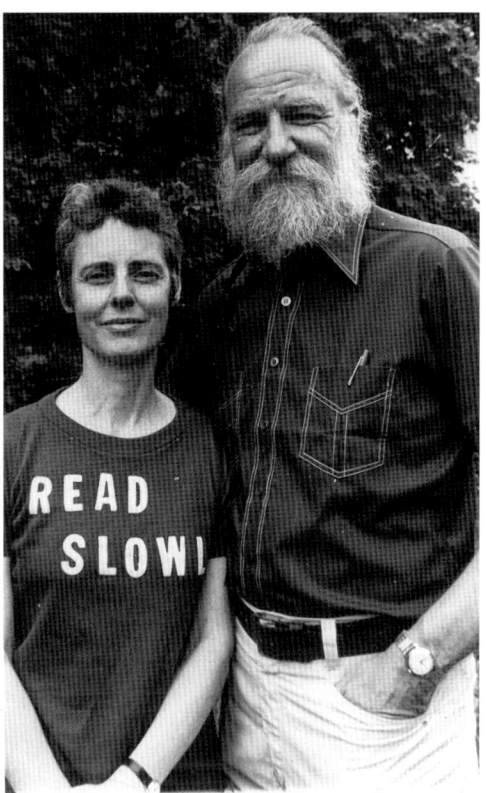

Carol and Ed, 1970.

All artists provide some sense of bewilderment to their family. It was an unusual way of life in Levittown with two creative parents. Peter Emshwiller remembers this time:

I occasionally was confused by our "lifestyle." It was very strange growing up in conservative, conformist, mass suburbia with hippie/artist/bohemian parents. It sometimes felt a little like we Emshwillers were the Munsters or the Addams Family of our neighborhood.

We were the weirdo-freaks of Wantagh, Long Island.

In hindsight, it was actually very cool. But as an insecure kid wanting to fit in, I was often mortified we didn't blend in better. Why couldn't we be like everyone else? No one else's dad had a huge straggly white beard, a long ponytail, and no nine-to-five job. No one else's mom rarely wore dresses, never put on makeup or high heels, and served her family organic health food instead of Frosted Flakes. No one else's family didn't attend church or temple but instead went to meetings of "The Ethical Culture Society."

And certainly no one else's parents cared deeply about art and politics but couldn't have cared less about making money or acquiring things....

My friends' homes were always spotless and carefully decorated and even had cool plastic covers on all their flower-printed living room couches! Why couldn't we have that?

Our house was always a cluttered mess: film, video, and sound equipment crammed into every free corner; mismatched, cat-scratched furniture piled high with books, papers, art supplies, and magazines. Our dining-room table was flanked by a pair of beat-up picnic benches instead of chairs. Right next to this table was what appeared to be a primitive love seat — but if you looked close you noticed that under its cushion was a homemade cage housing our three-foot-long pet iguana, Philip-the-Second. (Philip-the-First had been a snake, may he rest in peace.) Oh — and the color of our living-room rug was chosen specifically because it didn't show the cat-vomit stains. Yup.

As a kid I was convinced visiting neighbors were shocked to see that, once they made their way past our rarely-mowed, dandelion-filled lawn and entered our front door, directly to their left was a wall covered with stills from my dad's films — including some female nudes from "Relativity."

The horror! The shame! The embarrassment!

Occasionally, my folks'd have a party and all kinds of strange, bearded artsy-types would invade from

Manhattan. My dad would set up the projector in the backyard and screen some of his latest films that I just couldn't follow at all. What must the neighbors think of us?

On the rare occasions when Carol was away and Ed was left in charge of the kids, he would take them out for forbidden treats of donuts or fall back on a delicacy he discovered during his army days: pan-fried Spam. Peter Emshwiller's memory of these treasonous suppers is a small personal epiphany: "We totally loved it — greasy, salty, spiced mystery-meat ambrosia." Ed would top off his Spam dinner with a dollop of cream cheese.

Ed had the habit of holding a paintbrush in his mouth when not using it and his daughter Susan would yell at him, "Dad! You'll poison yourself!"

Susan remembers that as a child she would go to friends' homes, be introduced to their parents, and find herself frozen as to how to respond—unsure of the proper etiquette in meeting "normal people." No one had shown her the social grace of a handshake. She never knew when her father would be around the corner waiting to film her or her siblings. "Everything had to be for a movie or painting." She appeared as the nude toddler watching her robot "father" decorate the tree in one of the last SF Christmas covers Ed did (page 93, *F&SF*, January 1960). Susan resented this imposition while growing up, but later came to see it as part of their unique family dynamics.

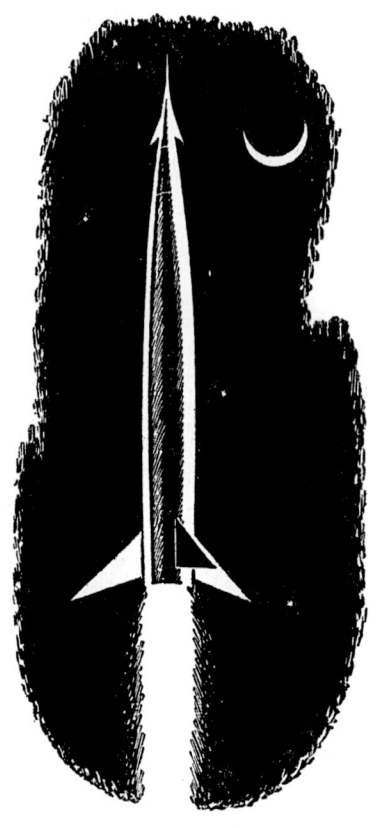

Ed told his kids, "You can smoke pot if you want, but don't bring it into the house." He did not want to give ammunition to any neighbor with ill will. Many times Ed would be away from Levittown for extended periods of time. On one occasion he returned home from such a trip and found everyone home in the living room. He jauntily asked, "How's school?" and was surprised when he was told, "You don't even know our teachers' names." This was an offhand teenage response, but Ed began to cry.

By the late sixties Ed was doing many

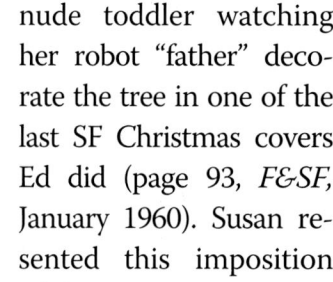

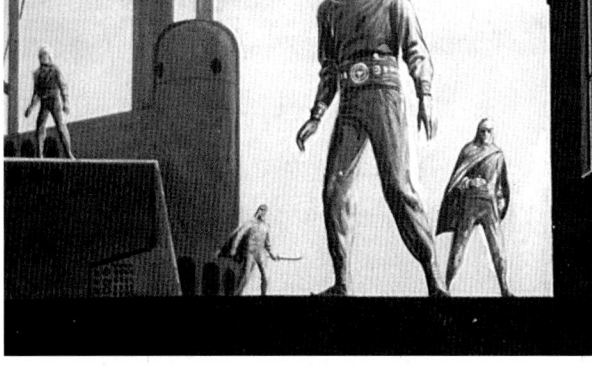

(top R) Spot art. IF SCIENCE FICTION. C. 1957.

(bot L) (bot L) BELIEVER'S WORLD by Robert Lowndes. 1961. Avalon

one night stands as a lecturer, short teaching stints at colleges across the country, and "show and tell" demonstrations at film festivals. While on a Canadian summer vacation trip in 1957, Ed had grown a small goatee on a bet and this gave him the appearance of a beatnik. With every passing year, Ed looked more and more like the guru Mr. Natural, a long-bearded cartoon character created by Robert Crumb that became a sort of mature hippy icon of the times.

At the Milford Conference in 1968, he filmed many of the writers in attendance to create *Image, Flesh, and Voice*. This was a strange quasi-narrative film that appealed more to science fiction's sub-culture than to a regular audience and some people saw it as an insular SF comedy. It included scenes like the one where a nude young woman appears repetitively from behind a door until the final time when she becomes Judy Merril. Ed shot the film with a 35mm Arriflex that he had acquired while doing his U.S. government films. "…I wanted to make a 35mm feature length film with the same freedom from commercialism as a personal 16mm film, a sort of 'it doesn't have to be made to sell tickets' attitude.

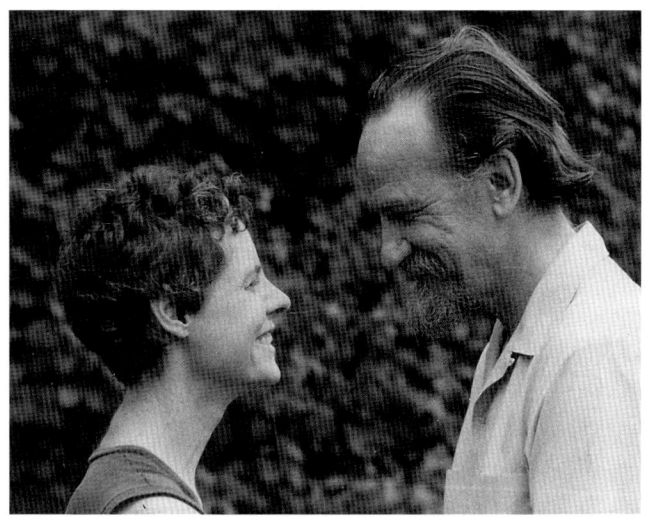

(top R) Carol and Ed. 1972.

(bot L) UNTAMED. Jan. 1960.

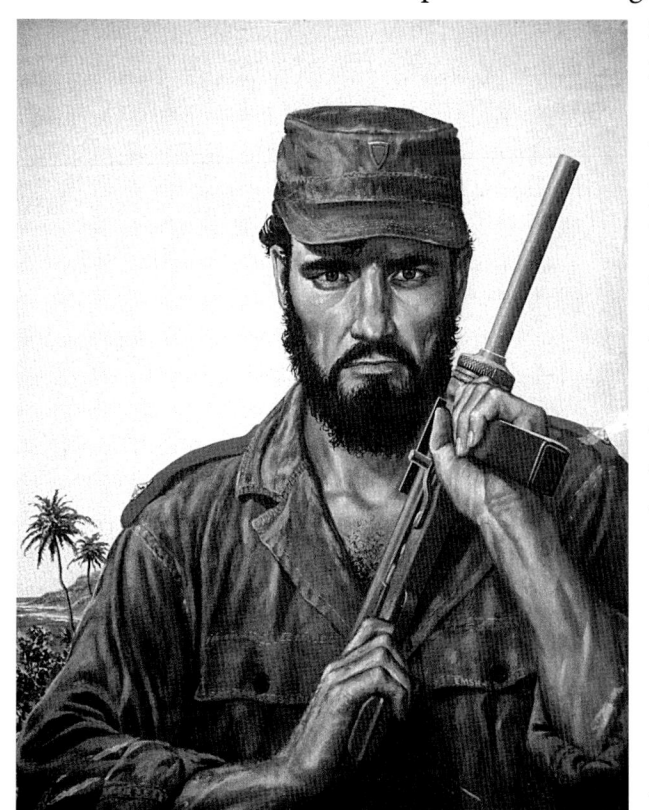

"I wanted to either catch people in, or provoke people into, emotional states. I did a lot of recording of many different people over a period of a couple of years. Sometimes the tapes were of conversations, sometimes they were of people responding to my 'provocateur's kit,' which was a set of 3x5 cards with questions about how they saw themselves and others, and a series of word associations, and a number of Polaroid photos of some of the 'interviewees' for others to react to. During this time I would occasionally film some of the people interviewed, though deliberately never sync sound as my concept of using voice in this film didn't call for it…. I was fascinated with the relative weight of word vs. picture."

Tom Disch had a voice-over telling tales of romantic woe while a party takes place. Ed had recorded conversations apart from the film's images and later combined the two, avoiding any direct correlation between voices and visuals. Disch wrote about the film: "That life offers too much data for art ever to be able to order; the movie had persuaded me that it was life — uncooked, uncalculated fact. Later I asked Ed whether he felt the same way, or if he had a constant sense of his own artifices. Could a modern Riefenstahl turn *these* techniques to sinister purpose? Or, put it this way: is there a language, after all, in which it is impossible to lie?"

Ed's fragmented life-style made it difficult to develop long-term projects, and he did not know what he would be doing from one year to the next. In the summer of 1970 he was at Cornell University, in Ithaca, N.Y., leading a school program to create a feature length film in six weeks. Ed liked the idea of working on a film from scratch without even knowing anything about the people who were going to participate. "I sometimes see the body of my work as like a tree—there's kind of a continuity and a trunk, but there are all kinds of branches. Literally, I made a film called *Branches* because it was concerned with the idea of possibilities. … It's a curious hybrid of collaboration."

Harlan Ellison had gotten Leo and Diane Dillon to create cover art and interior black and white illustrations for each story in *Dangerous Visions*. The book had wound up being a big success for Doubleday and Ellison sold them on doing a follow-up volume. This time Ellison asked Ed if he could do art for *Again, Dangerous Visions*. Ed thought it would be fun, and as a favor to Ellison threw himself into SF art again. Over the years he had done a few covers for the special author issues of the *Magazine of Fantasy & Science Fiction*, including Asimov, Silverberg, and Fritz Leiber (pg. 142). These were also done as a favor since Ed now saw himself as a filmmaker and not a painter. Ed's illustrations for *Again, Dangerous Visions* were created as a visual "soundtrack" to each story.

By the seventies Ed felt that he might be repeating himself in film. Video was beginning to gain some cachet over filmmaking in its ease of use and manipulation of recorded images. Ed had met and become friends with video artist Nam June Paik in the late sixties. Paik may have been one of the first artists to manipulate broadcast images on TV screens using magnets. Born in South Korea, he was living and working in Germany where he met and was heavily influence by John Cage.

(top) HEADGAME or PERCEPTUAL SPECTRUM LINES. Oct. 1968. "This film will involve concepts of art (dance, sculpture) and science (bio-psychology). It will be impressionistic, employing a wide range of styles.... It is intended to engage the viewer in a gestalt-like, C. P. Snow two worlds experience." — EE

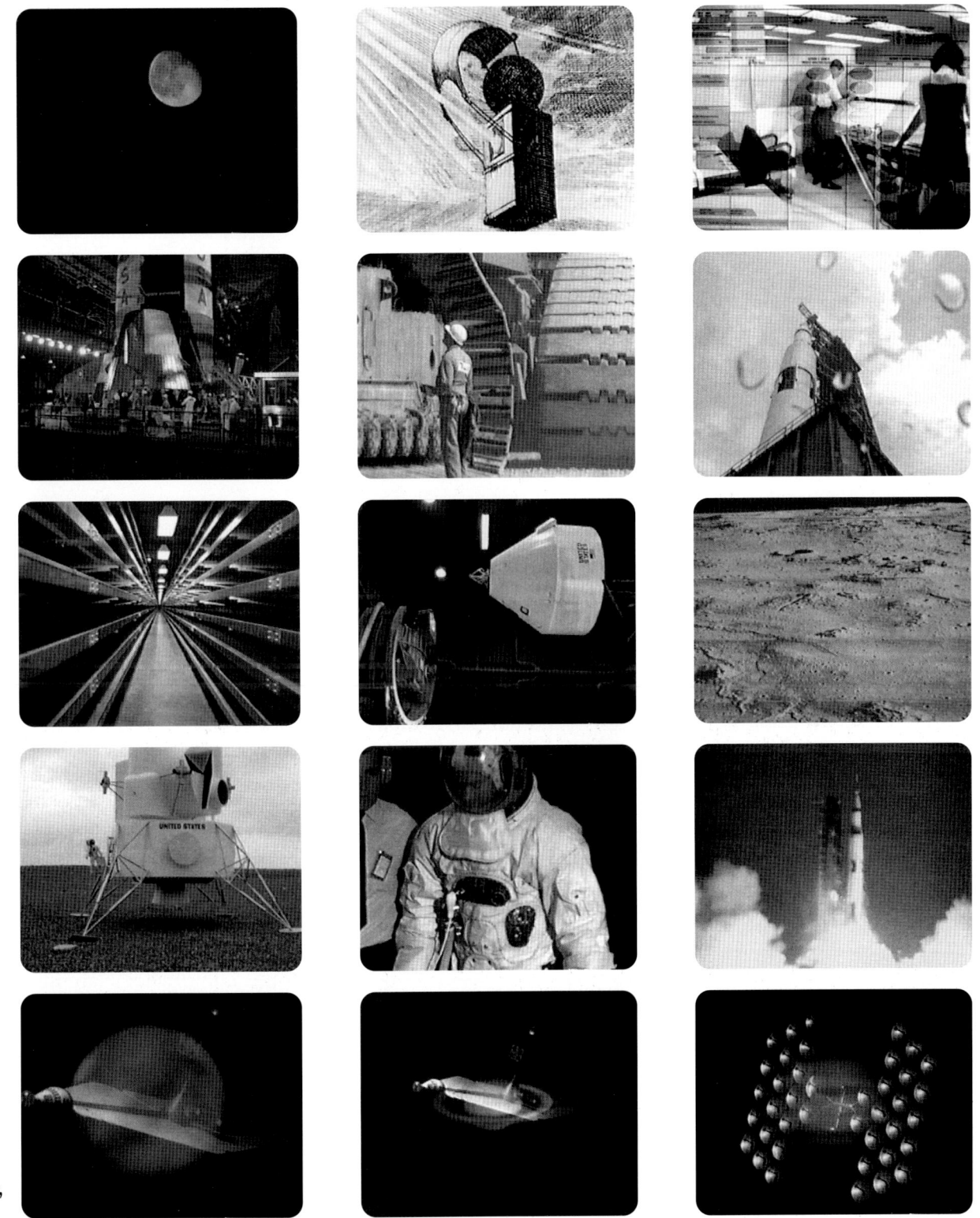

PROJECT APOLLO. 1968, color, 16mm, 32 minutes.

Ed still carried his Bolex everywhere he went, but was intrigued by the possibilities of video. "I like the idea of going through different careers. It's like being reborn a number of times. There is always a certain amount of frustration about growth because it seems to come in spurts ... you get the skill, capability and perception and then you become dissatisfied and question all the things you have been applying to your life and thought you wanted."

At first, Ed seemed at odds with video. "The painter is really the best off, the filmmaker is at sort of a second stage with video really at the bottom of the heap — that is, if you believe that control over the way in which your work is viewed is important."

After gaining more experience with the medium, Ed changed his mind. He liked the immediate playback and ease of mixing different kinds of elements. Using video synthesizers and colorizers to key in and manipulate images brought out the artist in him. It was like returning to painting. "I could see whether I had what I wanted or not right away."

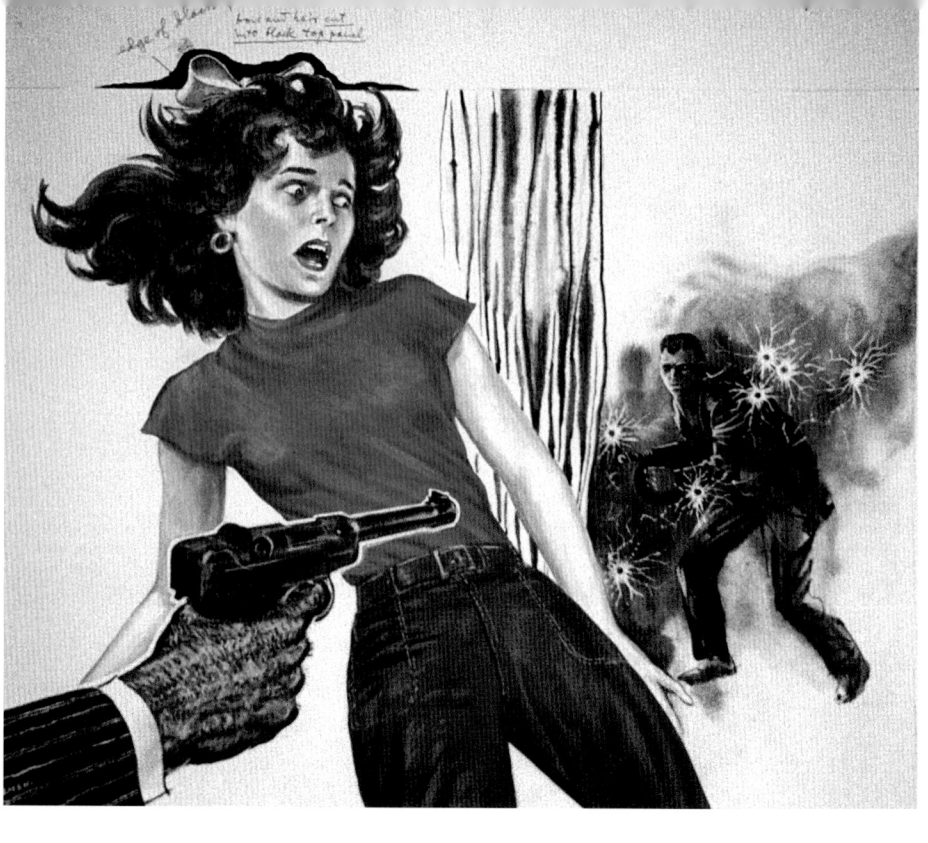

Ed worked by using different types of video cameras to tape images and scenes. When he thought he had enough videotape, he would make little notes, on separate pieces of paper, defining all the clips that seemed to have something to them. Then he would edit by putting these pieces of paper on a big table and assembling them into a storyboard. "Then I take those same pieces of paper, shuffle them, and say, This part doesn't work so I'll throw it out; and here are some things which would relate better in a different place and if I add some shots here which I didn't include in the first assembly."

WNET-TV in New York started its Television Laboratory in 1972 and Ed was one of the people it consulted with about how best to optimize their facilities. After trying a few permutations of technical to creative use of people, WNET began an artists-in-residence program. They invited Nam June Paik and Emshwiller, along with two other video artists, to work in their laboratory. Ed had only started in video the year before.

David Loxton, the WNET lab director, arranged for Ed to visit Dolphin Computer Image Corporation, which used a Scanimate System for real time analog image manipulation. This system worked by scanning in existing artwork, then manipulating and distorting it electronically before it reached the screen. The work Dolphin was doing appeared too commercial to Ed, nevertheless he decided to try their system. He made five small black and white felt tip marker drawings which were used to cre-

(top) **A SHROUD FOR MR BUNDY.** Mercury Mystery Books. Date unknown.

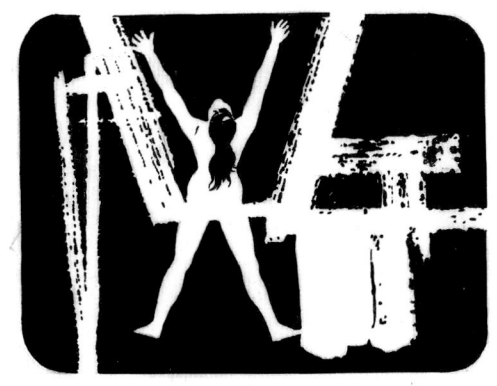

ate a forty-minute video in the single day of computer access. Back at the Television Laboratory, he edited the tape into the seventeen-minute *Computer Graphics #1*. This was edited further into the twelve-minute *Thermogenesis*.

At the time, Ed's idea of computer video animation was that of "pretty variations of Lissajous patterns," "stiffly mechanical transformations," or "flashy zap cute commercials."

"I was doubtful about how much I could control the pacing, the sensual quality of the movement, since, in this situation, once having made the drawings, the only action I could take was to tell [Dolphin technicians] Walter and Richard what kind of movements I wanted, what I wanted to avoid, and the tempo I wanted. …To be so far removed from…direct physical participation, as I was with the computers, I was afraid I'd be completely frustrated. Not so, as it turned out. … The experience was, once again, analogous to a musical performance. Watching the monitors, giving instructions, waving my arms, asking for changes, gave me plenty of sense of direct involvement."

Ideally, Ed would have liked to have the skills to make his own transformation personally on the Scanimate System.

Ed was intrigued enough with the results of *Thermogenesis* to try a more ambitious work. He used twenty-two standard sized Acme animation cels of artwork overlaid with five different gray levels. These were made from different tints of zip-a-tone (a clear material made up of tiny dots used for halftone printing) that Ed used as palette for the computer to render into color. This time Ed took two days working on the Dolphin computer graphics system, with the help of programmer Walter Wright, to complete his computer graphics. (He used two Scanimates—one for foregrounds and one for backgrounds.) Later, dancers were videotaped at the TV studio and chroma-keyed with the computer animation "environment." The soundtrack came last and, taking a week, was the longest component to complete. In 1972, *Scape-Mates* played on PBS stations and at festivals.

THIS PAGE
(top) High contrast frame from DANCE CHROMATIC. This art was also used by Ed for his letterhead throughout the 1960s.

(bot R) EARTH'S LAST FORTRESS by A. E. van Vogt. Ace Double Novel. April 1960.

PAGE 140
INSTA-MOVIE. NEW WORLDS magazine, No. 178.

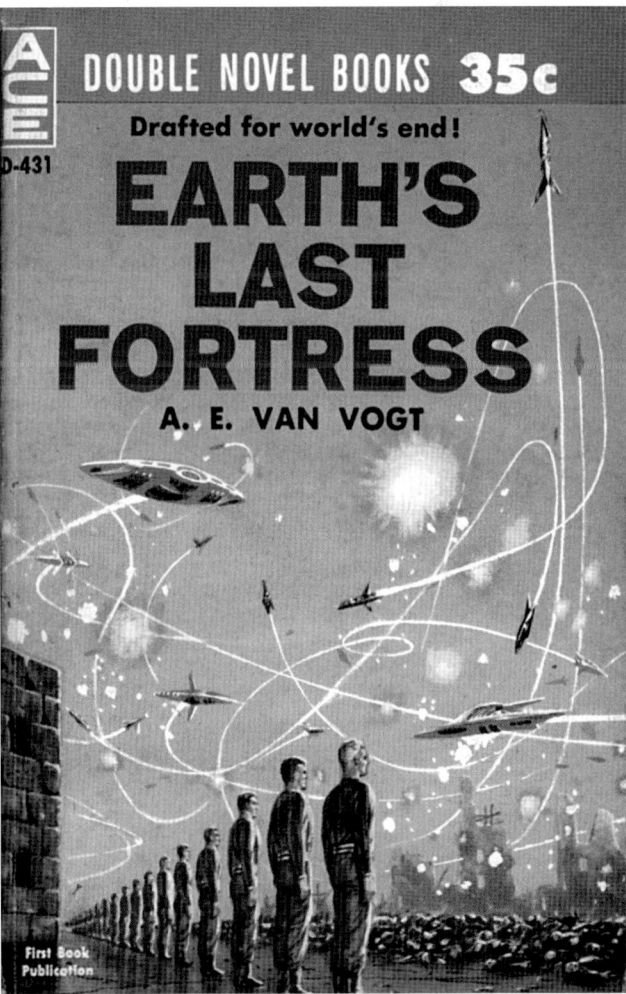

Ed was quick to see the immense flexibility of computers interfaced with video equipment. *Thermogenesis* and *Scape-Mates* were both free-form voyages through electronic environments. *Scape-Mates* especially combined a vast Escher-like setting with human figures and received an Emmy nomination in 1974 based on its visual inventiveness and novelty (this in a time when it seemed that the bland sameness of broadcast television had reached an all-time low).

Ed was seeking new visual possibilities at WNET Television's Laboratory. He wanted, above all, to figure out the creative uses of new technologies even while he was finding the new tools frustrating: "... well, there are so many variables." During the next few years Ed used analog video synthesizers, including the Paik-Able and the Rutt-Etra, but found these systems limited.

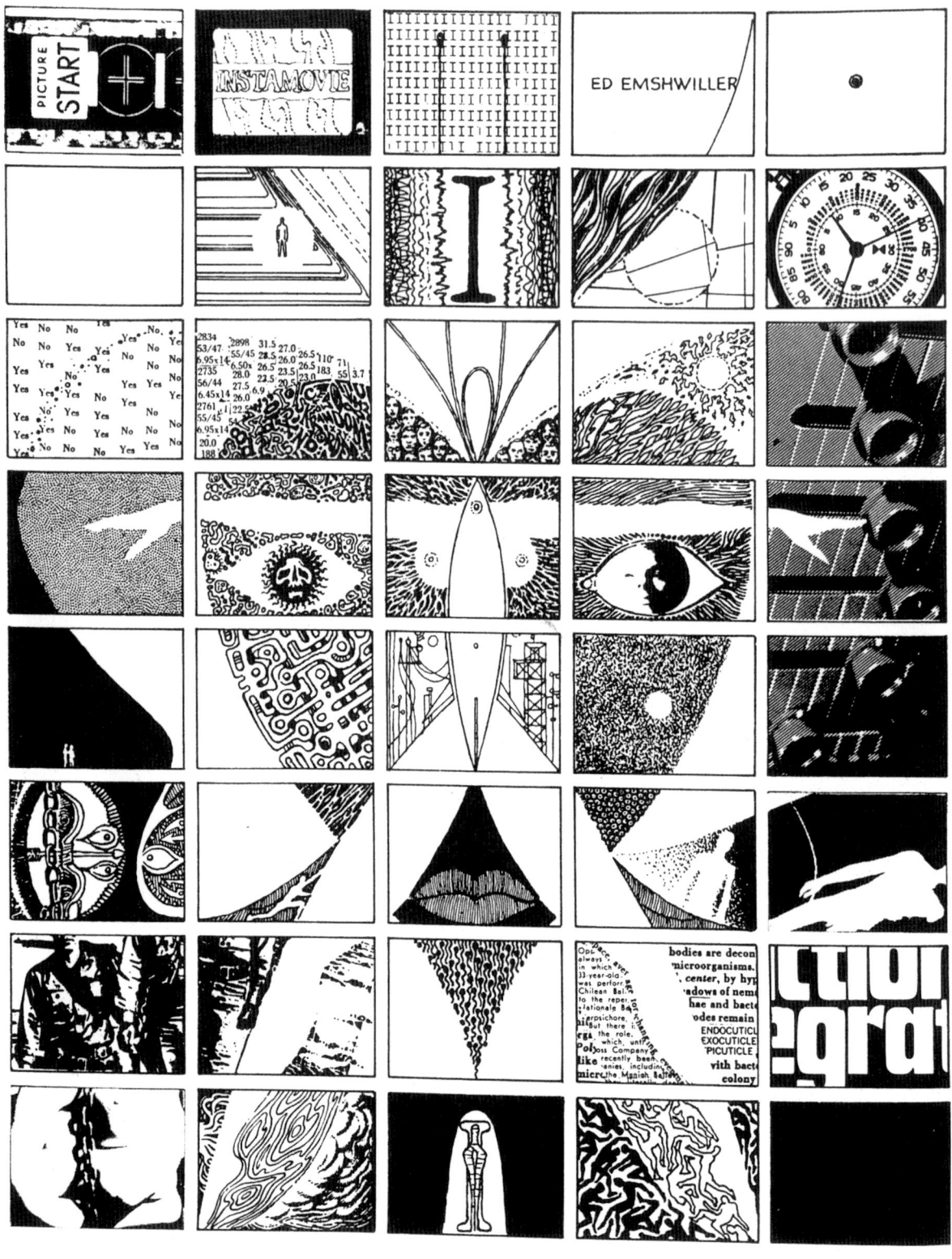

Twelve

ILLUSION OF REALITY

AS PART OF HIS INTRODUCTION to Carol's story in *Dangerous Visions*, Harlan Ellison wrote, "It would be a happy inevitability if Ed were to translate Carol's work for the screen." In 1974, with a grant from the National Endowment for the Arts and the help of the WNET lab, Ed created *Pilobolus and Joan*, a reversal of Kafka's *Metamorphosis,* wherein a cockroach wakes up to find it is a man. This was a video for which Carol wrote the narration. (Her title for the piece was "Metamorphosed.") Pilobolus was a dance group composed of four men who had impressed Ed with their acrobatic style of dance. The troupe portrayed the man-insect by interlinking themselves and moving in a carefully choreographed unity. Joan was singer-composer-actress Joan McDermott.

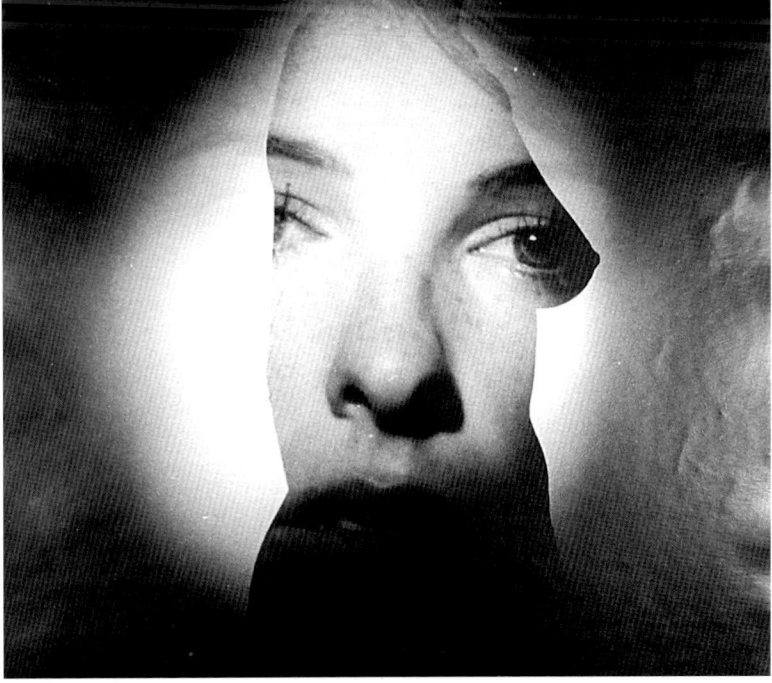

IMAGE, FLESH AND VOICE. 1969, 77 minutes, 35mm, black and white. A collage sound track of candid, self revealing voices is counterpoint to images of dance, everyday street scenes, nudes, impromptu party shots and semi-abstract or surreal actions.

During production of *Pilobolus and Joan*, Ed screened a rough cut for Carol in their living room. Carol's interpretation of one scene left Ed confused, and he reran the tape. "I felt she had missed the point of the scene, and I said 'look at it again.'" Carol still didn't see what Ed saw. Finally, she moved closer to the TV screen, a mere three feet away and then she saw what Ed was talking about.

Ed realized that the coarse resolution of the TV picture tube was simply not good enough for certain subtleties and details. "In this miniature space, I often feel that infinity lies about four feet behind the screen."

One afternoon Carol had been working on a story about how many angels could dance on the head of a pin. The radio was on and someone began reading a story about how many angels could dance on the head of a pin. *Arghh*, Carol cried out. The story was by Donald Barthelme.

Barthelme had developed a funny, surreal, enigmatic way of story writing, using a without-a-net narrative drive and sleight-of-hand wordplay that appealed to the fiction editors and readers of *New*

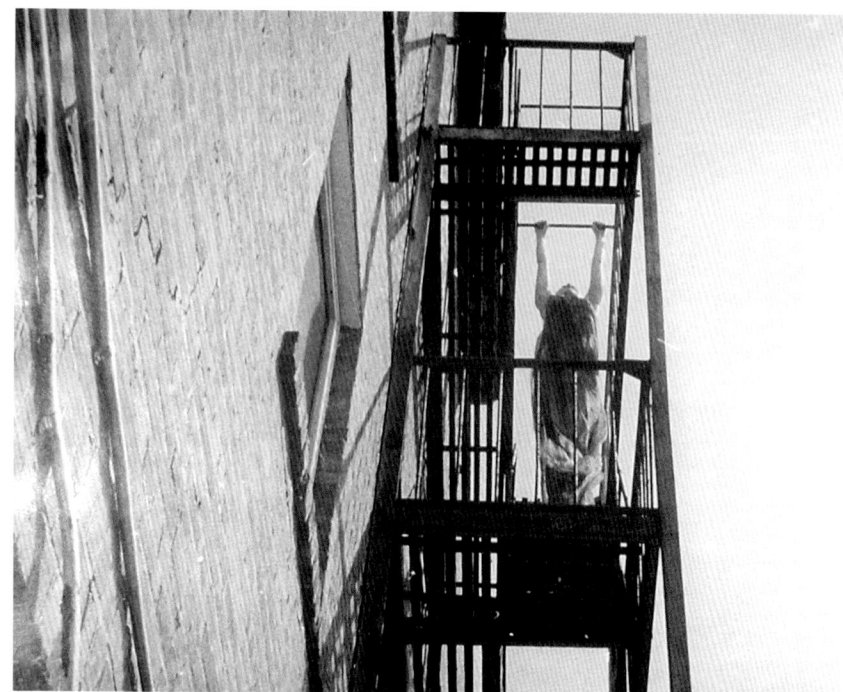

Yorker magazine. Barthelme's primary editor at the *New Yorker* said of his writing, "I've always had an interest in painting, and reading one of his stories was like looking at a work of art."

Carol had many of the same postmodern influences as Barthelme: Samuel Beckett, Kenneth Koch, sixties experimental film, and modern poetry. After Carol received some story rejections that called her stories ersatz Barthelme, she looked up his work and read it for the first time. She quickly realized she did write like him — quite without trying. Even though she had a natural inclination towards this style of storytelling, Carol threw out all her recent stories and set out by design to *not* write like Barthelme.

Carol always tells everyone that it was Kenneth Koch who showed her the literary brio outside of genre and mainstream fiction. Koch was a New York poet and fiction writer

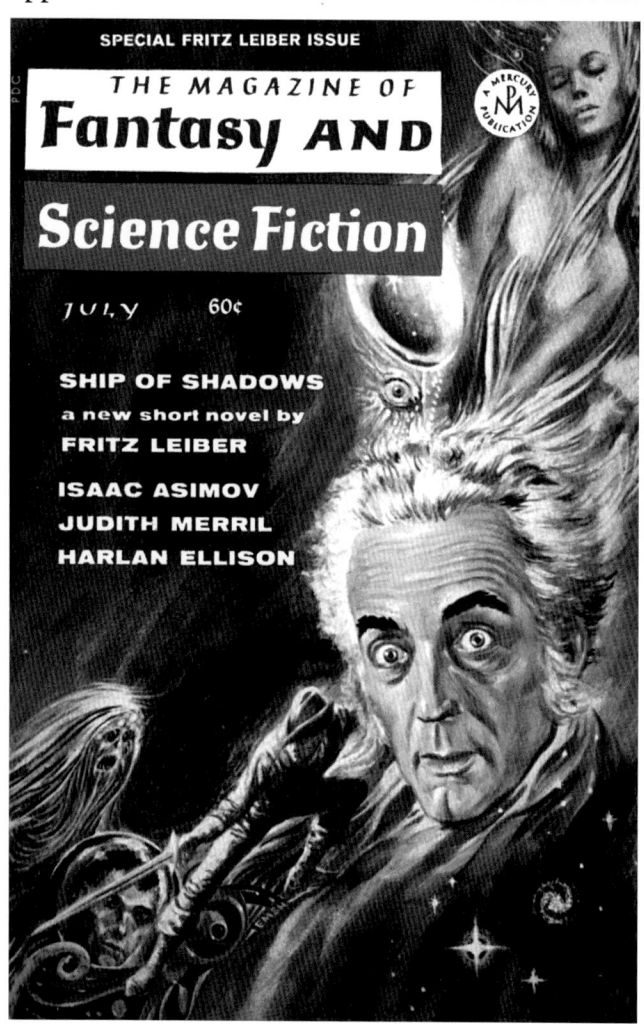

(top R) IMAGE, FLESH AND VOICE. 1969.

(bot L) MAGAZINE OF FANTASY & SCIENCE FICTION. July 1969. Special Fritz Leiber issue.

with a magpie's view of literary prose—anything that caught his fancy was fodder for his own work. He thought nothing of mimicking the prose of James Joyce, using words in the manner that the New York school of painters used paint, or taking word-trips that got lost between life, poetry, and art. Koch taught a writing class at the New School that Carol took in the late seventies. Koch's class gave her a sense of writing as fun, of playing with prose, and of forgetting plot entirely. (She may have been the only fiction writer in a room filled with poets, and Koch told her she had to write some poetry to get into his class.) After the class Carol could not write for a long time. Her mind was spinning with new ideas. *I learned too much at once.*

Carol compared the experience to studying art. *I can't say what I learned [in Koch's class]. I can say what I learned in art school. I thought I was a really good artist before I went to art school. And then I could see that I wasn't.* When she began to write again, she was trying to write short stories almost as poems. *I didn't want to have anything to do with science fiction. I wanted to be a "literary" writer.* A kind of literary artistry took over her prose where she didn't think in terms of prose being separate from poetry.

She went into Koch's class writing satire and fantasy and came out writing satire and fantasy, but her writing seemed entirely different, with a fresh atmosphere. Carol began to submit her experimental stories to literary magazines like *Trans-Atlantic Review* and *Tri-Quarterly*.

Ed was the kind of guy who if he thought Carol was behaving in an unreasonable manner

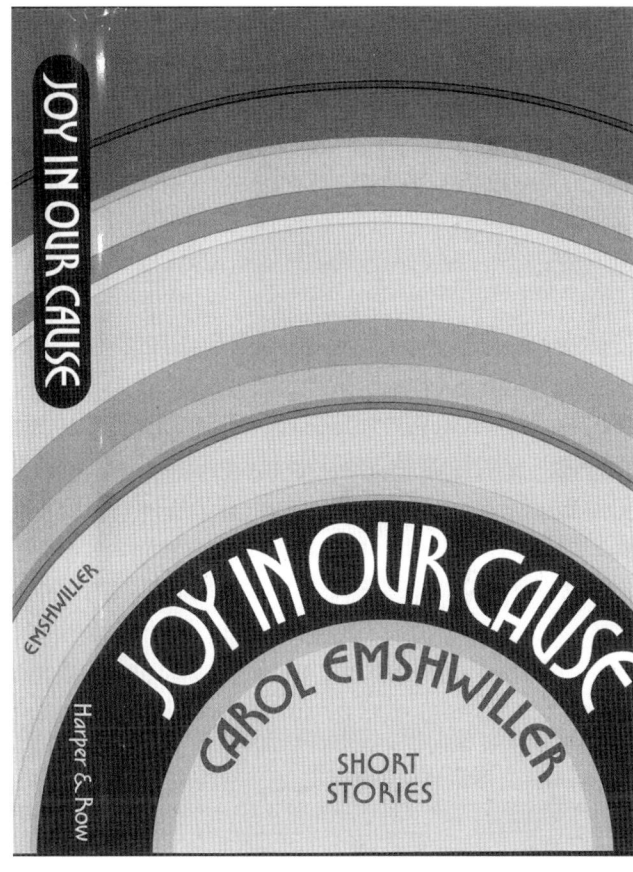

(top R) JOY IN OUR CAUSE. Carol's first book. 1974.

(bot L) art from unknown publication. C. late 1950s.

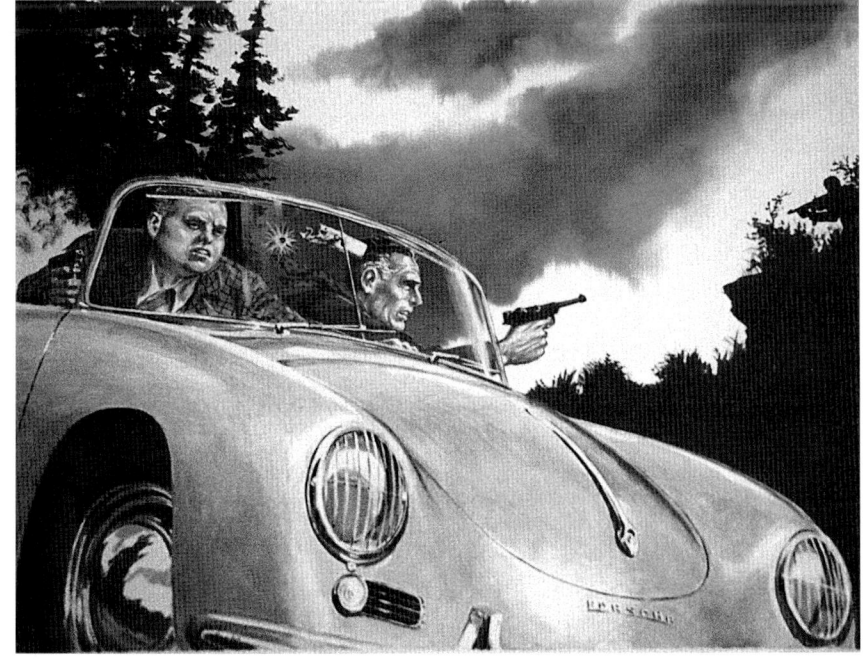

would say, "I'll get a divorce." Ed could be rude to her in many little ways, and for a long time Carol thought that she deserved this kind of treatment. Their daughter Susan pointed out her father's bad manners to him at CalArts, when Ed would get students to help him in his films and videos, then forget to thank them—much the same as he had done with Carol. Ed was for women's lib where it concerned his daughters, but not when it came to his wife.

Carol first began psychoanalysis when she discovered Ed was seeing other women. This was a commonplace "presentation" trigger for wives going into therapy. Carol stated later that going through psychoanalysis was the best thing she ever did, and she wished she had done it sooner. It gave her the strength to turn the tables on her husband and there came a time when Ed was afraid she would get a divorce. She learned to be forceful — taking a firm stance or walking away — and realized that she had become more dependent on her husband than in love with him. Not letting things overwhelm her had always been a problem for her. *It was really nice not to have arguments.*

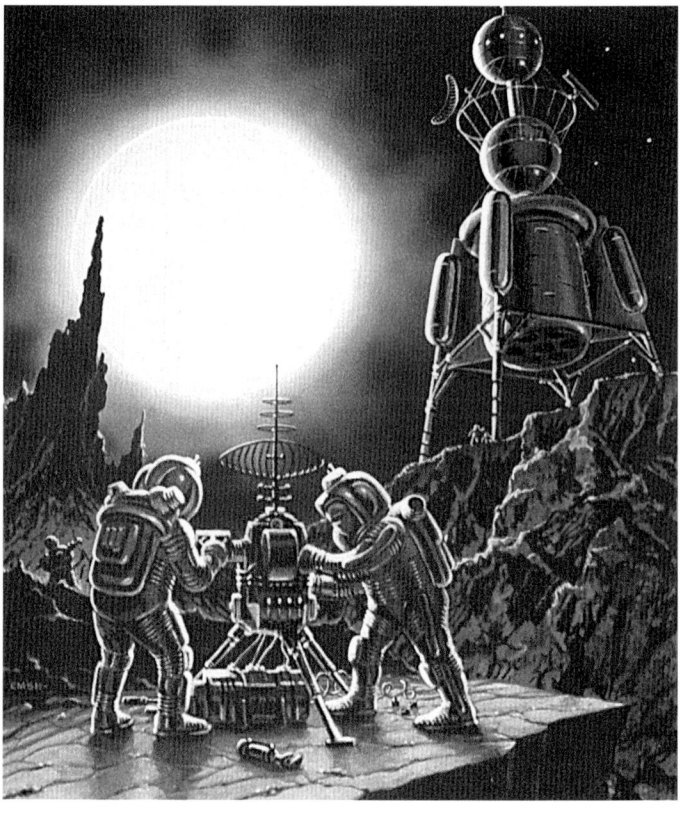

A story she wrote, "Fledged," has a mistreated wife who has left her husband, returning to him as a powerful bird. He is unable to cope with the changeling she has become. *She comes back as this wonderful, terrible thing. I know it's a metaphor for something.*

Carol desperately wanted to get a collection of her stories published. She had gone through four different agents by the early seventies, including Virginia Kidd and Candida Donadio. Most of her agents quickly lost faith in marketing her experimental writings. During the sixties Carol worked on an avant-garde novel. *A peculiar thing that kind of makes me think of Ed's "Relativity."* This went nowhere. Donadio was sending her stories to popular magazines that printed fiction and tried to

THIS PAGE
(top R) GALAXY. Sept. 1953, "Solar Weather Station on Mercury". The scorched pinnacle and the rocketship lean inward toward the Sun, making us more aware of its enormous size and heat. Emsh renders the shadowed mountains with deep red folds and scoriations, while he highlights the men and equipment in blazing white light. Every element conveys the feeling of a landscape baked by a merciless radiance.

(bot L)Pen and ink drawing. 1949.

THIS PAGE
(top R) FUTURE SCIENCE FICTION. December 1959.

(bot L) GALAXY. Feb. 1963. "Comic Inferno" by Brian Aldiss.

PAGE 146
(top R) THE STREETS OF GREENWOOD.

groom Carol into a *Saturday Evening Post* writer.

Tom Disch took Carol's story "Strangers" for his collection *Bad Moon Rising*, and some of the reviews of the book singled out the story for praise. This brought Carol's writing to the attention of Kitty Benedict, a senior editor at Harper & Row.

Harper & Row gave Carol a contract to put together a collection of her fiction and then left her to her own devices. Carol knew she did not want to use any of her old science fiction stories, though she did slip "Sex and/or Mr. Morrison" into the collection. Her editor gave her little input and Carol made the final selections, organized the order of presentation, and turned everything over to Harper & Row.

Joy in Our Cause was published in 1974, a barebones book of Carol's short stories. No one had told her that your best story should lead the book, and your second best story should end the collection. There was no introduction or ancillary copy added. Carol scattered her best stories in the middle of the book (this was the manner in which she read a story collection and thought everyone else did also).

Reviewers had a hard time categorizing *Joy in Our Cause*. One called her fiction "surrealism of

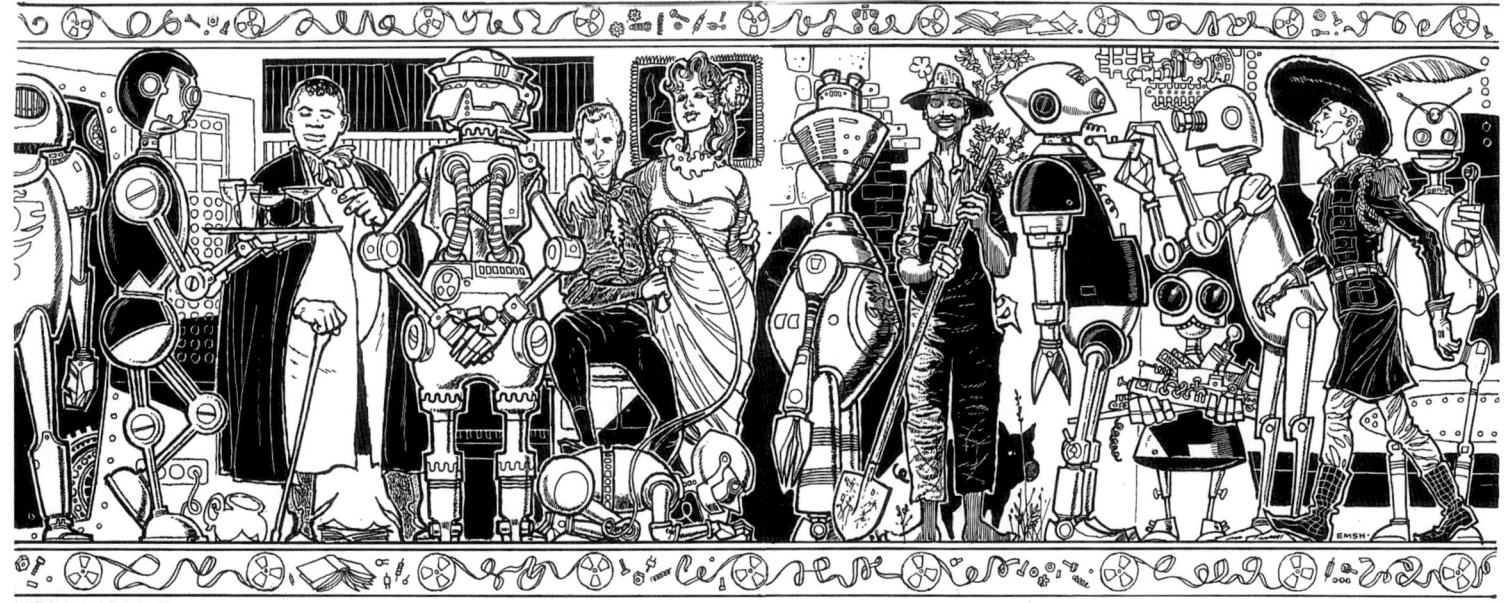

the fresh." Another, "stream of consciousness," while another said, "Elements in her stories are like elements in Godard's movies. ..." Carole Horn, writing in *The Washington Post*, characterized her fiction as having a "cockeyed élan."

Anatole Broyard, in his review for the *New York Times*, said of Carol, "She is perhaps the most extreme example of a new tone in women's writing. Making a virtue of necessity, she writes of what she has been confined to. She knows these things as no man can, because she has experienced them so many times that they have become rituals, religions, abstractions, art forms, anthropology."

One unsigned review infuriated Carol. *Kirkus Review* used quotes from her stories out of context and gave them a spin contrary to Carol's intent. She was dismayed at the complete misunderstanding of her sense of humor—and more so at *Kirkus'* confusion of her use of irony. *Am I wrong in thinking my stories were judged in women's lib terms? They were written over a period of ten or so years and perhaps I should have put them in the order of ascending consciousness (or descending).* One sentence from the petty review should suffice: "But anyone whose first thought after a kick in the crotch is that 'women don't hurt there as much as men do,' deserves everything she gets."

Another review, which described her writing as dealing with the "frustrations of her daily life ... her fantasies, sex, menstruation—the texture of her life," caused Carol to scribble in the margins: "No, I was striving for the illusion of reality." Marketing for the book was minimal — a spot in the Harper & Row catalog, a tiny mention in a full-page ad in the *New York Times Book Review*. Carol had no idea how to promote her book. Harper & Row was silent in this area, and before long the book was remaindered.

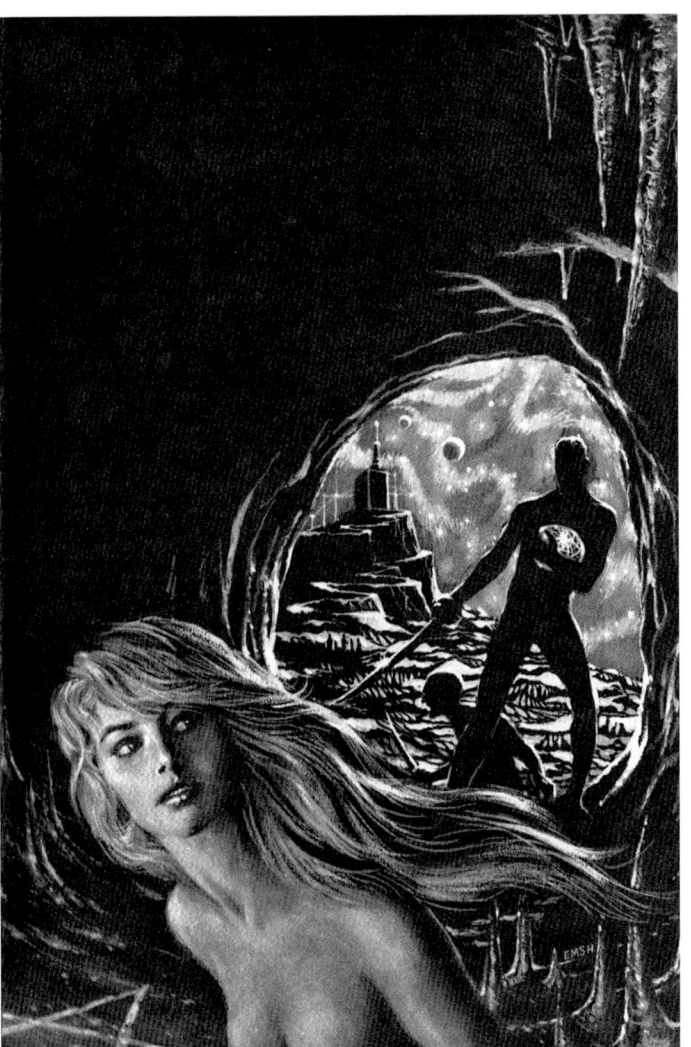

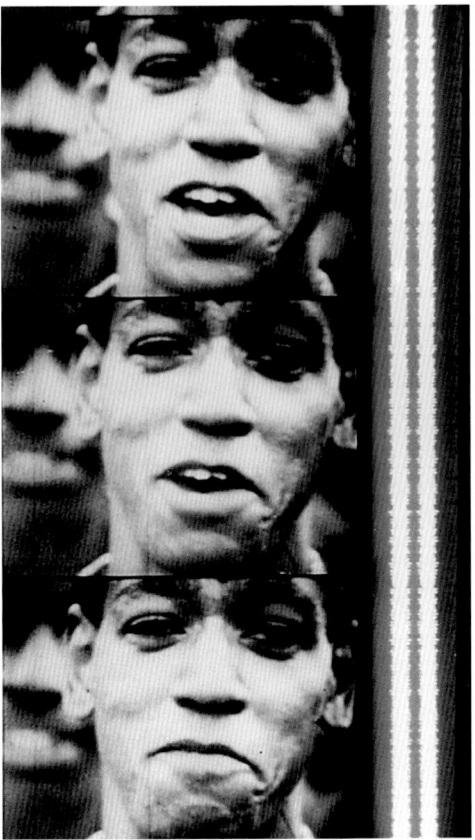

(bot L) F&SF. Sept. 1963, "Glory Road," Pt. 3, by Robert A. Heinlein. The Empress of 20-odd universes and her fighting man of Earth enter a mysterious cave, where a pentagram (lower left) will spirit them away to home base. The sky outside shows this to be a world with an over-active ionosphere, bilious green aurorae oscillating like snakes across a mauve-&-pink firmament. Sharp stalactites and stalagmites curve toward and away from the adventurers, like the fangs of some invisible demon which (but for the Empress's magic) might rend their flesh. Our hero carries the long-sought grail, "The Egg of the Phoenix," which glows like a universe in miniature. The beautiful naked "Star" (Ishtar?) throws him a backward glance, to be sure that her hired mercenary follows, ever faithful. As what man or boy would not, for a stunner like her?

Thirteen

digital blobs

IN THE FALL OF 1978 Ed appeared in Old Westbury, Long Island, at the campus of the New York Institute of Technology (NYIT). He had heard of a team of "hippy artist guys" creating computer animation inside a one-time four car garage (with living quarters for the chauffeurs). The building was part of a grand North Shore estate that could have seen the likes of F. Scott Fitzgerald and Zelda during the roaring twenties. The computer lab used DEC minicomputers, instead of room-sized IBM systems, to drive custom frame buffers (picture memory and video output units), and a new programming language simply called C (based on Bell Labs' Unix software).

The lab seems to have had unlimited funds and was ready to buy or create whatever it needed. Due to limitations at the time in computer-to-video/film interfacing, NYIT concentrated on creating high-quality video graphics optimized for television.

A few technically oriented filmmakers like John Whitney, working at IBM, and Stan VanDerBeek at MIT, had been creating computer-assisted animation since the sixties. As early as 1957 Whitney had used an analog computer, scavenged from a surplus military anti-aircraft gun controller, to direct picture elements on his animation stand.

The NYIT Computer Graphics Lab was developing the first digital paint systems and was at the creative forefront of computer animation. Throughout the hegemony of large mainframe computers, artists had been mostly neglected or

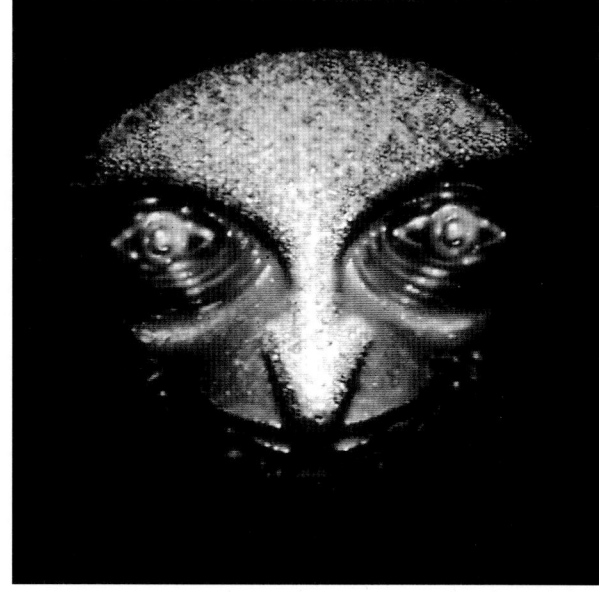

One of Ed's experimental faces done on the paint system at NYIT. 1979.

dismissed. Few had thought to invite artists to use the brute power of computers creatively. The curious part about Ed's appearance at NYIT was that he was expected.

One night in September 1978, some lab denizens including Alvy Ray Smith, Ed Catmull, and David DiFrancesco watched Ed Emshwiller demonstrate his experimental video work on a PBS program hosted by Dick Cavett. On the show Cavett asked Ed to define video art: "The use of video for me is more like a painter or a conceptualist would [work] than, say, a dramatist—not that there isn't an overlap."

The NYIT group was impressed by Ed's use of analog film/video technologies to create art and his openness to computers. When they learned that Ed lived in nearby Levittown, someone suggested they contact him. Alvy said, "If he's who I think he is, he'll find us."

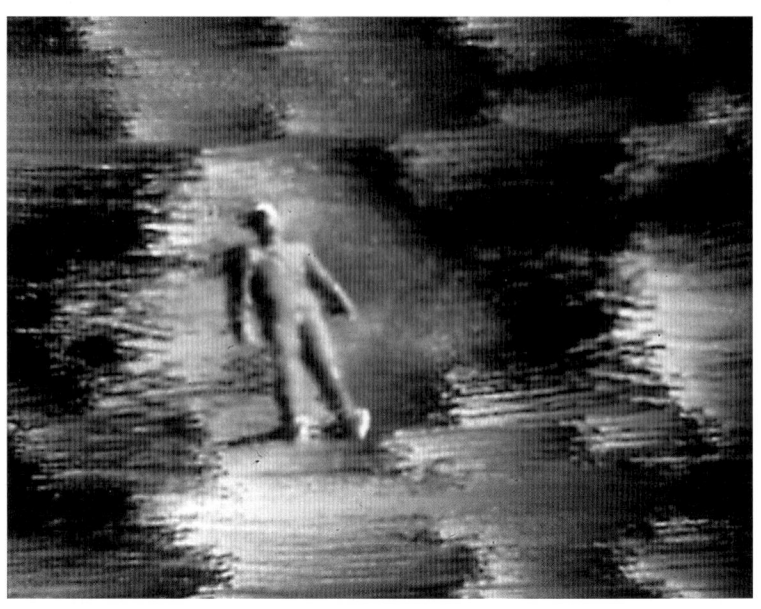

After receiving a Guggenheim Fellowship early in 1979, Ed arrived at NYIT one day and announced his plans to make a ninety-minute movie in six months. The lab team burst into laughter, unsettling Ed.

"You'll be lucky to finish a piece of three minutes in that time," Alvy explained.

Ed spent some time learning the capabilities of the paint systems at NYIT, using a stylus and a graphics tablet to create figures and faces made up of digital blobs. One early image was a face drawn entirely out of eyes. "Late at night I would get carried away," Ed explained. His original concept, of making a one-and-a-half-hour TV program about "go[ing] on location in software-land," was put aside.

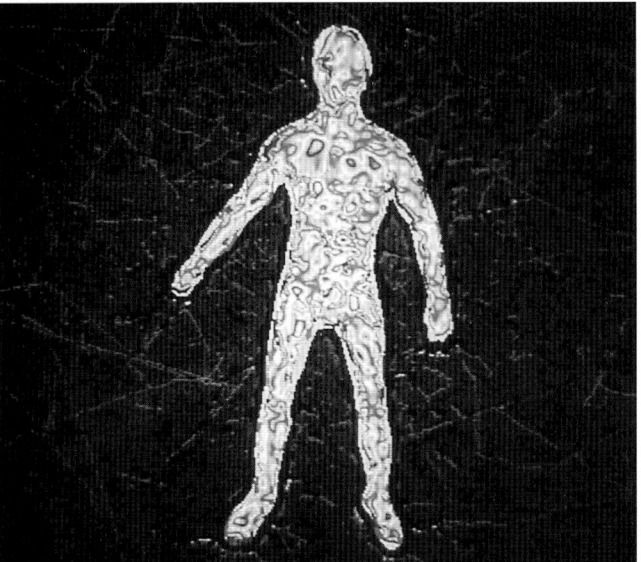

Ed made hundreds of grayscale digital images before proposing some scenes he wanted to develop. One early idea was to have a figure walking through water waves. Another idea was to push a 3D face through a solid 3D wall of brick or stone, but he was told these were too complex for their paint system. (Alvy Smith's favorite expression was "We can't do that yet.") Some compromises were made and Smith wrote code using 2D tricks to mimic some of what Ed wanted. Smith created a height map for each pixel of a head-on shot of the face — by turning pixels on or off frame by frame,

(this pg and bot L pg 151) Early on at NYIT, Ed attempted to develop figures in an environment, but was unable to animate them to his satisfaction and abandoned the idea.

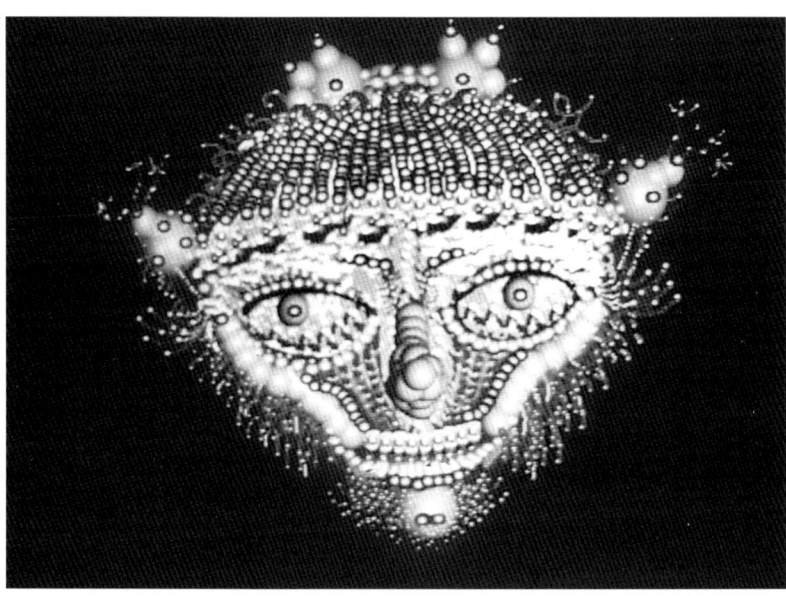

(top L) Another digital face done while Ed played with the NYIT paint system.

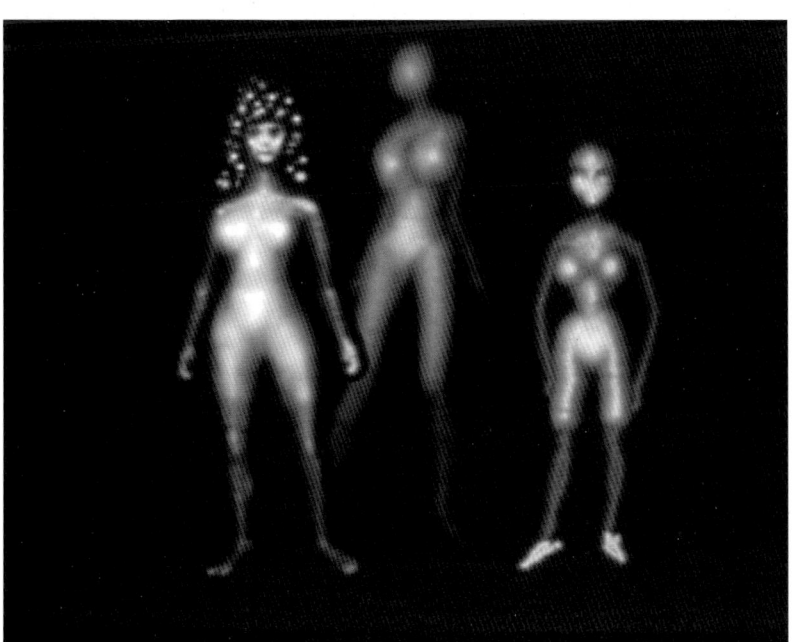

depending on how "high" they were in relationship to the background surface, the face appeared to come out of the wall.

Ed still had to create the corresponding height-map for the face. Smith's program would generate the frame animation for the image: combining the face with the wall using Ed's different height threshold at each frame, they would then tape the results with a computer-controlled frame-accurate 2-inch videotape recorder (a computer/video interface invented at NYIT).

Smith was one of the first programmers to develop a 24 bit color RGB system using three eight-bit frame buffers, but was surprised that Ed avoided using the full color capabilities of the NYIT system. "Too overwhelming," Ed told him.

Ed learned at his own pace, gaining more experience until he felt comfortable enough to allow his grayscale images to erupt finally into color. Smith was impressed by Ed's restraint. "Most early users were head-over-heels in love with the color (including me)." Alvy had been an artist before becoming a scientist, and the pair eased into a symbiotic rapport.

Alvy said of their working relationship, "[Ed] couldn't code, pure and simple, so I had to do that part if it, but he quickly learned what he could and couldn't ask for by our constant repartee. ... He would say, let's do A. I would respond, we can't do A (usually I would say, we can't do A 'yet' — the computers were VERY slow in those days). But, I would say, we can do B, where B would be inspired by A but in a 'doable' way. Then Ed would respond, well, if you can do B, what about B? And I would say, well, not quite, but we could do B."

The creation of art on the NYIT paint system was done in real time. Animation was more involved. Getting from art to animation typically took a day to process. One night Ed watched Alvy working on a piece of software called Texas, and they figured out a way to use the program to show a rotating cube with images appearing on the flat sides. The sequence took 56 hours to compute into an 18 second scene.

"The problem was not creating the images—it was choosing among them." Ed began concentrating on a single image: an androgynous metamorphic moon face floating in space and given life-like appearance by the use of manipulated colors and solarization of the image. Smith's coding would often be just an "exposure sheet" piece of a program that would invoke graphic routines he had already written. Eventually a short film, *Sunstone,* came together with NYIT colleagues Lance Williams and Garland Stern's help

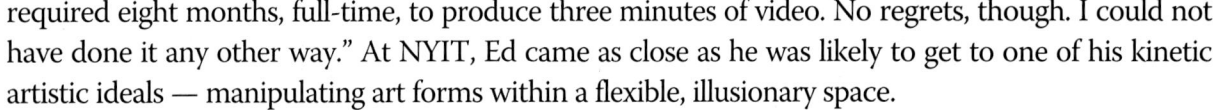

Ed described his use of a face icon as suggesting "... birth, death and rebirth..." and added, "... this visage, taken... through various transformations so that in turn it is startling and humorous, implying meditation, destruction, and radiance...."

Afterwards Ed said, "I learned a hard lesson at NYIT: computers may be fast, but, if you are using them to animate complex pictures, you must be prepared to spend a lot of time. I had never before required eight months, full-time, to produce three minutes of video. No regrets, though. I could not have done it any other way." At NYIT, Ed came as close as he was likely to get to one of his kinetic artistic ideals — manipulating art forms within a flexible, illusionary space.

Alvy Ray Smith left NYIT soon after *Sunstone* to work at LucasFilm, and later helped form Pixar, but to this day considers *Sunstone* the best artistic collaboration of his life. Though it is commonplace today for SF artists to create art with computers, Ed may have been the first to "paint" digitally: and he did this many years before the ubiquity of personal computers and graphic software. The face in *Sunstone* went on to become a classic icon of early computer animation. *Sunstone* also became Ed's favorite of all of his films and video.

The first PBS made-for-television movie came out of WNET's Experimental TV Lab in 1979. David Loxton wanted to initiate an anthology series based on science fiction stories and selected Ursula K. Le Guin's cautionary novel *The Lathe of Heaven* for the first installment. Working with a small budget of $250,000 for the complete movie, Loxton fell back on the TV Lab for special effects. Ed was assigned the alien invasion scenes and used his son Peter as assistant.

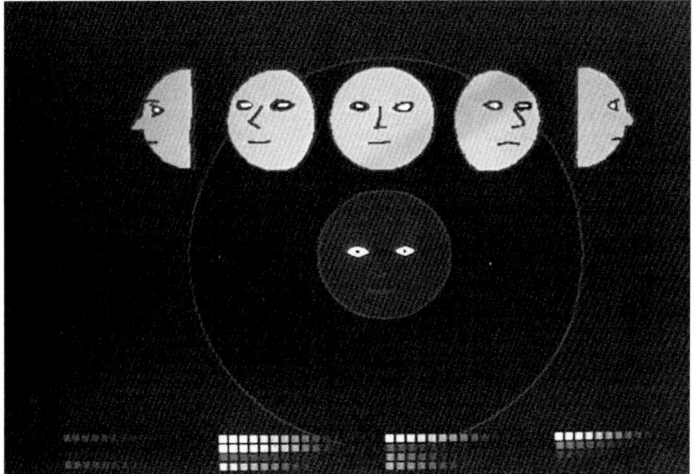

Back in Levittown, Ed turned his attic into a movie studio, completely covering the walls in matte-black seamless paper. An oversized photograph of the moon left over from *Project Apollo* was affixed to a three by three foot sheet of rear-projection material. Ed set up his

(top R) Unused concept from SUNSTONE.

(bot L) Digital elements developed by Ed and Alvy Ray Smith. The computer would create the "in-betweening."

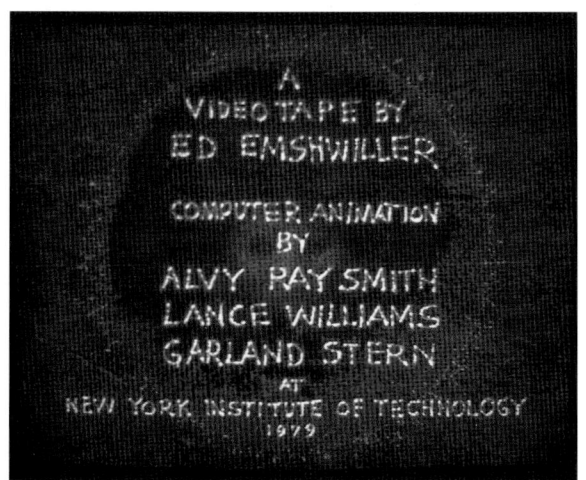

camera on one side of the sheet while Peter, dressed in black clothing, stood on the other side and used a penlight against the sheet to simulate spacecrafts taking off from the surface of the moon and arcing into space. Ed rewound the film to create double exposures and show multiple liftoffs taking place at the same moment. They also created explosions on the surface of the moon by flicking the penlight on and pulling it slowly away from the rear-projection sheet.

For one scene they laid the moon photograph on the floor for stability and rigged a mirror to the ceiling. Peter used some flash paper from an old magic kit to "blow up the moon" using a high-speed camera. In another shot showing a rocket ship in flight, Peter held one of Ed's old Hugo awards and filmed the golden trophy through a lens smeared with Vaseline.

For the alien invasion of earth scenes, Ed and Peter took store-bought lamp reflectors, miniature lights, and battery packs, and jerry-rigged them together to create flying saucers. A stand to hold the flying saucers was built out of wood and painted black. These were attached to Ed's beat-up Ford station wagon. That night Peter zigzagged the car, covered in black duvetine cloth, around a nearby grocery store parking lot while his father filmed the blinking spaceships from various angles. Ed Wood, Jr., oddball director of poverty-budget features like *Plan 9 from Outer Space*, would have approved. These shots were later combined with sky and buildings.

Ed also helped design the turtle-like aliens, which because of cost restraints had only one working arm, and he made many trips to the set in Houston to consult on other special effects. He could live with the cheaply-made alien costume, but was not happy with how it was lit and photographed. Despite the bargain basement budget, the reviews were enthusiastic for *The Lathe of Heaven*. One critic called it "a special effects lover's smorgasbord."

Frank Lloyd Wright once said, "Tip the world on its side and everything loose will land in Los Angeles." This applied more so to filmmakers. While Ed was wrapping up *Sunstone* and *The Lathe of Heaven,* he was contacted by the California Institute of the Arts, a school founded by Walt and Roy Disney in 1961, and offered a position as dean of

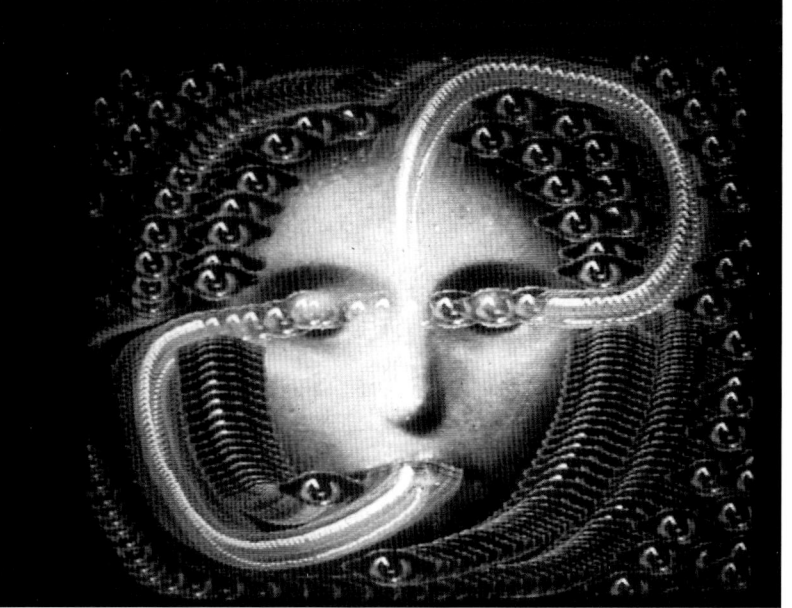

(top & bot) SUNSTONE images, 1979, 3 minutes. Techincal support by Alvy Ray Smith, Lance Williams, and Garland Stern.

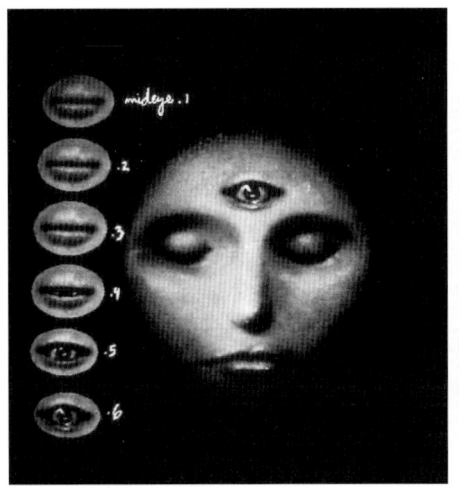
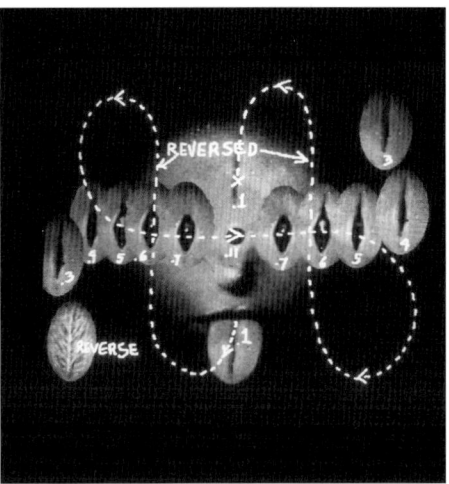

the School of Film and Video. The university was using artists in administrators' roles to help it get endowments and bring in fresh ideas.

Ed agonized over moving to California, telling people "I'm just going to try it out. I hate California. I'll go for a semester and see how it goes." Very quickly Ed fell into the academic routine and even found that he had some skill in administration and academic guidance. The school gave him an apartment near the campus that was used by visiting artists and had been decorated by a CalArts secretary in a suburban housewife style, with blue peacock fabric on the couch and floral print on the wall. Ed took no notice of the décor that went against everything avant-garde.

Ed had always yearned to be part of a community of artists, an idea that had its genesis during the sixties when he visited artist communes. Ultimately, he came to believe that CalArts fulfilled this role, if somewhat imperfectly, and fell in love with the job and California. He had been depending on freelancing and grants until CalArts. Soon after he arrived at CalArts, Ed talked his daughter Susan into studying at CalArts, and not long after she arrived she switched from painting to film.

Carol's writing throughout the seventies and early eighties had become more thoughtful, fluent—fully conscious of the thin line between what is fantasy and what is reality. She was linked to the feminist movement despite the sympathetic treatment of men in her fiction. This was a time when any woman author dealing with any sort of injustice was automatically given the "feminist" tag. Her stories appeared in the women's lib-tinged tomes *Women of Wonder, Bitches and Sad Ladies,* and *Edges.* Some readers still saw her as an SF author and she did appear in the 1980 anthology *Universe,* edited by Terry Carr, but she was more likely to show up in literary venues like *New Directions, Croton Review,* and *The Little Magazine.*

Modernist writers like Jorge Luis Borges, Robbe-Grillet, and Italo Calvino

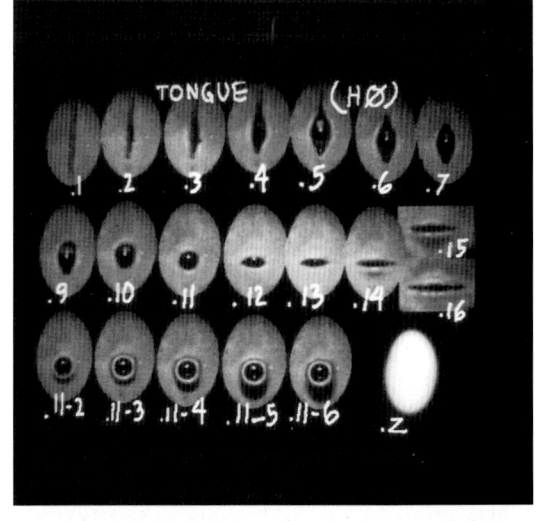

(top L & mid R) SUNSTONE. Digital facial elements in preparation for animation, done at NYIT. 1979.

(bot R) "Jellyfish" digital "sketch." done at NYIT, 1979.

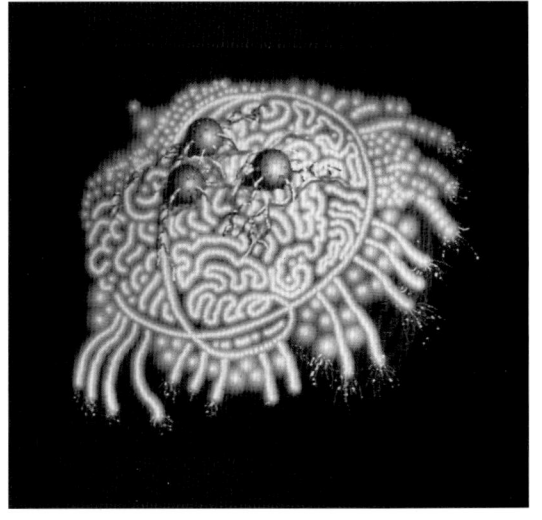

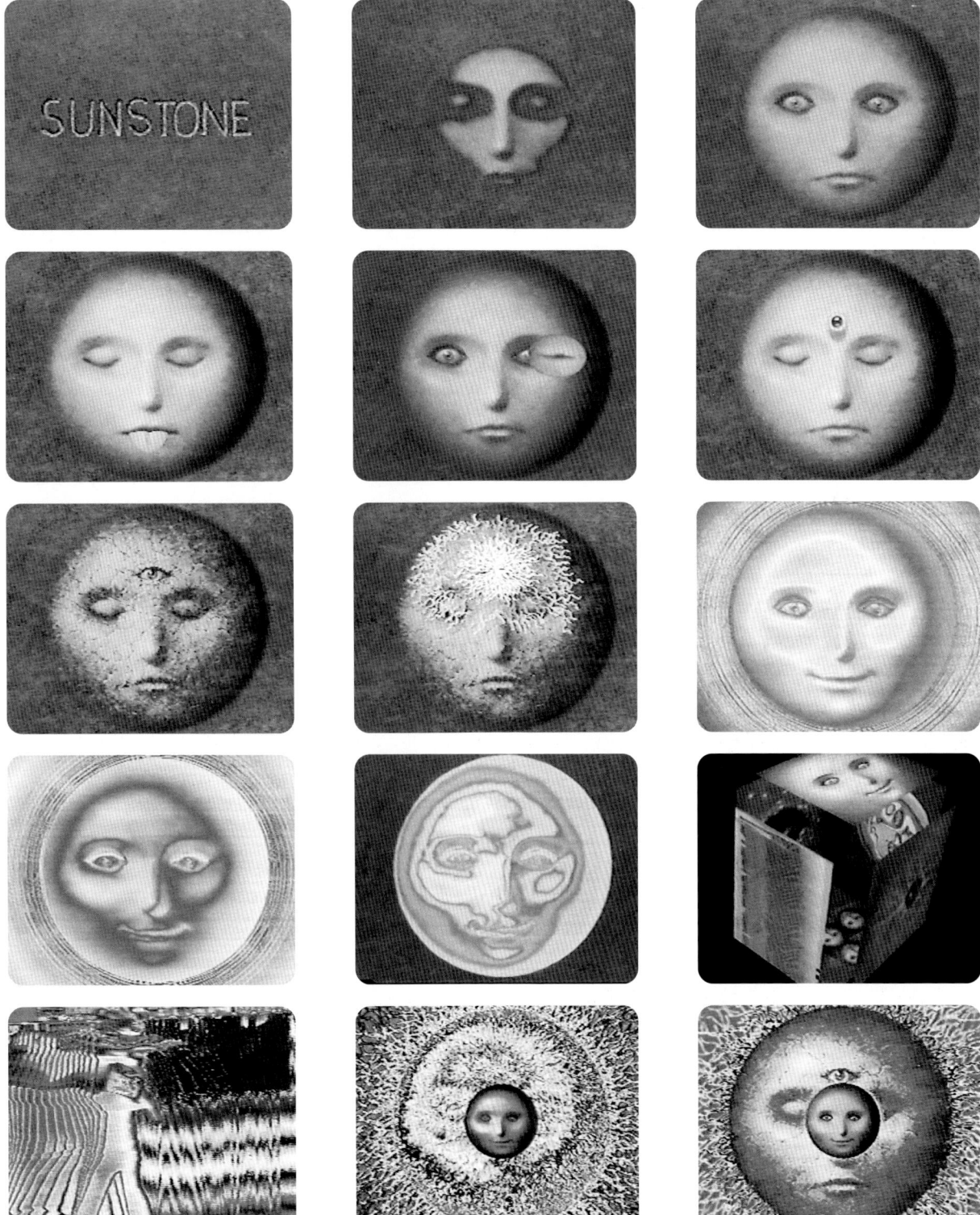

"SUNSTONE is a computer-animation videotape which begins with a blank "stone" surface. A moon like a face emerges from it. The face goes through a series of transformations suggesting heightened consciousness, death, rebirth, alternative universes, levels of reality, and the trace of prior existence in the cyclical return to the 'blank' surface."
- EE

had turned to detective fiction to manipulate literary and theoretical ideas and bring them back down to earth. A few authors used the mannerisms of science fiction: Doris Lessing, William Burroughs, Margaret Atwood, and again Borges and Calvino. These writers, looking for new ways of skinning the literary cat, found a new plaything in the blue-collar world of genre science fiction. In some cases they were unsuspectingly reworking SF ideas first used in old science fiction magazines. These authors did not always merge the earthbound and SF tropes smoothly, though their readers couldn't always tell the difference between the dreamlike actualization of modernism and the lucidity of SF, nor did they care. Atwood's otherwise engaging *The Handmaid's Tale* is an example of this.

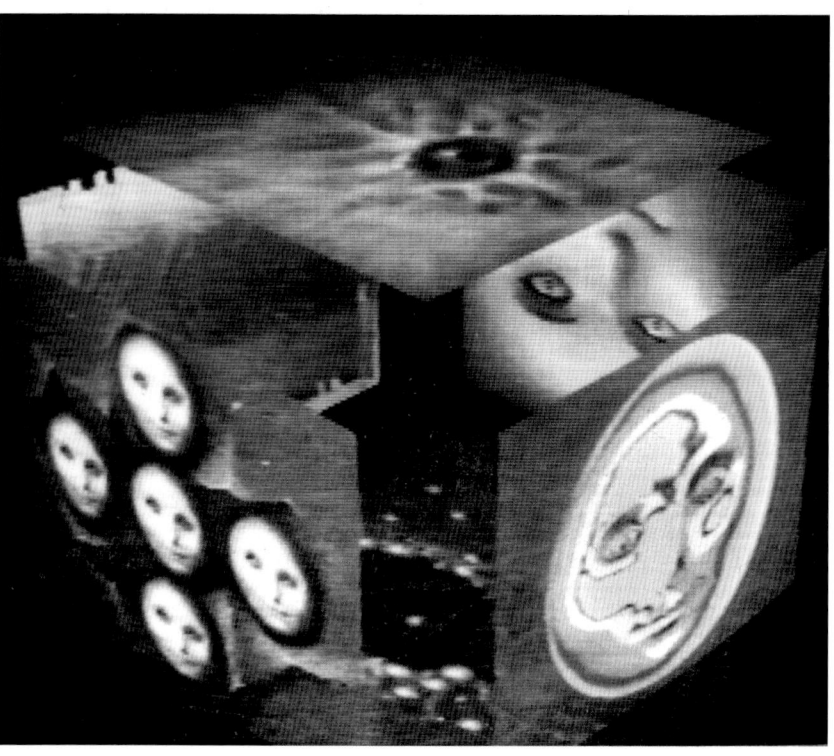

Carol read Samuel Beckett and William Burroughs, but while she appreciated what Beckett was trying to do in his fiction, she thought that there wasn't anything she could learn from Burroughs. Cyberpunk writers would absorb Burroughs later, along with English New Wave authors like J. G. Ballard and Michael Moorcock, to better effect. Carol was headed in another direction. She found herself returning to plotting, and writing science fiction stories.

Structuring strategies was the name that Ed and Carol called what they were trying to do, each through different mediums. They both believed that avant-garde filmmaking or writing still needed a structure to hold things together. *I'm not interested in stories where anything can happen at any time.... I try to have all, or most of the elements in [my] stories linked to each other.* Eventually Carol got tired of experimental writing.

She also began to teach writing—her first real job—at New York University, and started a bi-coastal marriage. Both Ed and Carol found that they loved their new academic jobs. They also got more work done while apart. He would return to New York during his spring break and Carol would go to California for summer vacation. In California they hiked and camped all over the Sierra Mountains.

They rented out the Levittown house, still not feeling secure enough to sell it outright, and Carol found a small Manhattan apartment in a tenement building on East 9th Street, between First and Second Avenues. It had taken years to find time to write. Now her children were away at college or getting on with their lives.

(top R) SUNSTONE

Fourteen

Avantopia

ED HAD SOME BOUTS with bad health throughout much of 1981 and in December found out he had chronic lymphasitic leukemia, a cancer of the blood and bones. His father had the same illness and lived for many years after his diagnosis. At the time, the general life expectancy for anyone with this form of leukemia was eight to ten years, but the doctor told Ed, "You're going to die from something else." Even before this Ed had problems with blood clots — one nearly killed him in 1984 when he developed gangrene in his intestines and needed an emergency operation — and before this he had been diagnosed with prostate cancer. Ed was lucky in picking up medical insurance from CalArts.

In 1982, Ed bought a tiny Sinclair computer and a Bally Arcade (really a low resolution video game system) and taught himself the programming language Basic. He eventually wrote over two hundred programs, using the Bally's paltry 4K of memory to make *Skin Matrix*. Ed was trying to see if he could make as effective a piece of artwork with the Bally as he could with the more sophisticated computers he had available at NYIT. "I … like to explore the characteristics of various tools and the way they make me think in order to produce an effective work."

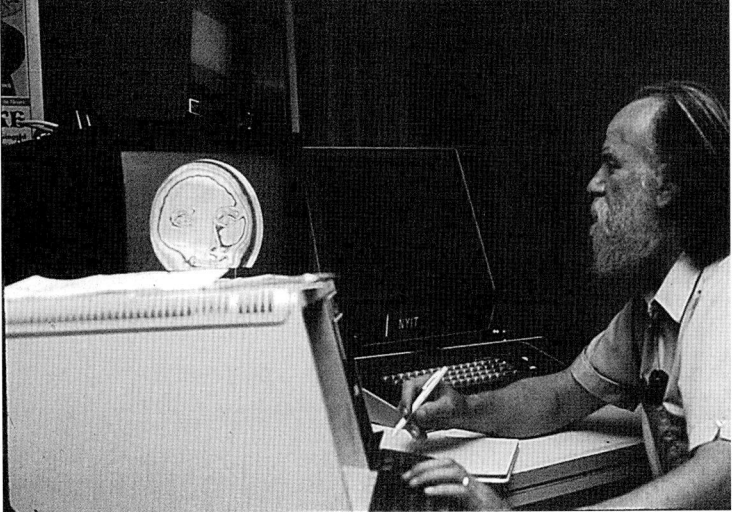

EE working on the computer paint program at a PDP-11 work station. 1979.

For *Skin Matrix* Ed shot between six and seven hundred 35mm slides with a Nikon camera. These were keyed in and combined with pre-recorded video and Ed added his own musical score created on a Roland synthesizer. Ed pared down and refined over 30 hours of footage into a first edit of three hours and 40 minutes, before getting to a final 20 minute video. Ed referred to *Skin*

Matrix as a "video tapestry" of energy, inorganic and organic textures, human figures, and imagination (flying figures). He used his Basic programs to atomize the video image into pixels that could be rearranged into new patterns. It took two years for him to complete *Skin Matrix*, while keeping up with his duties at CalArts, and when finished it was shown at the Los Angeles Olympic Arts Festival in 1984.

Ed was still learning, taking classes alongside CalArts students. "Although I've tried a lot of different things, we all have habits, ruts of thinking, so that we have a signature even when we try to be different. As we grow older, we become more selective, and that makes it more difficult to create new forms. It's my intention to keep growing. If I don't, then I know I'm not fulfilling my self-image."

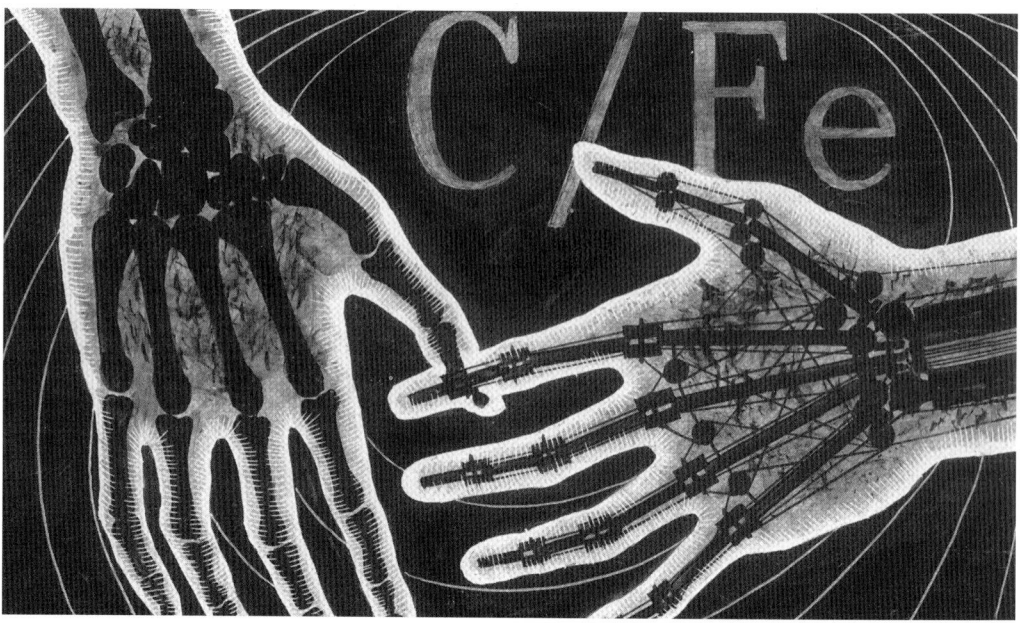

GALAXY SCIENCE FICTION, Oct. 1953, "The Caves of Steel" by Isaac Asimov, (b&w scratchboard). Another one of Ed's x-ray views of life, in this case both carbon-based and iron-based, symbolizing the partnership between Man and Robot, skin and steel.

At CalArts, Ed met and became friends with Alexander Mackendrick, the English director of *The Man in the White Suit* and the original *The Ladykillers*. Mackendrick called Ed the "artist" and referred to himself as the "craftsman."

When he started at Calarts, Ed would go to meetings and feel like the Roy Scheider character, in *All That Jazz*, who thought he was having a heart attack while sitting at the conference table. The meeting became background noise to Ed's mind, focused on the scratching sound of a pen on the paper before him. Though Ed would never have admitted to having an anxiety attack, this was most likely what he was going through. It took him a while to learn that the problems at the school were "like a cafeteria tray: every time you took one, another would pop up."

At a film program of his work at the science fiction convention Kubla Khan in Nashville in 1985, Ed stated that in everything he did he tried to "embody the principal of dynamic contrast." He meant this in every sense of the term, not just in dark and light, but in color contrast, and contrast of shapes. It started in his commercial art and paintings and continued with his films. Early on he was doing this without thinking. With experience he refined and consciously made this aesthetic ideal work for him. *Thanatopsis* is a perfect example of this, with the stationary man counterbalanced by the agitated angel of death frantically buzzing around him.

At the Kubla Khan, Ed had made his appearance there contingent on the committee also inviting Carol. They had not been together in months and some of the attendees remember them "mooning over each other." In these later convention appearances, Ed and Carol would appear together as a genial presence, easily accessible to all.

In the spring of 1986, Ed took a backpacking trip with some CalArts colleagues to the Grand Canyon at the height of the Halley's Comet reappearance. This was a once in a lifetime chance to see the event. Late one cool night on the canyon's floor, he decided that he wanted to sit along the rim, and hiked up the cliff. In the early hours of the morning he reached the top and looked up at the clear sky. It was as if the universe was on display for him, and he danced along the edge of the rim under the unknown mysteries of the night sky.

In late 1986, Ed fulfilled a long-held ambition when he began taking flying lessons. (Since childhood he had dreams where he saw himself flying.) His first solo flight was on February 11, 1987, in a two-seater Piper Tomahawk. Once he got his pilot's license Carol would join him in the tiny single-prop plane. During early trips she felt that she had to keep track of the flight checklist to remind Ed of what to do next. *The scariest thing I ever did in my life was going up with him in that tiny little plane.* Their own children always had a "previous engagement" when invited to fly.

It had been many years since one of her fictions appeared in a science fiction magazine when Carol sold "The Secret Library of Stone" to Ellen Datlow of *Omni* magazine at the end of 1986. By the eighties, with very few exceptions, fiction magazines had disappeared from newsstands, making it harder for writers to earn a living.

She also began work on her first real novel, based on ideas she had gleaned from Elaine Morgan's books *The Aquatic Ape* and *The Descent of Women*. Morgan wrote about the theory claiming that many human evolutionary features can only be explained in the light of an aquatic stage of evolution.

Carol's agent Virginia Kidd did not like *Venus Rising* when she read the first sections of it, and told Carol not to bother finishing it. Carol had planned to continue the story with the heroine and her mixed-species offspring. (Carol later wished she hadn't listened to Kidd.) The fifteen thousand-word section Carol had written sat around in her files for a long time, and appeared as a chapbook in 1992, some years after her first

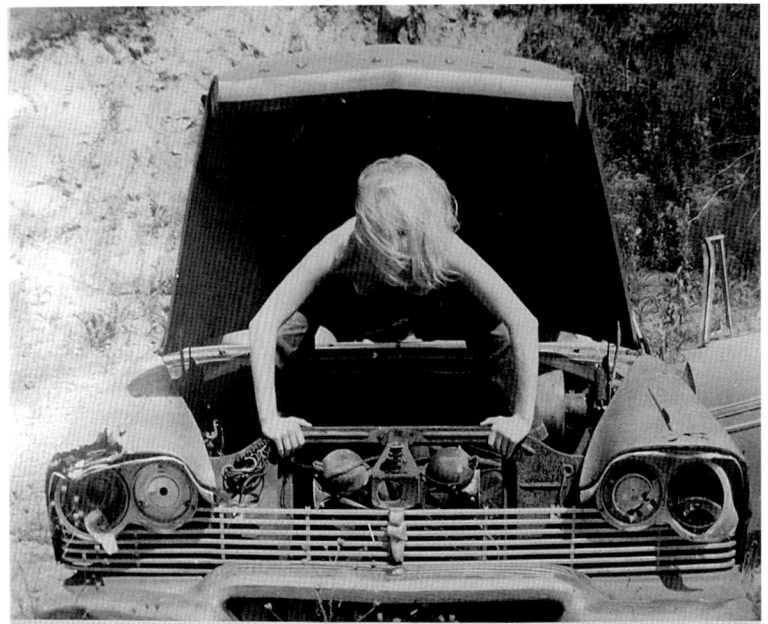

IMAGE, FLESH AND VOICE. 1969, 77 minutes, 16mm.

published novel, *Carmen Dog,* came out in 1989.

Carols admits that she did not know anything about writing a novel when she began *Venus Rising* and *Carmen Dog.* The latter's premise has female pets turning into intelligent humans while women become dumb animals. In a series of picaresque chapters, Carol presents the Manhattan perils of Pooch, a golden setter bitch turning into a woman with a love of opera. As usual the man of the house is oblivious to everything, except for the new womanly attributes of his pet. The good-hearted Pooch runs away from home when her master's wife becomes a snapping turtle and tries to bite the baby. She thinks she will be blamed.

Pooch takes the infant along with her. In workshopping the story, some readers pointed out to Carol that she had scenes where the baby is all but forgotten as Pooch is arrested and put into a series of ever-escalating perilous predicaments.

One reviewer called *Carmen Dog* a "hyper-Kafkaesque world," and compared the novel to Joanna Russ's classic *The Female Man.* In writing *Carmen Dog,* Carol was influenced by Olaf Stapledon's *Sirius,* wherein a super-intelligent dog's life is portrayed, and the Marquis de Sade's *Justine,* the story of an ingénue put through a wringer with every good deed she does.

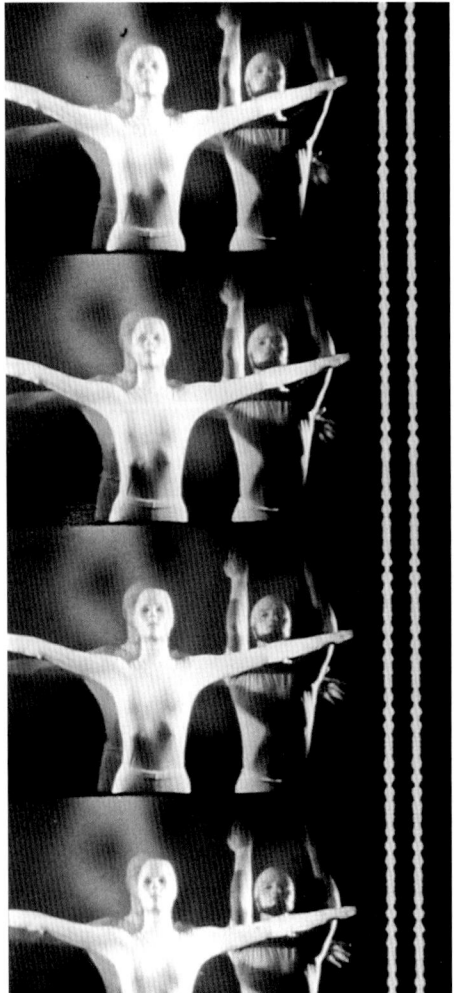

At the same time Carol was working on *Carmen Dog,* Ed began work on the last major artistic undertaking of his career. He collaborated with the composer Morton Subotnick in an interactive 3-D live performance, with sound and images manipulated by various autonomous computer-controlled devices. This came together as the electronic video opera, *Hungers,* that played at the Los Angeles Arts Festival in 1987. In *Hungers,* live performers interacted with motion-sensing devices to mutate the music and video so that no two performances were ever the same. Ed had chaos theory in mind with *Hungers* and described it as an attempt to "get film out of its can."

The multi-media *Hungers* appeared to mixed reviews, and Ed culled materials from the project into a single-channel, half-hour video that stood alone. Sometimes it seemed that these multi-media events worked or didn't work based on the mood or receptiveness of the audience.

Around 1988, Carol began to send around a manuscript of her uncollected stories to publishers. The collection went to progressively smaller publishing houses after each rejection. One small San Francisco publisher, Mercury House, sent her the readers' grades. All five readers were enthusias-

FILM WITH THREE DANCERS. 1970.

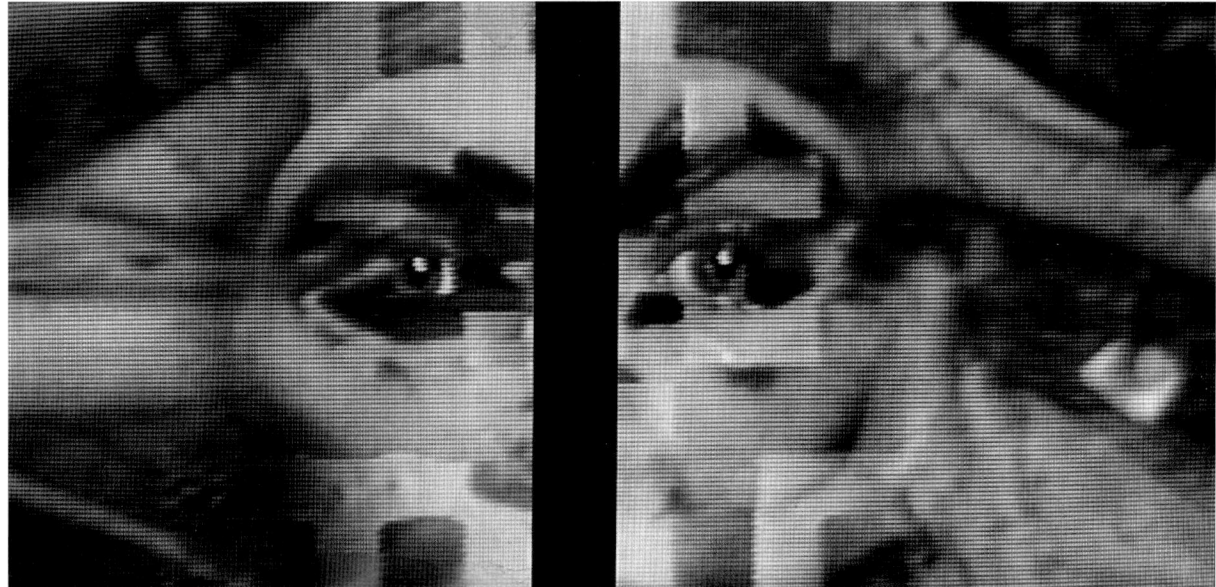

SKIN MATRIX. 1984, 17 minutes, video. Made at Calarts in association with WNET/13 NYC. "Skin Matrix is a video tapestry. It is a layering of traces of different manifestations of energy; electronic (light, video, computer), inorganic (sand dunes, rocks, baked mud), organic (wood grain, stumps, plants), human (skin, hair), individual (faces, eyes), and imagination (sculpture, robot, flying figure). It is a videotape which weaves the textures of nature and the mind into a unified form having multiple meanings." — EE

The human element here goes back to a short film idea Ed had in the spring of 1959 for "a close up study of many types of skin [done] as a film poem."

tic about publishing the collection, but Mercury House told Carol that they were too young a company. "We are showing you the readers' write-ups so you don't think we are rejecting you because of the quality of your work. We can't afford to put out a really super literary book." *Verging on the Pertinent* was eventually taken by Coffeehouse Press, and brought out in 1989. After this, Mercury House took Carol's next four books.

Carol later said: *What really bothered me, and dashed me, and made me realize you shouldn't say to yourself, 'I'm gonna get better,' was when these five readers all said publish it—and they didn't do it. That made me realize it doesn't matter how good you are.*

By this time Ed was dismissing his commercial art career and quietly turning down SF fan publishers when they approached him about doing a book of his art. Ultimately, he wanted to be known as a filmmaker. In his last year he was still thinking of new projects.

At a Christmas party given by Alexander Mackendrick in his home in December of 1989, Ed unknowingly fractured a bone in his spine while going down some steps. Most of the time he ignored aches and pains, but this time the pain bothered him enough that he drove himself to the hospital.

By spring he felt well enough to make his annual trip to New York, but on the cross-country return trip Carol found herself walking the streets of an unknown midwest town looking for a drugstore while Ed suffered in a hotel room. In California the pain became worse and he could hardly walk. Ed entered the hospital in May of 1990 and learned he had cancer throughout his body. The cancer had spread to his spine leaving it in a weakened state. Essentially he had suffered a broken back in December. Until the end, Ed never took seriously the thought that he was dying. In a hospital bed he was drawing storyboards for new projects.

Ed once stated: "Looking further ahead, I would like to see and work with a moving, color, holographic 3D image system. Beyond that, one thinks of the age-old science fiction-like dream of the child-artist-god who brings into being and transforms at will whatever his heart desires, whether the means be microsurgery combined with world bank computers and telepathy or the genii in Aladdin's lamp. The only limitation would be one's imagination."

All his life he had paid little attention to shelter, food, pets, or people. His art was his life. In the hospital, Carol would sit with him, and on one occasion observed him in a semi-comatose state holding his hands out and typing on an invisible computer keyboard while saying, "It's beautiful—I wish I could really do that." Ed's unseen dream machine art, at the edge of his awareness, may have been a hallucination, but it sustained him at the end.

Ed died quietly in the night on July 27. His ashes were scattered from a plane over the California coast. Students remember Ed for his patience and his sense of humor. Friends and family all said that he had a scientific *and* artistic brain. However freeform his films appeared, they were all done in a precise manner—like his life—even though he always gave the impression of winging it.

After Ed's death, Carol finally became a fulltime writer. She still split her time between New York City in the winter and the Sierras Mountains in the summer. She had grown fond of the western landscape and attending the Mule Festival every spring near her mountain home. As she entered her seventh decade, Carol continued putting together new collections of her stories, and began working on a new novel—a realistic western, and a love story of sorts. *Ledoyt* was a real novel, not a hodgepodge of short scenes or the movement of characters through space, but a story constructed with people and incident flowing back and forth towards a common end. Carol stitched *Ledoyt*'s pieces together like a freeform quilt, laying out manuscript pages and cut paragraphs on the floor to work out scenes and structure.

Ledoyt is an old family name that Carol had saved for the right occasion. She reworked incidents and memories from growing up, like the time her father broke his toe and jammed a boot over the injured foot. During the two weeks that it took his toe to heal he never removed his boots. *Ledoyt* was about the incoherence of family love. Carol has stated that she eased some of her loneliness, after her husband's death, through the characters in *Ledoyt*. *In Ledoyt I created a man for myself. I made him a difficult man otherwise he*

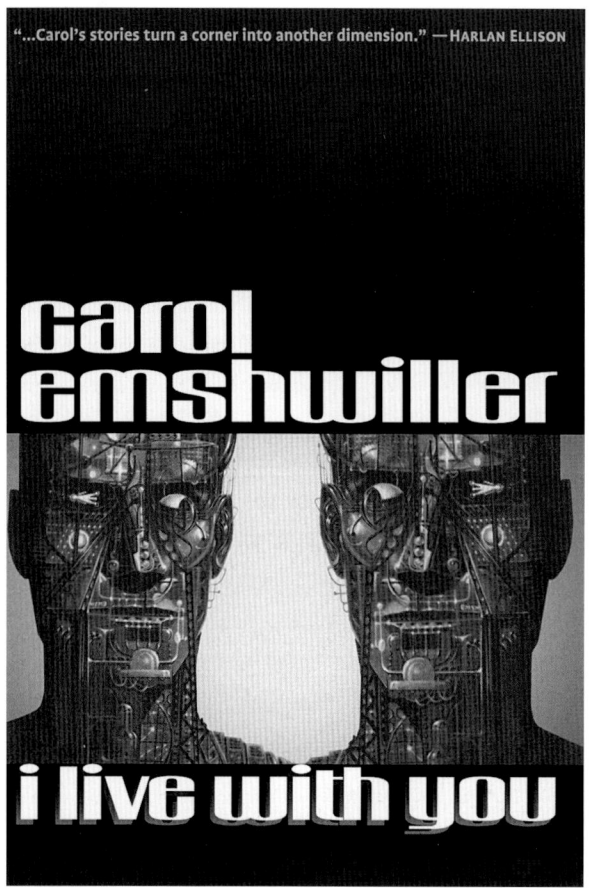

I LIVE WITH YOU. 2005. Tachyon Publications. Carol began using Ed's art for her book covers with this collection of stories.

wouldn't be at all interesting even to me. (I didn't make him as difficult as my real husband was...) I'm monogamous even to characters I created.

The novel *The Mount* came out in 2001 and developed a theme Carol had used before of upending the usual idea of prey vs. predator. She had gone to animal husbandry classes with ranchers to understand some of the psychology of horses. In *The Mount* Carol used the point-of-view of an unreliable narrator, a human ridden by hoots, diminutive aliens that have invaded and conquered earth. The human wants to be the best mount he can be. *I actually wanted the reader to feel torn about what was best, being looked after or having the hardships of being 'free'.*

In 1999 she was back in *Magazine of Fantasy & Science Fiction* —after a 33-year interval — with a story in the October/November issue. Her last story published there had been in April 1966. Going back to SF was a practical decision. Literary magazines took a long time to respond to submissions, while SF magazines were a lot faster in rejecting or accepting a piece of fiction. She had come around full-circle. In 2002 she won the Nebula Award for the short story "Creature" and the Philip K. Dick Award for *The Mount*.

It took a new century for critics and readers finally to catch up to her. Her prose had for many years defied easy classification, and in this sense, a marketing tag. At the end of Isaac Bashevis Singer's "Gimpel the Fool," the main character says: "No doubt the world is entirely an imaginary world, but is only once removed from the true world." Like Gimpel, Carol is unconcerned about the gap between a fabulist and plausible reality.

It would be easy to place Carol in a magic realist category, but her stories resemble no one else's in or outside that group. The disjointed Latin-American experience driving much of magic realism, fusing the old and the new, is missing from her writings, and the personal and the political do not quite intertwine as in much fabulist hybrid fiction. The war stories Carol began writing with the turn of the twenty-first century addressed some of her experiences during WWII.

(top R) AMAZING STORIES. July 1963. "Redemption" by Robert F. Young.

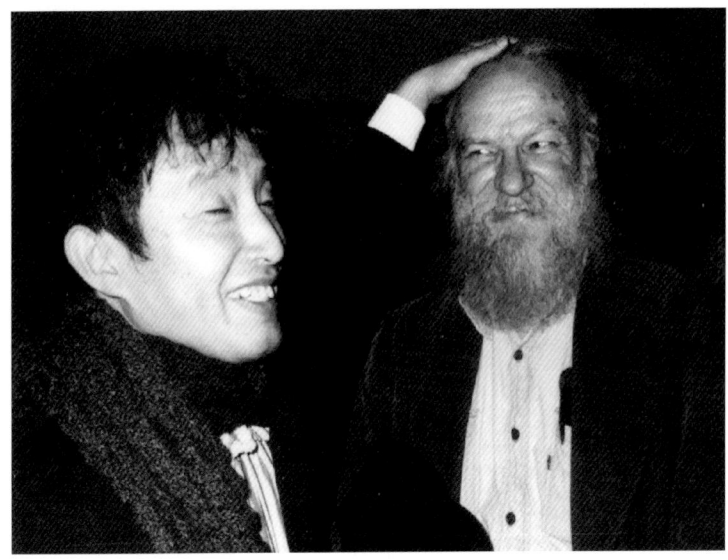

The cover art of science fiction magazines has changed since Ed's time, along with the themes of the fiction, which now blend in many more fantasy elements, but like the once-thought-gone coelacanth, science fiction magazines live on past the extinction of general fiction magazines. In 2005 Carol was given the lifetime achievement award at the World Fantasy Convention. She had to be coaxed into showing up to receive the award. After the event Carol said, *This should be typical of a mother of three's career.*

Much that is best in Ed's work came out of his sense of contrast and balance. Because he was always on the prowl for catch-as-catch-can moments, he had to know when the right relationship was in place for the best possible image or juxtaposition of kinetic images. It is as if Ed, holding a sheet of paper with metal filings on it in one hand and a magnet underneath with the other hand, tried to capture the moment just before the magnet touched the paper and the iron scraps snapped into place, that moment when everything is still in dynamic flux. Once established as a filmmaker, Ed worked to please himself without fear of an audience. He always had faith in his art opening the eye. "I'm interested in different ways of seeing," was one of Ed's favorite expressions.

Ed died too soon to have any real interaction with the high-speed world of desktop computers. He would have taken to it like a fish to water. His own work prefigured it and laid some of the foundation. He had always pursued new visual phenomena through twentieth-century American idioms of animation and science fiction. Many students emerged from CalArt's computer animation program in the eighties to make a mark. For many of them the unique exposure to both the avant-garde ideal and Hollywood, the artist and the craftsman, instilled in them the idea that images could create their own fiction or truth. This is one small legacy of Ed Emshwiller.

If Ed had lived to the present day, he would also have enjoyed the science fictional idea of people with handheld camera phones and iPods: recording, manipulating, and sending disembodied images and movie clips to each other — a universal community of image-makers sharing their personal vitality. Beyond the YouTube divide, short-length cinematic experimentation is seen as an affectation, something for the cineaste. Bewilderment had become a sin and art a liability to a marketplace searching for mass appeal. Ed's own mother once sat angrily through an avant-garde dance program because she could not understand the story, and Ed had to explain that the dance was meant to be watched as art in movement. He tried to explain this as the difference between reading fiction and a poem.

(top) **Ed with Nam June Paik. 1979.**

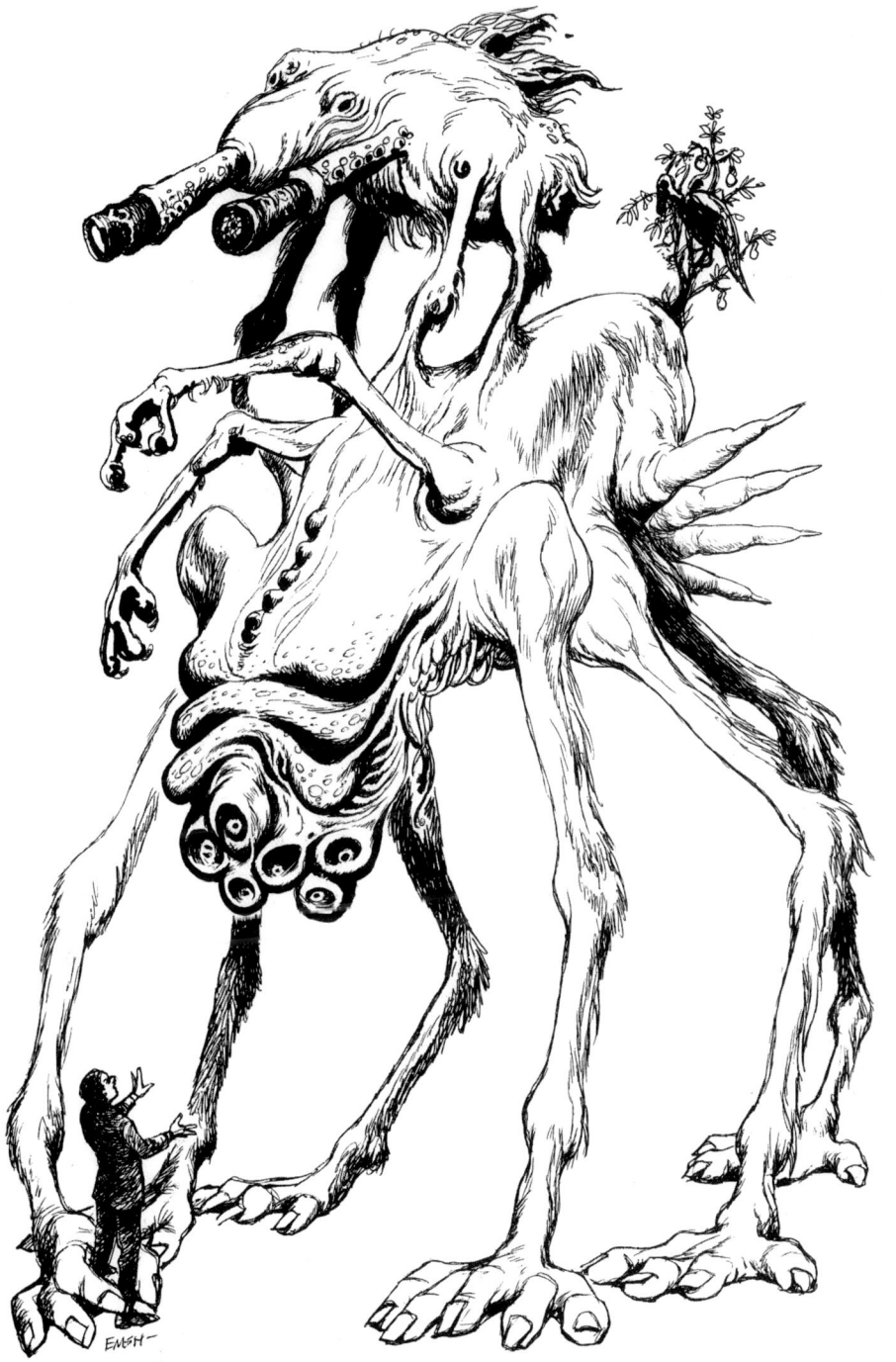

Demo drawing done in ballpoint and pentel at the 1985 Kubla Khan in Nashville, TN, where Ed and Carol were joint Guests of Honor.

Beyond *Relativity*, many science fiction people have been overlooked Ed's cinematic body of work in much the same way that many cinephiles have overlooked his science fiction art. Both sides miss how Ed managed to fuse these two elements together. SF elements are inherent in many of his films (*Relativity* and *Sunstone*, for example), and the lever of visual storytelling in his SF paintings (he was the premier *art first, story later* artist in the field) hinted early on at a creative energy that went beyond commercial art. Indeed, in an interview in an obscure Canadian film group newsletter, he was asked "Don't you regret not going back to drawing many-headed monsters?" Ed replied, "...I think that I did what I was going to do as an illustrator and painter, and I think that my particular way of seeing and doing has a greater range, a greater potential, in film than I was capable of giving to the static work. I more or less exhausted my vision in that area. That was the easiest change [I] ever made. I just got bored stiff."

In film, he was able to invoke new and odd juxtapositions, while giving the appearance of not trying too hard. As a cameraman, his athletic litheness along with his artistic eye exploited a virile movie style in much the same way his scientific bent helped him in developing apt science fiction images.

But it was always the moving image that excited Ed. "When I look at films I've made over the years I'm struck by the changes and continuities I see in them. They form a record of my interests and perceptions, going back over … years. In a way, they form a diary made without the self-consciousness of diary-keeping. Although there is virtually none of my day-to-day personal life in them, they do show the evolution of my preoccupations as a filmmaker and some of the general changes that have come about in society over the years."

NOTES

Looking into the Future

This chapter draws primarily from interviews with Carol Emshwiller and Mac Emshwiller.
19 "...we had a *Natural History* book: "EE: an interview," *Afterimage*, September 1974, Scott Hammen
20 *Why did he need a movie camera?:* Phone interview with Mac Emshwiller, June 2005
20 "... at 24 frames a second: "EE: an interview," *Afterimage*, September 1974, Scott Hammen
21 *my mother and grandmother just had each other:* Interview with CE, February 17, 2005
21 *We were one of those old-fashioned families:* Ibid
22 *"Américain, tete de chien,"* Ibid, from autobiographical manuscript in progress by CE
22 *I remember the exact word:* CE's Guest of Honor Speech, WisCon 2003, *Extrapolation*, Vol. 45, No. 1, 2004
22 *I'm sure he thought :* Interview with CE, February 6, 2006
22 *I would daydream while walking down:* Ibid
22 *My dad was one :* Ibid

Two x Infinity

This chapter is based on EE's army records, and on my interviews with CE.
26 *I was cursed at:* "Autobiography," CE, www.sfwa.org
26 *I was not a good violinist:* Interview with CE, March 14, 2005
26 *I was dexterous in art:* Ibid
27 *I was stationed in Tarcento:* Ibid
28 "Between waves": "The men behind *Amazing Stories*, Ed Emsler," *Amazing Stories*, October 1952

The Art of Things to Come

29 "Before *Galaxy* was a year old: *Galaxy 30 Years of Innovative Science Fiction*, introduction by Fred Pohl, eds. Frederik Pohl, Martin H. Greenberg, & Joseph D. Olander, 1980, Playboy Press
30 "Horace Gold earnestly believed: *The Engines of the Night*, Barry Malzberg, 1982, Doubleday
30 "... had been pretty well sheltered from: "The men behind *Amazing Stories*, Ed Emsler", *Amazing Stories*, Oct. 1952
33 "SF pulps leaves me puzzled: R.A. Lafferty, *Fantastic Lives*, 1981
34 "Paul made amends for: *Science Fiction Art; Yet More Penguin Science Fiction*, 1964, Brian Aldiss
34 "How marvelous were Paul's illustrations:: *Fantastic Lives*, 1981, Philip José Farmer
34 *I got mad cause he always lost*: interview with CE, February 17, 2005
34 "truly edit rather than: *Worlds of Science Fiction*, Robert P. Mills, 1963, Anthony Boucher
34 "Horace created a unique milieu: *Galaxy 30 Years of Innovative Science Fiction*, William Tenn
36 "faking of color" EE letter to parents, Feb. 4, 1954
37 "So many contentious, brilliant, and outrageous: "When De Kooning was King," *N.Y. Times Book Review*, Red Grooms, Dec. 12, 2004
37 "SF was once impoverished:" *Bury my Heart at W.H. Smith*, 1990, Brian Aldiss
38 "We were chosen: *Who Killed SF?*, (1960), comment by P. Schuyler Miller, ed. Earl Kemp
39 "The trouble has been that science fiction editors: "The Universe", by Sam Moskowitz, *Sky Hook* 19 (fanzine), 1953
40 "fat check" *Wonder Child: My life in Science Fiction*, Jack Williamson, 1984, Benbella Books
42 One incident: story told by EE to Alex Eisenstein at Kubla Kahn, 1985

Red Maple Drive

45 "There were certain things done: 'An Interview with Amos Vogel," *Wide Angle*, Cinema 16: Documents toward a history of the Film Society, part I, vol. 19, no, 1, January 1997, Scott MacDonald
47 "Possibly the rarest Gnome Press book: *The Science-Fantasy Publishers: A Critical and Bibliographic History*, Chalker & Owings
48 "I was in the gallery: "Video Art: EE: Combining Inner and Outer Landscapes," *Videography* 8, Sept. 1983, V. Ancona
49 "Kelly was great fun: *Pulp Era*, # 67, 1967, Robert W. Lowndes
49 "As far as I know it is the most symbolic: EE letter to parents. May 7, 1953
50 "The story on that Emsh painting: *Fantastic Story Magazine*, "Letters from our Readers", January 1953 (the cover in question is for September 1952)
51 there were six SF&f movies playing: *Philcon Reporter (WorldCon newsletter)*, 1953
51 "Would be Zoomies Meet In Philadelphia": *Bedford Gazette*, Sept. 8, 1953
52 "I've always been attracted more: EE: an interview,"*Afterimage*, Sept. 1974, Scott Hammen
52 "I was really interested in action painting: "An interview with EE;" by Gayla Jamison, *Filmmakers Newsletter*, Nov. 1977
52 "When I was an action painter: "Image Maker meets Video, or, Psyche to Physics and Back," by EE, *The New Television: A Public/Private Art*, eds. Douglas Davis and Allison Simmons. Cambridge, MA:MIT, 1977
52 "I worked at what I called doodles: "Four Artists as Film-Makers," *Art in America* 55, no. 1, Jan.-Feb. 1967, Adrienne Mancia and Willard Van Dyke
54 "LSD Christmas tree: Email interview with Robert Silverberg by author, July 2005

Science Fiction Boom

55 *I guess what triggered my first stories:* Interview with CE, March 14, 2005
55 *Something clicked: Magazine of Fantasy & Science Fiction*, May 1957

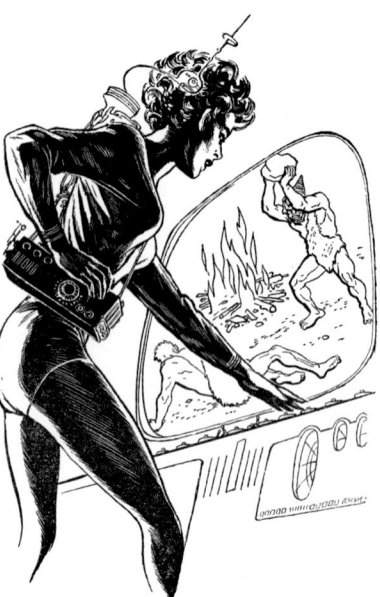

INFINITY SCIENCE FICTION. Aug. 1956. "The World in the Juke Box" by Edward Wellen.

164

56 *All the reading Ed did:* CE comment to author in reading draft of manuscript, August 2006
56 Ed believed that his most recent work: EE letter to parents, Jan. 23, 1954
58 "If things go through as hoped: EE letter to parents, July 15, 1955
58 "quite enthusiastic": EE letter to parents, undated, circa 1955
58 "One cover sold would pay for it.": EE letter to parents, Sept. 16, 1955
60 "It was like camp: EE letter to parents, Sept. 17, 1956
60 *That first time at Milford:* Interview with CE, February 27, 2005
60 *I was always a very slow reader:* Ibid
61 she found herself in agreement with Merril: CE letter to Judy Merril, Oct. 17, 1956, J. Merril Fonds, Library and Archives Canada, Ottawa
61 *He was kinda cute and pixie-like:* Interview with CE, February 27, 2005
61 Knight tagged Carol a "buttercup": Letter to CE from Judy Merril, 1956, J. Merril Fonds, Library and Archives Canada, Ottawa
62 "They aren't attempts to swashbuckle: *Future SF* No. 35; Feb. 1958, Robert W. Lowndes
62 "strange, off trail stories." Ibid, Robert W. Lowndes' blurb to CE's story
64 "The interesting new work tended: *SF: The Best of the Best*, J. Merril, 1967
66 the Emshwillers and Silverbergs shared a ride back to New York: Email interview with Robert Silverberg, July 2005
66 *It not only changed my feelings on writing:* Letter from CE to J. Merril, Sept. 18, 1956. J. Merril Fonds, Library and Archives Canada, Ottawa
66 In many cases she discovered this helped: CE interview, March 14, 2005

Art first, Story second

In this chapter I drew on my inteviews with CE, Harlan Ellison, and Robert Silverberg. Uncited quotes come from these sources.
67 "Instead of film: CE interview Apr 13, 2005
67 "We had…two different audiences: 'An Interview with Amos Vogel," *Wide Angle*, Cinema 16: Documents toward a history of the Film Society, part I, vol. 19, no, 1, January 1997, Scott MacDonald
68 By the late sixties he would joke: "Remembering EE", Joanna Frazier-Hudson *IM*
68 "Though the formal organization dictated: EE proposal to Ford Foundation Fellowship Program for studies in the Creative Arts, Nov. 10, 1960, Calarts EE Papers
69 "Time became a factor…in addition to form and color in two dimensions: Ibid
71 Ed was adept at "dreaming up ideas": "Ring around the Illustration," panel, *The Proceedings: DISCON 1965*, ed. Dick Eney, Advent Publishers
71 "Ed's cover ideas were always clever ones: per Robert Silverberg, *The Proceedings: DISCON 1965*
71 "[In] one situation Ed Emsh and Bob Lowndes presented me: Email interview with Robert Silverberg by author, July 2005
71 "amusing challenges": Ibid
72 "… poster[s] which [had] a gimmick [….]: Ibid
72 He wrote "Sunrise on Mercury" in a day. *Phases of the Moon*, Robert Silverberg, 2004, ibooks
72 Harlan Ellison remembers: Phone interview with H. Ellison October 2005
72 "I've been encouraged to do…flagrantly wrong ideas: Pittcon panel 1960

So be a Camera

Background on the 1950s science fiction field comes from various fanzines of the period.
75 *They were happy. I was the one*: CE's Guest of Honor Speech, WisCon 2003, *Extrapolation*, Vol. 45, No. 1, 2004
77 *I think that instead maybe I will manipulate:* Joy in our Time
79 "Campbell put everone: Email interview with Robert Silverberg by author, July 2005
80 "… having many battles about the response: 1971 "Conversation in Pittsburgh", *Intersecting Images*
81 *The little freebles floomped blurrily along*: "Science Fiction Covers in Ten Easy Lessons," *Peon* 29 (fanzine), 1953, Carol McKinney
83 "No, I would not: "Changing Trends in Science Fiction Art" John W. Campbell, Jr., Ed Emshwiller, and Sam Moskowitz on September 4, 1960 at Pittcon, 18th World Science Fiction Convention in Pittsburgh, PA, *Luna* #2 (fanzine), 1962 edited by Frank M. Dietz
84 "We found if we do not call a book science fiction: *Infinity Science Fiction* questionnaire to SF publishers 'Infinity's Choice" by Damon Knight, June 1958
84 "pulp's disease": *Spacewarp* 38 (fanzine), Bob Tucker
90 "I received assignments from a wide range of people: "Changing Trends in Science Fiction Art" John W. Campbell, Jr., Ed Emshwiller, and Sam Moskowitz. *Luna* #2 (fanzine), 1962 edited by Frank M. Dietz

"Oh, there he goes again"

For this chapter I drew on interviews with Bill Griffith, CE, and Peter Emshwiller, and correspondence between EE and his parents.
91 "…There were to be three stages: "Conversation with EE," 1969 Pittsburgh
91 "… an experience in the sense of the unfolding of a small universe." ibid
92 "I remember that when [it] was shown on the screen in the huge Needles Trades High School Auditorium: "Ed Emshwiller", Cecile Starr, *Intersecting Images*, Anthology Film Archives
95 "What a perfectly wonderfully perfect experience: Letter to EE from Stan Brakhage, Nov. 9, 1961, Calarts EE papers
96 "Oh, there he goes again.": "Conversation with EE", 1969, Pittsburgh, (CE denies having ever said this in comment to author upon reading draft of manuscript, August 2006)
96 "spontaneous" scene suggest what followed: Ibid
97 "The lines in your hand, procreation: Ibid
98 "…to get my own feeling for it: "Changing Trends in Science Fiction Art," Pittcon panel 1960

96 SF book covers showing a spaceship or at least one alien: "What does a woman know about SF Anyway" by Sharon Jarvis, *Inside Outer Space*, 1985
99 "Sometimes I think [the rejected ones] are *better*: *The Proceedings; DISCON*, 1964
99 First over $100 SF painting at SF auction per Andrew Porter, phone conversation June 2006
101 Carol was once asked if she was happy to have a technically minded husband around: "Wives panel", *The Proceeding; Discon and comment by CE to draft of manuscript*
101 *Ed's work ... made the money that kept us going*: CE interview with author April 22, 2005, with amendment via comment to manuscript
101 "I'm Quacky! I'm Quacky! : email from Peter Emshwiller, Mar 29, 2006
101 "man's man," tooling around on a motorcycle: Email from Bill Griffith to author, April 2005
102 "The first serious film I made: "Cine-Dance," by EE, *Dance Perspectives* #30, Summer 1967
103 *I've always wondered if the other writers*: CE letter to J. Merril, Feb. 2, 1960
103 *If I helped him it was the same as if he was doing it*: CE interview, Feb. 17, 2005
104 *I do know that I was very frustrated back [then]*: "Interview: CE," by Patrick Weekes, *Strange Horizons*, April 30, 2001
105 Ed invested $4,000: Letter from EE to parents, n.d.
105 "All my films up to that point: EE interview, *Afterimage*, Sept. 1974
106 "Natural inclination ... to remake his world: "EE interview by James Mullins", summer 1966, *Film Culture* #42

Rainy day scenarios

109 "I feel that I cannot be a party: Letter from Amos Vogel to EE, Apr. 4, 1963, Calarts, EE Papers
110 "It's great! See what this camera can do: "Ed Emshwiller," by Adolfas Mekas, *Intersecting Images*
110 "I always thought it would be nice to be in the museum: EE letter to parents, March 30, 1963
114 *I had to reject plot little by little*: CE: Autobiography, www.sfwa.org
114 *Each story was different*: SUNY Brockport Writer's Forum video interview with CE, 37m, hosts Jack Wolf & Stan Sanvel Rubin, Mar. 17, 1976
117 "It was very exhausting: "EE interview by James Mullins", summer 1966, *Film Culture* #42
117 "I wanted to create maximum tension: "Film as Autobiography", by EE, Feb. 1973, Calarts: EE Papers
117 "I think your meditation on death is brilliant: Letter by Stan VanDerBeek to EE, March 5, 1963, Calarts: EE papers
118 "The whole concept of LIFELINE: "EE interview by James Mullins", summer 1966, *Film Culture*
120 *We would use up every penny*: CE interview, Feb. 27, 2005
120 *grand old man of the avant-garde*: Ibid
120 *their token avant-garde filmmaker*: Ibid

Take a Number

121 "My principal project now: "A Statement," EE, *Film Culture* 29, Summer 1963
121 "[It's] probably the only field: Letter from Judy Merril to Richard M. Powers; 1962, J. Merril Fonds, Library and Archives Canada, Ottawa
121 He must have filmed the creation of hundred: Interview with Alex Eisenstein, Apr. 6, 2006
122 *Man alone; isolated*: "Project Description," c. 1963, EE papers, Calarts
123 "Ed, during our breaks, taking the lens: EE, by Jack Willis, *Intersecting Images*
124 Ed stated that he could have dreamed *Relativity*: Jonas Mekas on EE, *Movie Journal, Village Voice* June 25, 1970
124 "... sort of traveling bum: "EE interview N.Y. Film Festival 1966", *Film Culture* #42 Fall, 1966
124 "Shot largely in long, smooth, hand-held tracking shots: "*Relativity* Re-affirms Emshwiller's Stature," September 15, 1967
125 "Many filmmakers seem to have come to the medium: *Images from the Underground*, by EE, *Dialogue* 4, 1971
124 "A cine-dance in which the choreography often comes: "Dance Films" by EE, Calarts: EE papers
129 "I suppose it's the old proving yourself : "Biography of an Uncircumcised Man", *Joy in our Cause*, 1974, CE
129 "... somehow [they were] more textured than their counterparts: "2001: A Space Odyssey, a Review"; by EE, *The Year's Best SF no. 2*, ed by Harry Harrison and Brian W. Aldiss
130 "...Despite its conception as propaganda: "EE" by Samuel R. Delany, *Intersecting Images: The Cinema of Ed Emshwiller*
130 "If I'm going to spend the kind of time: "Eight Notes on the Underground," *Velvet Light Trap* 13, Fall 1974, Russell Campbell
130 Of course, it also means that the cutting edge of the avant-garde is : Ibid. (In 1963 Bernard Lodge designed the first *Doctor Who* titles using a technique called "howlaround", which was just a TV camera pointing at its own monitor. When Lodge redesigned the titles in 1973 "howlaround" was dropped and the then new technique of "slit-scan" used. This was the same method used in *2001: A Space Odyssey* for the hyper-space end sequence, where multiple exposures of light refracting in plastic were filmed through slots in a black card.)

All kinds of branches

131 That way I don't have to satisfy anyone: "EE: beginnings", by Letty Lou Eisenhauer, *Art and Artists*, Mar 1974
131 "I have turned down several requests: "EE: an interview", *Afterimage*, Sept. 1974, Scott Hammen
131 Ed watched the rehearsals: EE interview, WNET *The Film Generation*, 1970
132 "When the dancer is used in filmic terms: *Dance Perspectives* 30, summer, 1967, 1025
132 "Dancers are seen in different ways: EE description of his dance films, Calarts: EE papers
133 *I occasionally was confused by our "lifestyle."* : Peter Emshwiller, email interview, March 2006
134 "Everything had to be for a movie : Interview with Susan Emshwiller & CE; May 10, 2006
134 "Dad! You'll poison yourself!": Ibid
134 "You can smoke pot: Ibid
135 "I wanted to either catch people: Whitney Museum of American Art New American Filmmakers Series, program sheet, Feb. 24-Mar. 1, 1972
135 "That life offers too much data: "Re: Image, Flesh and Voice: Thoughts Ed's movie made me think," Tom Disch; CalArts EE Papers, n.d.

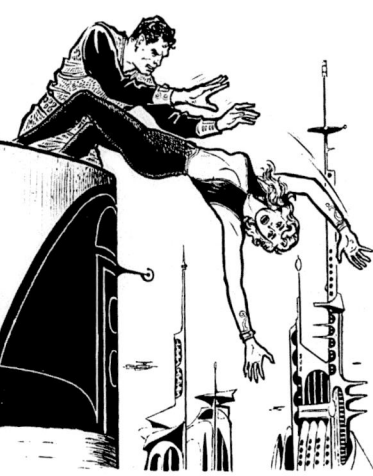

FUTURE SCIENCE FICTION. AUGUST 1959. Line art for cover.

136 "This film will involve concepts of art: proposal for Headgame, unrealized 16mm color film, Calarts EE Papers, October 1968
138 "The painter is really the best-off: "EE: interview", *Afterimage*, Sept. 1974, Scott Hammen
138 "I could see whether I had what I wanted or not:: "A Journey to Compute," EE, The Pacific Ring Festival program booklet, 1986, La Jolla, CA
138 "Then I take those same pieces of paper: "An interview with EE" *Filmmakers Newsletter*, Nov. 1977, Gayla Jamison
139 "pretty variations of Lissajous patterns,": "Image Maker meets Physics and Back," by EE, *The New Television: A Public/Private Art*, eds. Douglas Davis and Allison Simmons. Cambridge, MA:MIT, 1977
139 "environment." : *Experimental Animation*, by Robert Russett and Cecile Starr, 1976
140 "… well, there are so many variables.": "Emshwiller Completes New Work," *The Television Laboratory News*, May, 1974, Vol. 1, No. 3

illusion of reality

141 "In this miniature space: "Image Maker meets Video, or, Psyche to Physics and Back," by EE, *The New Television: A Public/Private Art*
142 "I've always had an interest in painting: attributed to Roger Angell, *About Town*, Ben Yagoda, 2000, Scribner
143 *I learned too much at once.*: Interview CE 4-17-05
143 "I'll get a divorce.": CE interview, Apr 13, 2005
144 *It was really nice not to have arguments*: CE interview, Feb. 6, 2006
144 *She comes back as this wonderful, terrible thing*: CE interview, *Science Fiction Chronicle*, Jan 1993(The story appeared in *Omni*, Dec 1988)
145 *A peculiar thing that kind of makes me think of Ed's "Relativity."*: CE letter to Judy Merril, May 17, 1967, J. Merril Fonds, Library and Archives Canada, Ottawa
146 "surrealism of the fresh.": "Women in Science Fiction," Veronica Geng, *Bookletter*, vol. 2, No. 6, Oct 27, 1975
146 "stream of consciousness,": "Two Collections," Rich Quackenbush, *Ann Arbor News*, Aug 4, 1974
146 "Elements in her stories are like elements in Godard's movies. …": "Joy in Our Cause" (review), The New Republic
146 "cockeyed élan.": "A Peaceable Kingdom," Carole Horn, *Washington Post Book World*, June 23, 1974
146 "She is perhaps the most extreme example: "The Panic of Being Alive", *New York Times*, May 15, 1974, Anatole Broyard
146 A*m I wrong in thinking my stories were judged*: CE, unsent letter to *Kirkus Review*, March 23, 1974
146 "frustrations of her daily life … her fantasies: Book review by John Alfred Avant, *The New Republic*, July 20, 1974

digital blobs

148 "If he's who I think he is: Email interview with Alvy Ray Smith, Mar. 14, 2006
148 "You'll be lucky to finish a piece of three minutes: Ibid
148 "Late at night I would get carried away.": "Digicon 83", Paul D. Lehrman, *Creative Computing*, vol. 10, no. 4, April 1984
149 "Too overwhelming,": Email interview with Alvy Ray Smith, Mar. 15, 2006
149 Most early users were head-over-heels in love: Ibid
149 "[Ed] couldn't code, pure and simple: Ibid
150 … birth, death and rebirth: "Video Art: EE: Combining Inner and Outer Landscapes," *Videography* 8, Sept. 1983, V. Ancona
150 "I learned a hard lesson at NYIT: Ibid
150 "SUNSTONE is a computer-animation videotape: auto-biographical handout, Calarts: EE papers
151 "blow up the moon": Email interview with Peter Emshwiller, Mar. 29, 2006
151 "a special effects lover's smorgasbord: *New York Times*, uncredited review, n.d.
154 *I'm not interested in stories where anything can happen*: CE interview, March 14, 2005

Avantopia

155 "You're going to die from something else.": Susan Emshwiller interview; May 10, 2006
155 "I … like to explore the characteristics: EE letter to Peter Sorensen, Jan. 24, 1985
156 "Although I've tried a lot of different things: "Video Art: Ed Emshwiller," by Victor Ancona, *Videography* Sept. 1983
156 Mackendrick called Ed the "artist" and referred to himself as the "craftsman.": Susan Emshwiller interview; May 10, 2006
156 "like a cafeteria tray: Ibid
156 "embody the principal of dynamic contrast.": Alex Eisenstein interview, April 6, 2006
157 *The scariest thing I ever did*: CE interview; May 10, 2006
158 "hyper-Kafkaesque world,": "Specialty: Science Fiction," by Thomas M. Disch, *Entertainment Weekly*, April, 13, 1990
158 "get film out of its can.": *EE: Computer Animation Lab Founder*, Calarts, facility web page; emsh.calarts,edu/facility/emsh.htm
159 "We are showing you the readers' write-ups: CE interview, February 6, 2006
159 *What really bothered me, and dashed me*: Ibid
159 "Looking further ahead, I would like to see and work with a moving, color, holographic 3D image system: "Image Maker meets Video, or, Psyche to Physics and Back," by EE, *The New Television: A Public/Private Art*
159 "Skin Matrix is a video tapestry: auto-biographical handout, Calarts: EE papers
159 "a close up study of many types of skin: "Project Ideas for Film," EE, May 16, 1959, Calarts: EE papers
160 *In Ledoyt I created a man for myself*. "How my husband's death changed my writing" by CE, Fantastic Metropolis (website)
160 *I actually wanted the reader to feel torn*: CE interview by Robert Greeman Wexler, Fantastic Metropolis, September 11, 2002
162 *This should be typical of a mother of three's career.*: Emshwiller takes lifetime award, Internet report
162 "I'm interested in different ways of seeing,": "An interview with EE", *Filmmakers Newsletter* 11, no. 1, Nov. 1977, Gayla Jamison
162 "Don't you regret not going back to drawing many-headed monsters?": EE interview, *Rushes*, Vol. II, number 2, Oct. 1972; Canadian Filmmakers' Co-op, Toronto, Ontario, CalArts EE Papers
163 "When I look at films I've made over the years: Ibid

Selected Bibliography

Aldiss, Brian W.; *Trillion Year Spree*; Avon,, 1988
Aldiss, Brian W.; Harrison, Harry, eds.; *Hell's Cartographers*; Futura Publications, London, 1975
Ashley, Michael; *The History of the Science Fiction Magazine, Vol. 3 1946-1955*; Comtemporary Books; Chicago 1976
Ashley, Michael; Tymn, Marshall B., eds.; *Science Fiction, Fantasy, and Weird Fictions Magazines*; Greenwood Press, 1985
Bower, Bill ed.; *Outworlds #52*, September 1987
Chapdelaine Sr., Perry A.; Chapdelaine, Tony; Hay, George, eds.; *The John W. Campbell Letters, Vol 1*; AC Projects, 1985
Disch, Thomas M. *On SF*; University of Michigan Press, 2005
Ellison, Harlan ed.; *Dangerous Visions*; Doubleday, 1967
Emshwiller, Carol; *Joy in Our Cause*; Harper & Row, 1974
Eney, Dick; The Proceedings: DISCON; Advent Publishers, Chicago; 1965
Frank, Jane; *The Art of Richard Powers*: Paper Tiger; London, 2001
Halas, John; Manvell, Roger; *Art in Movement*; Hastings House; New York, 1970
Haller, Robert A. ed.; *Intersecting Images: The Cinema of Ed Emshwiller*; Anthology Film Archives, 1997
Hickman, Lynn A. ed. ; *The Pulp Era #67*, May-August 1967
James, David E.; *To Free the Cinema: Jonas Mekas & the New York Underground*; Princeton University Press, 1992
Kemp, Earl & Nancy, eds.; *The First Safari Annual: Who Killed Science Fiction?*; Chicago, 1960
Keyes, Daniel; *Algernon, Charlie and I: A Writer's Journey*; Challcrest Press, 1999
Knight, Damon; *The Futurians*; John Day; New York 1977
Lovisi, Gary, ed.; *The Pulp Crime Digests*, Gryphon Books, 2004
MacDonald, Scott; *Wide Angle*, Vol. 19, no. 1 & no. 2; *Cinema 16: Documents Toward a History of the Film Society*; January & April 1997
Merril, Judith; Pohl-Weary, Emily; *Better to Have Loved: The life of Judith Merril*; Between the Lines,; Toronto, 2002
Parfrey, Adam ed.; *It's a Man's World: Men's Adventure Magazines, the Postwar Pulps*; Feral House, 2003
Pohl, Fredrik; *The Way the Future Was: a Memoir*; Del Rey Book, 1978
Pohl, Fredrik; Greenberg, Martin H.; Olander, Joseph D., eds.; *Galaxy: Thirty years of Innovative Science Fiction*; Playboy Press: 1980
Rosheim, David L.; *Galaxy Magazine: The Dark and the Light Years*; Advent Publishers, Chicago; 1986
Russett, Robert; Starr, Cecile; *Experimental Animation: Origins of a New Art*; Da Capo Press, 1976
Schreuders, Piet; *Paperbacks, U.S.A.*; Blue Dolphin Book; San Diego, 1981
Silverberg, Robert; *Phases of the Moon*; ibooks, 2004
Tyler, Parker; *Underground Film: a Critical History*; Da Capo, 1995
Weinberg, Robert; *A Biographical Dictionary of Science Fiction and Fantasy Artists*; Greenwood Press, 1988
Wood, Ed, ed.; *Journal of Science Fiction 4*; 1953

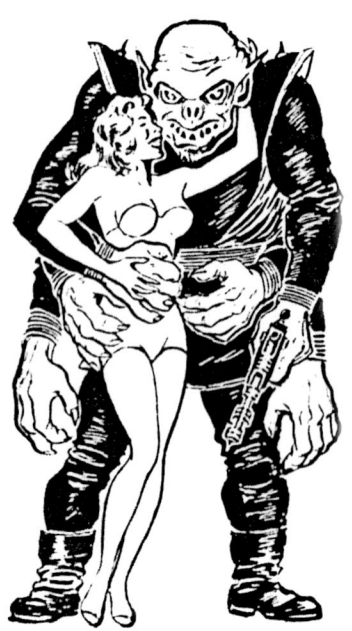

FUTURE SCIENCE FICTION. AUGUST 1959. Line art for cover.

Ed Emshwiller Filmography

PAINTINGS, 1957-1958, 16mm, color
MONSTERS, 1958, 16mm, 3 min., b&w
BIG VACATION, 1958, 16mm
DANCE CHROMATIC, 1959, 16mm 7 min., color
TRANSFORMATION, 1959, 16mm, 5 min., color
LIFELINES, 1960, 16mm 7 min., color
VARIABLE STUDIES, 1960-61, 16mm 5 min., color
TIME OF THE HEATHEN, 1961, 35mm, 75 min., b&w with color sequence. (In collaboration with Peter Kass.)
THE AMERICAN WAY, 1961, 35mm, 10 min., b&w. (cinematographer)
THANATOPSIS, 1962, 16mm, 7 min., b&w
TOTEM, 1963, 16mm, 16 min., color. (In collaboration with Alwin Nidolais.)
HALLELUJAH THE HILLS, 1963, 35mm, 80 min., b&w. (cinematographer)
FILM MAGAZINE #1, 1963, 16mm
SCRAMBLES, 1964, 16mm, 15 min., b&w
GEORGE DUMPSON'S PLACE, 1964, 16mm, 8 min., color
FACES OF AMERICA, 1965, 35mm, 20 min., color, USIA film
BODY WORKS, 1965, mixed media, live dance with 8mm and 16mm film, 25 min., (Performed at the Film-Makers Cinematheque, Nov. 1965.)
RELATIVITY, 1966, 16mm, 44 min., color
ART SCENE U.S.A., 1966, 35mm, 35 min., color USIA film, 16 min.
IN THREE ZONES (based on play by Wilford Leach), 1966, 16mm, b&w, 35 min.
FUSION, (with Alwin Nikolais), 1967, 16mm, color, 16 min.
NORMAN JACOBSON, 1967, 16mm, b&w, 60 min., (cinematographer)
PROJECT APOLLO, 1968, 30 min., color, 30 min.
IMAGE, FLESH & VOICE, 1969, 35mm, b&w, 77 min.
CAROL, 1970, 16mm, color, 6 min.
BRANCHES, 1970, 16mm, b&w, 103 min.
FILM WITH THREE DANCERS, 1970, 16mm, color, 20 min.
CHOICE CHANCE WOMAN DANCE, 1971, 16mm, color, 44 min.
IMAGES, 1971, video, 30 min.
COMPUTER GRAPHIC #1: THERMOGENESIS, 1972, video, color, sound, 12 min (also longer version)
WOE OH HO NO, 1972, video, 13 min.
THE CHALK LINE, 1972, 3 min.
PAINTERS PAINTING, 1972, 82 min., color. (cinematographer)
INSIDE THE GELATIN FACTORY, 1972, b&w, 10 min.
SCAPE-MATES, 1972, video, color, 29 min.
CHRYSALIS, (with Alwin Nikolais), 1973, 16mm, color, 22 min.
PILOBOLUS & JOAN, 1973, video, color, 58 min.
POSITIVE NEGATIVE ELECTRONIC FACES, (with Tony Bannon), 1973, video, b&w, 30 min
IDENTITIES, 1973, 10 min.\
CROSSINGS AND MEETINGS, 1974, video, color, 28 min.
INTERRUPTED SOLITUDE, 1974, 20 min.
INSIDE EDGES, 1975, video, b&w, 16 min.
FAMILY FOCUS, 1975, video, color, 58 min.
NEW ENGLAND VISIONS PAST AND FUTURE (with William Thompson), 1976, video, 28 min.
COLLISIONS, 1976, video, 4 min.
SELF TRIO, 1976, video, 8 min.
SHORT AND VERY SHORT FILMS, 1952-1976, 25 min.
SUR FACES, 1977, video, color, 58 min.
SLIVERS, 1977, multi-monitor video, 60 min.
FACE OFF, 1977, 12 min.
DUBS, 1978, video, color, 24 min.
SUNSTONE, 1979, video, color, 3 min.
SKIN MATRIX, 1984, video, color, 9 & 17 min.
HUNGERS, 1988, video, color, 28 min.
THE BLUE WALL, 1988, computer installation interactive video

Index

A
Adventures in Time & Space 78
Again, Dangerous Visions 136
Aldiss, Brian 14, 33, 37, 145, 164, 166
Amazing Stories 18, 32, 33, 34, 41, 49, 84, 108, 164
Ann Arbor, Michigan 17, 21, 24, 28, 31, 36, 55, 70, 167
Anthology Film Archives 4, 165
Aquatic Ape, The 157
Asimov, Isaac 21, 30, 32, 35, 38, 41, 51, 58, 60, 67, 70, 121, 122, 128, 136, 156
Astounding Science Fiction 12, 18, 29, 41, 51, 76, 78, 79, 80, 81, 83, 84, 85, 89, 112
Atwood, Margaret 32, 154

B
Bad Moon Rising 145
Ballantine (paperback publisher) 39, 80, 83, 88
Ballard, J. G. 32, 81, 112, 154
Bally Arcade 155
Barthelme, Donald 142
Beast from 20,000 Fathoms (movie) 51
Beckett, Samuel 103, 142, 154
Berkley Books 80
Bester, Alfred 36, 50, 85, 95, 113
Bettmann Archives, 103
Big Vacation, The (EE film) 95
Bitches and Sad Ladies (anthology) 152
Blood of a Poet, The (film) 68
Bok, Hannes 36, 37, 51
Bolex (16mm camera) 52, 138
Borges, Jorge Luis 152, 154
Boucher, Anthony 29, 34, 40, 42, 44, 66, 85, 164
Boyle, Kay 114
Brakhage, Stan 109, 117, 165
Broyard, Anatole 112, 146, 167
BSA (motorcycle) 23, 28, 35, 46
Budrys, Algis 34, 59, 83
Buñuel, Luis 45, 68
Burroughs 154

C
Cabinet of Dr. Caligary, The (silent film) 109
Cage, John 34, 76, 86, 133, 136
CalArts 6, 144, 152, 155, 156, 157, 159, 162, 165, 166, 167
Calvino, Italo 152, 154
Campbell, John W. 12, 29, 30, 32, 34, 41, 51, 76, 77, 78, 79, 80, 81, 84, 85, 112, 123, 165, 166
Canada Film Board 20
Carmen Dog 157, 158
Cartier, Edd 10, 34, 36
Catmull, Ed 148
Cavett, Dick 148
CBC (Canadian Broadcast Company) 111, 123
Century of Progress World's Fair 18
Chicago Divinity School 22
Chicon (SF convention) 121
Cinema 16 (NYC film society) 45, 46, 52, 67, 68, 164, 165
Clarke, Arthur 43, 59, 129, 161
Colliers (magazine) 31
Columbia Publications 40
Cornell University 136
Creative Film Foundation 92, 97
Croton Review 152
Cyberpunk 154

D
Dali 9, 45, 68, 75. 108
Dangerous Visions 113-114, 136, 141
Datlow, Ellen 157
De Kooning 36, 54, 164
Dean Drive 78
DEC minicomputers 147
Delany, Samuel R. 14, 116, 130, 166
Dell (paperback publisher) 80, 83
Demolished Man, The (Alfred Bester) 85
Deren, Maya 46, 67, 92
Descent of Women, The 157
Destination Moon (movie) 52
Dianetics 29, 39, 78
DiFrancesco, David 148
Digicon 83 167
Dick, Philip K. 32, 40, 98, 123, 161
Disch 50, 113, 114, 135, 145, 166, 167
DISCON 165, 166
Disney, Walt 69, 151
Dolphin Computer Image Corporation 138
Donadio, Candida 144, 145
Don't Look Back (documentary) 111
Dumpson, George 123, 132, 139
Dylan, Bob 111

E

Earth's Last Fortress (A. E. Van Vogt) 100, 139
Ecole des Beaux-Arts 28
Edges (anthology) 78, 152
Eisenstein, Alex 4, 7, 42, 164, 166, 167
Ellery Queen (magazine) 58, 71
Ellison, Harlan 6, 7, 14, 36, 38, 51, 59, 72, 113, 116, 136, 141, 165

F

Faces of America (documentary) 124
Freas, Frank Kelly 10, 49, 50, 51, 52, 59, 80, 85
Freiburg, Germany 23
French Cinematique 28
Future Science Fiction 49, 57, 69, 165

G

G.I. Bill 26, 28
Galaxy 7, 8, 9, 10, 11, 12, 15, 17, 19, 21, 29, 30, 31, 34, 35, 36, 37, 39, 40, 41, 42, 49, 50, 51, 54, 58, 60, 61, 62, 63, 81, 84, 88, 95, 112, 114, 125, 144, 145, 156, 164
Garrett, Randall 71
Gernsback, Hugo 32, 33, 66, 70
Gnome Press 10, 33, 34, 36, 47, 48, 76, 88, 164
Godard 146, 167
Gold, Horace L. 6, 7, 9, 29, 30, 31, 34, 35, 39, 81, 84, 85, 164
Greenberg, Clement 92, 164
Greenberg, Marty 36
Griffith, Bill 4, 44, 101, 166
Griffith, Nancy 127, 130
Grooms, Red 36, 164
Guggenheim Fellowship 148
Guinn, Robert M. 30, 42

H

Hallelujah the Hills 98, 110
Haller, Robert 4, 14
Halley's Comet 157
Handmaid's Tale, The 154
Harrison, Lou 92
Harper & Row 145, 146
Heinlein, Robert A. 70, 82, 99, 113, 146
Hubley, John 46, 69
Hugo Awards 51, 151
Hungers (multi-media event & video) 158

I

I Live with You (CE story collection) 160
If, Worlds of Science Fiction 112, 114, 121
Image, Flesh, and Voice (EE film) 135
Infinity Science Fiction 4, 5, 7, 14, 23, 56, 60, 73, 75, 78, 86, 89, 123, 142, 164, 165
Invaders from Mars (movie) 51
It Came from Outer Space 51

J

Joy in Our Cause (CE short story collection) 143, 145, 146, 166, 167

K

Kass, Peter 104-105
Kemp, Earl 4, 85, 164
Keyes, Daniel 85
Kidd, Virginia 144, 157
King Jr., Martin Luther 111, 164
Kirkus Review 146, 167
Kline, Franz 48, 54, 80
Knight, Damon 38, 50, 58, 59, 61, 62, 70, 75, 165
Koch, Kenneth 5, 142, 143
Korean War 35
Kornbluth, Cyril 58, 59, 64, 66, 70, 113
Kubla Khan (SF convention) 156, 163
Kubrick, Stanley 43, 128, 129

L

La Jetee (short film) 128
Ladykillers, The (movie) 156
Lafferty, R.A 33, 164
Lathe of Heaven, The 150, 151
Le Guin, Ursula K. 150
Ledoyt 160, 167
Leiber, Fritz 59, 70, 84, 86, 136, 142
Lessing, Doris 32, 154
Levitt, Bill 46
Lifelines (EE film) 97, 118-119, 121
Lion Adventure Magazine 43
Lovecraft, H.P. 32
Lowndes, Robert 35, 40, 49, 56, 57, 58, 62, 69, 70, 71, 72, 79, 84, 164, 165
Luros, Milton 40
Lye, Len 20, 46

M

Macabre Reader, The (ed. by Donald Wollheim) 83, 112

Mackendrick, Alexander 156, 159, 167
MacLean, Katherine 59, 66
McKendrick, Sandy 8
Malzberg, Barry 29, 116, 164
Man in the White Suit, The (movie) 156
Man who Japed, The (by Phillip K. Dick) 98, 123
McCarthyism 35
McComas, Mike 29, 44
McDermott, Joan 141
McLaren, Norman 20, 46, 95
Mekas, Jonas & Adolfas 4, 109, 110, 117, 166
Mercury House (publisher) 158, 159
Mercury Mystery Book-Magazine 58, 63, 86
Mercury Publications 58
Merril, Judith 31, 38, 59, 61, 62, 64, 66, 70, 76, 101, 112-113, 116, 121, 135, 165, 166, 167
Meshes of the Afternoon (film) 68
MGM Studio 128
Milford SF conference 59, 60, 61, 62, 64, 66, 75, 76, 85, 121, 135, 165
Mills, Robert 76, 85, 164
Mines, Sam 50
Mondrian, Piet 68
Moorcock, Michael 112, 154
Morgan, Elaine 157
Moskowitz, Sam 39, 164, 165
Motherwell, Robert 54
Mount, The (CE novel) 38, 76, 161
Muybridge, Eadward 21
Museum of Modern Art 111, 117

N
NASA 129
National Endowment for the Arts 141
Nebula Award 161
New School for Social Research 20, 69
New Worlds (SF magazine) 114, 139
New York Times 46, 146, 167
New York Times Book Review 146
New York University 154
New Yorker (magazine) 8, 64, 142
Nikolais, Alwin 124, 131, 132
North Dakota Agriculture College 24
NYIT 4, 147, 148, 149, 150, 152, 155, 167

O
O'Hara, Frank 76
Olympic Arts Festival, Los Angeles 1984 156

Omni magazine 157
Orbit (magazine) 116
Original Science Fiction 49, 57, 69, 83, 101, 110

P
Paik, Nam June 136, 138, 140, 162
Paul, Frank R. 33
Philcon 51, 164
Pilobolus and Joan (EE video) 141
Piper Tomahawk (two-seater airplane) 157
Pittcon 72, 165
Plan 9 from Other Space 151
Planet Stories (SF magazine) 8, 30, 49, 125
Playboy (magazine) 8, 55, 164
Plezzo, Italy 25
Poel Jr., Washington Irving van der 8, 17, 31, 40, 41, 49, 58
Pohl, Fred 29, 33, 34, 38, 58, 63, 81, 84, 112, 116, 164
Pollock, Jackson 48, 52, 54. 83
Popular Science (magazine) 55
Porter, Andrew 4, 165
Powers, Richard M. 12, 12, 51, 52, 60, 80, 81, 83, 121, 166
Pratt School of Art 26
Project Apollo (EE documentary) 129, 130, 132, 137, 150
Pynchon, Thomas 32

R
Rauschenberg, Robert 76
Relativity 7, 15, 121, 123, 124, 125, 126, 128, 129, 133, 145, 163, 166, 167
Rehn Gallery 81
Richmond, Virginia 24
Riefenstahl, Leni 130, 136
Robbe-Grillet 5, 152
Rocket Stories 37, 41, 49
Rocketship X-M (movie) 52
Rockwell, Norman 54
Roland synthesizer 155
Rosset, Barney 92
Russ, Joanna 158

S
Salter, George 12, 40, 49
Saturday Evening Post 29, 31, 54, 145
Scanimate System 138, 139
Scape-Mates (EE video) 139, 140
Scared Stiff (movie) 51

Schoenherr, John 12
Science Fantasy Bulletin (fanzine) 36
Science Fiction Stories 7, 41, 49, 57, 69, 81, 145, 150, 154
Science Wonder Stories 18
Scientific American 5, 55, 128
scratchboard 30, 32, 36, 50, 54, 156
Seeger, Pete 111
SF Quarterly 57
Shaw, Larry 56
Silver Springs, Maryland 27
Silverberg, Robert 6, 38, 54, 56, 59, 62, 64, 71, 72, 75, 78, 85, 113, 116, 134, 136, 164, 165
Sinclair computer 155
Singer, Isaac Bashevis 141, 161
Skin Matrix (EE video) 155, 156, 159, 167
Smashing Detective 57
Smith, Alvy Ray 6, 34, 41, 75, 76, 148, 149, 150, 151, 164, 167
Space Stories (SF magazine) 9, 38, 41, 42, 43, 48
Spivak, Lawrence 49
Star Science Fiction (magazine) 81
Starr, Cecile 92, 165, 167
Stars My Destination, The (Alfred Bester's 1956 novel) 12, 13, 36, 85
Startling (SF magazine) 9, 9, 35, 41, 48, 67, 70
Stella, Frank 48
Stern, Garland 150, 151
Street & Smith 34, 41, 76
Streets of Greenwood, The (documentary) 111, 146
Sturgeon, Theodore 59, 66, 70, 72, 113
Stuyvesant Town 34
Sunstone (EE computer animation) 15, 150, 151, 152, 153, 154, 163, 167
Super-Science Fiction (SF magazine) 9, 18, 73, 86

T
Tanguy 9, 10, 80
Tarcento 26, 27, 164
Tarzan 22
Tenn, William 34, 35, 164
Thanatopsis (EE film) 13, 121, 128, 131, 156
The Quiet Takeover (documentary) 123
Thermogenesis (EE video) 139, 140
3rd Battalion, 351st Infantry 88th Division 25
Thrilling Wonder Story (SF magazine) 49
Time of the Heathen (movie) 104-106
Thrilling Wonder (SF magazine) 7, 41
Toronto Planetarium 130

Totem (cine-dance) 124, 131
Trans-Atlantic Review 143
Transformation (EE film) 96, 139
Tri-Quarterly 143
True Detective 58
Tucker, Bob 83, 165
12 Monkeys (movie) 128
2001: A Space Odyssey 128, 129, 166

U
Unix 147
Un Chien Andalou (film) 68
Untamed (men's magazine) 44, 56, 73, 78, 90, 135
University of Michigan 6, 21, 24, 25, 26, 27, 48
UPA 46, 69
USIA 124, 129, 130

V
Vance, Jack 85
VanDerBeek, Stan 117, 122, 147, 166
Venture (SF magzine) 7, 10, 57, 72, 83, 86
Venus Rising 157, 158
Verging on the Pertinent (CE story collection) 158
Vogel, Amos 45, 67, 164, 165, 166
Vogt, A. E. Van 139

W
Wantagh, Long Island 46, 66, 133
Warhol, Andy 95, 96, 121
Whitehall, Richard 124
Whitney, John 147, 166
Who Killed Science Fiction? (fanzine) 85, 168
Wilhelm, Kate 61, 116
Willis, Jack 123, 166
Wilson, Richard 9, 39, 70
WNET-TV 138, 140, 141, 150, 159, 166
Wolfe, Bernard 35
Wollheim, Donald 81, 99
Women of Wonder (anthology) 152
World Editions (Edizioni Mondiale) publisher 29, 30
World Fantasy convention 161
World Trade Center 17, 33
Wright, Walter 139, 151

Z
zip-a-tone 139
Zippy the Pinhead (comic strip by Bill Griffith) 44, 101

About the Author

Luis Ortiz was born in Hoboken, New Jersey and grew up in New York City where he works as editor, art director, computer artist, and writer. His previous book *Arts Unknown: the Life & Art of Lee Brown Coye* was on *Locus* magazine's recommended reading list for 2005. He lives with his wife Karan, and a bale of turtles, in the southern most tip of Manhattan.

By the author of EMSHWILLER: INFINITY X TWO

Praise for

Arts Unknown
The Life & Art of Lee Brown Coye

by Luis Ortiz

"... a smashingly beautiful book .... Reading this fine biography is like riding a train through the history of three-quarters of the twentieth century, and seeing Coye's monsters through every window."
    Paul di Filippo, "On Books"
    —*Asimov's Science Fiction*

"... well-researched biography .... a must for lovers of the weird and fantastic."
    — *Publishers Weekly* (issue also includes interview with author)

"... it turns out that the man himself was as interesting as his work."
    Charles de Lint, "Books to Look For"
    — *Magazine of Fantasy & Science Fiction*

"... [Coye's art] has a raw, primitive, and dark power ..."
    — *Illustration Magazine*

"... Splendidly realized, long overdue illustrated bio of the extraordinary, eccentric illustrator of the macabre; derived from interviews with Coye's friend and family, as well as unprecedented access to the artist's archives, diaries and letters. Essential!"
    — *Bookfellows*

" ... you feel as if you are unearthing forgotten masterpieces of the macabre the further you delve into Coye's interesting life .... the biographical content alone will be worth pursuing for anyone interested in tangents of the Cthulhu Mythos and pulp terrors ....The anecdotes in *Arts Unknown* range from the heart warming to the hilarious .... an inspiring read for anyone involved in the arts."
    — *Liarsociety.tripod.com/blog*

available from www.nonstop-press.com

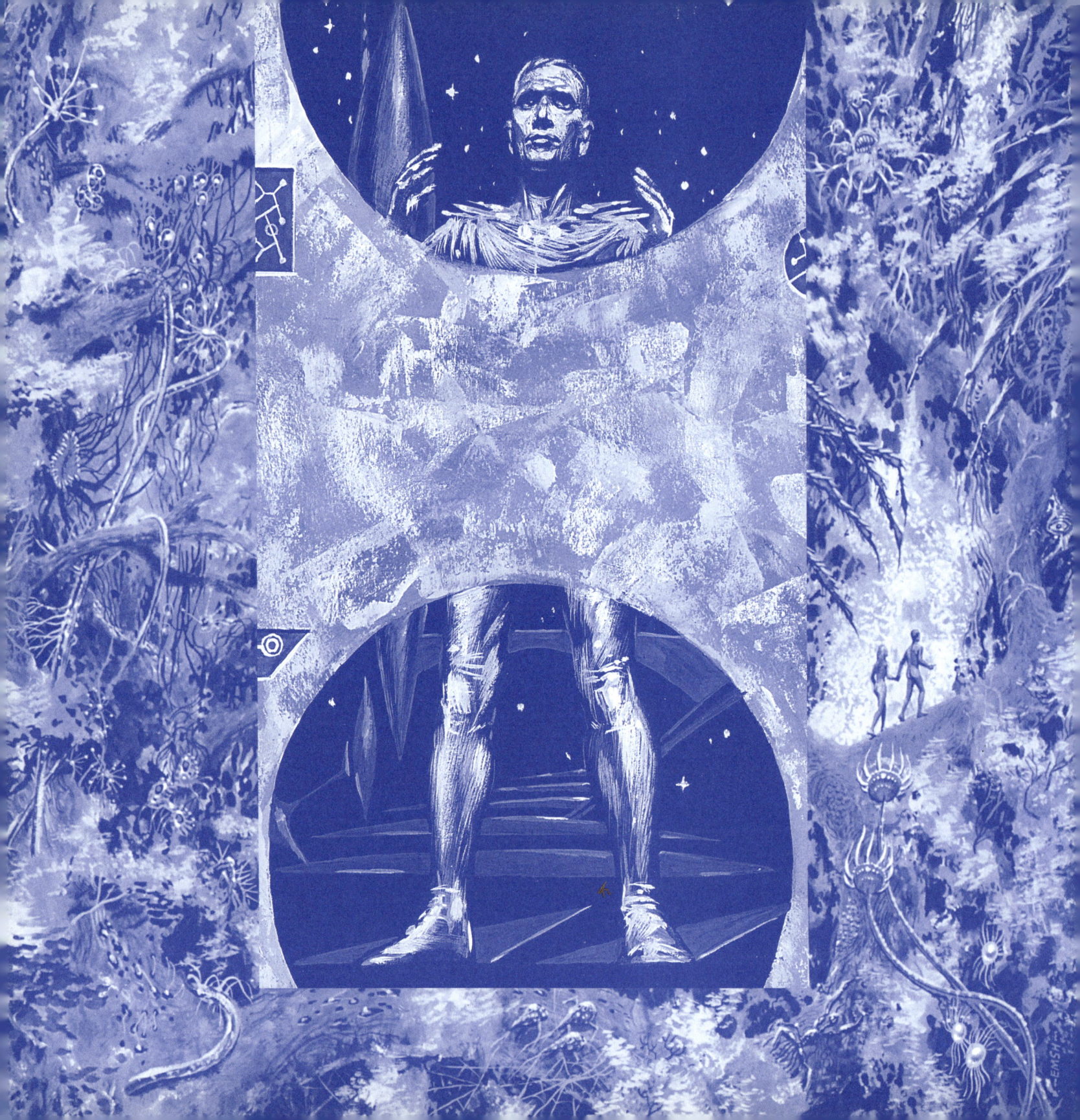